THE POWER OF THE PURSE

Other PEP Publications

Commonwealth Preference in the United Kingdom

Company Boards. Their Responsibilities to
Shareholders, Employees and the Community
BARBARA SHENFIELD

The Company. Law, Structure and Reform in Eleven Countries
CHARLES DE HOGHTON (ed.)

The Containment of Urban England
PETER HALL *et al.*

European Advanced Technology
CHRISTOPHER LAYTON

European Political Parties
S. HENIG AND J. PINDER (eds)

European Unity
Growth in the British Economy
The Member of Parliament and His Information
A. BARKER and M. RUSH

Politics and Bureaucracy in the European Community
DAVID COOMBES

Sex, Career and Family
MICHAEL FOGARTY, RHONA RAPOPORT AND ROBERT N. RAPOPORT

State Enterprise. Business or Politics?
DAVID COOMBES

Ten Innovations
CHRISTOPHER LAYTON

Women in Top Jobs. Four Studies in Achievement
PATRICIA WALTERS, A. J. ALLEN, ISOBEL ALLEN AND
MICHAEL FOGARTY

THE POWER
OF THE PURSE

THE ROLE OF EUROPEAN PARLIAMENTS
IN BUDGETARY DECISIONS

DAVID COOMBES
et al.

PEP

Political and Economic Planning
12 Upper Belgrave Street, London

LONDON   GEORGE ALLEN & UNWIN LTD
Ruskin House · Museum Street

First published in 1976

© George Allen & Unwin Ltd., 1976

ISBN 0 04 336061 0

Printed in Great Britain
in 10 point Times Roman type
by Willmer Brothers Limited, Birkenhead

PREFACE

This book results from a multi-national, inter-disciplinary symposium directed by PEP with financial support from the Social Science Research Council and from the Wolfson Foundation. The Symposium was co-ordinated by David Coombes, who was attached to PEP as Visiting Research Fellow during the academic year 1970–71. Professor Coombes was assisted at PEP, first by Miss Mary Preston and then (since May 1973) by Mrs Sarah Wood. Additional translations were done by F. T. C. Carter, Lecturer in German at Loughborough University, and by Mrs Carla Standing of PEP.

In addition to the contributors of articles to this book, acknowledgements to whom appear in the text, PEP is grateful to a number of other individuals and organisations who collaborated in the project. The Instituto Affari Internazionali of Rome not only assisted in finding suitable Italian contributors to the project, but also joined in its planning and execution. Professor Paul Gaudemet of the Faculty of Law and Economic Sciences, University of Paris, contributed invaluable guidance in the early stages and was responsible for our contact with most of the French contributors. The Hochschule für Verwaltungswissenschaften at Speyer also gave invaluable encouragement, and Professor Heinrich Siedentopf, a member of its staff, acted as co-ordinator for the German contributions. Three colloquiums were held as part of the project. These were organised with the help and joint sponsorship of other institutions, and PEP wishes to acknowledge the value of their participation: the College of Europe in Bruges; the Instituto per gli Studi della Programmazione Economica in Rome; and the Fondazione Agnelli in Turin. Among other individuals who gave freely their advice, criticism and time for the project we would also like to thank the following: Professor H. J. Arndt, Dr G. Bonvicini, Dr E. d'Aniello, Dr G. Granaglia, Professor W. Hennis, Dr Joachim Hirsch, Dr R. Lo Re, Mr F. Médard, Mr Riccardo Perissich, Dr S. Ristuccia, Professor R. Schnur, and Professor A. Wildavsky.

Needless to say, the sole responsibility for views expressed in the contributions published here rests with the individual authors.

CONTENTS

THE CONTRIBUTORS

SABINO CASSESE is Professor in the Facoltà di Economia e Commercio, Università degli Studi di Urbino, Ancona.

DAVID COOMBES was formerly Professor of European Studies at Loughborough University and is now a director of research at the Hansard Society for Parliamentary Government.

HANS DAALDER is Professor of Political Science at the University of Leiden.

JEAN-CLAUDE DUCROS is maître-assistant in the Faculté de Droit et des Sciences Economiques of the University of Nancy.

ALAIN DUPAS is chef du secretariat de la Commission des Finances of the French National Assembly.

PETER ELSE is senior lecturer in the Division of Economic Studies of the University of Sheffield.

KARL HEINRICH FRIAUF is a professor and director of the Institute for Constitutional Law of the University of Cologne.

SONJA HUBÉE-BOONZAAIJER is a lecturer in political science at the University of Leiden.

PIERRE LALUMIÈRE is a professor of public law of the University of Paris I.

DAVID MILLAR, previously of the Committee Office of the House of Commons, is now Head of Division in the Directorate General of Research and Documentation of the European Parliament.

JOEL MOLINIER is a professor of the University of Social Sciences of Toulouse.

VITTORIO MORTARA is Professore incaricato di Scienze dell 'Amministrazione of the Universita della Calabria, Cosenza.

VALERIO ONIDA is Professor of Regional Law in the Department of Law of the University of Pavia.

ALFRED SCHMIDT is Wissenschaftlicher Assistent in the Department of Economics and Social Sciences of the University of Dortmund.

PAOLO URIO is Assistant Professor in the Department of Political Science of the University of Geneva.

STUART WALKLAND is senior lecturer in the Department of Political Theory and Institutions at the University of Sheffield.

ALBRECHT ZUNKER is Wissenschaftlicher Assistent in the Seminar fur wissenschaftliche Politik of the University of Freiburg.

CHAPTER 1

INTRODUCTION

David Coombes

The project which led to this book really began on the Gianicolo hill in Rome four years ago when I was talking with Riccardo Perissich (now *chef de cabinet* of Altiero Spinelli, member of the Commission of the European Community) – in unusually grand surroundings for such a discussion – about possible subjects for research combining relevance for European integration with significance for political or administrative reform in the nation state. We shared an anxiety about the apparent divorce between the study and practice of European integration, especially as manifested in the European Community, on the one hand, and the practical study of problems of government in our various European states, on the other. Although European integration seemed to imply the creation of common political institutions, a persistent weakness in the foundations of these institutions seemed to be the lack of communication and understanding among national scholars and experts in the relevant disciplines and organisations, arising not so much from differences of language, as from the failure to confront each other on important common themes. Since that time, the establishment of the European Consortium for Political Research has done a great deal to improve communication and contact, with very constructive results, among political scientists. Our idea was less strictly academic than this, since we had it in mind to bring together not only university teachers, but also practitioners of government, and to choose a theme which would be relevant to contemporary policy-makers at both European and national levels.

At that time (summer of 1969) it seemed that one likely way out of the stagnation then affecting the European Community lay in the proposals to give the European Community its own financial resources and to increase at the same time the budgetary powers of the European Parliament. Yet the subject of parliament's 'power of the purse' was not significant only for European integration; it seemed to be an area where change was taking place in most Western European states. Moreover, while in the Community fundamental questions were being asked about the nature of parliament and the need to adapt its role to modern circumstances of government, it seemed especially timely to study as fundamental an aspect of the role of parliament as budgetary control.

It is important to emphasise, therefore, that the symposium reported in this book arose not only from an interest in European integration, but also from an enthusiasm for the study of parliament. There are of course other perspectives from which to study budgetary procedure and public expenditure. These subjects have been widely studied by economists, and at least one European symposium has been published from this point of view.[1] There have been a number of collections of studies, many of them also by economists, some of them inter-disciplinary, of budgetary decision-making seen mainly as a problem of the public administration and of government as a whole.[2] There is a very comprehensive and stimulating comparative work on the role of public audit and accountability, covering the United States as well as most European countries.[3] Our own focus in this project has been at once more general and more directly parliamentary. It has certainly not been possible to exclude aspects touching on the economic significance of budgetary decisions, on developments in budgetary decision-making within government, and on financial audit. The symposium does not, however, offer a specialised contribution in any of these respects. Its central concern has been to assess the modern significance in selected Western European states of what it takes to be the traditional powers of parliament over the national budget: first, by tracing recent changes in the procedures and practices of parliament; secondly, by testing the importance still attached to budgetary powers in relation to other powers of parliament; and thirdly by examining the relationship between budgetary procedure and the wider economic responsibilities of the state, in particular the impact of new techniques of decision-making where these can be

---

[1] R. Regul (ed.), *The Budget Today* (Bruges, de Tempel, for the College of Europe, 1967).

[2] See, for example, F. J. Lyden and E. G. Miller, *Planning, Programming and Budgeting: a Systems Approach to Management* (Chicago, Markham, 1968); *Public Administration Review*, vol. xxix, no. 2, (March–April 1969) (Symposium on Planning–Programming–Budgeting system); S. B. Chase (ed.), *Problems in Public Expenditure Analysis* (Washington, The Brookings Institution, 1968); I. W. Davis, jr, *Politics, Programs and Budgets: A Reader in Government Budgeting* (Englewood Cliffs, Prentice-Hall, 1969).

[3] E. L. Normanton, *The Audit and Accountability of Governments* (Manchester University Press, 1965).

said to have had a practical influence. Finally, some conclusions have been drawn from this for the role of the European Parliament, and a separate study of budgetary procedure in the European Community has been made.[1]

THE MEANING OF THE 'POWER OF THE PURSE'

With such broad aims in mind there were bound to be difficulties of definition and communication, especially in a symposium of six countries. Since the idea was to focus on the budget, the first problem was to define this concept, which does not mean the same thing in all European countries. In Britain, parliamentary procedure does not even recognise formally anything called a 'budget', expenditure and revenue being presented to parliament separately and being voted in different procedures. The 'budget statement' made by the Chancellor of the Exchequer, usually in March or April every year, is related officially to the revenue side, although the occasion is used to consider the government's financial and economic activity as a whole. By contrast in France, Italy and the Netherlands the budget is a law (or set of laws) which must pass through the various stages of legislative procedure before the government is authorised to collect revenue or commit expenditure. In Switzerland, on the other hand, the budget takes the form of an executive decree. These differences do of course affect the nature of parliamentary procedure, as well as the form of the proposals making up the budget. However there is still some value in treating the budget as something which a large number of parliamentary systems of government have in common. In all countries considered in this symposium some statement (or statements) of expenditure and income estimated by governments for a future financial year is submitted to parliament annually for approval. It is in this general sense that we shall use the expression 'budget'.

A second problem arises from the concept of 'control'. In common (and orthodox) English usage this word is ambiguous, including as possible meanings, not only inspecting, but also restraining, and even guiding and influencing. It is in this ambiguous meaning that it is commonly used in the expression 'parliamentary control', and doubtless many hours of debate have been spent on the subject of the powers of parliament resulting mainly from the ambiguity of that expression. Nevertheless it is certainly far too late to call for greater precision in using the word

[1] D. Coombes, *The Power of the Purse in the European Community* (London, PEP/Chatham House, Joint European Series No. 20, 1972).

'control', and one thing which this symposium revealed at an early stage was that the loose English usage has been welcomed on the mainland of Europe. Strictly speaking, *contrôle* in French, *controllo* in Italian, and *controle* in Dutch have much more precise meanings as inspection, verification, checking against fixed standards, and are used especially in the field of expenditure (public and otherwise) to refer to the process of auditing. (The German meaning of *kontrolle* seems to come closer to the wider English usage.) In the contributions which follow, the word 'control' is used in its widest, typically English meaning. Most of the contributors even used its counterparts in their own languages in that sense. In fact the ambiguity of this usage is not a disadvantage, since the symposium was concerned with parliament's role in the budgetary process in the broadest sense, and since one of the things which we were trying to elucidate was exactly what that role implied for parliament's relationship with the executive. Starting from the broad sense of 'control' the contributions generally try to reach more precise notions of that relationship; and in the concluding chapter I try to distinguish among different forms which it can take.

Moreover, as we shall see, the distinction between different phases of the expenditure process is not always clear in practice. In France, for example, the activity of auditing government expenditure is entrusted to the administration, and parliament is not thought to have a significant part to play in it. In Italy, however, the regulatory functions of the Corte dei Conti are exercised before and after expenditure takes place. The German Bundesrechnungshof can lend its services to members of parliament when they are considering proposals for expenditure. In general the activity of auditing can be seen as having significance beyond both the checking of regularity of accounts, and the *a posteriori* stage of control.[1] This symposium has tried to avoid treating parliament's role in the budgetary process in terms of a series of distinct formal steps, and in the concluding chapter we shall develop the view that it is not usually helpful to see it in that way. The contributors have included *a posteriori* control of expenditure in their studies whenever they thought it necessary in order to give an adequate account of parliament's role.

Another problem arises because public expenditure, especially in modern circumstances, is itself an ambiguous concept. As Peter Else shows in the next chapter, there are a number of ways of defining it depending on the interest from which it is approached, so that from a macro-economic point of view, for example, the widest

[1] See in particular Normanton, op. cit.

possible definition will be required. Forms of public expenditure such as the financial activities of nationalised industries, regional and local authorities, and of the number of miscellaneous State-sponsored bodies which exist in most industrialised, liberal democracies raise a number of special problems. The subject of this symposium was felt to be sufficiently wide already, so that no special treatment of these forms of expenditure is included, with the following exceptions: that the expenditure of the states of the Federal Republic of Germany is considered in relation to the problems of parliamentary control at federal level; that a particularly important form of 'para-fiscal' institution in Germany is given special consideration; and that French and Italian authors refer in passing to the role of autonomous public agencies and corporations. As far as possible, however, the symposium has been confined to dealing with receipts and expenditure of the central government. This is not to imply that other forms of public finance have no relevance for parliament's 'power of the purse'; on the contrary authors have dealt with these other forms where they felt that there was no alternative in giving an adequate explanation of parliament's role in budgetary procedure.

Since the symposium is not pitched at the level of formal rules of procedure, these difficulties are not really so daunting. We begin with the vague, but apparently widespread, conviction that the 'power of the purse' carries some special significance for the power of parliaments in Western Europe. At first sight there seems to be little in practice to support this conviction – either in its implication that financial procedure can be reduced to a set of rules giving parliament special privileges, or in its suggestion of generality across different countries. Nevertheless the conviction persists in one form or another, and uncritical acceptance of it is no more dangerous than unthinking scepticism.

In view of the differences and obstacles which can be noticed, what then do people usually mean by the expression? Perhaps the best way to interpret it at the level of conviction is to see it as three interdependent rules: first, that in some way parliament's prior approval should be required for all expenditure and all revenue proposed by the government; secondly, that parliament's approval should also be required for the allocation of expenditure among different items; and finally, that parliament should have the right to approve the accounts of expenditure, in order to check that the government has conformed to what was approved. These 'traditional rules' of budgetary procedure may or may not have been applied in practice in all the states of Western Europe; in so far as they have been applied, it has presumably been in different ways. However this is as good a starting point as any for the work of the following symposium, which is concerned essentially with the applicability of these rules in modern conditions of government.

THE METHODS OF THE SYMPOSIUM

The first step was to bring together a group of specialists in the field from different Western European states and with this group to define an approach to the subject and find possible contributors. It was decided that as far as possible the contributions to the symposium would contain original material; thus, rather than ask for a general paper on each country providing a synthesis of previous research, we looked for contributors who were either currently doing research on the subject or were willing to write short, original papers on particular aspects of it. In an attempt to ensure that the project was truly collective, it was agreed that the contributions should be seen only as the result of a number of meetings, each marking a particular stage in the development of the symposium.

With the co-operation of the College of Europe in Bruges, in November 1970 a colloquium was organised at the College's premises to which a fairly mixed group of academics and others from five European countries was invited. At this meeting the fundamental nature of the symposium was determined. Although a fairly elaborate paper was presented setting out a common approach to the subject, it emerged immediately that no general rule, even regarding content, would be acceptable, if the twin criteria of topicality and originality were to be observed. To give two examples, aspects which seemed to be of current importance in Italy were of mainly historical significance in other countries, while in Germany there was not much point in approaching the subject without special consideration of the effects of the federal system. Part of the contribution which the symposium itself would have to make would be to point out what were the important aspects of parliamentary control of the budget in the countries concerned. Moreover, since the criterion of originality meant that many contributions would have to be based on current research, some contributions would be too specialised to give an adequate picture of the role of parliament in the country concerned. Consequently it was decided to ask for more than one paper per country, at least in the larger states. Thus for Germany, France, Britain and Italy special groups were formed with their own co-ordinators and these were entrusted with preparing outline papers for a later colloquium indicating what subjects would be covered, and how. Similar outline papers were requested from the Netherlands and (subsequently to the Bruges meeting) from Switzerland. It did not prove possible to find a contributor from a Scandinavian country, so that, rather than delay the start of the project, it was decided to go ahead with the six countries from which participants had come forward.

The next meeting of the group was held in Rome in June 1971. The representatives from each country were asked to justify the outline papers presented (and previously circulated). A discussion then ensued on a host of problems which these papers threw up about matters of terminology and translation. (These outline papers, like all others, were for the most part submitted in the author's own language and then translated into French or English.) It was apparent moreover that the national groups left to themselves would produce highly specialised contributions which would not make much sense on their own to a foreign readership. Consequently it was agreed that for each of the larger countries at least one contribution should be prepared dealing with the historical and legal background to parliamentary control of the budget, attempting with some care to explain aspects which might be difficult for anyone not intimately acquainted with the political system to understand. The authors for the Netherlands and Switzerland agreed to include sections designed for the same purpose in their own contributions. It was also decided at this stage to include two contributions dealing especially with economic aspects of the budget, so much did these aspects impinge upon the subject-matter of the work of other contributors. Thus Peter Else was asked to contribute an introductory chapter dealing with the changing scope and content of public expenditure in all the countries considered, as well as in other similar countries, and to provide as part of the conclusions to the symposium a survey of the impact in the six countries covered of new techniques of economic analysis and decision-making in government (these appear as Chapters 2 and 17 respectively).

The fourteen national contributions were mostly produced in draft in time for a final meeting of the group in Turin in April 1972. There remained considerable difficulties of overlapping treatment, important gaps in information for particular countries, and many problems of translation and understanding. The contributors split up into working parties, selected not according to nationality, but according to subject-matter, to iron out the remaining difficulties and also to draw up, for each main theme of the symposium, a set of general conclusions. The results of the working parties were then debated in general session. The final contributions were received for the most part about a year later.

They are presented here, translated where necessary, in the form in which they were received. They are grouped together in countries (in alphabetical order in French). The contributions providing general background (Chapters 4, 7, 9, 12) are not necessarily placed at the beginning of a country's contributions; it appeared logical to begin the German contributions with a study of the effects of the federal system (Chapter 3), and the French contributions with Dupas's account of current parliamentary procedure, since it is criticised in some respects by the ensuing contribution of Lalumière. Molinier's comparison of France and Britain (Chapter 9) serves as an introduction to the two British contributions.

The contributions fall into four main types: the background contributions just mentioned (Chapters 3, 4, 7, 9, 12), those dealing directly with parliamentary procedure and practice (Chapters 6, 10, 13), those dealing with special topics of particular significance in one country (Chapters 5, 8, 11, 14), and the two final ones covering all relevant aspects of the two smaller countries included (Chapters 15 and 16). Two of the contributions are by parliamentary officials (Dupas and Millar). The remainder are by academics with backgrounds either in public law or political science.

THE POWER OF THE PURSE IN THE EUROPEAN COMMUNITY

It was possible to make use of preliminary findings of the symposium in writing a special study of changes proposed in budgetary procedure in the European Community consequent upon the decision to introduce a system of own resources for the Community.[1] This subject proved to be separable from the main topic of parliamentary control of the budget in the nation-state, since the question of budgetary procedure in the Community had been treated largely in terms of the special problems of that organisation and particularly of the competences of its institutions. However, much opposition to the granting of extensive powers to the European parliament had been based on suspicion of the role of parliaments in general in budgetary affairs. One argument in the debate which took place in the Community during the winter of 1969–70 was that the European parliament should not be given powers which were greater than those enjoyed by any national parliament, although a counter-argument was that it should not, on the other hand, receive fewer powers than would be considered acceptable at

[1] Coombes, op. cit.

the national level. The compromise reached in the treaty of April 1970 left the European parliament with budgetary powers which were extremely restricted and at the same time extremely vague. One problem was that most Community expenditure was said to flow automatically from previous Community acts, so that the parliament could not be given the power to alter it without upsetting the existing balance among the institutions.

Our study made the general criticism that the question had been approached far too narrowly in terms of the legal competences of the parliament and Council, while what was really needed following the establishment of the Community's own sources of revenue was a general review of the whole decision-making process leading to expenditure. In fact it did not seem as if self-financing would be used as an opportunity to reform the methods for deciding and managing Community expenditure. The budget would still be treated essentially as that of an ordinary international organisation. The trouble here was that it had in fact grown into something nearer to that of a national government – if not in quantity then at least in the nature of the bulk of expenditure made (which already involved a redistribution of income among social groups and was already to some extent an instrument of economic policy).

At the time of the 1970 decisions, the Commission and Council had promised to look at the whole matter of the parliament's powers again and this they have been doing during 1973. The Commission itself meanwhile seems to have gone some way to improve its methods of drawing up the budget (as it happens rather along the lines outlined in our study). However, the main emphasis in the Commission's new proposals for reforming budgetary procedure is on the creation of better *a posteriori* control of Community expenditure. The other institutions still seem to look begrudgingly upon the parliament's demands for powers similar to those traditionally associated with national parliaments' power of the purse. The publication of the results of the present symposium is likely to come too late for the present round of decisions on this issue. However, we doubt very much whether this will be the last time that the budgetary procedure of the Community is going to be changed, so that the findings presented here can certainly be of value in this respect. We are indeed of the opinion that some of the conclusions set out in the final chapter could have a useful influence on this wider European debate.

CHAPTER 2

THE SCOPE AND CONTENT OF GOVERNMENT EXPENDITURE

Peter Else

Expenditure by governments has long been a significant item in the national accounts of individual countries, and it has over time tended to become an increasingly important one. Moreover, its growth has been associated with marked changes in attitudes towards it. A century ago in Britain, for example, the old 'liberal' doctrine that government expenditure should be minimised subject to the provision of adequate protection from the Queen's enemies abroad and the maintenance of law and order at home was still widely accepted, and retrenchment was the guiding principle of public finance.[1] By the 1880s, however, more expansionist policies began to find favour, and in Germany, Adolph Wagner was formulating his 'law' predicting an increasing expansion of governmental activities and expenditure.[2] This law, he claimed, was formulated as a result of 'empirical observation in progressive countries, at least in our Western European civilization'.[3]

It is not entirely clear from Wagner's writings whether he was expecting just an increase in government expenditure or whether he was making the more specific prediction that it would rise over time relative to national income. Subsequent writers have tended to assume the latter, and in doing so have, on the whole, been supported by the factual evidence, some of which is discussed later in this chapter. First, however, in examining the scope and content of government expenditure it would seem useful to review the basic reasons for it, and this will provide a framework within which recent trends can be examined. In this discussion, for the most part

[1] P. Einzig, *The Control of the Purse* (London, Secker and Warburg, 1959), ch. 26.

[2] A. Wagner, *Finanzwissenschaft* (Leipzig, 1883).

[3] A. Wagner, three extracts on public finance (an English translation from Wagner's writings) in R. A. Musgrave and A. T. Peacock, *Classics in the Theory of Public Finance* (London, Macmillan, 1958), p. 8.

government expenditure will be considered as a whole, although some of the implications of the division of responsibility for expenditure between the various levels of government will be noted where necessary. Moreover attention in this chapter will be concentrated on expenditure by governments as such, excluding the expenditure of public enterprises and the like.

REASONS FOR GOVERNMENT EXPENDITURE

The most basic reason of all for government expenditure arises out of the need for some form of government. No community can operate without a set of rules or laws which regulate the economic and social relationships of its members. As soon as primitive man realised the advantages of specialisation, he must have realised the need for rules of some sort establishing property rights and trading conventions, even if they could only be rules of a rudimentary and informal nature. At the very least, therefore, a community must have some machinery for framing laws, and once the laws have been established it will also need some machinery for enforcing them and for settling disputes between members about rights under the law. In small simple communities these requirements need not give rise to monetary expenditure, but they would involve costs in the sense that those called upon to carry out public duties would have to spend time on them which could be spent doing other things. The more complex nation-states of the modern world also make extensive use of voluntary labour for this kind of work, but in addition they find they need to pay for the services of some of their legislators, and to buy the services of administrators, lawyers, ancillary workers of many kinds, buildings, equipment, and the like through normal market channels. The need therefore for some means of framing laws, seeing they are carried out and settling disputes provides an important basic and continuing reason for government expenditure. Further, the increasing complexity of social relationships in growing economies almost inevitably means that the resources required for such activities tend to increase over time.

Few governments, however, have restricted their activities to legislation, administration and adjudication. They have in addition taken on the responsibility for providing certain goods and services, either because adequate provision through the private sector of the economy cannot be relied upon, or because such provision would have undesirable consequences of one sort or another. It is sometimes possible to control some of the more undesirable consequences of private provision through legislation, but usually there remain areas of activity in which the deficiencies of private provision are found to be more intractable. Some communities have taken the extreme view that the provision of goods and services on the initiative of private individuals or concerns acting through a market system will in all cases have such undesirable consequences that the only solution is the public provision of all (or nearly all) goods and services. In the Western world, the relative advantages of the private provision of many goods and services tend to have been more highly regarded. Indeed, whilst there are variations between countries, the underlying principle would appear to have been that goods and services should be provided through the private sector (subject to such legislative restrictions as are considered appropriate) unless specific advantages for public provision can be demonstrated. Moreover, even then, the public provision of goods and services need not necessarily impose any financial obligation on governments, since it may still be possible for the goods and services in question to be bought and sold through normal market channels. Whilst production would then be by public enterprise rather than private firms, production expenses could be met in the normal way out of revenue from sales, and decisions on the quantities of resources to be used by the enterprise would still essentially be business decisions made in response to market signals rather than political decisions. For this reason, expenditure by public enterprises is not here considered as a part of government expenditure.[1] Governments do, of course, influence the behaviour of public enterprises by determining their terms of reference, the conditions under which they operate, their financial objectives and the like, but this is all part of their legislative function to which reference has already been made.

Nevertheless, there are certain goods and services which, if provided at all, have to be provided through non-market channels, since they have characteristics which prevent even the most perfect market system from working properly. These are goods and services which, following Samuelson,[2] are referred to as 'public' or 'collective' goods – terms reflecting the necessity of providing such goods on a public or collective basis.

A market system breaks down with such goods because the exclusion principle cannot operate; no one can be excluded from the

[1] Any grants-in-aid paid by a government to a public enterprise, whether to cover losses or subsidise specific activities, are of course included as part of government expenditure.

[2] P. A. Samuelson, 'The Pure Theory of Public Expenditure', *Review of Economics and Statistics*, vol. 36, no. 4 (Nov. 1954), pp. 387–9, and subsequent articles in the same journal.

benefits of them once they are provided. With ordinary 'private' goods like loaves of bread or bus rides or even theatre performances, potential consumers can be prevented from using the goods or services in question unless they are willing to pay for them. The prices consumers are willing to pay will depend on the benefits they expect to enjoy from the goods in relation to the benefits they could expect to receive by spending their money in different ways. Further, these prices will ultimately determine the quantities of the particular goods provided. With public goods or services such as defence, public health schemes or street lighting, where it is not possible to restrict the enjoyment of their benefits to those who are willing to pay for them, a potential consumer's willingness to pay will tend to reflect not so much the benefits he might expect to receive as the knowledge that as long as the goods are provided, he will be able to benefit from them irrespective of the amount he pays towards the cost of their provision. In general, therefore, his willingness to pay will probably fall short of the value of the benefits to him, and with everyone reacting in the same way, the market would respond by providing fewer public goods than would be desirable, taking into account their potential benefits, and may even provide none at all. Governments can, and of course do, get round this particular problem by providing public goods themselves and using their powers of coercion to extract the money to pay for them through taxation. But whilst taxation provides a means for financing the provision of public goods, it does not perform the other function of the market, which is to determine what quantities of particular goods and services should be produced. A properly working market system provides a means through which the preferences of consumers can influence the quantities of the various goods and services provided. By contrast, the quantities of publicly provided goods and services are determined through the decision-making processes of government, which are of course the main concern of this book. For the moment, however, it is sufficient to note that a second reason for government expenditure is to satisfy the demand for certain necessary public goods which because of their nature cannot be provided through a market system.

The third reason for government expenditure is closely related to the second and arises where the provision of particular goods and services through a market system is possible, but where it is thought that the amounts provided and used would be insufficient. This might be the case if it was felt that the individuals buying the goods or services did not fully appreciate the benefits to them of more consumption, which might arise, for example, if the benefits accrued after some elapse of time, as with education, health insurance or pension rights. Public provision could then ensure that more of the goods in question was provided than would be provided in response to private demand, and the government's powers of coercion could again be employed to ensure that the services provided were used and paid for. Goods and services in this category have been termed 'merit goods',[1] but exactly the same problems are raised with goods and services with which an individual's consumption gives the community benefits over and above those which he himself might receive. For example, whilst a literate person benefits from his literacy, so do many others since the costs of communicating with him are reduced. Similarly, a person innoculated against infectious diseases protects himself and also others to whom he might otherwise pass the disease. Yet another case raising similar problems is where individuals might be prevented from purchasing as much of a good or service as it is felt they should consume, in their own or the community's interests, by inadequate means. The private demands of individuals will again in both these cases tend to lead to too little of the good being produced and consumed and public provision could help to rectify this deficiency. In all these cases, however, the alternative of subsidising private producers or consumers might be preferred to complete public sector provision, but whatever the arangement, some government expenditure will be involved.

Apart from expenditure arising from the basic functions of government, all the motives for government spending mentioned so far arise out of the desire by governments to influence the allocation of resources, and in particular to ensure that adequate resources are devoted to the production of those goods and services for which private sector provision might be deficient. Another important motivation for government expenditure arises from the desire to alter the distribution of income and wealth within a community. In a market economy, individuals can obtain the means to buy the goods and services they need by selling or offering for hire whatever goods and services are at their disposal. Most people, however, possess little more in the way of goods than they require for their own personal use and hence have to rely on what they can get from the sale of their labour services for income. In addition some people find their earning power is further restricted because of age or other disability, or because there is not much demand for the services they can offer. Governments may therefore attempt to redistribute income by making payments to their less-well-off

[1] R. A. Musgrave, *Theory of Public Finance* (New York, McGraw-Hill, 1959), p. 13.

citizens financed by taxes or other levies on the rest of the community. Of course, governments need not be confined to redistribution through cash payments. Indeed the possibility that governments might finance, or help to finance, the provision of particular goods and services to ensure that inadequate means do not unduly restrict their users' enjoyment of them has already been mentioned. In fact cash payments and the provision of specific goods and services are simply different ways of redistributing income, and in many countries both methods appear to be employed. Also relevant in this context is the structure of the tax system, as some distributive changes can be obtained by appropriate modifications to it. Nevertheless the desire to redistribute income in some way can give rise to government expenditure over and above that accounted for in the previous discussion, although in practice there may not always be a clear distinction between expenditure carried out for distributional reasons and that carried out for other reasons.

One further type of government expenditure to note is interest on debt. This arises because governments often find it expedient to finance a proportion of their expenditure through borrowing rather than current taxation. There is obviously some justification for this with expenditure on durable assets such as roads, buildings and the like, since the benefits from them are likely to be spread over a number of years after the asset is obtained, but there are also circumstances when some more obviously current expenditure is also financed by borrowing. In either case borrowing will create an obligation to pay interest in the future, and in most countries interest on the public debt does constitute a small but significant proportion of government expenditure.

With all these reasons for government expenditure, it does not seem unreasonable to expect that its total will tend to increase as a country's national income increases. Just as a private individual buys more goods and services for the satisfaction of his own private wants as he gets better off, a nation will tend to devote more resources to the satisfaction of its collective wants as its economy expands. However, whilst this suggests increasing government expenditure in absolute terms, it does not necessarily follow that it will also lead to government expenditure rising relatively to national income as predicted by the interpreters of Wagner's Law. However, the latter seems to have been a common experience, and a number of additional influences have been identified which, it has been argued, have contributed towards this outcome to a greater or lesser extent.

Peacock and Wiseman, for example, in their study of government expenditure in the United Kingdom[1] identified what they referred to as a 'displacement effect' whereby government expenditure is substantially increased as a result of war or other social upheaval. The basic notion is that at such a time of national emergency, accepted ideas on what is the maximum tolerable level of taxation necessarily have to be set aside. Then, as people get used to higher taxation, these ideas are revised, permitting a continued higher level of government expenditure after the emergency is over. This seems a plausible hypothesis, but subsequent empirical work has suggested that in practice this is likely to be, as Musgrave put it, 'a factor of short-run timing rather than long-run trend'.[2] In other words, whilst it would lead to an increase in the rate of growth of government expenditure in the short run, the long run trends would not be materially affected.

A more significant influence in the long-run growth of government expenditure has probably been the impact of technical developments in various fields. The most obvious example is the development of the motor vehicle which has led to considerably increased expenditures on road networks in many countries, particularly since the Second World War,[3] but other developments in transport (e.g. the development of air travel) and in other fields such as medicine must have had similar effects. In addition there has been the effect of population growth and its increased concentration in urban areas. Greater urbanisation, it can be argued, increases the need for government action to alleviate some of the less pleasant 'spillover' effects of the actions of individuals or groups. Such action may take the form of smoke control programmes, expenditure to reduce noise nuisance from airports or main roads, and similar activities. Further, an expanding population tends to mean that the proportion of children and retired persons in the economy increases, leading to increased government expenditure on education and social welfare programmes. Moreover, attitudes towards this kind of expenditure have also changed over the years in the sense that the view that people should not be prevented from using certain basic services, particularly in the education and health fields, by inadequate means seems to have become an almost universal basis for policy. The reasons for the

[1] A. T. Peacock and J. Wiseman, *The Growth of Public Expenditure in the United Kingdom* (Princeton, National Bureau of Economic Research, 1961).

[2] R. A. Musgrave, *Fiscal Systems* (New Haven and London, Yale University Press, 1969), p. 109.

[3] e.g. in the UK total expenditure on roads increased from £74·4 million in 1950 to £630 million in 1970, or from 0·6 per cent of GNP in 1950 to 1·5 per cent in 1970. British Road Federation, *Basic Road Statistics 1971*, and earlier years.

change are not entirely clear. Some writers have attempted to explain it in terms of the reactions of vote maximising politicians to the enfranchisement of the less well-off sections of society;[1] others have suggested that it may reflect the realization that politically the interests of the public as consumers of public services have become more important than their interests as taxpayers.[2] Whatever the reason, the fact remains that the responsibilities assumed by governments in the educational and social welfare fields are generally considered wider now than they were fifty or so years ago.

One final influence on government expenditure in comparatively recent years which deserves particular attention has been the realisation, following the work of J. M. Keynes, of the potential role of government expenditure, and indeed of fiscal policy generally, in the macro-economic management of the economy. This is of comparatively recent origin since, although Keynes set out his ideas in the 1930s,[3] their adoption by governments has been largely a postwar development. The implications of Keynesian ideas for government expenditure depend on the precise objectives of economic policy, but many governments now regard it as part of their responsibilities to keep the level of unemployment within acceptable bounds and at the same time to control, as far as possible, inflationary tendencies. Hence, if private demand is insufficient to maintain full employment, government expenditure can be increased to create additional demand and raise the level of employment. Conversely, if the total demand for goods and services is excessive, in relation to the resources available, a reduction in government expenditure can help to ease the situation. This can lead to problems since an inflationary situation is not likely to restrain the long-run trends increasing the demands for publicly provided goods and services. Nevertheless fiscal policy is not the only tool of economic management that governments have at their disposal; monetary policy can also be used. Indeed, an influential school of thought, led by Milton Friedman, the Chicago economist, argues that, as far as the control of inflationary tendencies is concerned, monetary policy, and in particular the control of the money supply, is the key factor. Friedman himself goes further and argues that because the effects of both monetary and fiscal policy are uncertain in timing and extent,

[1] e.g. A. Downs, *An Economic Theory of Democracy* (New York, Harper Row, 1957).

[2] See Sir Richard Clarke, 'Parliament and Public Expenditure', *Political Quarterly*, vol. 44, no. 2 (April–June, 1973), p. 142.

[3] In his *General Theory of Employment Interest and Money* (London, Macmillan, 1936) and other works.

the use of either to counteract short-run fluctuations in an economy is likely to do more harm than good by introducing additional instability into the system.[1] Instead he argues that inflation needs to be controlled more on a long-term basis by limiting the increase in the money supply to a rate just sufficient to allow the long-run growth potential of the economy to be realised.[2] However, there are few signs that governments, faced with demands to 'do something' about rising unemployment, are willing to turn away from Keynesian orthodoxy and adopt the more austere doctrines of Friedman.[3] The announcement of an increased programme of government expenditure can give the impression of purposeful action even if its effects are uncertain. Even so, some governments find they have to place more emphasis on monetary policy because the effectiveness of fiscal policy is restricted by institutional factors. In Germany, for example, the division of powers between the federal government and the *Länder* means that the former's budget is relatively small, and its constitutional powers are such that its ability to influence the budgets of state governments is limited, whilst in Italy delays in the implementation of budgetary decisions restrict the efficacy of fiscal policy.[4]

TRENDS IN GOVERNMENT EXPENDITURE

Some indication of the actual trends in government expenditure in Germany, the United Kingdom and the United States since the end of the nineteenth century can be obtained from Figure 2.1. This diagram suggests that in all three countries government expenditure rose relative to gross national product (GNP) more or less continuously over the period and that by the 1960s, again in all three countries, government expenditure expressed as a percentage of GNP was more than three times its level at the turn of the century. The experience of these countries thus provides considerable empirical support for the operation of Wagner's Law. Comparable data for other countries covering the same period, however, are not

[1] M. Friedman, 'Statement on Monetary Theory and Policy', in *Employment, Growth and Price Levels* (Hearing before the Joint Economic Committee of Congress 1959), US Government Printing Office, p. 611.

[2] ibid., loc. cit.

[3] Indeed the first Nixon administration in the USA tried to follow monetarist policies but, in the face of rising unemployment, abandoned them in 1971 in favour of expansionary fiscal policies. *Survey of the United States*, April 1972, OECD.

[4] See Chapters 3 and 14, and also W. Heller *et al.*, *Fiscal Policy for a Balanced Economy* (OECD, 1968), which is a report of a more detailed study of the use of fiscal policy in a number of countries including West Germany and Italy.

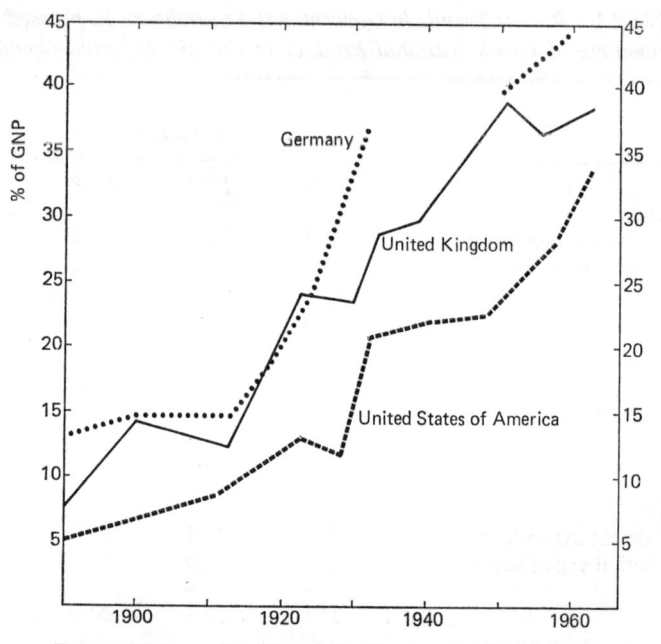

FIGURE 2.1 Long-Run Trends in Government Expenditure

Notes 1. The underlying figures for the different countries are not exactly comparable with each other (or with those in the tables) because of differences
in national income accounting conventions.

2. The discontinuity in the German trend reflects the change in national
boundaries; the post-war trend relates to the German Federal Republic.

3. War-time peaks are omitted from the trends.

Source: R. A. Musgrave, *Fiscal Systems* (New Haven and London, 1969),
pp. 94–5.

readily available, but the development of national income accounting techniques and the influence of certain international bodies
in organising the collection of data has meant that more detailed
comparisons can be made for the period since the Second World
War. Table 2.1 thus shows government expenditure expressed as a
percentage of GNP in selected post-war years for all the six countries
which are the particular concern of the following chapters.

The figures are derived from national accounts data compiled by
OECD and the United Nations and arranged by them, as far as
possible, in a standardised form based upon internationally agreed
definitions. Government expenditure is defined in Table 2.1 (and
following tables), following the discussion of the preceding section,
to include expenditure by all levels of government from central
government down to the smallest local authority, but not expendi-

Table 2.1 *Recent Trends in Government Expenditure Expressed as a Percentage of Gross National Product in the Six Selected Countries*

		% of GNP at market prices			
		1953	1961	1969	1970
France					
Current expenditure		31·1	31·2	33·1	32·6
Capital expenditure		1·9	2·5	3·2	3·2
	Total	33·0	33·7	36·3	35·8
Germany (Fed. Rep.)					
Current expenditure		28·7	28·6	32·2	31·6
Capital expenditure		2·3	3·4	3·9	4·3
	Total	31·0	32·0	36·1	35·9
Italy					
Current expenditure		22·7	25·4	31·9	31·6
Capital expenditure		3·1	2·9	2·3	2·4
	Total	25·8	28·3	34·2	34·0
Netherlands					
Current expenditure		24·4	28·4	36·8	38·5
Capital expenditure		4·4	4·3	4·9	4·8
	Total	28·8	32·7	41·7	43·3
Switzerland					
Current expenditure		18·9	19·5	23·2	..
Capital expenditure		..	3·5	..	..
	Total	..	23·0	..	..
United Kingdom					
Current expenditure		30·3	29·6	32·5	32·4
Capital expenditure		1·3	1·8	2·7	2·6
	Total	31·6	31·4	35·2	35·0

.. = not available.
Sources: OECD, *National Accounts of OECD countries 1963–69*; United Nations *Yearbook of National Accounts Statistics 1970 and 1971*

ture by government enterprises and public corporations. Current expenditure includes all expenditure by governments on goods and services for current consumption, all transfer payments such as pensions, social security benefits and the like, subsidies and interest on public debt. The figures for capital expenditure similarly cover investment by governments. Expressing this expenditure as a percentage of GNP means simply that it is being related, conceptually, to the total value of all the goods and services produced with the aid of the productive resources owned by the individuals and organisations of that country. The resultant figure does not, of course, provide a measure of the goods and services produced which are used by governments, since some government expenditure normally consists of transfer payments which help to finance private consumption of goods and services; it simply gives an indication of the size of government expenditure relative to GNP.

Table 2.1, like Figure 2.1, shows a tendency for government expenditure to rise relative to GNP in all the countries covered, although that tendency has been stronger in some countries than others and perhaps more generally stronger in the 1960s than in the 1950s. Moreover, of the six countries, the experience of France, West Germany and the United Kingdom appears to have been fairly similar; in all three government expenditure expressed as a percentage of GNP was around the same level in 1953 and had increased by about the same amount by 1970.[1] The percentages for West Germany and the United Kingdom incidentally appear less in Table 2.1 than those for the corresponding period in Figure 2.1, principally because for the latter government expenditure has been expressed as a percentage of GNP at factor cost (i.e. net of indirect taxes), whilst in Table 2.1 and following tables it has been found most convenient for the purpose of making comparisons between different countries to express government expenditure as a percentage of GNP at market prices which, of course, include indirect taxes. Of the other countries in Table 2.1, in Italy government expenditure was significantly lower relative to GNP in 1953 than in France, West Germany and the United Kingdom, but by 1970 it had caught up, whilst in the Netherlands government expenditure appears to have grown faster relative to GNP than elsewhere and by 1970 amounted to a rather higher percentage of GNP than in the other five countries. Switzerland, by contrast, is notable for maintaining over the whole period a much lower level of government expenditure relative to GNP than the others.

Further comparisons can be made with the help of Table 2.2

[1] Too much significance should not be attached to small differences between percentages, since although OECD and UN national income accounts are set out in a standardised form, variations in the estimating procedures of member states who provide the basic data mean that the figures are not always exactly comparable.

B

Table 2.2   *Recent Trends in Government Expenditure Expressed as a Percentage of Gross National Product in Other Selected Countries*

		% of GNP at market prices			
		1953	*1961*	*1969*	*1970*
Belgium					
Current expenditure		25·9	27·4	32·8	33·8
Capital expenditure		1·6	2·0	3·2	3·5
	Total	27·5	29·4	36·0	37·3
Sweden					
Current expenditure		25·3	28·5	37·2	37·8
Capital expenditure		3·4	2·7	3·1	..
	Total	28·7	31·2	40·3	..
United States					
Current expenditure		25·5	26·9	29·3	30·7
Capital expenditure		2·0	2·6	2·5	2·3
	Total	27·5	29·5	31·8	33·0
Japan					
Current expenditure		15·6	12·9	14·0	14·3
Capital expenditure		..	5·0	5·1	..
	Total	..	17·9	19·1	..

.. = not available.
Sources: as Table 2.1.

which provides comparable information for two additional European countries, Belgium and Sweden, and two other countries with developed market economies, the United States and Japan. This table suggests that experience in Sweden over the period has been almost identical to that of the Netherlands, in terms of both the level and increase in government expenditure relative to GNP. In Belgium government expenditure has not increased by quite as much, relative to GNP, as in Sweden and the Netherlands, but the increase there has been more marked than in France, Germany and Britain. Of the European countries covered in the two tables, therefore, Switzerland appears to be very much the extreme case with a significantly lower level of government expenditure relative to GNP than the others. In fact, according to OECD figures, in 1969, of all the countries of Western Europe, only Spain and Portugal had a

Table 2.3 *Growth of GNP and Current Government Expenditure 1953–70*

	At current prices		At constant prices	
	Annual average rates of growth			
	GNP	Current govt. expenditure	GNP	Current govt. expenditure
	%	%	%	%
France	10·5	10·8	5·5	5·3
Germany (Fed. Rep.)	9·4	10·1	6·3	6·4
Italy	9·3	11·3	5·5	6·6
Netherlands	9·4	12·5	5·0	6·7
Switzerland[a]	7·8	9·2	4·4	5·5
United Kingdom	6·6	7·0	2·8	2·3
Belgium	6·9	8·5	4·1	5·9
Sweden	8·2	10·9	4·2	5·8
USA	6·1	7·2	3·4	3·6
Japan	14·9	14·0	10·0	7·0

[a] Average rates of growth for 1953–69 only.
Estimated from the sources used in Tables 2.1 and 2.2.

lower level of current government expenditure relative to GNP than Switzerland.[1] Switzerland also had relatively less government expenditure than the United States (where government expenditure expressed as a percentage of GNP was not much less than in France, West Germany and the United Kingdom), but its position appears less extreme when compared with Japan, where not only was current government expenditure considerably lower relative to GNP than in the other nine countries, but it was also lower in 1970 than in 1953. Nevertheless, this cannot be taken to imply that Japanese governments have been less willing to increase their expenditure than their Western counterparts. In fact, in Japan, current government expenditure rose at a faster rate between 1953 and 1970 than in any of the other countries, but there, taking the period as a whole, it was more than matched by the growth of GNP, whereas in the other countries government expenditure tended to grow at a faster rate than GNP.

Details of the average rates of growth per annum of current government expenditure and GNP over the period of 1953–70 for all

[1] The corresponding figures for Spain and Portugal were 17·9 and 18·1 per cent respectively. OECD, *National Accounts of OECD countries* 1953–69.

ten countries are shown in the first two columns of Table 2.3. The growth rates relate to expenditure in money terms and so reflect price changes as well as changes in the real volume of goods and services provided by governments and in the real value of transfer payments. The last two columns of Table 2.3, therefore, show estimates of the corresponding rates of growth at constant prices (i.e. in real terms). These growth rates need interpreting with extra caution as particular difficulties arise in estimating expenditure on public services in real terms. The usual procedures imply that there is no change in the productivity of public service employees. Where their productivity does increase, therefore, the growth of expenditure in real terms tends to be underestimated, and this may account for the fact that in most cases the growth of government expenditure appears to be lower in relation to the growth of GNP when measured at constant prices than when measured at current prices. Taking the figures at their face value, however, Japan again stands out as having a higher rate of growth of government expenditure in real terms than any of the other nine countries, whilst the United Kingdom appears at the opposite extreme with the lowest rate of growth of both government expenditure and GNP. In fact the table suggests some association between the growth of government expenditure and the growth of GNP. This need not be unexpected since governments in rapidly growing economies naturally find it easier to increase their expenditure, but clearly there are also other influences at work: the Netherlands and Sweden, for example, both appear to have experienced a greater increase in current government expenditure (whether measured in terms of current or constant prices) than some countries with a greater growth of GNP. Perhaps the most important point to be derived from Table 2.3, however, is that apparently similar movements in government expenditure expressed as a percentage of GNP may conceal very different increases in government expenditure. In West Germany and the United Kingdom, for example, government expenditure expressed as a percentage of GNP was roughly the same in 1953 and increased by a similar amount over the period to 1970, yet in that time whilst government expenditure in the United Kingdom (at current prices) trebled, government expenditure in Germany increased more than fivefold. This should be borne in mind in the following paragraphs where the discussion turns to the composition of government expenditure, because it will be convenient to continue to make comparisons between countries in terms of percentages of GNP.

The OECD and UN national accounts data for most countries are not sufficiently detailed to permit comparisons of the com-

Table 2.4 *Composition of Current Government Expenditure*

% of GNP at market prices

	Civil	De-fence	Total	Sub-sidies	Transfer payments	Interest on public debt	Total[a]
		Direct expenditure on goods and services					
France							
1953	7·9	7·9	15·8	1·2	13·0	1·1	31·1
1961	7·6	5·3	12·9	1·8	15·2	1·2	31·2
1969	8·7	3·5	12·2	2·3	17·4	1·2	33·1
1970	..	..	12·1	1·9	17·5	1·0	32·6
Germany (Fed. Rep.)							
1953	10·1	4·3	14·4	0·3	13·4	0·5	28·7
1961	10·5	3·5	14·0	0·8	13·2	0·7	28·6
1969	12·7	3·1	15·8	1·3	14·2	0·9	32·2
1970	13·0	2·9	15·9	1·4	13·4	0·9	31·6
Italy							
1953	8·6	3·0	11·6	1·1	8·4	1·7	22·7
1961	9·4	2·4	11·8	1·1	10·4	2·1	25·4
1969	11·1	2·1	13·2	1·9	14·4	2·3	31·9
1970	10·7	2·0	12·7	1·6	14·7	2·4	31·6
Netherlands							
1953	8·4	5·5	13·9	0·4	7·4	2·8	24·4
1961	9·8	4·0	13·8	1·1	10·7	2·7	28·4
1969	12·5	3·2	15·7	1·0	17·2	2·9	36·8
1970	12·6	3·5	16·1	1·3	18·1	3·0	38·5
Switzerland							
1953	8·3	3·0	11·3	0·7	5·1	1·9	18·9
1961	8·3	2·5	10·7	1·0	6·5	1·4	19·6
1969	9·3	2·2	11·5	1·1	9·2	1·4	23·2
1970	..	..	..	..	..	..	..
United Kingdom							
1953	9·4	8·9	18·3	2·1	5·8	4·0	30·3
1961	10·7	6·1	16·8	2·1	6·6	4·0	29·6
1969	12·8	4·9	17·7	1·8	8·9	4·1	32·5
1970	13·2	4·8	17·9	1·7	8·8	3·9	32·4

.. = not available.

[a] Totals are not always exactly equal to row sums because of rounding.
Sources: As Tables 2.1 and 2.2.

Table 2.5   *Distribution of Government Expenditure by Function*

% of GNP

	France 1966	Netherlands 1955	Netherlands 1965	Switzerland 1961	Switzerland 1966	UK 1955	UK 1965
Defence	4·2	5·4	3·8	2·7	2·5	8·9	5·9
Education	5·4	3·5	6·2	2·8	3·5	3·1	4·4
Health	4·4	} 6·8	13·3 {	1·4	1·7	3·0	3·5
Social security	11·2			5·5	7·0	5·6	7·1
Housing and community amenities	0·8	0·7	0·6	—	0·1	3·3	3·5
Agriculture	1·1	0·7	0·7	1·1	1·1	1·4	0·8
Transport and communications	3·1	1·0	1·5	2·8	4·2	1·1	2·0
Other	6·8	7·9	8·4	4·9	5 6	6·6	6·9
Total	36·9	26·0	34·4	21·2	25·6	31·9	34·1

[a] Including both current and capital expenditure.
Source: Mary Garin-Painter, 'Public Expenditure Trends in OECD Countries',
OECD Economic Outlook, Occasional Studies July 1970.

position of government expenditure in other than broad aggregate
terms, but it is possible to compare the trends of certain major
categories of expenditure. Table 2.4 thus shows the distribution of
government expenditure between a number of major categories, in
the six countries covered in Table 2.1, for the years 1953, 1961,
1969, and 1970, and again certain similarities in their experience
become apparent. In fact over the period 1953–70 as a whole, all six
countries experienced an increase in civil expenditure on goods and
services and in transfer payments, together with a decline in defence
expenditure (all relative to GNP) – the latter in most cases being
more marked between 1953 and 1961 than in the later part of the
period.

Additional information on the distribution of government
expenditure for four of the six countries is provided in Table 2.5
which is derived from a special OECD study of public expenditure
trends. The figures there cover capital expenditure as well as current
expenditure, whether it takes the form of direct expenditure on
goods and services, transfer payments or whatever, but the same
broad pattern emerges as from Table 2.4. In fact, taken together the
tables provide some support for the ideas suggested earlier in this
chapter,[1] in that it has been the growth of expenditure on the civil

1 pp. 28–29 above.

Table 2.6 Composition of Current Government Expenditure 1965–8
Average % of GNP

	France	Germany	Italy	Netherlands	Switzerland	UK
Direct expenditure on:						
General administration	..	2·6	4·2	..	..	1·8
Justice and police						
Education and research	..	3·8	4·1	5·2	..	3·5
Health services	..	..	0·9	..	..	3·6
Special welfare services	..	..	0·9	..	..	0·3
Other civil expenditures	..	..	1·3	..	..	2·7
Total civil expenditure	8·6	12·2	11·4	12·0	9·3	11·9
Defence	3·9	3·7	2·3	3·6	2·4	5·7
Total direct consumption	12·5	15·9	13·7	15·6	11·7	17·6
Subsidies	2·2	0·9	1·7	0·7	1·0	1·8
Transfers to households on:						
Education and research	..	0·1	..	0·1	..	0·8
Health	..	1·2	..	3·7	..	0·9
Social security and assistance	..	12·5	..	8·7	..	5·6
Other	..		..	2·8	..	0·5
Total transfers to households	16·4	13·8	13·6	15·3	7·6	7·8
Transfers to rest of world	1·0	0·6	0·1	0·2	0·2	0·5
Interest on public debt	1·1	0·8	2·0	2·6	1·4	3·9
Total current government expenditure	33·2	32·0	31·1	34·4	21·9	31·6
Expenditure by central government	18·4	12·0	17·1	20·3	7·9	23·0

.. = not available. Source: *UN Yearbook of National Accounts Statistics 1966–9*.

functions of government that has led to the commonly experienced upward trend in government expenditure relative to GNP, and, as far as can be seen from Table 2.5, it would appear that most expansion has been in the fields of education, health and welfare and, to a lesser extent, transport and communications.

Whilst the trends in the various categories of expenditure appear to have been similar in all six countries, there appear to have been continuing differences between some of them in the actual distribution of expenditure. Tables 2.4 and 2.5 give some indication of this, but Table 2.6 perhaps gives a better picture of expenditure in more recent years, despite the fact that a complete set of figures is not available for all six countries, since it shows expenditure under each heading expressed as an average percentage of GNP for the years 1965–8,[1] thus reducing the influence of minor fluctuations.

Table 2.6 covers current expenditure only, but it can be seen that, in the particular years considered, the differences between five of the six countries in terms of total current expenditure expressed as a percentage of GNP were at the time small, and three of them, West Germany, Italy and the Netherlands, also had a similar distribution of expenditure between the major categories. The United Kingdom had roughly the same proportion of its resources devoted to civil expenditure on goods and services as these three, but spent relatively more on defence[2] and on servicing the national debt, and correspondingly less on transfer payments. In particular it would appear, from the limited information that is available, that social security transfer payments, covering pensions, unemployment benefits and the like, were rather low relative to GNP in the UK compared with the others (except Switzerland). Some confirmation of this impression is provided by Table 2.5, and also by an earlier British study which found that in 1960, social security cash benefits amounted to 10·4 per cent of GNP in West Germany, 8·3 per cent in France, 7·9 per cent in Italy, 7·7 per cent in the Netherlands and 6·4 per cent in the UK.[3] In contrast to the United Kingdom, France had a higher level of transfer payments over the period covered by Table 2.6 than West Germany, Italy and the Netherlands, but relatively less civil expenditure. In fact, in terms of the distribution of current government expenditure between direct consumption and

[1] It proved impossible to include later years in these calculations because of changes in the classification of expenditure in the UN national accounts data.

[2] It is worth noting that in relation to GNP the UK spent rather less on defence than the USA, when defence expenditure amounted to 8·6 per cent of GNP in 1969 (and 13·2 per cent in 1953).

[3] 'Social Security in Britain and Certain Other Countries', *National Institute Economic Review*, no. 33 (August 1965), p. 56.

transfer payments, France and the United Kingdom would appear to have been at the opposite ends of the spectrum formed by the six countries. However, the difference between them arises in part from institutional differences in the financing of health services. In the United Kingdom, publicly provided health services are financed directly by the central government (with some charges to users), but in France, patients pay medical fees which are then reimbursed from public funds. The expenditure thus appears in the national income accounts as a transfer to households.[1] Similar institutional differences presumably account for the relatively low direct expenditure on health services in Italy as compared with the United Kingdom, but it is interesting to note that this difference is almost offset by a higher level of expenditure relative to GNP in general administration, justice and police.

The tables also provide further information relating to the comparatively low level of government expenditure relative to GNP in Switzerland. Table 2.6 suggests that it was the result of relatively less expenditure under nearly all the main headings. Swiss transfer payments relative to GNP were admittedly considerably less. Table 2.5 provides a little more detail on this, and suggests that the Swiss government's involvement in the provision of education and health services is rather less than that of governments in other countries, an impression which is supported by additional information in the report of the special OECD study from which Table 2.5 is derived. In fact it was estimated that in 1966 direct government expenditure accounted for 54·6 per cent of the total (public and private) expenditure on education in Switzerland compared with 71·5 per cent in the UK (in 1965) and 100 per cent in the Netherlands (again in 1965). With expenditure on health services, the corresponding percentages were 31·5 per cent in Switzerland compared with 93·8 per cent in the United Kingdom.[2] Transfer payments and subsidies (not included in the above percentages) may have accounted for some of the differences, but not all, as according to Table 2.5 government expenditure (including transfers and subsidies) on education and health was lower in Switzerland than in the United Kingdom relative to GNP, yet, again according to the OECD study, total expenditure (i.e. public plus private expenditure) appears to

---

[1] In 1965, 99 per cent of current government expenditure on health in the UK was direct expenditure on goods and services; in France (in 1966) only 11 per cent was direct expenditure; the rest was on transfers and subsidies. Mary Garin-Painter, 'Public Expenditure Trends in OECD Countries', *OECD Economic Outlook; Occasional Studies July 1970*, p. 50.

[2] ibid., p. 52.

have been relatively higher in both areas in Switzerland than in the United Kingdom.[1]

One final item in Table 2.6 of particular interest in the context of the present study is the last line of the table, indicating the expenditure in each country (again expressed as a percentage of GNP) which is the direct responsibility of central governments and therefore of most interest to national parliaments. These figures, which include any grants by central government to non-central governments, reveal significant variations between countries. As might be expected, the central governments account for a much smaller proportion of government expenditure in the countries with federal constitutions (West Germany and Switzerland) than in the others, but even among the latter there is some diversity, ranging from Italy, where central government expenditure amounted to just over 17 per cent of GNP, to the United Kingdom where it was 23 per cent. By showing the size of central government expenditure relative to GNP, these figures also give some indication of the potential role of fiscal policy in the management of the economy, which would appear to be much greater in, for example, the United Kingdom than West Germany, although it has to be remembered that central governments may be able to exercise considerable influence and even control over the expenditure of lower-tier governments even where the latter have their own independent powers of raising finance.

IMPLICATIONS FOR THE CONTROL OF GOVERNMENT EXPENDITURE

If there is any conclusion to be drawn from this brief survey of recent trends in government expenditure in the six countries that are the particular concern of later contributions to this symposium, it is the obvious one that whilst there have been continuing differences between them, particularly in the distribution of expenditure between areas of government activity, there have also been important similarities in their experience. In all six countries government expenditure has increased both in absolute terms and relative to GNP, but to put the discussion of the following chapters into perspective, it is perhaps also important that the full magnitude of the increase in government expenditure should be realised. From the figures in Table 2.3, the average rate of increase in current govern-

---

[1] In Switzerland in 1966 public and private expenditure on education and health amounted to 6·6 per cent and 5·3 per cent respectively of total expenditure on the consumption of goods and services. In the UK in 1965, the corresponding percentages were 5·1 and 4·4. Garin-Painter, op. cit., p. 53.

ment expenditure over the period 1953–70 (in money terms) works out at just over 10 per cent per annum, implying that on average, government expenditure in 1970 was *five times* as great as it was only seventeen years earlier. The available evidence suggests that government expenditure has tended to grow faster in the post-war period than in earlier years, but even so, when a period as long as a century is considered, the increase begins to look almost astronomic. For example, in the United Kingdom, where the growth of government expenditure in the post-war period has actually been slower than the average, it would appear that government expenditure was more than 200 times as great in 1970 as in 1870.[1] Increases of this magnitude would, by themselves, have placed a considerable strain on government and parliamentary budgetary procedures, but, as suggested earlier in this chapter, over the years there have also been significant changes in attitudes towards government expenditure, which in turn have had fundamental implications for the type of question those concerned with the control of expenditure have had to consider.

As long as the prevailing view was that government expenditure should be minimised subject to the maintenance of essential services, on the grounds that its main effect was to divert useful resources from productive industry, it followed logically that the emphasis of control should be on providing the machinery for a detailed scrutiny of estimates before the expenditure was approved, to make sure that the proposed expenditure was no more than necessary, and then, at a later stage, for checking that there had been no unauthorised expenditure and that expenditure had nowhere exceeded the approved limits. As the view that government expenditure might have a rather more positive role came to be accepted, however, other considerations also became relevant.

First of all, where governments take over responsibility for the provision of goods and services, problems of efficiency can arise. Where goods and services are provided through a competitive market system, the pressures of competition, actual or potential, should theoretically ensure the efficient use of resources by producers, and the prices consumers have to pay should encourage efficiency in the consumption of the goods and services produced. But when goods and services are provided outside the market sector there are no such automatic pressures leading to efficient pro-

---

[1] J. Veverka (in A. T. Peacock and J. Wiseman, *The Growth of Public Expenditure in the United Kingdom* (Princeton, NBEC, 1961), Table 1, p. 37) has estimated that in 1870, government expenditure in the UK was £93 million. The corresponding figure for 1970 was more than £19,000 million.

duction, and if they are made available without charge to consumers, no incentive to efficient consumption. This suggests that attention needs to be directed towards the efficiency with which publicly provided goods and services are produced and consumed.

Secondly, when governments attempt directly to manage their economies, it becomes important for them to be able to control total government expenditure in relation to the other main macro-economic aggregates. Total government expenditure is, of course, the aggregate result of literally thousands of individual decisions made at different times and at different levels of government, but it is nevertheless important, at least for central governments, to be able to take account of the impact of their decisions on aggregate expenditure both in the present and in the future if macro-economic goals are to be achieved.

Thirdly, macro-economic considerations may, under certain conditions, bring other issues to the fore. For example, if conditions require restraint in the growth of public expenditure, problems of choice arise over which expenditure programmes should continue unchanged, which should be cut back, and so on. Such problems become more acute at times of budgetary constraint, but they are obviously always present. It will always be the case that resources are scarce, so that some expenditure proposals have to be modified or rejected or given less priority than others. Hence consideration has to be given to the relative importance of particular types of expenditure and the ends they are meant to serve.

On top of all this, the widening scope of government expenditure has raised the question of the time horizon of expenditure decisions. As long as the volume of government expenditure was relatively small and mainly on routine administration, a budgetary system which looked no farther than the year ahead was perfectly adequate, but as governments became involved in longer-term expenditure commitments, and as it became necessary to plan the provision of services several years in advance, the development of budgetary procedures with a longer time horizon became a necessity.

Altogether then, the control of government expenditure has over time become a more complex problem, not only because of the vastly increased scale of expenditure, but also because of the wider issues which control procedures now need to encompass. Realisation of this need has led widely to changes in budgetary procedures and to experimentation with new budgetary techniques. Chapter 17 will examine some of these techniques, drawing on material presented in the contributions relating to individual countries, and will attempt to make some assessment of the way in which parliaments in the six countries have been able to take advantage of budgetary innovation to equip themselves to deal with problems posed by the changing and expanding role of government expenditure.

CHAPTER 3

CONSEQUENCES OF THE FEDERAL SYSTEM FOR PARLIAMENTARY CONTROL OF THE BUDGET OF THE FEDERAL REPUBLIC OF GERMANY

Albrecht Zunker

Any attempt to analyse parliamentary control of the budget in the light of the federal structure of West Germany must start with the observation that there is no such thing as *the* budget of the Federal Republic. There are in fact around 24,000 public budgets: that of the central government (*Bund*), those of the eleven member states (*Länder*)[1] making up the Federal Republic, and finally the estimates of the various local authorities.

The *Länder* are not simply the institutional expression of a decentralisation of the political authority of the centre. It is rather the case that all governmental powers are distributed between them and the central government, i.e. the *Länder* are member *states* with their own sovereignty (albeit limited by the constitution and by federal law), which is exercised by democratically elected parliamentary governments. Since they bear responsibility for the independent execution of certain functions of government, they enjoy, as does the central government itself, a large measure of autonomy in the planning and supervision of their budgets, an autonomy which is enshrined in the constitution. This constitutional arrangement between *Bund* and *Länder*, and especially the principle of budgetary autonomy, might lead one to the view that in any analysis of budgetary control by parliament it is possible to isolate the two levels of government from one another and to ignore the existence of a federal system altogether. Such an approach would only be justified, however, if it were possible to separate sufficiently clearly from one another the functions of the *Bund* and the *Länder*, and if questions of economic interdependence could be ignored.

In fact none of these conditions can be met. On the contrary, the

[1] In order of population size: North-Rhine Westphalia, Bavaria, Baden-Wurttemberg, Lower Saxony, Hesse, Rhineland-Palatinate, Schleswig-Holstein, Saarland, Berlin (West) (the special status of Berlin is of no significance in the context of the present study), Hamburg, Bremen.

execution of the central government's powers is constitutionally dependent in a variety of ways on the agreement or co-operation of the *Länder*. Moreover the development of a modern industrialised welfare state has been accompanied by a marked diminution in the self-sufficiency of both levels of government. In the economic field it is enough to point out that less than half of the proportion of the national product constituted by public expenditure (altogether about 30 per cent, or if social security payments[1] are included, about 40 per cent) is determined and spent by means of the federal budget, and that only about 20 per cent of public investment, important as it is for growth and a stable economy, is carried out by the *Bund*.

These observations provide some indication of the difficult problems facing the modern federal state in determining and executing its functions and its economic and financial responsibilities. In the final analysis the problems arise from the basic question of how the federal system in West Germany can be reconciled with the requirements of an industrialised society and the responsibilities of the modern state. Public finance is of course today the most important instrument available to implement economic policies aimed at such goals as growth or full employment. The conditions for the success of such an economic policy are difficult enough, even before we consider the complications of a federal state, whose economic resources are fragmented, and in which there is a large measure of autonomy of expenditure. The federal structure requires a separation of political decision and of parliamentary responsibility and control between *Bund* and *Länder*. In view of these circumstances, how can a unity of purpose which would be adequate for determining, planning and executing *Bund* and *Land* functions be achieved?

Only half-solutions have been found so far in the Federal Republic. On the one hand in recent years there has been a tendency towards more or less complete centralisation in some areas; on the other hand, to balance the separation of central and member states many different forms of co-operation and co-ordination, of reciprocal representation, and of institutional combinations and interactions have appeared. The parliaments at both levels of the system have naturally been affected by these developments. It is therefore not possible, even in an analysis limited to budgetary control by the central parliament, to ignore the existence of the federal system whose political, constitutional and administrative structures must necessarily affect parliamentary control. In what

[1] See A. Schmidt, Chapter 5 of this book.

follows we shall trace the consequences for parliamentary control of the budget of the existence of a federal state in West Germany. As a point of departure it will be necessary to give a brief outline of German federal constitutional and financial arrangements, and of their evolution up to now.

Main Characteristics of the Federal System

In 1948, when it was decided to give the western parts of Germany a constitution, a federal structure was more or less inevitable from the outset. The newly-created *Länder* set up by the occupation forces – new, that is, compared with pre-1933 territorial units – had already been functioning since 1945; the Western military governors had made a federal system a pre-condition for their acquiescence; the Parliamentary Council (*Parlamentarischer Rat*)[1] also came out in favour of such a system, believing that the new state would be legitimised by taking over what had been, after all, a traditional principle in the creation of German unity. And so a federal constitution was agreed, which included some traditional elements, such as a second chamber at federal level to represent *Land* governments. Furthermore the constitution gave great weight to the *Länder*, largely as a reaction against the *'Gleichschaltung'* of the *Länder* under National Socialism.

Considerable differences exist between the *Länder* in size, population and economic strength. They range from North-Rhine Westphalia with 17·1 million inhabitants to Bremen with 0·74 million, from Hamburg, which has a gross internal product per caput of DM 17,519 (1970) to Rhineland-Palatinate with DM 8,177. On the other hand there are no significant variations from *Land* to *Land* or between the *Länder* and the *Bund* in the type of constitution adopted. With minor exceptions the constitutions of both *Bund* and *Länder* provide for parliamentary systems of government. In view of the fact that in such a system there is usually a strong connection between the executive and the parliamentary majority it follows more or less naturally that relations between the

[1] The Parliamentary Council met from September 1948 to May 1949 in order to work out the Basic Law (*Grundgesetz*). The title of 'constitution' (*Verfassung*) was avoided in order that any future all-German settlement might not be prejudiced. The Basic Law was worked out for the three western zones and came into force in April 1949, following its acceptance by the Allies and by ten *Land* parliaments. The Council was composed of sixty-five members of *Land* parliaments, and was therefore not a national assembly (*Nationalversammlung*).

two levels of the federal structure are largely controlled by the governments.[1]

The most significant characteristic of a federal state is without doubt the existence of two levels of government, i.e. the distribution of functions between the federation and the member states. Compared with a unitary state the significance of this division lies mainly in a series of limitations: effective political responsibility, and with it parliamentary control, are limited to the functions and sphere of influence of the relevant level of government served by the parliament in question. In order to show where and how these boundaries are drawn in the present structure of the Federal Republic, we must sketch in some of the outlines of the constitutional system.

The Basic Law of the Federal Republic is based on the principle that the *Länder* should perform all governmental functions other than those specifically reserved for the *Bund*. It lays down the powers of the *Bund* very clearly. The boundary between *Bund* and *Land* powers can be changed only by amending the constitution itself. Such a move would depend on the fulfilment of special conditions and on specified majorities both in the Bundestag, the central parliament elected by universal suffrage, and also in the Bundesrat, which represents *Land* governments at federal level.[2] This means that the Bundestag is not the sovereign law-making body like, for example, the British Parliament, which acts as the parliament of a unitary state.

The distribution of powers in this federal system is *not* made, as it is traditionally, by allocating to the central government certain areas in their entirety, these areas of decision then becoming the sole preserve of the federal legislature, executive and judiciary. In fact the distribution of powers is based on a separation into three areas: with few exceptions functions of government are arranged initially into legislative, executive and judicial spheres, and only then are allocated between the two levels of government.

Thus both the *Bund* and the *Länder* have powers of legislation. Although federal law overrides *Land* law, the legislation of the *Bund* is limited to those areas laid down in the constitution. In reality the *Bund* has taken over most of the functions of legislation, on account of the increasing tendency to establish unified regu-

[1] Congress in the US presidential system has been able to develop a more independent role in the federal sphere.

[2] An amendment to the constitution requires a two-thirds majority in the Bundestag and in the Bundesrat. For further conditions see Art. 79, paras. 3 and 20, para. 4, *Grundgesetz*.

lations for the whole Federation. This was achieved by making the fullest possible use of such powers as were originally allocated to it by the constitution and by the introduction of a whole range of constitutional amendments, which arose out of the need to modernise the federal structure. The legislative areas remaining to the *Länder* are mainly those of cultural affairs and education, police and their own internal structure (largely local authority regulations). But even those areas are not safe; education, for example, is increasingly influenced by the central state. Thus the *Länder* parliaments have lost ground as legislative bodies. Of course this does not mean that the member states have no influence on federal legislation. On the contrary, limited though the legislative powers of the *Länder* may be, their powers of influence on *Bund* legislation are all the more apparent.

The Bundesrat is the central institution through which the *Länder* participate *directly* in *Bund* legislation, as well as in many other aspects of the political control of the federal state. It is a federal organ, composed of members of *Land* governments; a special kind of second chamber, it is in essence a 'chamber of ambassadors', since its members are bound by the directives of their governments.[1] The Basic Law and subsequent legislation allocate to the Bundesrat extremely important powers. It enjoys an unlimited, albeit rarely exercised right to introduce legislation; all draft bills and proposals of the federal government are submitted to it for its views, and it has the 'last word' on all laws passed by the Bundestag. The so-called 'laws of assent' comprising approximately one-half of all federal laws (e.g. all constitutional amendments and all legislation concerning financial provisions for the *Länder* or affecting the *Länder* financially) can pass into law only if the Bundesrat gives its assent. The same holds for all legal and administrative decrees of the federal government touching the interests and functions of the *Land* governments. In the case of other laws passed by the Bundestag, e.g. the budget of the *Bund*, the Bundesrat is entitled to enter an objection. The Bundestag can overrule such an objection only by an equivalent vote, i.e. a majority of members or a two-thirds majority as appropriate.

---

[1] The Bundesrat is composed of forty-one members appointed by the governments of the *Länder*. They are members of the *Land* governments which they represent. *Länder* with over 6 million inhabitants have five seats each (North-Rhine Westphalia, Bavaria, Baden-Wurttemberg, Lower Saxony), those with over 2 million hold four seats (Hesse, Rhineland-Palatinate, Schleswig-Holstein), those with less than 2 million three seats (Hamburg, Saarland, Bremen). West Berlin sends four representatives, but they do not have voting rights. The votes of every *Land* must be cast *en bloc*.

The extension of *Bund* legislative powers at the expense of those of the *Länder* has considerably added to the importance of the Bundesrat within the parliamentary system, because the requirement for the assent of the Bundesrat has been made statutory in almost every case in which *Land* functions have either been limited in favour of the *Bund*, or transferred completely to the latter.

In the execution of laws, that is, in administration, the weighting between *Bund* and *Länder* is differently distributed. Here, in spite of increasing federal influences on *Land* administration, the form envisaged by the Basic Law has been preserved: the main body of public administration is concentrated in the *Länder*, while federal administration is limited to a few exceptions. As well as executing their own laws, the *Länder* are entrusted in principle with executing federal laws. Thus part of their administrative function is laid down by federal law, although as a rule they execute laws independently *on their own responsibility*. The federal government can only supervise the legality of the execution of these laws; it cannot issue instructions or directives to the *Länder*. In a few cases determined by the Constitution, the federal legislature can transfer certain administrative functions to the *Länder*, which the latter must then carry out as agents, i.e. *under the direction* of the *Bund*. The *Land* authorities are bound by directives of the federal government, and federal supervision also implies controlling the effectiveness of administrative behaviour as well as the execution of federal directives. A federal administration proper exists in only a few special areas, such as the administration of the armed forces, foreign affairs, shipping and waterways. However, there is no *overall* central administration of taxation, for example, and by far the greater part of the administration of justice falls to the *Länder*.

This 'administrative federalism' acts as an impediment to parliamentary control and ministerial responsibility, for it is hardly necessary to point out that parliaments find themselves in a peculiar position as a result of these delineations of powers. Thus, a *Land* parliament controls an executive responsible for giving effect to laws which the parliament itself had no part in passing. A *Land* parliament has no control over the interpretations or amending of these laws or over their budgetary consequences. They control executives which in some administrative areas are subject to directives from another level of government, and which are to that extent not responsible to the very parliaments on whose confidence they depend for their existence. On the other hand the Bundestag is attached to a government which in wide areas of executive activity lacks its own administration and therefore has no direct control over the execution of its policies. Moreover in some areas, where its action is based on budgetary rather than legislative provision, this government's measures can in certain circumstances be countered by the *Länder*.

The picture so far presented of the Basic Law's allocation of powers has stressed the separation of powers between the two levels of government. This leaves out significant features. The development of a modern industrialised state has brought with it far-reaching changes in the federal structure, which point towards a 'unitary federal state'.[1] In this process the *Länder* have had to subordinate political independence to the needs of the federation as a whole. In some areas the separation of powers has yielded to a centralisation of powers in the hands of the *Bund*; in others it has been weakened by new forms of co-operation and co-ordination. Above all it has been superseded by the need for a successful economic and financial policy dedicated to national economic goals.

Not only has the *Bund* taken over more legislative powers, but a complex system of *Bund-Länder* links has emerged from the increased intermeshing of what were originally separate areas of control. This has occurred where the *Bund* pays financial subsidies to the *Länder*, and especially where the administration operates freely, exercising discretionary rather than legal powers. Some of these new forms of co-operation have found their way into the Constitution. In this way joint planning and financing of certain *Land* activities has been introduced, limiting the principle of distribution of functions – so-called joint planning functions (*Gemeinschaftsaufgaben*). To quote another example, joint consultative committees (*gemeinsame Beratungsgremien*) have been established by law to reach agreement on economic and financial policies. The pressure to unify political decisions has affected more than *Bund-Länder* relations. Even in areas where they operate independently the *Länder* have been forced to co-operate more closely *with one another*. This has resulted in a kind of third level, finding its expression in specialist conferences between individual ministers, and a wide range of treaties and administrative agreements between *Länder*.

We shall return in detail to the consequences of this development for parliamentary control of the budgets. But before we can do this we must take a look at the financial arrangements as provided by the constitution.

---

1 This process is described by K. Hesse in *Der unitarische Bundesstaat* (Karlsruhe, 1962).

The Distribution of Financial Powers

It has frequently been asserted that the distribution of financial powers is the cornerstone of a federal order, because it is on this that the vitality of the system depends.

The main difficulty lies in securing on the one hand adequate financial (and thus political) independence of the two levels of government from one another, and yet on the other hand satisfying the citizens' demands for equal treatment over taxation and a uniform level of public services.

At the same time it is also necessary for federal economic and financial reasons to ensure adequate co-ordination of financial policy within the various *Länder*. The Basic Law sets out to achieve this goal by means of a complex arrangement of legislative powers, a network of revenue distribution, by means of a device for financial equalisation (*Finanzausgleich*), and finally by setting up the legal framework for the co-ordination of all economic activities on the state and local level in order to ensure the implementation of federal economic goals.

Ever since the Federal Republic was established, the organisation of finance has been a regular bone of contention between federal and *Land* governments. Controversies in the Parliamentary Council (*Parlamentarischer Rat*) led to compromises (due in no small measure to the intervention of the Occupying Powers), compromises which were seen as a victory for the *Länder*, which however affected adversely the powers of the federal government to regulate federal finances in the interest of the whole. In the period which followed, the inadequacy of these arrangements became apparent. They were unable to cope with the increasing functions which had to be allocated, the complexity of the problems which had to be solved, and the demands for an equilibrium in public intervention designed to ensure an even spread of economic welfare over the country as a whole. There *were* major reforms in 1955–6, 1967, and 1969, but it was only very gradually (and the process is not complete even now) that the idea took root that 'in a modern federal state finance and budgets are to be seen as a totality, in which there can be no separate financial arrangements and no isolated financial policies pursued by a particular political unit within the system, if the total political structure is not to suffer damage'.[1] However clear the justification for this step-by-step (and still incomplete) adaptation of the financial structure to modern

---

[1] H. Laufer, 'Föderatives System und Finanzordnung', in *Festschrift für K, Loewenstein* (Tübingen, 1971), p. 300.

governmental conditions and objectives, it must nevertheless be recognised that the very creation of such a 'totality', such an 'overall framework' threatens to limit the opportunities for parliaments to initiate and to control.

It is possible to mention here only a few of the most important features of the present arrangements. The central government now enacts virtually all tax legislation although the Bundesrat safe-guards the rights of the *Land* governments to influence and veto federal tax legislation. This concentration of tax legislation in the hands of the *Bund* means that *Land* governments and parliaments can no longer pursue an independent taxation policy. However the Bundestag is in a similar position, since any important decision in this area depends on the assent of the Bundesrat. Thus the method by which revenues are distributed between the *Länder* and the *Bund* becomes a key issue. Since the most important regulations regarding distribution of revenue are written into the Constitution, they can be changed only by majorities in the Bundestag and the Bundesrat large enough to amend the Constitution. In practice this means they are inflexible, at least in the short term. In the first instance there are elements of a separating system: the proceeds of different taxes are going to different levels of the federal structure. Thus the federal government receives, for example, customs and excise revenues, yields from fiscal monopolies and most of the consumer taxes and taxes on the transport of goods while the *Länder* receive taxes on property, inheritance and motor vehicles and the municipalities and other local authorities are allocated real estate taxes. This system of division, which was much more clearly defined in the original pro-visions of the Basic Law, has been gradually modified in favour of a compound system: income tax, corporation tax, and (since the finance reforms of 1969) turnover tax are shared between federal and *Land* governments. More than 60 per cent of all taxation revenues, and more than 70 per cent of *Bund* and *Land* revenues, flow into this pool. After deduction of the local authorities' share of income tax revenues, the federal and *Land* governments each receive one half of this tax and of corporation tax. Revenues from turnover tax are also shared, with the difference that the ratio is not laid down in the Basic Law, but is fixed by a federal law, which requires the assent of the Bundesrat. After the usual sharp disagree-ments between federal and *Land* governments, the 1972 and 1973 ratios were fixed at 65 : 35.

According to the present constitutional provisions turnover tax is the only moveable component in revenue–distribution by means of which adjustments can be made to an imbalance between the expenditure of the *Bund* and that of the *Länder*. In order to correct even partially the great differences between 'poor' and 'rich' *Länder*, this distribution is supplemented by an extremely complicated system of adjustment. Its elements are also laid down in the Constitution, but individual provisions require a federal law, for which the assent of the Bundesrat is required. Here too the Bundestag is not in a position to introduce changes independently of the Bundesrat.

It is worth noting in passing that there is a separate federal and *Land* revenue administration. The customs, monopolies and main consumer taxes are administered by the federal government, the remainder by the *Länder*. Efforts to introduce a uniform federal revenue administration, such as had existed in the Reich from 1919–45, were foiled by opposition from the *Länder*. Nevertheless it did prove possible in the financial reforms to improve the dual system in the direction of a 'mixed' *Bund–Länder* administration.

Only the parliament concerned may in principle determine the expenditure of those financial resources which, as a result of the processes of distribution and adjustment, are allocated to the *Bund* and *Länder* and which can be supported by bond issues. Following the principle of division of functions, the parliament concerned must make provision for whatever expenditure is required to fulfil the functions prescribed. The Constitution states: '*Bund* and *Länder* are autonomous and independent of one another in their budgetary arrangements.'[1] Federal German practice has shown that these principles can be applied only if considerable exceptions are made. Mention has already been made of one limitation of the principle of the division of functions, namely the 'joint projects' (*Gemeinschaftsausgaben*), which at present embrace higher-education building, economic improvements in the regions, agriculture, and coastal protection. In addition federal and *Land* governments co-operate in educational planning and scientific development. Finally, the federal government is able, through the financial assistance it provides, to participate in local and *Land* investments which are of significance for the Federal Republic as a whole, and which are necessary to combat economic imbalance in the federation as a whole, to balance differences in economic strength in the various parts of the federation, or to encourage economic growth. This shows that the principle does not always apply that any particular government level allocated a project must bear the financial burdens necessary for its fulfilment. The unrestricted application of this principle would mean that any *Länder* carrying out federal laws on their own responsibility and which involved, for example, distribution of savings bonuses, building grants, and so on, would have to bear the costs out of their own resources. In fact, the federal

[1] Art. 109, para. 1, *Grundgesetz*.

government takes over all or part of the expenditures involved in such cases. These breaches of the principle happen to be expressly permitted in the Constitution; in practice there are many others. All in all this justifies the claim that 'only in a few areas today are there public undertakings in the financing of which federal, *Land* and local authorities do not in some form or another participate jointly'.[1] This of course represents a major challenge to the capacity of *Bund* and *Land* administrations and parliaments to plan and to control policies and budgets rationally and independently.

From the economic point of view of the whole federation this is obviously true. Unrestricted budgetary autonomy, as laid down in the section of the Constitution quoted, cannot be reconciled with the fact that economically the Federal Republic is a single entity. The overall economic responsibilities of the modern state cannot be reconciled with a situation in which 'revenues and functions are shared out, so that everyone can be left to do what he thinks best'.[2] Yet this is a reflection of the situation in the Federal Republic as it existed into the second half of the 1960s: 'This autonomy [was] *de facto* a right to share the responsibility for financial chaos.'[3] It was only then (the late 1960s) with the experience of the economic recession in 1966-7, that all those concerned were forced into an awareness of the need for an agreed budgetary policy for the whole economy and for all levels of government, within the framework of longer-term planned growth, and for a co-ordinated fiscal and credit policy. It was only at this point that a tentative limitation to the autonomy in budgetary planning of the *Länder* became possible, and, based on it, the passing of the Stability and Growth Law (*Stabilitäts- und Wachsturmsgesetz*). This bound both federal and *Land* authorities to take account in all economic and financial measures of national economic requirements, and pledged them to co-ordinate their budgetary planning. At the same time the federal government was granted a number of powers to issue decrees, requiring the assent of the Bundesrat, by which, for economic reasons, tax-rate changes, credit limitations, or the creation or winding up of so-called 'balance reserves', can be prescribed for both *Bund* and *Länder*. These powers can be applied if an economic council, composed of members of *Bund* and *Land* governments and also of local authority representatives, cannot mutually agree to a solution. In addition the Stability Law binds federal and *Land*

---

[1] J. Hirsch, *Haushaltsplanung und Haushaltskontrolle* (Stuttgart, 1968), p. 96.
[2] H. Haller, 'Wandlungen in den Problemen Föderativer Staatswirtschaften', in H. C. Recktenwald (ed.), *Finanzpolitik* (Köln 1969), p. 142.
[3] Hirsch, op. cit p. 98

authorities to the setting up of a policy for medium-range financial planning. Finally the finance reform of 1969 created the constitutional prerequisites for substantially the same legal provisions governing drafting and executing the budgets in *Bund* and *Länder*. It also set up a finance planning council (*Finanzplanungsrat*), corresponding in its structure to the economic council (*Konjunkturrat*), to co-ordinate budgetary policies and financial planning.

For the parliaments this trend towards increased co-ordination and combined planning, which understandably falls mainly in the sphere of the executive, means that there emerges a large area of 'intra-federal foreign policy' (*innerbundesstaatliche Aussenpolitik*). In this they face the prospect of losing all but the functions of ratification.

The foregoing rough outline of the constitutional and organisational *structure* of the German Federal State has shown some of the basic problems and limitations for the parliaments in realising their 'power of the purse'. It is now time to turn to the federal aspects of the budgetary *process* itself.

FEDERALISM IN THE BUDGETARY PROCESS

The Länder *and the Budget of the* Bund

The *Länder* have plenty of opportunities to exercise a controlling and corrective influence on all phases of the budgetary process at federal level, both directly and indirectly. The institutions which can be used for this purpose include the economic and finance planning councils, the large number of *Bund-Land* administrative committees, specialist ministerial conferences, and of course the Bundesrat. Because of its direct role in the federal budgetary legislation process, it is primarily to this last body that we must now turn.

Since the federal budget must appear in the form of a law and the Bundesrat plays an integral part in federal legislation, the *Land* governments have through its medium a direct means of control assured to them by the Constitution. The federal government presents its draft budget and its medium-range financial plan (the latter on a consultative basis only) simultaneously to the Bundestag and the Bundesrat. Subsequently the Bundesrat has a period of six weeks in which to debate these proposals and present its proposed amendments. For the preparation of its response the Bundesrat makes use of its committees, mainly the Finance Committee. Normally the *Land* governments are represented on this committee by their finance ministers, together with high-ranking *Land* civil servants as *their* representatives. The ministerial bureaucracies of the *Länder* are at their disposal for support in the preparation of their work. For this reason and because the *Land parliaments* do not participate in the decisions of the Bundesrat, it is often claimed that control of the federal bureaucracy by the *Land* bureaucracy has been institutionalised.

The committee recommendations, which are worked out in private session, are discussed in a plenary session of the Bundesrat, and since these recommendations carry great weight, they are largely taken over by the whole chamber and passed. The reply of the Bundesrat is then passed to the Bundestag via the federal government, which first adds its reply. Only after this can the second reading of the budget take place in the Bundestag. On completion of the legislative process in the Bundestag the Bundesrat has a second opportunity to express its views. During this second procedure it mainly examines whether and to what extent its reactions to the first procedure have been taken into account, and whether fresh reservations arise from any budgetary changes undertaken in the Bundestag. Since the budget law is not one of those which require the assent of the Bundesrat, the latter can vote only for a suspensive veto against a budget which has been passed by the Bundestag. The suspensive veto would only be required should a mediation procedure fail, and it could be negated by a majority in the Bundestag corresponding to the majority by which the Bundesrat raised its objection.[1] However, the Bundesrat has never made use of this right in the case of a federal budget.

Not only are there measures for the execution of the budget which may require the assent of the Bundesrat, as under the Stability Law; the Bundesrat is an equal partner of the Bundestag in the last phase of the budgetary process, which is the statement of accounts, although this is an exercise to which it has never attached much importance.

The viewpoint of the *Länder* (or to be more precise of the *Land governments'* interests) is the centrepiece of the strategy of the Bundesrat in its work on the federal budget. Key issues are the financial relationships in the federation, more especially the protection of *Land* finances from attack by the *Bund*, but also the influencing of budgetary policy and federal programmes to the advantage of the *Länder*. Where individual budgetary measures affect the *Länder*, they are in the forefront of their deliberations: for example supplementary payments by the *Bund* to the *Länder*, general finan-

1 cf. p. 50.

cial adjustments, investment grants and federal funds designed to promote *Land* projects, reductions which the *Bund* intends to make at their expense, corrections of minor points in the budget which are based on the administrative experience of the *Länder*, and so on.

The widespread mixing of federal and *Land* projects causes the Bundesrat to work for somewhat contradictory ends, first, of warding off attacks by the *Bund* on the financial autonomy and competences of the *Länder*, and then, of participating in the finances of the *Bund* by grants and joint financing projects.[1]

It has hardly ever managed to exert a comprehensive or positive influence directly on budget proposals; just as it has failed, in spite of its increased importance following the extension of federal activities, to become a forum in which expert discussion is held on federal policy and practice.

The Bundesrat is likely to hold a debate dealing more with principles or with systematic examination of fundamental questions concerning the federal budget, only when no agreement is reached in another forum of conflict, for example, in the Economic Planning Council. Even if such an agreement has been reached, the Bundesrat acts only as a formal, ratifying body.

There has been a certain enlivening of budgetary debates in the Bundesrat since the Social-Democrat and Liberal coalition of 1969. For the first time the opposition party in the Bundestag has had a majority in the Bundesrat.[2] Even this politically interesting situation leads only occasionally and under exceptional circumstances to party conflict in the Bundesrat. This may sound surprising, but the party political confrontations which characterise Bundestag debates tend to be neutralised in the Bundesrat by such things as conflicting interests among the *Länder*, conflicts between *Länder* and *Bund*, confrontations between 'poor' and 'rich' *Länder*, the fact that political parties at *Land* level are more or less independent of their federal organisation, and so on.

We should not underestimate this self-imposed limitation on the political activity of the Bundesrat, which has far-reaching consequences for the functioning of the federal system.

In order to judge the performance of the Bundesrat this point should not be ignored: both the *Land* governments and their ministerial bureaucracies are brought in for consultation in the pre-

[1] Hirsch, op. cit., pp. 123–4.
[2] At present the Christian Democrats form the governments in Schleswig-Holstein, Rhineland-Palatinate, Baden Wurttemberg, Saarland and Bavaria.

liminary stages of drafting the budget by the federal government, especially by individual ministries. This occurs not only because time-tabling makes this early contact compulsory, but largely because the *Bund* is dependent for the realisation of its projects on information from the *Länder* and also on their readiness to co-operate in the stage of execution. To plan a project and to plan expenditure it is necessary to control the execution of the plans themselves, but this is to a large extent an affair of the *Länder*. Pre-budgetary collaboration reduces the amount of 'visible' work which the Bundesrat performs later on.

Moreover the *Land* governments participate in the deliberations of the Bundestag, since they are entitled (and can be obliged) to take part in consultations during plenary debates of the Bundestag (although this opportunity is seldom taken) and in Bundestag committees. For example, representatives of the *Länder*, in the form of officials of the *Land* governments, are usually present at sessions of the Budget Committee of the Bundestag. On their own initiative they can use the offer of information and expert assistance from their departments for the service of committees and of individual members of parliament to promote the interests of a particular *Land* or of the *Länder* as a whole. Thus the Bundestag is given 'the opportunity in its budget deliberations to deal with experts from various "camps" ',[1] even though it sees itself confronted by *Bund–Land* plans and measures which have already been agreed at government level, and which force the Bundestag to assume the role of intruder.

The Bund and the Budgets of the Länder

Of course there is no institution at *Land* level comparable to the Bundesrat, by which the *Bund* could be directly involved in the parliamentary stage of the budgetary process. This does not mean that the *Bund* exercises no influence on *Land* budgets. Indeed as a regular feature of federal policy the *Bund* encroaches directly and indirectly on to *Land* affairs. The brief treatment of financial powers has already shown what can happen. This does not mean that the *Bund* has the financial and budgetary policies of the *Länder* under strict control. Nevertheless this influence has been increasing since the birth of the Federal Republic. This can be explained in a number of ways, although we shall mention only one here. In the past the *Länder* and the local authorities seem to have taken no account in their expenditure of the effect of general economic fluctuations and to have based expenditure and their liabilities on

1 Hirsch, op. cit., p. 125.

estimates of revenue. *Land* revenues vary 'pro-cyclically' with general fluctuations of the economy, so that it is quite possible that the federal government could be frustrated in any attempt to implement an 'anti-cyclical' economic policy. Indeed the government's interventions could have the opposite effect to the one intended. As has already been shown, the federal government has no direct influence on the structure or quality of revenue or expenditure in the *Länder* and the local authorities, nor can it apply the relevant clauses of the stability law without the agreement of the majority of the *Länder*. Therefore it has to rely either on voluntary co-operation or on indirect means of influencing these bodies.

This interdependence of functions and of financial responsibility together with the increase in joint planning and co-ordination have had a marked effect on budgetary control by the *Land* parliaments.

The functions of control of the *Land* parliaments are limited mainly because basic questions of project planning and of expenditure policy are frequently decided by agreements between *Land* governments, or between federal governments and *Land* governments. These agreements are usually concluded to the exclusion of parliament; it is extremely difficult to bring an individual government to account either *ex ante* or *ex post facto* for its responsibility in concluding these agreements. *Bund* subsidies limit the areas of self-determination of the *Länder* even further because they can be used only according to the special instructions accompanying them. Information from the *Bund*, which is needed before control can be exercised, is often not available. In the *Länder*, as in the *Bund*, input-orientated budgetary planning methods governed by specific administrative considerations are applied which are ill-suited to political planning and control.

Faced with this situation the *Land* parliaments see their prime function as being to exercise intensive control over detail in the committees. Plenary sessions seldom lead to debate on the broad principles of economic and financial policy. The freedom of action of an individual *Land* is scarcely adequate to provide for controversial parliamentary debates on the basic principles of budgetary policy. When they *are* held, all that usually emerges is a repetition or a continuation of discussions already held or to be held at federal level, and so plenary debates almost never go beyond the statement of position of the various parliamentary parties, and are then followed by discussion on individual items of the budget. One might imagine that in view of this the *Land* parliaments would pay close attention to *ex post facto* control, to auditing and performance control. Yet this is as weak as it is in the Bundestag. On the other hand the *Land* parliaments act vigorously in the executive phase of the budget via their budget committees, and thus try to compensate for the limitations on their powers to enact the budget. However this attempt at 'participation in government' through the committee system undermines the detachment without which criticism of government actions is unlikely.

Co-operative Federalism

In the early stages of the Federal Republic it was only through the Bundesrat that co-ordination and co-operation between member states and the *Bund* were practised to any real extent. Nowadays there is a multiplicity of newly created co-ordinating bodies, which have become an indispensable element of the federal system. In response to the challenge presented by the range and complexity of the tasks confronting a highly developed, industrialised welfare state there has been a great deal of interlocking of the two levels of government, and an extensive overlapping of their powers of decision. Many features of the contemporary system can be traced to this development: limitations on regional independence, more power to the executive, a decline in the independence of *Land* governments acting alone in the federal decision-making process, all have made it much more difficult to safeguard parliamentary responsibility and control.

With regard to the budgetary powers of parliament we should examine two kinds of co-ordinating procedures and two bodies having co-ordinating functions. First, there are the Economic Council (*Konjunkturrat*) and the Finance Planning Council (*Finanzplanungsrat*). Both are composed of members of federal and *Land* governments together with representatives of the local authorities. The Economic Council discusses the application of all economic policy measures laid down in the Stability Law, and considers the means available for meeting the credit requirements of *Land* governments and local authorities. In short, it deals continually with the drafting of budgets, and so with the economic measures considered necessary to execute them. The Finance Planning Council also deals with decisions on budgetary planning. Its main function is to make recommendations regarding the drafting of budgets, and the medium-term financial planning of both *Bund* and *Länder*. The adoption as policy objectives of real and nominal rates of growth in gross domestic product, and of a rational expenditure programme for the country as a whole, calls for a comprehensive and co-ordinated plan. Thus the duties of the Finance Planning Council include providing the 'technical' prerequisites of macro-economic decisions, such as the design of a system of budgetary and financial planning using uniform economic and functional criteria. It also has to define the political, economic and financial concepts which will serve as a foundation for all the budgetary and financial planning of *Bund* and *Länder*. Finally, it is the council's duty to set priorities of time and of scale for the completion of all official policy objectives on the basis of long-term forecasts and an assessment of the needs of the economy as a whole.

Both Councils have a purely advisory function, and are enpowered only to make recommendations; neither has been completely successful. For example at their meetings, which take place on average four times a year, they have regularly agreed on recommendations for guide-lines in the drawing-up of budget and finance plans, but these have not been implemented very often, even by the *Bund*. They had rather more success in their attempts to regularise credit-drawing and participation in the capital market. They recommended the creation of 'balance reserves' (*Konjunkturausgleichsrücklagen*)[1] and this was subsequently passed by the Bundesrat. They agreed on adjustments to the distribution of revenues from certain taxes and these were ratified by the relevant parliamentary bodies. The range of subjects discussed has even included civil service salaries.

In spite of their purely advisory powers they exert a considerable influence on the decisions of the Bundesrat and Bundestag, as on those of the *Land* parliaments; their deliberations precede those of parliament, both in time and in terms of procedure. If agreement can be reached at government level, the parliamentary committees very often forgo their rights of discussion, criticism and control over the issues concerned.

The influence of the joint undertakings (*Gemeinschaftsaufgaben*) is even more apparent. On account of their national importance these are jointly financed and planned by *Bund* and *Länder*, the *Bund* bearing at least half of the costs involved. Joint planning committees are set up by *Bund* and *Land* governments to formulate structural plans for these undertakings (*Rahmenpläne*) (say, a plan to reform and expand higher education). The committees have powers of *decision*. They are composed of the relevant federal

[1] Balance reserves (*Konjunkturausgleichsrücklagen*) are an instrument for creating reserves, e.g. for the financing of additional expenditure in a period of anti-cyclic financial policy. In periods of rapid growth some *Land* and *Bund* revenues are held by the Federal Bank. They can be released when the economy is weak, with the object of producing a boost to the economy overall; see the Stability Law.

minister, the federal finance minister and one minister from each *Land*. Their decisions, if passed by a three-quarters majority (each *Land* has one vote and the *Bund* has a vote which corresponds to the number of *Länder*), are binding on the *Land* governments. They are obliged to provide in their financial and budgetary proposals for any expenditure which is envisaged in a structural plan. Although the *parliaments* are not bound by these decisions, this is the legal, not the political position. In practice parliaments must vote the necessary credits unless they are prepared to reject the plan as a whole and lose the federal subsidies involved. The reason for this is that if a parliament turns down a government request for credits to finance a joint undertaking, the plan has to be redrafted and agreed again.

Parliaments have tried to free themselves from this strait-jacket by binding their governments to inform them in advance of projects to be included in the structural plans, and to continue to keep them informed before decisions are taken in the planning committees, so that parliament may retain an opportunity to exercise prior influence and control in the executive sphere. The very complexity of these planning processes makes parliamentary control extremely difficult.[1] Some *Land* parliaments intend to set up special committees for this purpose.

It remains to be seen whether it will prove possible to limit the consequences of joint planning and finance enough to satisfy the parliaments, without on the other hand so far limiting the freedom of decision of governments that they become unable to negotiate and compromise. Some *Land* politicians are very ready to suggest that the joint undertakings, brought in only in 1969, should be abolished on the grounds that the *Länder* were being denied the opportunity to demonstrate regional initiative and individuality, in areas covered by joint undertakings, and that therefore one of the great advantages of a federal state was being lost. It was claimed that regional initiative was being handed over to the *Bund*, which, because of its larger finances, was able to push its own ideas through and then leave the *Länder* to deal with the subsequent costs arising from the joint investment. However, what happens with joint undertakings only illustrates especially well a tendency in other areas of activity.

It would be wrong to interpret the above remarks on the forms and practice of *Bund–Land* co-operation as an argument against co-ordination and long-term planning. No one can dispute the fact

[1] For discussion on parliamentary problems over joint undertakings see *Bundestag Drucksachen*, VI/1057, VI/1651, VI 1705.

that a modern State is unable to perform its function without planning. The question is, what are the procedures and instruments most suitable for a democratic system? No really satisfactory answer has yet been found to the question of how parliament in a unitary State can effectively participate in the planning process. How much more true this is in a federal State!

CONCLUSION

We could point to even more consequences of the federal system for parliamentary control of the budget. There is the lack of public information available on the co-ordinating practices of governments and bureaucrats. The financial and budgetary planning techniques and methods used today are inadequate for a rational control of projects undertaken in the complex structures of the federal state. The federal system of public finance is so complex – an aspect we have only broached so far – that while parliamentary control and influence are limited, the role of experts within parliament is becoming more decisive. Finally there are the various ramifications arising from the fact that the opposition in the Bundestag is the governing party in some of the member states.

Taken together, the observations made in this chapter could be misinterpreted as a demand for a strict division of roles between central and member states, and the allocation to parliament of clearly defined areas of control. But a strict division is not possible in view of the interdependence and complexity of the functions of a modern State. The federal State can cope with the tasks of planning, direction and welfare for modern society only with 'an interplay of various decision centres, in a fine web of powers and functions, of possibilities for co-operation and influence'. Indeed, the problems of parliamentary control considered here take on a 'third dimension' with the beginnings of economic and financial co-operation within the framework of the EEC.

These problems require different solutions. Initial steps lie for example as much in the revision of the regulations governing federal powers (especially for finance), as in the restructuring of parliamentary committees, or in new techniques of gathering and processing information.

The chief aim must be to put the responsibility of governments to parliament on a practicable, comprehensible footing. For it is in the preservation of government responsibility, involving argument, proof, justification and publicity, that the principal task of the Bundestag, and also of the *Land* parliaments, must surely lie.

C

CHAPTER 4

PARLIAMENTARY CONTROL OF THE BUDGET IN THE FEDERAL REPUBLIC OF GERMANY

Karl Heinrich Friauf

INTRODUCTION

The control of the nation's finances – the 'power of the purse' – is one of the key constitutional arrangements of the modern State, since the execution of political plans, indeed of any governmental activity at all, is dependent on the availability of the necessary resources. Thus the right to decide on the goals involved in the application of public monies lies at the centre of the State decision-making process. However, the power of any government agency to define its aims and priorities can be fully exercised only if the agency concerned is also given the right to allocate the appropriate funds. In other words full political authority can be exercised only if policy-making and financial powers are combined.

This combination of powers means that the budgetary system of any given country will necessarily reflect the country's constitutional structure. The extent and degree of parliament's power to control the budget are thus bounded by the relationship between parliament and government as set out in the Constitution. A government is not 'strong' unless constitutional law or practice provide it with a measure of financial control which is independent of parliament. Conversely, the 'weakness' or 'strength' of parliament depends on the financial control which it is able to bring to bear on the government. *The question of parliamentary control of the budget is therefore inextricably bound up with the general constitutional structure.* Where this relationship between Constitution and parliamentary control is not specifically laid down in the text of the Constitution, then it will perforce resolve itself through a series of constitutional confrontations between the executive and the legislature, which could lead either to a situation in which the body controlling the budget exerts a decisive influence on the whole machinery of state, or to a devaluation of budgetary powers to those of mere ratification.

THE DEVELOPMENT OF THE BUDGETARY SYSTEM IN GERMANY

The accuracy of the above observations is borne out by the history of the budgetary system in Germany, or, to be more exact, of the individual member states of the former German Reich.[1] The constitutional structure of the German states was a dualist one, comparable to the presidential structure of the United States of America. Overall executive power was vested in the Crown, which was solely responsible for appointing and dismissing ministers, who in their turn were responsible only to the monarch. The government was in no way answerable to parliament. Ministers could be impeached by the supreme courts (*Staatsgerichtshof*) only for breach of the Constitution, which in practice rarely occurred; this meant that they could not be unseated by a parliamentary vote of no confidence. In fact parliaments did participate in the legislative process. Without their assent no new law could be passed, and no taxes levied. On the other hand the Constitution allowed them no influence on government policy. In such a situation it became a crucial question whether parliaments were in a position to decide on, or at least influence, the application of financial resources, and in this way to bring an indirect influence to bear on the general trend of policy.

In a number of (mainly southern and central) German states, whose Constitutions came into force before 1850, the parliaments were from the outset excluded from any participation in budgetary legislation. Indeed the budget was decided by the government alone, usually for periods of two to five years. After it had been passed, the budget was only presented to parliament in order to show the need for any additional taxation. The question then arose whether the government was subsequently bound by the budget which it had produced, after parliament had voted the taxes needed for its execution, and whether the government was obliged to refrain from any expenditure not expressly granted by parliament. For decades the government concerned opposed any such limitations. They took it as their prerogative to dispose of State resources at their own discretion, and to depart as they saw fit from the provisions of the budget which had been the basis of the tax legislation. The parliaments protested frequently and with some emphasis against this government position, but they were unable to change it. It was only after decades of conflict that a compromise solution was worked out

[1] For details cf. K. H. Friauf, *Der Staatshaltsplan im Spannungsfeld zwischen Parlament und Regierung*, vol. I (Bad Homburg, Berlin, Zurich, 1968), pp. 37–269.

which gave parliaments a small, but very limited, influence over State expenditure.

In the remaining German states, above all in Prussia, the Constitutions provided for an annual budget bill along the lines of the Belgian Constitution of 1830. Since the Crown could not put laws into effect without parliamentary assent, this meant that every budget required a parliamentary majority. Since government policy was dependent on the availability of resources, this situation seemed on the face of it to provide a means of overcoming the dualism of Crown (government) and parliament, by giving parliament a decisive influence over government policy. However, such a development would have been in stark contradiction to the constitutional basis of the whole system (i.e. the monarchic principle), according to which the Crown held all State powers and parliament was only allocated certain advisory functions (but not a share in power).

In the inevitable political conflicts arising from the situation, governments were largely able to hold their own against their parliaments. The Prussian constitutional crisis of 1862–5 was one of the key conflicts of this period. During these four years no budget bills were enacted for the kingdom of Prussia, because parliament refused to accept the government's draft budget, objecting to the expenditure involved in army reform. The government in its turn was not prepared to bow to the amendments proposed by the parliamentary majority. The dissolution of parliament and subsequent elections still failed to resolve the conflict, and so the government decided to carry on its business without the support of a budget bill passed by parliament. In justification it put forward its original budget proposals, in spite of the fact that these had been rejected by parliament. In this way it carried through the reform of the army, for which parliament had refused to vote the necessary credits. It was only four years later, following more elections and a changed political climate, that parliament accepted the actions of the government with a retroactive law of indemnity.

The Prussian constitutional conflict ended in a clear victory for the Crown and its appointed government. The solution of this conflict was of far-reaching significance for the interpretation of parliament's budgetary role, an interpretation which was to dominate German political thinking for the next fifty years. Extensive discussion of this question can be seen in the constitutional commentaries of the day. Between 1870 and 1918 there is probably no other question in the whole field of constitutional law which was so frequently and intensely analysed as that of the legal consequences of the budget.

The overwhelming majority of leading commentators on constitutional law found that the position of the Prussian government was constitutionally fully justified. Their view was based on the claim that according to German constitutional law the budget had no political significance, and in particular that it did not involve the empowering of government by parliament to engage in expenditure. After all, the government was already empowered by the constitution to carry out such expenditure as it held to be necessary, while the budget passed by parliament contained mere estimates of expected expenditure and not real appropriations, and was only necessary for the sake of good accounting procedures.

Furthermore the constitutional commentaries of the day did not even allocate to parliament in its passing of the budget those political powers which it enjoyed in other fields of legislation. Its role was seen as being comparable with that of an administrative body. Leading writers on constitutional law took the view that parliament's budgetary role was not to decide on the basis of 'legislative freedom', but on that of 'administrative obligation'. All expenditure which seemed necessary for the execution of existing laws and for the maintenance of existing State institutions in their present form should be passed without question.

Parliament was thus not entitled to deny credits with a view to abolishing or modifying these institutions; it was only free to take certain decisions over granting additional credits for new public enterprises.

The 1861 Constitution of the German Reich took over the budgetary principles which had applied in the Prussian Constitution. It is worth noting that a solution was found for the military estimates, at that time the most important part of the budget. In order to remove these estimates from the annual debate over budget proposals they were fixed for periods of seven years at a time (the so-called *Septennat*). This was a compromise reached between government and parliament. Only following the expiry of the seven-year period was it necessary to fix expenditure for a subsequent seven years.

All in all it can be seen that the budgetary system operating in Germany until 1918 did not become an effective *political instrument of control* of the government by parliament. Parliaments seldom made any serious attempt to exert influence on government policy by means of the budget. Where they did try, they enjoyed scant success. By and large they tended to obtain certain concessions from the government by way of compromise. Any thought of parliament seizing supreme power by controlling the finances of the State would have been foreign to the majority of elected representatives. Moreover it would have been incompatible with the practice of constitutional monarchy.

The *overall economic significance* of the national budget was in practice not adequately realised during this period. Although the State took over a gradually increasing proportion of the domestic product, little account was taken of the effects its expenditure might have on the economy as a whole. A study of the lengthy budget debates, which were frequently held in German parliaments, yields little evidence of any awareness of the interaction of public expenditure and the economy as a whole. There was certainly no attempt to influence economic performance via the budget. The budget therefore remained an economic instrument in the narrower sense. It did not become an instrument of intervention.

In this situation the chief function of the budget proposals and of parliament's participation in them lay in the *administrative sphere*. Parliaments saw as their main duty the need to ensure the most economic application of public resources. In essence they saw themselves as representatives of the taxpayer, whose first duty was to minimise government expenditure and in so doing keep down the tax rates. Proposed government expenditure was far more often attacked on the grounds that it was unnecessary or extravagant, than because it was considered politically inappropriate.

Resulting from this overriding *function of thrift* exercised by parliament, accounting procedures were developed and refined with a view to increasing the responsibility of the administration for exercising all possible economies.

Courts of audit (*Rechnungshöfe*) were set up in the German states, which carried out extremely strict and comprehensive audits. The attitudes of the day are reflected in the fact that these courts of audit were not made subordinate to the parliaments, as aids in the latter's control of the executive, but were instituted as supplementary organs of the government in order to supervise bodies responsible to those governments. They had to report on their investigations to the finance minister, not to parliament.

The Weimar Constitution of 1919 introduced a parliamentary system of government in Germany. However it allocated to the President a considerable area of executive power. He was elected directly and was not responsible to parliament. Thus certain elements of a dual system of government survived in spite of the introduction of a government which was responsible to parliament.

In the Weimar period the budgetary process was considerably developed and refined. The 'general law on budgetary procedure' of 1922 (*Reichshaushaltsordnung*) regulated the whole budgetary procedure in what was for those days an extremely progressive manner: from the report of the various ministries on their financial requirements, the adoption by the Cabinet of the budget proposals, the debate on the proposals and their acceptance by parliament, through to the expenditure of the funds by the executive, the statement of accounts and the audit by the court of audit, and finally the acceptance by parliament of the statement of account.

Although this represented a considerable advance in budgetary procedures, it did not mean that there was any understanding of the function of the budget as an instrument of parliamentary control. However, it was generally understood that the budget proposals were more than a mere instrument of administrative routine and that they represented a decisive political function. Consequently they were designated 'a fundamental act of general state policy' (*staatsleitender Gesamtakt*). However the dominant view in both constitutional theory and practice was coloured by the traditional theory of the separation of powers. Thus as an 'act of government' the budget was allocated to the sphere of the executive, not to that of parliament. As a result financial decision-making was regarded as a matter for the government, while parliamentary *participation* in formulating budget proposals was considered to be of only secondary importance. Thus, although it was based on the traditional separation of powers and showed little understanding of how a fully developed parliamentary system of government works, German constitutional theory at that time arrived at conclusions about the interrelated roles of parliament and government in setting up the budget which coincided with the situation in some genuinely parliamentary systems. In the period from 1933 to 1945 there was no parliamentary control of the budget, although the passing of annual estimates was retained. However those were prepared and decided on by the government alone. They served only as an instrument of control by the government over subordinate administrative bodies. The government itself was neither bound by legal norms nor was it politically responsible to any other body.

CHARACTERISTICS AND PROBLEMS OF THE PRESENT BUDGETARY SYSTEM[1]

1 In the *federal system* of the Federal Republic of Germany *Bund*

[1] The most important regulations are contained in:

(i.e. central government) and *Länder* (i.e. member states) are autonomous and independent of one another in their budgetary arrangements (Art. 109, para. 1, Federal Constitution). In principle *Bund* and *Länder* must each provide for such expenditure as is needed for the fulfilment of their various functions (Art. 104, para. 1). As a result we must consider not only the budget of the *Bund*, but also the independently prepared budgets of the individual *Länder*, as well as those of the thousands of local authorities.

This multiplicity of independent budgets within the framework of an overall state structure (a structure in which moreover the total volume of the *Land* and local authority budgets together far outweighs that of the *Bund*) has led to considerable problems for the economy as a whole. In recent years the role of the public sector as an interventionist instrument has become more apparent. It has become equally apparent in this situation that the fragmentation of public finances into a multiplicity of independent economies runs counter to the requirements of an effective, rational economic policy. On the other hand the rights of the *Länder* to control their own budgets are guaranteed under the Constitution, so that any unilateral modification of this position would have jeopardised the entire framework of the federal structure. Clearly, some mutually accommodating solution had to be found, and this took the form of a constitutional amendment, plus the enactment of the Stability Law (*Stabilitätsgesetz*), both in 1967. These preserved the division of budgetary powers between *Bund* and *Länder* (including the rights of the *Länder* to determine their own expenditure), but allocated to the *Bund* powers to effect economic co-ordinating measures.

It will not be necessary here to go into details of economic co-ordination between *Bund* and *Länder*.[1] The object of the present analysis is solely budget arrangements at federal level. However the reader should bear in mind that this is only one half of the German exchequer.

2 Reference has been made (in the introduction to this paper) to the close interrelationship existing between budgetary control and the constitutional framework as a whole. We must now look at the budgetary law and practice in the Federal Republic of Germany

> (*a*) Art. 109–15, Federal Constitution (*Grundgesetz*) in the constitutional amendments of 12.5.1969 (*GG*).
> (*b*) Gesetz über die Grundsutze des Haushaltsrechts des Bundes und der Länder, vom 19.8.1969 (*HGrG*).
> (*c*) Bundeshausnaltsordnung, vom 19.8.1969 (BHO).
> (*d*) Gesetz zur Förderung der Stabilität und des Wachstums der Wirtschaft, vom 8.6.1967 (*StabG*).

[1] For details see Chapter 3.

against the background of the governmental system laid down in the federal Constitution.

The federal Constitution set up a full *parliamentary system of government*, which, while not corresponding exactly to the British model, resembles it in all its main characteristics. Legislative powers are vested in parliament, with the emphasis on the universally elected Bundestag, while the Bundesrat, representing the various governments of the *Länder*, enjoys certain participatory rights in legislation. The centre of executive power is the federal government, within which the *Bundeskanzler* (federal chancellor) plays a dominant role both by virtue of his constitutional position and also in political practice. The federal chancellor is elected by the Bundestag; he appoints all other members of the government, who for their part do not require any confirmation by parliament. The federal chancellor is responsible to the Bundestag, but cannot be dismissed by a simple vote of no confidence. He can fall only if the Bundestag elects a successor by absolute majority (i.e. by more than half of the total membership). The federal president, who is not elected directly but by a parliamentary assembly, has no significant executive powers. He is very largely restricted to a representational role in the execution of the political decisions of the Bundestag and of the government. As far as the budget is concerned he is both *de jure* and *de facto* excluded from any participation, with the single exception that he must formally promulgate the budget law after its final passage through parliament. This excludes the possibility of even the smallest influence being exercised by the federal president on budget proposals.

There is a close political relationship between the parliamentary majority and the federal government. Members of the government are almost without exception also members of parliament, while the federal chancellor is customarily also leader of the largest government party. This situation necessarily leads to political domination of the parliamentary majority by the government.

At the same time it cannot be said of the Federal Republic that the government 'controls' its parliamentary majority in quite the same way as is clearly true of other states with parliamentary systems of government. Government and parliamentary majority are not regarded as politically identical, as is the case elsewhere. It is rather the case that a certain consciousness of separation-of-powers has survived in the relationship between the two, which acts as a barrier to the political identification of one with the other. Although they carry the government, members of the parliamentary majority do not regard themselves simply as tools of its political will, but rather as holders of an independent control function. To some extent this is probably due to the fact that the Federal Republic has not had one-party rule, but coalition governments, with a consequently limited sense of political homogeneity. Also, party discipline seems to be less obviously exercised than is the case in, for example, Britain.

The effect of this situation can also be seen in the way in which parliamentary prerogatives regarding the budget are exercised. A federal government which rests on a majority in the Bundestag can be sure that the budget which it presents will, on the whole, be accepted. However it cannot necessarily expect that all individual items will meet with the agreement of members of parliament – including members of its own party. In other words, the confidence of the parliamentary majority in the government does not imply that every single government proposal will be accepted by that majority. This means that although we have a comprehensive parliamentary system of government, German budgetary practice retains aspects of dualism.

3 One of the chief problems involved in setting up the annual budget arises from the fact that by far the greater part of available finances is committed from the outset by permanent finance laws and by long-term expenditure programmes agreed in the past. These commitments have to be taken into account in budget deliberations and the sums involved cannot be varied by parliament. Compared to these sums, the amounts which remain (at least in theory) at the disposal of parliament are very small indeed. For this reason the annual budget tends increasingly to consist of little more than arithmetical additions of long-term items of expenditure already committed.

This situation has long been criticised on the grounds that most of the laws committing the *Bund* to large, long-term expenditure were passed independently of the budget, and that their economic effect was not harmonised with the trend of other national economic needs. While it is true that these laws all expressed the political will of parliament, it is also true that they were not the expression of a rational economic decision, because their overall budgetary implications were not known to parliament. This range of *ad hoc*, unharmonised financial measures was bound to endanger the financial stability of later years. The first serious financial crisis in the federal economy was brought about in 1967 when long-term, uncoordinated blocks of expenditure coincided with stagnation in the amount of tax revenues.

The experience gained in this crisis resulted in the law for the promotion of stability and economic growth in 1967 (*Gesetz zur Förderung der Stabilität und des Wachstums der Wirtschaft*). Paragraph 9 of this law requires that the federal economy be placed on a *quinquennial footing*. This five-year plan must show probable expenditure together with the sources of revenue proposed to cover it; it must also show both of these items in relation to the projected development of the economy as a whole. Particular attention must be paid to the financial effects of current legislation and economic programmes as well as the projected costs of any programme which is to begin in the course of the five-year period. Financial planning as foreseen in Paragraph 9 is dynamic, not static. This law also expressly lays down that the quinquennial plan must be revised each year to include actual performance for that year, and that projections also be correspondingly revised. The financial plan is thus not set out in inflexible segments, each of five years' duration, but rather keeps five years ahead of actual developments, and can absorb any annual budget changes. If for example a new category of expenditure is agreed in the budget of any particular year, the financial plan must automatically be revised to include estimated expenditure changes over the next five years which this new category will involve.

Quinquennial financial planning is an instrument of the executive. It is set up and presented by the federal finance minister. It needs a decision of the cabinet in order to take effect, and is only presented to parliament for information, so that there is no parliamentary vote on its acceptance. As the federal government stressed in its financial report for 1968, financial planning is in essence 'a government programme in figures, in which priorities of time, and all main positive and negative heads are set out'. Financial planning by government does not *de jure* affect the budgetary sovereignty of parliament, since parliament is not legally bound by the plan. Theoretically, therefore, any number of departures from the quinquennial plan are possible in the course of the proceedings on the annual budget. However it would make no sense of financial planning if frequent use were made of this possibility. But it is above all political pressures, together with a number of institutional provisions, which ensure that parliament will in the main adhere to the basic principles of the financial plan.[1] One eminent specialist in this area has claimed with some justification that the quinquennial financial plan (decided on by the government) may well exceed in its

---

[1] Cf. for details Friauf, *Öffentlicher Haushalt und Wirtschaft, Veroffentlichungen der Vereinigung der Deutschen Staatsrechtslehrer*, vol. 27 (1969), p. 1, et seq.

political significance and effect the annual budget passed by parliament.

The introduction of compulsory quinquennial financial planning shows then, in its practical consequences, a marked tendency to limit parliamentary powers of decision, above all in those areas concerned with the development of programmes involving new expenditure. Similar tendencies can be seen in a number of other areas; for example most of the economic measures provided for by the Stability Law are allocated either to the government or to other executive bodies. Parliament was granted only limited, *ex post facto*, rights of participation, and even then only in the case of a number of these measures. For example if the federal government decrees borrowing limits for public authorities, then the Bundestag has the power within six weeks to demand that this measure be withdrawn (Art. 20, Para. 5, Stability Law).

The fiscal powers of the executive have also been increased by developments in the federal components of the German constitutional system. Important functions which were originally undertaken independently by individual *Länder*, and which were also financed wholly from their budgets, have now been made subject to a joint *Bund–Land* decision (*Gemeinschaftsaufgaben* – joint undertakings). The governments of the *Bund* and *Länder* are represented on the committees dealing with these joint undertakings, but not the parliaments. Here too, of course, the parliaments are not bound by the decisions of these committees, just as they are not bound by medium-range financial plans. Theoretically their budgetary sovereignty is completely preserved. Nevertheless they are in practice under an irresistible political pressure to accept the findings of these committees without amendment, and to vote the necessary credits, since these findings will have been reached only by a complex system of compromises arrived at between the government of the *Bund* and those of the *Länder*. They have invariably accepted them up to now. To this extent it is no longer possible to speak *de facto* of any parliamentary freedom of decision in the adoption of the budget.

Similar developments occur wherever public expenditure is subject to an institutionalised process of long-term planning. By its very nature planning tends to produce pressures which change the whole political decision process. When it is rationalised and placed on a long-term footing it ceases to be simply one of a number of possible preparations for political decisions, but rather tends by its content to predetermine the decisions themselves, especially parliamentary decisions on legislation and the budget. Unless it is prepared to question the entire basis of the plan, parliament is subsequently left with no option but to pass its individual provisions into law, and is thus robbed of the chance of presenting a political alternative. Up to now there has been no evidence in the Federal Republic of Germany of any readiness to accept the continual loss of parliament's political powers caused by all these developments, nor is there any widespread acceptance of the view that they represent a normal expression of the relationship between legislature and executive in a fully developed parliamentary system of government. On the contrary present developments are regarded as constitutionally dubious, as a limitation on the constitutional position of parliament. This view to some extent results from the separation-of-powers attitudes described earlier in this paper, attitudes which hold that parliament is entitled to an expression of political will which is independent of that of the government it upholds.

The parliamentary committee for questions relating to amendments to the constitution (*parlamentarischer Ausschuss für Fragen der Fortbildung des Verfassungrechts*), set up by the Bundestag in October 1970, has devoted a considerable amount of time to this matter.[1] While it recognises that political planning is a legitimate government activity, it nevertheless demands that parliament be informed at all times of planning carried on at government level, and claims that parliament has the right to express a view on the various alternative plans, going so far as to say that the last word on acceptance of the plan is the prerogative of parliament. It recommends that a Bundestag standing committee on planning should be set up, in order to make the influence of parliament on government more effective.

4 The technical *procedure for setting up the annual budget* is regulated in detail in the BHO (*Bundeshaushaltsordnung* – budgetary standing orders). In the first instance each ministry must prepare estimates for its own area. The actual budget draft is then prepared by the federal finance minister (*Bundesminister der Finanzen* (BdF)) on the basis of these estimates. Some cuts in the ministries' estimates are usually involved at this point. If, on important issues, no agreement is reached regarding these cuts, and the minister concerned opposes the finance minister, a decision from the cabinet can be called for. However, the finance minister occupies a strong position within the cabinet. He can be outvoted only on budgetary issues; if the federal chancellor supports his

---

[1] cf. *Interim Report of the Commission of Inquiry into Constitutional Reform*, 21 September 1972, German Bundestag, 6th legislative period VI/3829, pp. 44–52.

views, the finance minister can defeat all the remaining members of the cabinet.

After any clashes between expenditure proposals of various ministries have been thus resolved, the draft budget proposals are finally agreed by the government and then laid before both the Bundestag and the Bundesrat. The decisive political weight in budget deliberations rests with the Bundestag, as the directly elected parliament. As the representative body of the *Land* governments the Bundesrat can enter an objection to a decision of the Bundestag in budgetary matters, and thus force a renewed debate. However the Bundestag, by satisfying certain majority requirements, can over-rule the objection and thus maintain itself against the Bundesrat.

The budget which the government lays before parliament (and which requires the latter's assent) is extremely complex in structure. Traditionally it is set out under the heads of the various departments making the expenditure. This frequently means that expenditure on allied programmes is shown in fragmented form, where these programmes are carried out by several ministries and authorities. This means that the federal budget is an administrative budget, not a programme budget. Members of parliament therefore have no overall view of the budget, an inevitable result of this form of presentation. To modify the effects of this situation, it has been compulsory since 1969 to add to the draft proposals specifications of groupings of undertakings and functions. It is claimed that this has made the interrelations between various expenditure heads clearer than was the case in the past.

In general the layout of the draft budget satisfies the requirements of administrative control (and thus above all the requirement for the most economic transaction of the administration's affairs), rather than those of political control and economic intervention. For the most part the various expenditure heads are extremely specialised. Individual items are set out in countless columns, frequently with details of the most minute amounts of money. As a result the draft usually amounts to around 3,000 pages. Lump sum appropriations appear for only a few areas, such as military purchases or for agricultural subsidies.

5 The major part of *parliamentary work on passing the budget*, above all deliberations on individual objectives, is not carried on in plenary sessions but in the Bundestag's budget committee[1] This committee is composed of thirty-three members, elected by the parliamentary parties in proportion to their representation in the

---

[1] Apart from the budget committee there is a finance committee, which is concerned not with appropriations, but with taxation.

Bundestag. It is thus a reflection in miniature of the composition of the Bundestag. Most of its members belong to this committee for a number of legislative periods, so that they tend in time to become specialists in one area or another. Because these members specialise in differing areas, and because they have worked together over many years, the situation has arisen that party divisions between majority and opposition are much less obvious in the budget committee than they are in Bundestag plenary sessions. This provides the opposition with a better opportunity to assert their view on one expenditure head or another (of course, without breaching basic government policy) than could ever be the case in plenary session.

Committee deliberations on the government draft tend to be thorough and intensive. However, they are often criticised for paying too little attention to the political significance of the various expenditure heads. The traditionally 'administrative' layout of the draft is one reason why the committee spends a great deal of time on the recurrent costs of the administration, neglecting the much larger appropriations for new programmes. It is by no means unusual, for example, for exhaustive discussion to be held on the need to establish two new typists' posts, or to acquire an additional ministerial car, while the many millions required for a subsidy programme go through on the nod.

A large number of amendments arise in this way every year during the course of parliamentary discussion on the government draft. Politically and financially, however, these amendments are not significant. In the 1966 budget, for example, 1,100 amendments to the government draft were accepted. The total amount affected by these amendments was no more than 2·1 per cent of the budget total (i.e. about $1\frac{1}{2}$ thousand million DM).

In the Bundestag plenary debate on the budget the emphasis is placed on general political questions which often have little to do with the narrower subject of public finances. This is especially true of the first reading. During the second reading it is possible to propose changes in individual expenditure heads, but in general such proposals have scant chance of being accepted unless they have the backing of the budget committee. Occasionally the government itself encourages sympathetic members of parliament to propose amendments. On doing so it is either taking account of developments which may have occurred after the draft had been laid before parliament, or it is attempting to shift the responsibility for unpopular economies (which the government itself considers necessary) on to parliament.

6 The *Bundestag's powers of decision* over the draft budget are

to a great extent unlimited, as far as *cuts in expenditure* are involved. At its own discretion it is free to reduce or to cut altogether the expenditure requested by the government. The only limitation here is that the Bundestag is not permitted to deny the government such appropriations as are necessary for the execution of existing laws. As has already been mentioned, however, parliament makes little use of these powers in practice.

On the other hand the Bundestag is subject to severe limitations when it comes to *increasing the appropriations* requested by the government, or to introducing new expenditure not proposed by the government. When the Constitution was set up in 1949 it was originally proposed to insert a clause along the lines of standing orders in the British House of Commons, which would have made parliamentary proposals for an increase in expenditure, or for new expenditure, admissible only if the government agreed beforehand. However this proposal was not accepted. Instead Article 113 of the Constitution was included. This states that decisions of the Bundestag or the Bundesrat which involve increasing the appropriations requested by the government, or which involve new expenditure in the present or future, require the assent of the government. Parliament is free then to consider proposals for increases in expenditure, and also to pass them. However, if the proposals obtain a parliamentary majority, they can become law only if the government agrees to them. In effect this gives the government veto powers over parliamentary proposals for increases in expenditure.

Article 113 of the Constitution has not however played any significant part in parliamentary practice. The main reason for this is probably the fact that the power of the government to refuse its agreement could only be exercised after the Bundestag had carried such proposals, and the Bundestag in turn could only carry such proposals if at least some of the members of the government party were to vote for them, since otherwise they would never have obtained a majority in parliament. In these circumstances a refusal by the government would have been the signal for open conflict between the government and its own parliamentary party. The federal government has always avoided such a conflict. During Dr Adenauer's long period of office as Chancellor the government only once refused to accept a decision of parliament based on Article 113. In all other cases it used its weight to try to have proposed amendments to increase expenditure turned down in parliament itself. When occasionally it failed in this attempt it acquiesced in the proposed additional expenditures.

In 1969 the veto powers of the government were extended by a constitutional amendment to cover parliamentary decisions which would involve a reduction of revenues. At the same time the procedure was changed to improve the government's chances of making use of its powers in practice. In the case of parliamentary amendments involving increased expenditure the government can require parliament to postpone its decision for six weeks and to await a governmental response. In addition it can require parliament to re-examine an amendment after it has been passed. If the members of parliament subsequently confirm their earlier decision, the government can refuse to give its assent, although no such refusal can be traced since 1969.

In this context it is noteworthy that the Bundestag passed a standing order in the 1950s according to which MPs moving amendments which involve new expenditure have to add concrete suggestions showing how the related costs are to be covered, before their amendment can be moved. However, this order was declared invalid by the Federal Constitutional Court, on the grounds that it represented an unconstitutional limitation on MPs' rights of initiative. All in all it can be seen that up to now the Bundestag has frequently added items to the budget which were not contained in the government draft, and that the government has accepted these additions. In individual cases these changes can be of some political significance. However, the total amounts involved in additional expenditure voted by parliament are usually insignificant when set against the total volume of the budget.

7 The criticism has often been made that the *political dimension* does not receive adequate weight when the budget is debated and voted. This criticism is certainly justified to some extent. The member of parliament's main interest is to influence individual heads of expenditure, frequently involving insignificant sums, and thus to exercise some control on the administrative consequences of the budget. Acceptance or rejection of the budget are not seen as a political act in the sense of expressing a general approval or disapproval of government policy. Approval of the budget does not imply any basic vote of confidence in the government.[1]

One is bound to ask whether it is even necessary, in the monistic structure of a fully developed parliamentary system of government, to regard the vote on the budget as an expression of confidence. After all, the government is appointed by parliament and should it

---

[1] There are of course occasional exceptions to this rule. For example the rejection of the budget which had been produced by the chancellor's office in spring 1972, arising from the split vote (248:248), can certainly be regarded as a political vote against the federal chancellor.

lose the confidence of the majority, can be replaced by a new one at any time, outside budgetary procedure. Whether or not the loss of confidence derives from financial policies is of no account. The rejection of the budget can take on the specific function of a vote of no confidence only in a dual system, in which parliament has no direct opportunity to bring down the government. What really matters in a parliamentary system is making government financial policy clear, giving the public and the opposition the opportunity to criticise, and giving the parliamentary majority (where it sees itself as a separate political centre which is independent of the government it supports) an opportunity to amend this or that cabinet proposal, without undermining its basic loyalty to the government.

Awareness of the fundamental significance of the budget has been slow to spread in German politics. However, it has, in political economy, finally found expression in the above-mentioned Stability Law of 1967 (*Stabilitätsgesetz*). This law states expressly that budgetary policy must serve fundamental aims of economic policy: namely price stability, high employment, external balance and steady economic growth. Thus the budget as a whole is declared to be *de jure* an instrument of rational economic control. The composition and extent of programmes according to Paragraph 5 of the Stability Law, must be so organised as to take account of these overall economic goals, while at the same time maintaining economic balance. It should be clearly understood, however, that using the budget as an instrument of economic intervention is a task which must be carried out by the government, which must prepare its draft accordingly. This limits parliament in practice to accepting the government's initiative.

Quite often in recent years a so-called conditional budget has been passed in addition to the regular budget. This included investment expenditures which are initially blocked and can be made available only by special permission of the finance minister to deal with undesirable economic trends. The use of public finance as an instrument of economic intervention seems increasingly to be a matter of executive action rather than part of the budgetary proceedings.

8 Not surprisingly the *execution* of the budget is a matter for the executive. The budget empowers the relevant authorities to effect the expenditure prescribed. On the other hand it has no influence on the rights and duties of the individual citizen. Administrative bodies are strictly tied to the amounts and objectives laid down in the appropriations (in other words the budget is divided into specialised sectors on both qualitative and quantitative grounds). Sums which

an authority may save on any particular programme cannot be applied to others, unless special permission has been given for specified amounts. In this way the budget provides administrative control.

For a number of years now the annual budget laws have provided for the exercise by certain Bundestag committees (chiefly the budget committee) of certain rights of control over the execution of the budget. Probably the most important example is provided by appropriations for military purchases. Here it has been frequently laid down that the minister of defence may only apply these funds with the assent of the relevant Bundestag committee. The constitutional propriety of this practice is a little doubtful. It has been claimed that parliament is interfering in an unconstitutional way in the execution of the budget, which is solely in the hands of the government. On the other hand it should be remembered that these new participatory rights of parliament in the *execution* of the budget are meant as no more than partial recompense for the fact that parliamentary control over the *setting up* of the budget has been subjected to numerous restrictions.

The strictly binding nature of the budget in administrative terms is qualified in two important respects: (*a*) by the so-called emergency appropriation powers of the finance minister (Article 112 of the Constitution), and (*b*) by a number of economic powers allocated by the government. The emergency appropriation powers (*Notbewilligungsrecht*) entitle the minister of finance to authorise, in the event of 'unforeseen and unavoidable need', expenditure which is not laid down in the budget. For years there has been a tendency to extend these powers. Originally they were limited to cases of urgent necessity, but they are being applied more and more frequently when certain political considerations suggest that expenditure is urgently called for, without any serious claim being possible that it is 'unavoidable', i.e. urgently and absolutely necessary. Parliamentary majorities have generally acquiesced in the extended use of his emergency powers by the finance minister, and in so doing have surrendered their right to any prior control of the funds being applied. In one unique case the opposition in one of the *Länder* attempted to obtain a ruling in their favour from the Constitutional Court on the unconstitutionality of one such 'emergency appropriation' by the finance minister. However the attempt met with failure.

The Stability Law empowers the federal government to make expenditure over and above the budget on programmes (above all investment) which are laid down in the quinquennial finance plan, should the economy begin to falter and the overall economic goals laid down in the law be endangered. The funds needed to cover this expenditure are taken initially from special reserves which the *Bund* is obliged to deposit in times of excessive economic expansion with the Federal Bank. Should the funds available in these special reserves not suffice for the purpose, the minister of finance is empowered to take up additional credits up to 5,000 million DM over and above the credit totals laid down in the budget. The projects proposed in this context must be laid before parliament, which can reject them. Its assent is assumed to have been given unless it expressly rejects the proposals within four weeks. This secures for the Bundestag a measure of political control; on the other hand the government's economic powers to initiate are only countered if they are positively rejected by a parliamentary majority.

In the reverse situation, an overheating of the economy which endangers stability, the federal government has the power (Article 6, paragraph 1, Stability Law) to decree an economic bar on certain funds already allocated. The effect is that the relevant authorities can only use the blocked funds if the finance minister gives his express approval in each case. Monies saved by this block must either be used to amortise debts or be deposited with the special reserves.

CHAPTER 5

FINANCIAL LEGISLATION IN THE BUNDESTAG: THE CASE OF COMPULSORY PENSIONS INSURANCE

Alfred Schmidt

THE DEFICIENCIES OF THE BUDGETARY PROCESS BEFORE THE REFORMS OF 1967–9

In a parliamentary democracy the budget is supposed to serve as an instrument of political leadership and as a means of control over the machinery of the State. Although in a sense the budget is the instrument of the government, elected by the majority party, the budget should also give parliament, and in particular the opposition, the opportunity to exercise control over the government, and make it possible for the electorate to form judgements on the intentions and actions of the political institutions which they have elected. In a model such as this, parliament holds the key position because of its right of initiative in budgetary planning, the decision it takes on the annual budget law, the current information it receives on the execution of the budget and also because of its right to subsequent audit of the budgetary accounts on which the government depends.

The political and economic functions of the budget are inseparable. In a circular process, the goals of economic policy are politically determined, while political activity itself depends on economic factors. In the Federal Republic, deficiencies in the budgetary process were apparent on both the political and the economic levels before the reforms of 1964–9.

The legal framework which regulates the budgetary process in the Federal Republic reflects a tradition dating from the era of constitutional monarchy, in which the annual budget is primarily concerned with the financial effects of current laws, existing institutions, and current projects. Decisions on new projects are mainly excluded from the annual budget debate, and the budget merely takes note of the financial effect of these decisions. Both in the budget and in approving decisions on individual projects according to normal legislative procedure, the role of parliament depends on the supply of adequate information. This

> means that the costs of clearly defined project aims are determined and presented in their entirety in relation to the time the project will take and its scope; that in certain cases information on the costs of alternative projects is available; that the economic side effects and the financial repercussions of the measures planned are disclosed, and that the entire programme of tasks in the public sector is available in a form which is sufficiently comprehensive and detailed for comparisons to be made and for decisions on the order of priorities to be taken.[1]

The failure of the annual budget debate to meet all these criteria would not matter if the appropriate information was considered when the laws relating to individual projects were themselves passed. However, prior to the reforms there was no way of doing this, for in legislative decisions there could be no consideration of the programme as a whole and therefore no possibility of making comparisons and setting priorities. But even in the annual budget debate no one looked at the situation as a whole; the experts in the budget committee frittered away their time with marginal details as did the members of parliament who have a special interest in particular sections of the budget. Moreover the members and, to some extent, also the ministers had insufficient information from the administration. 'Alternative programmes, even if they are in fact ever worked out, rarely leave the realm of administration, are available to the Finance Minister and the Cabinet only to a limited extent and almost never reach parliament.'[2]

Since in individual legislative decisions it is naturally the material content of the programme which is of most interest, and not its financial implications, a survey of the long-term effects of current programmes was needed as a background to annual budgetary planning, in order to show the scope existing for future financial decisions. Such a survey was made available only from 1965 (in the financial report of the Finance Minister). This has only tended to show that 'increases in fixed expenditure arising from legislation with long-term effects, limit the opportunities for action at the time of the annual budget to such an extent that one can only speak of

[1] Joachim Hirsch, *Parlament und Verwaltung*, part 2: *Haushaltsplanung und Haushaltskontrolle in der Bundesrepublik Deutschland* (Stuttgart, 1968), p. 105.
[2] ibid., p. 107.

planning in a very limited sense'.[1] This was one reason why medium-term planning became necessary, but it was also necessary as a framework for short-term financial policy and growth policy involving indicative planning of the economy as a whole.

There was another reason why the budget covered legislative programmes only in an unsatisfactory way. Their financing had been shifted out of the area of State activity as registered in the budget. There had in fact been a return to the pre-parliamentary 'system of funds'. This system offends the budgetary principles of clarity, comprehensiveness, and non-specific appropriation and cannot easily be subjected to ex-post control. Furthermore the system of funds makes it more difficult to survey the various parts of the public sector of the economy, which is necessary for a co-ordinated fiscal policy. This problem, which arose anyway from the federal nature of the Federal Republic, was complicated by the existence of 'para-fiscal bodies'.[2] We refer here first to certain areas of responsibility, which in other countries are often directed by the State itself, but which in the Federal Republic are transferred to organisations such as Chambers of Industry and Trade; and secondly to special tasks, above all in the field of social policy, which have been transferred to institutions, set up expressly outside the State machine. A common factor in all these para-fiscal bodies is that the State bestows on them the receipts from special taxes to cover their expenditure.

We have mentioned only some of the deficiencies which were apparent in the Federal Republic before the reforms of 1967 to 1969. We shall now look at an example which is relevant both to the way in which the financial implications of individual pieces of legislation are dealt with, and to the special problems which arise from para-fiscal bodies in the Federal Republic.

CASE STUDY: THE PENSION REFORM OF 1957 AND ITS FINANCIAL ASPECTS

At the beginning of the 1950s the Adenauer Government announced an extensive programme of social reform for the Federal Republic in response to a political initiative by the opposition party, the Social Democrats. During the 1950s and 1960s the social reform programme was split into a series of 'mini-reforms' which is not yet complete. The reform of compulsory pensions insurance was con-

[1] ibid., p. 109.
[2] Henry Laufenburger, *Théorie économique et psychologique des finances publiques* (Paris, 1956), vol. 1, pp. 130–5.

sidered urgent and was removed from the proposed general reform during the second legislative session of the German Bundestag, 1953–7, and took the form of the introduction of so-called 'productivity pensions'.[1]

The essential result of this reform, as its name indicates (albeit somewhat obscurely), is that new old-age pensions are pegged automatically to an annual index of the wages and salaries of all those insured. However, existing pensions are adjusted to changes in this index of wages and salaries only semi-automatically by a federal law. In this way consideration can be given to the financial position of the insurance bodies and to the economic situation as a whole. The pension insurance scheme is financed principally from payroll contributions, half of which are made by persons insured and half by the employers. In addition, it receives general tax revenue from the federal budget in the form of so-called federal subsidies.

Technically a method of 'pay-as-you-go' is being used, which is adjusted to make revenue and expenditure balance for a period of ten years at a time (now three years), with the proviso that at the end of this period a liquidity reserve should exist adequate to cover expenditure for a period of one year (now reduced to three months).

The organisation of the pension insurance scheme for workers and employees is the responsibility of nineteen public corporations, which are to some extent independent of one another and of the federal authorities. These insurance institutions are supposed to be administered by the insured, the pensioners and the employers themselves, but in fact they are governed entirely by agreements between trade unions and the employers' organisations. In addition the bureaucratic machine of the insurance institutions has a good deal of dynamic force of its own. The income and expenditure of the pension funds is however governed by common rules laid down by federal law, while the insurance institutions are subject to administrative and financial control by both federal and *Land* ministries of labour. The use of federal subsidies is scrutinised by the Bundesrechnungshof (Federal Audit Office). Only the federal subsidies appear in the federal budget, so that only these are subject to budgetary control by parliament.

A number of financial problems arising from the 'productivity

[1] See Paul Braess, 'Alcuni problemi della riforma tedesca delle rendite nel 1957', in *Assicurazioni*, vol. 24, part 1 (1959), pp. 119–33; Kurt Jantz, 'Pension Reform in the Federal Republic of Germany, in *International Labour Review*, vol. 83 (1961), pp. 136–55; Elisabeth Liefmann-Keil, 'Index-Based Adjustments for Social Security Benefits', in ibid., vol. 79 (1959), pp. 487 et seq.; Gaston V. Rimlinger, 'The Economics of Postwar German Social Policy', in *Industrial Relations*, vol. 6 (1966–67), pp. 192–9.

pensions' and from the parafiscal nature of the insurance institutions were discussed during the passing of the reform law and afterwards.[1]

The fact that in the Federal Republic today the greater part of the population is included in an old-age pension scheme provided and enforced by the State has to be justified. Those who support the legal arrangements which have been made point to the fact that old-age pensions are not sufficiently guaranteed if left to the open market and to individual preference, because individuals underestimate future needs. In order to avoid the social tensions which could possibly result from this, the State has to intervene. How far competition from the State affects the business of private insurance firms or discriminates against other forms of individual provision (for example, saving) depends essentially on the level of contributions. Part of the political resistance to the pension reform of 1957 was certainly influenced by this competitive aspect.

Public old-age pensions compete not only with private goods but also with other public goods. At the beginning, they competed with military expenditure which accounts for roughly the same as expenditure on social benefits in the federal budget. Nowadays such consumption expenditure competes more and more with 'social overhead investments', as in the educational sector. Competition between different public goods is increased because demographic and sociocultural factors worsen the ratio of the old-age pensioners to the active labour force. The solution to this problem has been found, up to now, not in a reduction of benefits or in higher federal subsidies, but in raising payroll contributions.

If social policy consists, as it mainly does in the Federal Republic, of transfers of income, then the redistributive function of the budget will be of prime importance. Today, the overwhelming majority of the population is insured by compulsory pension insurance. Therefore it does not seem possible by means of this scheme to have a 'classically' vertical redistribution, seeking an egalitarian distribution of income. Although it appears that the burden of financing is divided among three groups, that is, the insured, the employers and the State, in fact this is misleading, since there is no coincidence between the formal and material incidence

[1] These problems are discussed generally in a series of articles in *Public Finance*, vol. 24, no. 2 (1969). See especially S. Steve, pp. 101–13; A. van Buggenhout, pp. 114–92; A. Oberhausen, pp. 215–31; C. Zeitel, pp. 334–51; F. Forte, pp. 405–13. The contributions are also published under the title *Finances publiques et sécurité sociale* (Lyon, 1969) (le Travaux de l'Institut International de Finances Publiques. Congrès Turin, September 1968, 24th session).

of taxes, including payroll contributions. Therefore the compulsory pension insurance involves mainly a horizontal redistribution of income, from people who are involved in the work process to those who have left the work process.

During the political discussion which accompanied the introduction and elaboration of 'productivity pensions' the macro-economic aspect was of most interest. Although it affected the special interests of the pressure groups influencing the decision-making process least of all, nevertheless it raised what seemed to be disinterested objections to 'productivity pensions'. For there are many arguments which are supposed to prove that 'productivity pensions' are really one of the main sources of inflation. The sum involved in old-age pensions seems in fact to be too small for 'productivity pensions' to be a sole cause of inflation. However, they may have intensified inflationary tendencies which already existed. When 'productivity pensions' were set up, for the sake of short-term economic policy a three- to four-year time-lag was built in when adapting pensions to changes in the income index. This was supposed to increase the effect of old-age pensions as a 'built-in stabiliser'. In fact the lag has a pro-cyclical rather than anti-cyclical effect. Thus there are frequent demands to keep as small a time-lag as possible between the alteration in incomes and that in pensions.

The capital stock of the pension funds which is built up from current surpluses and which acts as a liquidity reserve seems particularly suitable for monetary policy measures. Before 1967 it was not at all certain whether the capital assets of the pension funds were managed in harmony with the monetary policy of the central bank. Indeed, the capital assets of the insurance institutions were free from the Bundesbank's monetary restrictions. The insurance institutions were forced by law to be prepared to consider public loans which the *Bund* and the *Länder* wished to negotiate. Moreover the *Bund* concealed undesirable deficit-spending by paying federal subsidies partly in the form of public securities. It was argued in academic circles that, while social aims should have priority over the use of economic tools to achieve stability or even growth, social measures should at least be compatible with general economic aims.

THE POSITION OF THE BUNDESTAG IN THE DECISION-MAKING PROCESS

The discussion of the financial problems of 'productivity pensions' will be used as an illustration of the role of the Bundestag in the decision-making process. I shall not deal with the formal steps in the legislative process, since it is more important to gain a realistic picture of the decision-making process and to compare the real significance of parliament with the central role which it occupies in the traditional model of parliamentary democracy.

The Internal Structure of the Bundestag

Political decisions are now hardly ever taken in open discussion in the plenary assembly. The plenary debates are used instead to make 'declamatory statements before the House and the public'.[1] This general impression is verified by the debate on the reform of the pension scheme. The decisive phase in legislation seems to be discussion in committee. The committee members, usually in closed session, come into direct contact with the government and the ministerial bureaucracy and get further information on the subject under discussion from experts and representatives of interest groups.[2] For example in 1956, the government's draft of the reform bill was changed fundamentally during discussion in the Committee for Social Affairs. This committee also held hearings in which experts made statements about the financial consequences of the reform. Since the various wings and groups within the parties are not represented in all committees with equal strength, the fate of a bill is often determined by its allocation to a certain committee. During the debate in 1964 on the Stability Law, for example, a controversy arose between the committtee primarily concerned with the bill, the Economic Committee, and the Committee for Social Affairs on the question of whether or not the reserve funds of the compulsory insurance institutions should be involved in the open-market operations of the Bundesbank. The views of the Economic Committee prevailed but the legal precautions surrounding these operations still reflect the controversy.

This shift of decision-making from plenary to committees is paralleled by the shift of debates and decisions to the parliamentary parties and to inter-party deliberations. The 'power of the committee' is derivative in so far as the committees have become

[1] Bruno Dechamps, *Macht und Arbeit der Ausschüsse. Der Wandel der parlamentarischen Willensbildung* (Meisenheim, 1954), p. 99. For the concrete case, cf. Günter Hoenig, *Die Entstehungsgeschichte der Rentenversicherungs-Neuregelungsgesetze für Arbeiter und Angestellte*, thesis (Bonn, 1961), pp. 30–5, 84–7, 94–102.
[2] Dechamps, op. cit., pp. 73–5; Hoenig, op. cit., pp. 55–8, 84–96, 108; Gerhard Loewenberg, *Parliament in the German Political System* (rev. German ed., Tübingen, 1969), pp. 186–7, 331, 347, 387, 391, 396.

'groups of party delegates'.[1] For example, the outcome of the Committee's discussion on the reform bill in 1956 depended on a compromise agreed within the parliamentary party of the CDU/CSU. In modern parliamentary democracy 'the confrontation of parliamentary majority and parliamentary opposition within parliament' is more important than the 'fundamental confrontation of executive and legislature which appears in the classical model of the separation of powers'.[2] However this confrontation was not always evident in the behaviour of the Social Democratic Party (SPD) when it was in opposition from 1948 to 1966. In one way, in taking an active role in pensions legislation from 1952 to 1957 the SPD was following up its ambitions of the time when it was in opposition in the early years of the Federal Republic. On the other hand, there was considerable agreement on the pensions legislation and from 1957 onwards both parties were able to keep a majority supporting the existing organisation of the compulsory pensions insurance scheme, which shows that there is plenty of scope for bi-partisanship in a social policy which tries to avoid sharp conflicts of interest. In these circumstances the opposition confined itself to airing tactical differences with the government, rather than making fundamental criticisms.

The result of the voting on the pension legislation of 1957 was symptomatic of this. The SPD voted with the CDU/CSU for the legislation, whereas both the CDU/CSUs' conservative coalition partners, the Free Democratic Party, and the German Party, either voted against the legislation or abstained.

To explain how 'productivity pensions' were set up and developed we have to go beyond the prevailing parliamentary relationships and proceedings. In the pensions reform of 1956–7 the legislation, as well as the compromise which made its passage possible, was brought into parliament from outside.

The Relationship Between the Majority Party in the Bundestag and the Cabinet

In fact the real opponent of the parliamentary opposition is not the majority party in parliament but the federal government. The system of parliamentary government calls for close personal and functional co-operation between the executive and the parlia-

---

[1] Dechamps, op. cit., pp. 106, 112. For the concrete case, cf. Hoenig, op. cit., p. 94.

[2] Jürgen Domes, *Mehrheitsfraktion und Bundesregierung. Aspekte des Verhältnisses der Fraktion der CDU/CSU im 2. und 3. Deutschen Bundestag zum Kabinett Adenauer* (Köln, Opladen, 1964), p. 11.

mentary majority. For many reasons the government tends to dominate the majority party. This impression comes mostly from the long years of CDU/CSU government under Adenauer. However one should not accept the image of the 'yes-man party' unconditionally even in the Adenauer era. Especially on economic and social policy, within the CDU/CSU parliamentary party the group representing workers and those groups representing the middle class, agriculture and the employers opposed even the Adenauer cabinet from time to time.[1]

The legislation on pensions reform seemed to illustrate the observation that the 'nerve centre of government is likely to be somewhere in the Chancellor's Office'.[2] In fact it was in this office that the bargaining process took place which resulted in the compromise between the workers' and employers' wings of the CDU/CSU on the pensions reform. It is true that there were no 'kitchen cabinets' like Adenauer's under later governments. Nevertheless even under later coalition governments the main controversies between government and majority party, and among the coalition parties, have been settled by 'coalition committees' or 'coalition discussions'.

The different groups within the majority party are always in close contact with the federal ministry relevant to their special interest. In this way the Federal Ministry of Labour in governments led by the CDU/CSU was traditionally connected with the workers' wing of the majority party. The central department responsible for social affairs is in this ministry. However, the areas of responsibility of other ministries were also affected by pensions legislation, above all, those of the Ministries of Finance and Economic Affairs. Here the position of the finance minister in the Cabinet was particularly important. His responsibility 'for the financial consequences of all social measures..., in so far as these... are financed from tax revenue',[3] certainly explains his strong intervention in the years 1955 and 1956 against the preliminary drafts on pensions reform worked out in the Ministry of Labour. The finance minister put forward the argument that an increased burden on the federal budget would make tax increases necessary, an argument well in the tradition of 'economical and thrifty housekeeping'. Erhard, the Federal Minister of Economic Affairs, similarly showed concern from a monetary point of view, as did certain economic interest

[1] Domes, op. cit., pp. 130, 134–5, 160–1, 168.

[2] F. F. Ridley, 'Chancellor Government as a Political System and the German Constitution', in *Parliamentary Affairs*, vol. 19, (1965–66), p. 459. For the nerve centre in action, cf. Domes, op. cit., pp. 157, 164, 172, 174, 188 (n. 257).

[3] Viola Gräfin von Bethusy-Huc, *Das Sozialleistungssystem der Bundesrepublik Deutschland* (Tübingen, 1965), p. 233.

groups; his fundamental philosophy was an almost paleo-liberal opposition to State responsibility for social welfare benefits.

The action of representatives of extra-parliamentary opposition to the pensions reform, such as the Ministers of Finance and of Economic Affairs, forced the Cabinet to reach a compromise, although the compromise worked out in the Chancellor's office depended mainly on the direct influence of various interest groups.

The Influence of Experts and Interest Groups

In the Federal Republic the opportunities for interest groups to influence parliament and administration are considerable. Representatives of interest groups get access to parliament through the political parties, but they can also be summoned as 'experts' before Bundestag committees. There are over sixty permanent advisory bodies attached to federal government departments, and most of them include various experts and interest group representatives. In addition to these institutionalised forms of direct access for organised interests, there are many opportunities to gain informal access to the administration. Both the institutionalised and the informal forms of access diminish the importance of parliament and they reinforce parliament's dependence on the ministerial bureaucracy for adequate information.

Both the trade unions and the employers' organisations, which confront one another in the labour market, are interested in decisions on social policy, especially those on the financing of the compulsory pensions insurance. The top industrial organisation, the Federal Association of German Industry, takes part in financial discussions about the compulsory pensions insurance scheme as do the private insurance firms and the banks which represent the sectors of the economy more or less directly affected.

Of these interest groups the trade unions were most eager for pensions reform and for improved welfare benefits, and they succeeded in having some of these demands accepted not only by the SPD but also by the government for inclusion in its bill on pensions reform. This 'grand coalition' representing trade unions, SPD and the workers' section of the CDU/CSU stuck firmly to the arrangement made in 1957 and strove for more improvements in welfare benefits wherever possible.

A fairly heterogeneous opposition was formed, including the economic interest groups named above, to oppose the idea of pensions reform. The opposition employed the tactic of drawing up a comprehensive catalogue of damaging effects for the whole national economy which were said to be likely to result from the attempt at reform, particularly from the point of view of monetary policy. The professed belief in stable monetary values ... was the catchword under which the forces of the massive opposition gathered.[1]

At the preliminary stage of work on the government's bill (and not only in committee discussion) this opposition, which also had representatives of course within the government coalition, succeeded in weakening the benefits of the compulsory insurance scheme, and particularly the method of pension adjustment, contrary to the original ideas of the Labour Ministry. The same attacks were made during the 1960s when the compulsory pensions insurance scheme was debated again. They are continually heard as a reason for limiting the number of members and the level of benefits in the scheme, especially in view of the financial dangers.

Both sides employed a series of academic camouflages. Several semi-academic advisory groups were attached to the Labour Ministry, in which attempts at reform ran the risk of being bogged down right at the beginning. This tendency to delay progress by bringing in academic advisors to lengthen discussion (for example, on how to overcome financing difficulties of the compulsory pensions insurance scheme) also played a part in the appointment of the Sozialenquête-Kommission (Social Inquiry Commission) in the early 1960s.

The way in which 'politics' and 'expertise' are mixed in advisory groups such as these is particularly clear in the Sozialbeirat (Social Advisory Council) which was appointed to aid the federal government in 1957 in connection with the pension reform. This body, composed of representatives of the trade unions, employers' organisations and the Bundesbank and including expert sociologists and economists, was supposed to have as one of its principal tasks that of working out suggestions for the annual pension adjustment. Advocates as well as opponents of the scheme introduced in 1957 are represented, so that the political conflict in the discussions on reform was brought into this body and, as it were, institutionalised. This was in effect an attempt to use the force of expert arguments in the advisory council to curb the seemingly excessive spending zeal of parliament. However, it failed because parliament has still been able to pass the necessary law on adjustment every year (with the

[1] Hoenig, op. cit., p. 73. For the following cf. ibid. pp. 84–96, 108; Bethusy-Huc, op. cit., pp. 170–2, 243, 245–8.

exception of 1958) and the Sozialbeirat has usually recommended an adjustment in anticipation of parliament's reaction and in spite of economic and financial anxieties.

COMPULSORY PENSION INSURANCE AND THE RATIONALISATION OF BUDGETING

In connection with the attempts at rationalising budgeting in the Federal Republic during the 1960s, two of the problems which arose with regard to the public pension schemes are relevant. These were:

1 That in short-term economic policy monetary disturbances could appear as a result of the Bundesbank's lack of control over the capital assets of the insurance institutions.

2 That in the long term financial provision for the existing arrangements, and its extension for future needs, must be ensured, while competition with other responsibilities in the public sector must be considered. In both these respects the institutional autonomy of the insurance funds seems to be an obstacle, since it encourages an isolated point of view in political decisions.

An attempt was made at solving both problems within the framework of the budgetary and financial reforms of 1967–9. According to Paragraph 30 of the Stability Law of 1967 the federal government is allowed in certain conditions to include the capital assets of the public pensions funds in the open market operations of the Bundesbank. This it was hoped would provide the solution to the first problem. The new instruments of pluri-annual forecasting and planning are of significance for the second problem. The following paragraphs deal with these instruments and their successes and failures in rationalising the public sector of the economy.

Pluri-Annual Financial Planning and the 'Social Security Budget'

Income and expenditure of public pensions funds appear in a variety of ways in the federal quinquennial plans required by the stability law:

1 Financial planning must be 'presented in its interrelationship to the projected development of the economy as a whole' (Stability Law, paragraph 91). This is done on the basis of medium-range projections of economic development. The size of government revenue, including payroll contributions to the public pensions scheme, and the size of certain items of government expenditure (such as transfer payments which are tied to income growth), can all be deduced from projections of the development of national income.

However only the general trend of changes in pensions funds expenditure are given in the financial plans of the federal government.

2 Paragraphs 51 and 52 of the Budgetary Principles Law of 1969 provide that the projected income and expenditure of public pensions institutions should be taken into account by the Financial Planning Council, whose duty it is to co-ordinate the financial plans of federal and *Land* governments.

3 In the financial plans of the federal government only federal contributions to public pensions schemes are set out explicitly. However these contributions amount to more than 10 per cent of all statutorily binding expenditure which has appeared since 1965–6 in the 'Medium-Range Economic Preview of the Federal Budget'.

In *theory* pluri-annual financial planning involves functions which have wide political consequences. In particular it is supposed to assist in the process of making financial and economic decisions. In *practice*, however, the financial plans published so far by the federal government have failed to realise these expectations. Some inadequacies are revealed in the methods by which the compulsory pension insurance funds are included. The dovetailing of medium-range economic projections with financial plans requires 'that pluri-annual financial planning should embrace all the institutions of the "state" sector, i.e. the federal and *Land* governments, local authorities and social security organisations'.[1] In fact, however, para-fiscal institutions like the pensions funds are only partly included in financial planning. Only a part of their expenditure is covered by federal payments, and only these payments are shown specifically in the plan. Furthermore it is not clear at first glance how much money the federal government spends overall on care of the aged, because the amounts spent on this programme are shown under a variety of headings. This kind of 'programme budgeting', which has been the practice since 1968, does not reflect the actual decision-making process. Like the annual budget, financial plans are constructed within individual departments from the bottom up. The various longer-term plans of the different departments are co-ordinated and combined into specific programmes only at the end of the process. Thus the programmes do not really serve as budgeting guidance.

Financial plans are based on medium-range economic forecasts, the quantities of which are adjusted to take account of developments from year to year. Thus this 'statement of government policy

---

[1] Karl-Heinz Raabe, *Projektionen der Mittelfristigen Wirtschaftsentwicklung in der Bundesrepublik Deutschland (Methode und Verfahren)*, ed. by Pressestelle des Bundesministeriums für Wirtschaft (Bonn, 1969), p. 27.

D

in figures' is hardly binding on the government itself. Although parliament has the right to demand that alternative figures should be preserved, up to now neither the prognostic nor the possible alternatives forming the basis of financial plans have been communicated to parliament. Furthermore the reasons for differences between actual and proposed expenditure are not given. This reduces the value of financial plans as information both for parliament and for the public at large. Opportunities to set out priorities in financial planning, or to give new programmes priority over old ones, are limited by the statutory nature of so much expenditure. For example, federal payments for compulsory pensions insurance are given as the priority in almost all financial plans, the political tactic being to allocate most expenditure to a priority of this type. It is much more difficult in the short term 'to push through a budget or a financial plan if those features of the government's programme are implemented which penalise [that is, deal "negatively" with] any particular section of the population'.[1]

Every year since 1968 the federal government has brought in a so-called social security budget (*Sozialbudget*) as a supplement to the pluri-annual financial plan. This is a confusing title, since in no sense of the word is any budget involved. The social security budget is simply an overall view, largely quantified, of welfare measures in the Federal Republic since 1950 or 1960; and at the same time it is a preview of their further development over the next three to four years. The social security budget embraces not only the whole field of public welfare expenditure by *Bund, Länder*, local authorities and para-fiscal institutions, but also indirect expenditure based on tax-relief, and assistance given by firms, either voluntarily or to meet legal obligations and agreements on pay and working conditions. From this point of view the social security budget covers much more ground than the financial plan of the federal government.

At the same time the social security budget has features in common with the pluri-annual financial plan. It rests on the same basic assumptions about economic and financial developments; all projections are based solely on the law as it stands, there is no evidence of alternative calculations being made or of any attempt to orient projected expenditure at a programme worthy of the name. The social security budget is based on institutions and functions. The functions are described as those social factors to which welfare payments are applicable, such as old age, sickness, housing and

[1] Kurt Schmidt and Eberhard Wille, *Die Mehrjährige Finanzplanung Wunsch und Wirklichkeit* (Tübingen, 1970), p. 82.

education. An attempt is then made to relate the most important institutions to these functions. The welfare institutions in the public sector are fully integrated with national income accounting. However, the social security budget says nothing about the financial and macro-economic effects of any changes proposed in social security legislation. The costs of social-security payments in particular annual budgets can only be extracted indirectly from the social security budgets by carrying out additional calculations. Thus the financial plans of federal and *Land* governments cannot be replaced by the social security budget; the two instruments complement one another.

The Second Pensions Reform

The second pensions reform may be considered as a test of the functioning of these new instruments. At the end of 1971 the coalition government formed by the SPD and FDP laid before the Bundesrat and the Bundestag draft bills for a 'second pensions reform', which had already been announced in the government declaration of 1969. The CDU/CSU Opposition countered with its own proposals, which were laid before the Bundestag as draft bills in October 1971. The introduction of a flexible retirement age was the centrepiece of the government draft; in certain conditions insured persons were to be entitled to choose between drawing a pension at current rates from their sixty-third year onwards, or continuing in employment up to sixty-seven (at most), thereby obtaining a higher pension. The Opposition suggested in a counter-proposal that the timing of the annual adjustment of pensions be brought forward by half a year. The aim of this was to reduce the time-lag between pensions and changes in incomes, a time-lag which had been introduced in 1957 and increased by the failure to adjust pensions in 1958. This would have led *de facto* to a general increase in pension levels.

To improve the schemes was possible as a byproduct of a gradual increase of payroll contributions from a rate of 14 per cent to 18 per cent of earned income between 1968 and 1973, which had seemed necessary, in view of the recession of 1966–7, to secure the financing of existing schemes. Following the subsequent powerful economic recovery these earlier projections were seen to be too pessimistic; indeed there resulted a public pensions fund surplus which by 1985-6 would exceed the legally prescribed reserves by more than 100 thousand million marks. At first sight each of the main reform proposals of both government and opposition seemed likely to use up these resources. Thus in its proposals the Opposition sought essentially to prevent the introduction of the flexible retirement age favoured by the government.

However the unexpectedly high growth rates of the gross national product (in terms of current prices) made it possible repeatedly during 1972 to revise the estimates of pension-fund surpluses upwards. Thus the end of 1972 saw a compromise solution between government and Opposition combining both sets of proposals. Subsequent political developments in the Federal Republic wiped out the coalition majority, ultimately causing early elections to be held. In this situation both government and Opposition had to accommodate one another's views. The government took over from the Opposition a general increase in pension levels, and the Opposition in turn developed counter-proposals for a flexible retirement age, which must have looked to the population group concerned even more attractive than the government's original proposals. During the second reading on 20 September 1972 the Opposition was able to force through so many amendments to the government bill that the Opposition reform programme was accepted *de facto* by all three parliamentary parties.

The accusation frequently made in connection with pensions legislation in the Federal Republic is that it is used as an election 'sweetener' on a massive scale. This accusation has now been so obviously justified that no one is likely to put forward the second pensions reform as evidence of advances in policy planning, although this claim was made by Professor Ehmke, Minister in the Chancellor's Office, as late as the end of 1971 in connection with the introduction of the flexible retirement age.[1] Professor Ehmke mentioned some of the socio-economic factors which had been taken into account in coming to a decision over the flexible retirement age: the effect on labour potential might put a brake on economic growth and thus reduce tax revenues; if the reserves of the pension funds were reduced, the capital market might be affected and the financing of public investments by credits be impaired; the introduction of a flexible retirement age is only one improvement needed in pensions insurance, and competes with others aimed at different groups; finally additional costs would be involved (although these in turn would be offset by other benefits to be jointly financed by *Bund, Länder* and local authorities). In their preparatory work the ministerial departments and the groups of experts

[1] Horst Ehmke, 'Computer Helfen der Politik', in *Die Zeit*, no. 51 (17 December 1971), p. 42.

associated with them certainly took these matters into account.[1] However, there is astonishingly little reference to them in that part of the political debate which has reached the public so far.

The political debate had turned largely on the major question of how future resources can be exploited to provide improved benefits within the framework of compulsory pensions insurance. Although it is being increasingly demanded by the public and by politicians it is difficult to subordinate the heterogeneous parcel of reforms to an overall welfare strategy for the improvement of the quality of life in old age. Electoral tactics always take precedence; the aim is always to benefit the largest possible number of potential voters. Although it is true that the second pensions reform does contain features related to the aims highlighted in the government declaration of 1969, these are the only programmes being realised, and many of the 'internal reforms' cannot be put into effect because they must be paid for out of the federal budget and cannot be financed from para-fiscal institutions which can dispose over ample resources in spite of heavy restrictions on general public expenditure.

In the final analysis the execution of urgent programmes depends, not on the degree of urgency, but on the financial manoeuvrability permitted by fragmented State budgets. In spite of financial planning and the social security budget, the old way of looking at problems in isolation is still dominant.

If the second pensions reform is regarded as a test case for the new instruments of planning and forecasting, then it can only be concluded that the latter will fail completely. For one thing they do not supply the information required for an analysis of the complex of circumstances mentioned by Professor Ehmke. At most it is possible to extract from pluri-annual financial planning and from the social security budget a few premises concerning general economic and financial developments. These might be of some assistance in making specialised, wide-ranging forecasts. However, it is just the *non*-specialist members of parliament who ought to be able to use this kind of information, if they are to be in a position to take rational decisions in plenary session. The Opposition has the additional disadvantage of being largely cut off from the additional information provided by government departments, and this was illustrated by the fact that their proposals for reform were based on financial calculations which were more scanty and uncertain than those of the government, and were available only after long delays. The weaknesses of these new instruments are apparent from the fact that it was only in the hubbub surrounding the passing of these

[1] cf. *Bundesarbeitsblatt,* no. 1 (January 1972), pp. 5–25.

electoral 'sweeteners' (which were approved by all parties) that the departmental experts confirmed that their proposals were financially viable by hasty upward revision of their forecasts of future resources in face of calculations already made by the Opposition.

CONCLUSIONS

This case-study enables us to draw a few tentative conclusions, which illustrate the role played by the new instruments of planning and forecasting in directing and controlling the machinery of the State in a parliamentary democracy.

Even before the introduction of these 'aids to decision', a specialised, quasi-scientific flavour had already been lent to political debate by means of consultative committees of specialists and experts. As was the case with the pension reform of 1957, expert opinions can be advanced by both proponents and opponents of a political decision. There is some ground for believing, therefore, that behind these experts there are politically active interest groups. Financial controversies among experts have been used more to bring about compromise on pensions legislation than to integrate compulsory pensions insurance funds into the national budget.

The quasi-specialist character of the discussion in the case discussed here is both a symptom and a cause of the tendency to remove political decision-making from the full session of parliament. Initially this is brought about by committee deliberations, which are more important than plenary debates. The committees are centres of gravitation for the expertise and the special interests of members of parliament. It is furthermore characteristic of the position of parliament in the decision-making process that in the 1957 pension reform both the draft bill and the decisive compromise were formulated outside parliament. The conflict among experts which precedes the decision in parliament means that both specialists giving evidence, and representatives of interest groups, are gaining in influence. However, these extra-parliamentary experts have even more influence in West Germany on government departments and their ministerial leadership than on parliament itself. This is a further indication of the relative loss of importance of parliament and strengthens the latter's dependence on an adequate supply of information from the executive.

One major objective of the new instruments for planning and forecasting should be to reduce the advantage of the executive in information. Such new instruments as the financial plan and the social security budget do lay before parliament and the public a wealth of information not previously available. However a whole range of facts necessary for more rational political decisions is either not included at all, or can only be obtained after lengthy additional calculations. Moreover up to now the new processes have not succeeded in lessening dependence on the traditional budgetary processes (constrained as they are by the multiplicity of separate departmental measures) in favour of a programme-orientated approach. The effects of the institutional fragmentation, of which para-fiscal bodies are an example, have not yet been overcome. The apparent victory of parliament over the executive in the second pensions reform, which was possible only because of the impending election, does not mean that the advantage of the ministerial bureaucracy over members of parliament in access to information has been reduced, as the discussions behind the legislative scenes shows. Nor do political decision-makers take any more account than in the past of the complex interrelationships which lie behind the new instruments. Indeed the danger has become more apparent that these economic and financial instruments can be misused and manipulated by bureaucrats and the interest groups behind them. All in all from experience in the Federal Republic to date it is doubtful whether attempts to rationalise the planning and budgetary process can reverse the tendency for parliament to lose power, a trend which runs counter to the conventional model of parliamentary democracy.

POSTSCRIPT

The final draft of this contribution was written shortly after the legislation on the 'second pensions reform' had been passed. After the Bundestag election in November 1973, the SPD-FDP coalition formed the federal government anew. It was not very surprising that one of its first acts was another bill which redressed the pensions reform according to the original intentions of the government. In the meantime, no important changes occured in this sector of financial legislation. Moreover, neither the institutional arrangements nor the problems changed in such a way as to have a serious effect on the conclusions drawn from the case under consideration.

CHAPTER 6

PARLIAMENTARY CONTROL OF THE BUDGET IN FRANCE: A VIEW FROM INSIDE THE NATIONAL ASSEMBLY

Alain Dupas

In France, as in many representative democracies, the decline of parliament has become a favourite theme for political theorists. It is a theme with many variations, of which one of the most popular is the withering away of the financial powers of the nation's representatives. The belief that parliament's examination of the budget must now be considered an unimportant ritual is one which many experts and politicians of all shades will support. They maintain that in times gone by the budget was the work of parliament, which sifted through all its elements and could at will turn the proposals inside out. Today, all real power has passed to the executive; the debate on the budget is no more than conversational and the parliamentary role is limited to the registration of governmental decisions.

It cannot indeed be denied that great changes have taken place. From a political point of view, in the first place, the constitutional transformation and the existence of a relatively homogeneous government majority have come to upset old habits; the National Assembly, once the main source of the delegation of executive power, is now limited to the admittedly important functions of legislation and control. Secondly, public finance has taken on a new form. The annual inventory of the cash needs of the State is still made, but the main problems of budgets are no longer decisions as to whether such and such a ministerial department should or should not recruit two or three extra clerks; the problems nowadays relate to complex technical proposals intended as instruments of economic control for operating cyclical policy, and as stages on the road to economic and social objectives set by medium-term planning.

These changes by themselves, however, in no way imply that parliament's financial prerogatives have been lost. The fact that the National Assembly has a majority of government supporters certainly excludes any spectacular rejection of budget proposals, but it does not prevent, and indeed rather promotes, the full exercise of parliamentary control over the revenue and expenditure of the State.

The increasingly technical nature of budgetary decisions certainly calls for a change in the Assembly's working methods, towards modern administrative procedures. Although strong resistance to such a change must be expected, there is no reason to suppose that it is impossible to effect. The conflict between technicians and politicians, in which government and parliament find themselves in the same camp, must be reduced to its actual proportions; the function of technical innovations is to clarify problems and not to solve them, to prepare decisions, but not to assume responsibility for them.

In order to assess the actual role of parliamentary assemblies in budgetary decisions today, these two aspects of information and decision must be examined. This study proposes to abandon the ethereal sphere of general ideas, and to describe on the basis of practical experience the real extent of the prerogatives of parliament. For parliament's means of acquiring information and powers of decision-making are more important than is sometimes believed, even though it does not always know how to make the best use of them.

PARLIAMENT'S ACCESS TO INFORMATION

An examination of parliament's access to information in budgetary affairs is a good measure of the extent of its functions. Access to information actually conditions the exercise of parliamentary control, although it is not itself the only means of control.

It would be very interesting in this respect to know how the problems of budgetary information have been solved in other European parliamentary democracies. The best solutions might eventually be translated from one country to another. Unfortunately financial publications in this field are very inadequate.

As far as France is concerned, it is useful to distinguish between those types of information received by parliament in document form, and those which involve active research by parliament.

Budgetary Documentation

French members of parliament are supplied with a strikingly large amount of budgetary documentation. Between the beginning of September and the middle of October more than eighty papers are distributed to them, and these are supplemented in the course of the year by another forty.

The first document is the draft *loi de finances* (finance bill) itself, each article of which is given a separate summary (*exposé des motifs*). Some of these articles are expressed in figures and constitute the genuinely budgetary part of the *loi de finances*. In these the national accounts are divided into three parts: the general budget, which consists of the total expenditure of the different ministries and the total of non-allocated revenues; the appended budgets (*budgets annexes*), which are eight small separate budgets with their own expenditure and revenue; and the special accounts of the Treasury or nearly seventy separate accounts grouped under six headings, some of which relate to temporary borrowing or lending operations. For each of these three parts, linked to each other in a general balancing article, recapitulatory tables provide the global formulae for legislative authorisation, and make comparisons possible between one year and another.

The draft bill is accompanied by several explanatory annexes, some general (*horizontales*) and others particular (*verticales*). The most important of the general annexes is the economic and financial report. This report, after analysing the situation and perspectives of the national economy, puts the government's proposed budgetary policy in its economic and social context. In support of this report are published major studies of the national accounts: retrospective accounts for the past year, estimated accounts for the current year, and prospective accounts or the 'economic budget' for the coming year.

Among the other general annexes there is the assessment of 'ways and means' which sets out in detail, line by line, the estimates of fiscal and non-fiscal receipts in the general budget. The report of the Economic and Social Development Fund deals with the financing of public investment, particularly that made by public enterprises with or without state assistance. The statement on the execution of the plan gives an indication of the extent to which programmes included in it have been achieved. A document on the regionalisation of the budget, unfortunately published with some delay, shows how the overall *crédits d'équipements* have been allocated among different regions and presents the most significant statistical data on the economic and social situation in these regions. There are other general annexes, which for the most part bring together expenditure dispersed between different ministries but designed for the same end: aid to developing countries, research activities, professional training, and so on. The special annexes contain proposals for expenditure applicable to each ministerial department. The way in which these documents are drawn up calls for a more thorough study.

A first series of papers known in the technical jargon as *'bleus budgétaires'* breaks the expenditure proposals of each ministry down into relatively small units, the *'chapitres'* or headings of the budget. Where investment is concerned, there is a distinction between two sorts of supply: the *crédits d'engagement*, or programme authorisation, which enable ministers to incur debts relating to the initiation of a programme, and *crédits de paiement*, which allow these debts to be settled.

For each heading, the sums granted for the current year (or *'crédits votés'*) are accompanied by the *'services votés'*, in other words the sums which would be necessary if the steps to be taken by the State in the course of the coming year were to be completely analogous to those which had been adopted in the previous budget.

As far as ordinary expenditure is concerned, the difference between *services votés* and *crédits votés* can result from two sorts of operations in contrary senses: in the first place from additions, for example in recording the extension over a complete year of provisions which only came into effect some months after the beginning of the previous year; and in the second place from subtractions, for example to take account of sums voted under the previous budget for extraordinary items which have no legal basis for continuation into another year.

The total of these additions and subtractions constitutes what are known as the *mesures acquises*, which are divided into six codifications on which *bleus budgétaires* provide detailed comment. Where capital expenditure is concerned the *services votés* are similarly defined; they correspond to the *tranches* of expenditure estimated necessary for the programmes authorised in previous years, but here the *bleus* provide much briefer comment and only under the larger headings of the *chapitres*.

That part of the budget proposal which is actually new, consisting of the modifications which the government is proposing for the *services votés*, is presented in a similar form. These modifications are known as *'mesures nouvelles'*; they can be positive (increasing expenditure) or negative (reducing it). An algebraic addition of the *mesures nouvelles* and the *services votés* gives the total expenditure envisaged by the government under each *chapitre*. *Mesures nouvelles* for current expenditure are divided into nine classes, each of which is given detailed explanation. Explanations relating to investment expenditure are presented for each *chapitre* and not for each *mesure*.

A second series of papers, coloured yellow, completes the series of *bleus*. These contain a list of *chapitres* for current expenditure with references to the *mesures acquises* and *mesures nouvelles* which belong to them, though of course one *mesure* can affect more than one *chapitre* and any one *chapitre* can cover several *mesures*. Another subdivision of a chapter, the *article budgétaire,* also appears here.

After the *loi de finances* has been promulgated, other documents, coloured green, are circulated to parliament and provide a basis for the scrutiny of the subsequent budget. Apart from a certain amount of special information, these papers contain details of the expenditures accepted by parliament for the separate ministries. Detail here goes down to the level of the 'paragraph', which is a subdivision of the article.

A recent reform has provided for the reclassification of budgetary articles and paragraphs according to the codification which is sectoral in character for the first, and economic for the second. This reform should make it possible, by the use of information techniques, to obtain a rapid 'functional' summary of State expenditure.

How is this documentation to be assessed? In the first place it must be recognised that for every *chapitre* of the budget French members of parliament have at their disposal precise details as to the costs of maintaining the existing situation and detailed information on the increases or cuts in expenditure currently being proposed by the government. The annexes to the budget, sometimes criticised for their profusion, constitute in this way a remarkably useful tool, and one which it would seem is far superior to those at the disposal of most foreign parliaments.

Although it is amply sufficient for current expenditure, however, the documentation does leave something to be desired where capital expenditure (*crédits d'équipement*) is concerned. It is not possible to follow as exactly as is desirable the performance in bulk of public investment, and in particular to measure the performance of individual investment programmes against the provisions laid down in the plan. After they have been approved, the *crédits d'engagement* (programme authorisations) subside into an undifferentiated mass to which are added all previous authorisations, and parliament does not always have the means of discovering which contracts undertaken by ministers in the course of the financial year apply to which authorisations. For the *crédits de paiement,* the explanatory annexes are very detailed, but refer only to totals, not to individual operations, and provide no information on the course of a particular investment.

An alternative would be for each programme requiring parliamentary approval to be accompanied by a timetable of all foreseeable contracts. Any alteration to this could then be presented as a *mesure nouvelle*, positive or negative according to whether it delayed or speeded up the programme concerned. This technical improvement would certainly be of considerable use to parliament, and its value would in fact be much greater than that of other reforms campaigned for with far more energy.

Means of Investigation

Apart from this basic documentation the French parliament has at its disposal means of investigation which are far from ineffective.

In the first place there is nothing to prevent it from employing the normal procedures for parliamentary control in order to enquire into public finance. These are written and oral questions, government statements followed (or not) by debate, and (in permanent or special committees) the hearing of evidence from ministers or other public figures, from commissions sent out within France or abroad, the receipt of written reports, the organisation of working parties, etc. Parliament can also have recourse to committees of enquiry 'appointed to collect information on particular questions' or to supervisory committees entrusted with the examination of 'the administrative, financial or technical management of the public services or of national enterprises'. This latter method is hardly ever employed by the National Assembly, but is more often used by the Senate and could well be extended in future.

Among the means of investigation which are specifically financial we should underline the importance of the public debate on the budget, which each year takes up the main part of the autumn session of parliament. Although it has been widely criticised and suffers at the present moment from a certain unpopularity, the few solutions for replacing it often neglect the real advantages which this long debate offers in terms of information. In fact it is the unique occasion for parliament as a whole to interrogate all the ministers in succession and in public on the different aspects of government policy.

However, in conformity with their traditions, the plenary assemblies confine the essential task of obtaining information to permanent and special committees. The preferred channels for budgetary information are the finance committees, the members of which – sixty for the National Assembly and thirty-six for the Senate – are nominated by proportional representation of the political groups. These committees arrange a division of labour by designating among their members special *rapporteurs*, each of whom is entrusted with the task of controlling the *crédits* of a particular ministry. Thus the Finance Committee of the National Assembly contains forty *rapporteurs*, all chosen from the groups of the majority. Above the special *rapporteur* there is a general *rapporteur* charged with following budgetary activities as a whole. For their part the permanent committees other than the finance committees also appoint *rapporteurs* to advise on the sectors falling under their terms of reference.

These members of parliament are given specific powers under several organic or regulatory texts. For example one provision requires that the members charged with

> presenting in the name of the relevant committee the report on the budget of the ministerial department shall watch over and control in a permanent manner, and at first and second hand, the use of *crédits* entered in the budget of this department. All information, whether financial or administrative, likely to assist them in their task must be given to them. They are entitled to receive any official document, of whatever nature, with the exception, on the one hand, of matters subject to secrecy relating to national defence, foreign affairs, and the internal or external security of the State, and, on the other hand, of the principle of the separation of the judicial power from other powers.

Another text extends the right of each *rapporteur* to cover the public enterprises subject to the sponsorship of the ministry which he is required to supervise.

In principle the work of the *rapporteurs* continues throughout the year, during and after the session, and they must cover at the same time the execution of the budget for the current financial year as well as the preparation of the budget for next year. They are provided with technical assistance by specialised officials. For example in the Finance Committee of the National Assembly these officials make up a team of about fifteen people, belonging either to the staff of the Assembly or to that of the Ministry of Finance or Ministry of National Defence. With the assistance of these technicians the *rapporteurs* maintain close relations with the ministerial departments, on both an oral and a written basis, and both regularly and occasionally. It has been the practice to send to the departments through the Finance Ministry, two sets of written questionnaires, one when the budget proposal is prepared, the other in September after the official documents have been received.

The *rapporteurs'* inquiries, their visits at home and abroad, and their questionnaires lead to the drafting of reports, which are distributed to all members of parliament after having been approved by the committee. These reports contain a description of budgetary data, destined in principle to ease the task of members of parliament and to give them the means of going through the mass of documentation. They also contain a critical analysis of the government's proposals, underlining the good points and the improvements, but also insisting on the inadequacies or on the limitations implicit in certain actions. This depiction of light and shade leads to the conclusions, that is to say, to proposals for adopting, rejecting or altering what is contained in the budget. Thus in the public session the general *rapporteur* and the special *rapporteurs* play the role of spokesmen of the committee before the full Assembly. However, since the committee's composition reflects that of the Assembly and since the political forces take part in its proceedings just as they do in full session, they are also led to play the role of spokesmen of the Assembly to the government. These, then, are important figures with whom ministers must be tactful, especially in satisfying their requests for information.

For his part the functions taken on by the chairman of the Finance Committee are in this area decisive. He is in touch with the First President of the Court of Accounts to whom he addresses requests for inquiries. Moreover the committee for supervising the accounts of public enterprises sends him at his request the special and confidential reports which it is required to make. The chairman must see to the provision of the documents which the committee has the right to obtain, in particular the annual reports of the financial controllers[1] of the ministries. With the help of the committee's *bureau*, composed of three vice-chairmen, three secretaries and the general *rapporteur*, he arranges the programme of budgetary meetings and of the hearings to which they lead. These are hearings of ministers, and, should the case arise, private individuals or representatives of professional organisations. His initiative will determine the effectiveness of the committee's control. The committee should be seen, according to one of its chairmen, as a 'laboratory of economic and financial thought', whose recommendations and discoveries can serve as a useful guide to government action.

As it has so far been described, the French parliament's array of

[1] See chapter 9, p. 172.

instruments for investigation might seem fairly complete. It is not, however, in practice considered satisfactory by the majority of observers, nor by many members of parliament.

The critics are in the first place concerned with the collection of information. Ordinary members of parliament can complain of a system which reserves the leading roles for the *rapporteurs spéciaux* who, as the Opposition will hardly fail to remember, all belong at least as far as the National Assembly is concerned to the majority parties. It is also argued that a disproportionate share of information originates from the government itself, and that more diverse sources would be valuable.

For their part, the *rapporteurs spéciaux* stress the difficulties they find in carrying out their work, arising partly from the short time which the system provides for them to do it in, and partly from reluctance on the part of the departments and services under scrutiny to provide the information necessary for this purpose; their questionnaires sometimes remain unanswered, or the answers when they finally arrive have lost any content in the course of their passage through the hierarchical and political structure.

The most serious problems arise in the processing of information. Here criticism is made of the availability of resources of persons and material. The *rapporteurs spéciaux* for example have to rely on the services of civil servants whose numbers would appear to be extremely small, at least in comparison with the general staff at the disposal of each member of the US Congress, for example.

For members of parliament who have no particular official responsibility, the scantiness of these resources is even more evident. Some improvement could result from recent initiatives, such as the establishment of a new information service for the National Assembly, which would include an economic research team, and the organisation of a training scheme for parliamentary staff.

Other questions remain unsettled, including for example that of direct access for parliament to public or private organisations capable of analysing this kind of information. More specifically, there is the possibility of arranging for the Assembly to be able to commission research or enquiries on data or subjects of its choice by the Institut National de la Statistique et des Études Économiques. The idea has long been debated that public organisations for economic research could be protected by a statute establishing their independence from the executive power, which would confer on them the status of a *magistrature* for information.[1]

1 See Chapter 8, p. 159.

However, the improvement of parliament's information requires a change more in spirit and attitude than in institutions. As far as the *rapporteurs spéciaux* are concerned, for example, it is quite true that the numerous obligations which they carry as ordinary members of parliament make it difficult for them to exercise permanent supervision over every detail. It is also true that it is hardly reasonable to press for a parallel administration to be created round them which would effectively duplicate government departments. Nevertheless, the quality of their work could undoubtedly be improved without much change in their prerogatives and by using current resources. For example, they could give up the attempt to collect and distribute information in depth on all the budgetary problems under their authority, and concentrate their attention instead on a small number of chosen subjects each year, which could then be treated in detail. Similarly, an increase in the help which the Cour des Comptes is ready to give to parliament would not meet with any opposition, provided that such help continued to be of a technical nature. Finally, the budgetary debate would cease to be so much criticised as an instrument of information if the political groups were to exercise greater discipline over the number, length and nature of their contributions to it.

One last problem is the role of parliament as a giver rather than a receiver of information. Although everything which is said in the Assembly is of course public, the work of its various sub-groups is on the whole conceived as being for internal use, and consequently remains little known by the public as a whole or even by specialists. Certain reformers believe that the budgetary problems discussed by specialised committees should be the subject of a great public confrontation of all opinions and attitudes. Apart from the hearing of evidence from ministers, which is now common, and evidence from private individuals which is becoming more common than it was, high-level civil servants could be required to appear before parliamentary committees, and all hearings could be given wide publicity, in particular by being televised. This formula, which is that adopted by Congress in the USA, has been proposed on several occasions in France, but public access to committee proceedings does not seem likely to be introduced in the near future.

PARLIAMENT'S POWERS OF DECISION-MAKING

Parliamentary approval of the budget has always been seen in France as one of the keystones of the parliamentary system. According to classical theory, the sovereignty of the legislature can be neither limited nor shared in this sphere, and the government may only implement the budget decided on by parliament. This theory has never corresponded with practice, and is very far from it at the present time.

The government has in fact its own powers of decision-making in the drafting stage of the budget and in its execution. For its part, the legislative authority is burdened with all sorts of constraints which reduce its reach and its importance. Here the factors always quoted are the short time allowed for the examination of the budget proposals, the global nature of the headings to be voted, the rigorous restrictions on the right of amendment, and the powerful procedural tools used by the government to get its own way. Besides these legal considerations, the political factor of the existence of a large majority at the government's disposal must also be taken into account; this in effect reduces the intervention of the legislature to a simple registration of the government's proposals.

An objective analysis of these different elements nevertheless leads to the conclusion that parliament's powers of decision-making, even though restricted and divided, still remain very considerable.

The time allowed for examining the budget proposals is certainly very restricted. From the appearance of the proposal with its principal annexes parliament has a total period of seventy days in which to examine in turn the revenue side of the budget, the expenditure of each ministerial department and the legislative articles. Out of this, forty days are allocated to the debate on the first reading in the Assembly and twenty days to the debate in the Senate. The remaining ten days are used for the '*navettes*' ('shuttles') for solving disagreement between the two chambers.

For example, the budget proposal for 1972 was delivered on 8 October 1971. The forty days allowed for the National Assembly ran out on 17 November; its Finance Committee, which had received the outline of the project in mid-September and subsequently received the various annexes one by one as they were produced, only took one month to finish its work. Consequently it was between 19 October and 17 November, or only twenty working days, that the approximately thirty-five separate discussions which made up the debate as a whole had to be included in the orders of the day for the session. This illustrates the highly compressed character of what is known as the budget marathon, the organisation of which involves many all-night sittings and which requires conscientious members to engage in an effort which could well be described as Olympic.

The object of the constitutional time limits is to make sure that the vote on the budget has gone through before 1 January, when the financial year begins. If at that date and despite these limits the budget has not been adopted, two things can happen. If the delay is the fault of parliament, for not finishing its debate within the time limit, the government has the right to put the budget into effect by ordinance. The seventy days can, however, end after the beginning of the budgetary year through no fault of parliament. This happens when the appearance of the budget proposals has been delayed, or when after a negative vote in both chambers the government is obliged to redraft a proposal (a procedure which involves a new time limit). In these eventualities, the government depends entirely on legislative authorisation to obtain revenues; it must receive this authorisation either by a special law being voted, or by a separate vote on the first part of the budget proposal. As far as expenditure is concerned, it can effect this itself by decrees corresponding to the existing *services votés*, and debate on the new proposals then continues in normal conditions after 1 January.

It is therefore only when parliament makes a deliberate decision not to reach a vote within the prescribed time that an ordinance may be substituted for a law. In the other situations, the procedures laid down in no way affect parliamentary prerogatives; their only purpose is to ensure the flow of cash to public services while the debate in the legislature continues. Occasion arose to operate these procedures in 1962, when the dissolution of the Assembly intervened; they were put into effect for the new Assembly without any problems arising.

It is often said that the authorisations of expenditure given by parliament are too general, and that this is another sign of the decline of parliament's decision-making powers. This criticism cannot apply to the voting of revenue, but it is relevant for votes on expenditure. In practice, only new measures involve individual votes and the *services votés* (see page 107) are covered by a very small number of authorisations. For example, *services votés* included in the general budget are all covered by one single vote.

Moreover, this expenditure accounts for about 85 per cent of the general budget; for 1972, 160 thousand million francs out of a total of 183 thousand million francs. It is often maintained that to vote such a mass of expenditure at once is analogous to holding a referendum on public spending as a whole and that it eliminates all real possibility of control over the greater part of the budget.

This argument, however, collapses if it is recalled that *services votés* are no more than a basis of reference for the real votes on expenditure, which take place when new measures are examined in detail. The evaluation of the *services votés* is a technical exercise which could easily be done without parliamentary approval; parliament's sole interest in it is to allow members to give their views on the accuracy of the experts' calculations. In any case, at the time of the debate on new proposals, members of parliament are not in any sense bound by their vote on the basis of reference. If certain items appearing under *services votés* displease them, they can eliminate them by voting corresponding new measures with a negating effect. In the last resort, members of parliament can exercise the right to pass negative proposals totalling the *services votés*; negative proposals totalled 160 thousand million francs in 1972, thereby cancelling all expenditure corresponding to the repetition in 1972 of the budget for 1971.

The trap which various experts fall into is to confuse the concept of the '*mesure nouvelle*' with that of the '*supplément de crédits*'. For them, the general budget for 1972 involved expenditure of 183 thousand million francs, divided between 160 thousand million for *services votés* covered by one vote, and 23 thousand million francs of supplementary expenditure covered by various special votes. In fact this 183 thousand million francs was subjected to detailed discussion; it was the result of adding to the last year's 160 thousand million francs the positive and negative *mesures nouvelles* proposed by the government. But parliament, within the constitutional limits of its right of amendment, was free to adopt different proposals whose net effect could have fixed the final budget total between nothing and 183 thousand million francs.

To understand this mechanism better, let us take the hypothesis of a budget of 100 thousand million francs, in which *services votés* also total 100 thousand million francs. Misinformed experts could deduce that this budget did not differ in any way from that of the previous year. If however its total had been reached by the adoption of 100 thousand million francs of negative *mesures nouvelles*, balanced by the adoption of positive *mesures nouvelles* to the same amount, the new budget would in fact have no features in common with the old one at all, and would be introducing a radical change in the existing state of the law.

Following from this, it may well be asked what interest parliament has in the system of *services votés*. Why not start afresh each year, from nothing, or from some simple reference such as last year's expenditure? The answer is simple: it is only by calculating the cost of existing authorisations that an accurate assessment of the cost of new proposals can be made. Let us suppose that an administrative item is allocated 10 million francs in 1971 and 11 million francs in 1972; the legislator could reasonably suppose that it is a question of increasing expenditure under this heading by 1 million francs. But if, for this same item, the *service voté* (or the sum which allows the administration to carry out its work under the same conditions as in the previous year) amounts to 12 million francs, the true allocation for 1972 becomes clear; there is in fact a saving of 1 million francs under this heading. The concept of the *service voté* is therefore a source of order and accuracy for the legislator. Far from reducing the rights of parliament, it improves the quality of its information while taking nothing away from its powers of deliberation.

This deliberative power is exercised on the occasion of voting on *mesures nouvelles*, which takes place as an annexe to the budget, under the category of special accounts, and by ministry and by heading in the general budget. The vote on these measures, which will affect the basis of reference of *services votés*, either increasing or reducing it, gives to each expenditure item its definitive form. Admittedly the detailed division into *chapitres* for the general budget and the annexes, and into special accounts, is done by the government, through decrees. But the government's powers here are purely formal, since the decrees for this division can only repeat the explanatory information given in the annexes to a project, and include the modifications which result from votes in parliament.

Legislative authorisations do consequently reach a fairly high level of precision, and it would be wrong to consider the finance bill as a general provision within which the government can dispose of the global items voted according to its own inclination. It must, however, be admitted that there are different means by which, in the course of the budgetary year, the government can deviate to some extent from the initial authorisation.

Sometimes the government can obtain additional finance without recourse to parliament. In an emergency supplementary expenditure can be authorised by decree and is allowed automatically under those headings representing expenditure required by law. Some of the decrees concerned must ultimately be submitted for parliamentary ratification, which is in general also necessary for corrections to projects included in the finance law. Nobody knows precisely what the legal position would be if ratification were ever refused.

More frequently, the initial distribution of expenditure between the different headings of the finance bill undergoes some alteration in the course of the year. Transfers which do not affect the nature of the expenditure, but only the department which is to carry it out, need no more than a simple *arrêté* by the Ministry of Finance. Certain headings of the budget, known as the *chapitres-reservoirs*, are in fact designed to facilitate such operations in the course of the year. Other types of transfer, which do affect the expenditure itself (*virements*), are subject to stricter rules; they must be authorised by decree and can only be made between *chapitres* which fall under the same ministry, and then within certain limits. Finally, expenditure is sometimes then carried forward, frequently in the case of capital items, and this can result in the prolongation of parliamentary authorisation beyond the financial year.

There is therefore a class of budgetary authorisation in which the legislative power takes no part. Parliament's intervention is limited to *a posteriori* supervision, which takes place with greater or lesser effectiveness, and in particular during the debate on the *loi de règlement*.

Another question arises here, which is whether parliament has any scope for altering government proposals by means of amendments on the occasion of the relatively numerous and detailed legislative votes. Can it do anything other than accept or reject these proposals?

This question is often answered in the negative. The freedom of initiative of members of parliament is strictly limited at the time of the debate on the finance bill. For the bill as a whole, Article 40 of the Constitution lays down a general rule which forbids members of parliament to take initiatives tending either to 'reduce public revenues or create or enlarge an item of public expenditure'. Although it is extremely restrictive, this rule does recognise the existence of a freedom of initiative and restricts it under only two aspects. For the separate finance laws, however, the regulations are even stricter; interdiction becomes the rule and freedom the exception. This is the aim of Article 42 of the *loi organique* of 2 January 1959, which begins purely and simply by suppressing the right to amend the budget proposal, before giving a very short list of kinds of amendments which are not actually forbidden, namely those which would 'prevent or reduce an item of expenditure, create or increase a revenue, or increase control over public spending'.

If we ignore the general influence of members of parliament, the permanent control exercised by the *rapporteurs spéciaux*, and the eventual effect of the views which emerge in the course of budgetary debates, then indeed parliament plays no part in the preparation of the budget (although a sort of 'pre-debate' on the options open for the next finance bill is currently being suggested). The final appearance of the proposal, after a long procedure of arbitration which begins early in the year and does not finish before September, is consequently the government's exclusive responsibility. In so far as this project cannot be modified in any way, it can certainly be concluded that parliament's powers of decision over the budget are restricted to its approval or rejection.

In fact observation of parliamentary practice shows that this is too summary a conclusion. For example, at the time of the first reading in the National Assembly of the budget proposal for 1972, 40 amendments were put before the finance committee and 150 proposed at the public session, and of these less than 10 per cent were declared unconstitutional. The right of amendment, whatever may be said, can still be exercised, and the constitutional and structural limits are so interpreted as not to constitute an insurmountable barrier to realistic initiatives which are intelligently mounted.

As far as revenue is concerned, and especially taxation, the only amendments forbidden are those which would have the effect of bringing the total amount of public revenue to less than that which would result from existing legislation. It is allowed to introduce initiatives to increase revenues, as well as balanced proposals to reduce taxation, in which one tax would be reduced and another increased in such a way that the overall level of revenue would remain unchanged.

This rule of compensation, the subject of much subtle jurisprudence, opens the way to much parliamentary initiative both in theory and in practice.

'Compensation' is not allowed in the case of expenditure. Initiatives which would lead to any extra expense, even if balanced by an economy elsewhere or by an increase in revenue of the same amount, are forbidden; amendments to reduce expenditure are the only kind possible. Faced with government proposals to increase or reduce expenditure, however, parliament is skilled in reducing the one and increasing the other. Amendments of this sort may be very precise and can have some particular measure in view, even a budgetary heading; it is enough to mention the contested measure or the heading which the proposing member would like reduced or suppressed in his *exposé des motifs*.

Of special interest are amendments which seek to alter the allocation of expenditure between the different headings of the budget in the finance bill. These are analogous to a *virement* or transfer of expenditure from one heading to another, and the operation consists of two stages. The first involves making a cut in the original heading, and the second in adding to the other. It is easy for members of parliament to launch this procedure, simply by moving permissible amendments to reduce expenditure with their accompanying *motifs*. The government alone, however, is in a position to carry it through.

Finally, nothing prevents a member of parliament from putting forward amendments to reduce expenditure for every heading of the budget. By this expedient the ancient ceremony of voting on the budget heading by heading, to which some still look back with nostalgia, could at any time be revived. This would not of course help to keep the budget debate within the set time limits.

Members of parliament wishing to change the government's proposals can therefore attempt to obtain either votes against articles or headings of the finance bill, or the adoption of amendments which pass the constitutional hurdle. But these are only tentative strategies; to succeed, proposals for changes must obviously be ratified by the various institutions involved, either a committee of the Assembly and the Assembly itself in full session, or the Assembly alone. It is also necessary for the two chambers to adopt identical proposals. In the course of all this legislative procedure, the government could be making use of its powerful technical or political weapons which sometimes enable it to set aside initiatives about which it feels very strongly and to retain only those which it has decided to accept with a more or less good grace.

We shall not spend much time on the technical weapons which the legislative procedure places in the hands of the government, since these are not specific to the finance bill.

In the first place, the parliamentary debate takes place on the basis of the government's text, or of the text passed from one chamber to the other, and not as once was the case on the basis of the text as it has been altered by the finance committees. Amendments made by these committees have thus no privileged position, legally speaking, as against those by individuals or by other committees. The government is not therefore obliged to concern itself with the re-establishment of its original text during the first reading before the National Assembly, and so is very rarely itself in need of concessions.

The government can also have recourse to the *'vote bloqué'* which allows it to ask for a single vote on all or part of the text under discussion, retaining certain amendments only. This procedure is used less and less, since at the present time it is not liked by the majority parties. These have nevertheless on certain occasions asked for certain votes to be *bloqué*. This most often arises when a popular measure, for example the reduction of a tax, is accompanied by an unpopular one, such as the increase of another; the majority is not in this case anxious to share popular approval for the first measure with the Opposition, while bearing responsibility for the latter on its own. Consequently the *vote bloqué* is not always nor solely a weapon used by government against parliament; it is also often a weapon used by the majority against the minority.

Before the vote on the project as a whole, a second debate may intervene which allows the government to recover the articles, revenues or expenditures on which it has been beaten. It is usually at the end of the first reading before the National Assembly that this procedure is set in motion; the government's greatest danger is that its defeats in the National Assembly might be confirmed in the Senate and so become irreversible. Defeats in the Senate are on the other hand less serious in so far as the Assembly does not vote to confirm them.

There remains the question of government influence on the mixed committee of deputies and senators. The decision to call a meeting of this committee, or to present its conclusions to the Assemblies for a vote, rests with the government alone. It is often at this stage that the last elements of resistance disappear. The *navette* between the two assemblies can be avoided by this measure, and at the end of the *navette* process the National Assembly always has the last word.

From a political point of view, it is clear that important consequences for the budgetary procedure flow from the fact that the government has enjoyed a stable and relatively coherent majority in the National Assembly for several years – a very new phenomenon for our country and one to which it may be doubted that it will ever become accustomed. It is to the existence of this majority that many observers attribute what they see as the decline in parliament's powers of decision-making in financial affairs. The minority, they say, no longer has any chance of success in its attempts to alter a government proposal. As for the majority, the timidity it reveals in its relations with the government causes it to leave the legal means at its disposal unused; its idea of its own role is such as to shelter the government from any disagreeable surprise.

This argument, which goes far beyond the problem of budgetary control, is not wholly convincing, even when presented in a more general and elaborate form. While it is true that the financial initiatives which are defeated usually come from members of the Opposition, this does not necessarily imply a decline of parliament. Rather it suggests a decline in those small political groups whose political influence was once disproportionate to their size. Proportional representation in decision-making has never been the main aim of the parliamentary system. Participation by a majority of the nation's representatives in a coherent and united policy would be a better way of describing its advantages.

Moreover, the relations of trust which unite the government with its majority do not always work in favour of the government. It is more usual to give way to one's friends than one's enemies, and the parliamentary majority, if it is united and determined, has sufficient weight to extract support from its partner, in the course of the final bargaining, for such proposals as it really cherishes. The government is occasionally asked for favours with special insistence, and can be persuaded either not to make full use of its weapons against certain parliamentary initiatives, or itself to propose modifications to its own proposals for which the initiative would be forbidden for members of parliament. Apart from these 'presents' which the government makes to its majority, some of which are prepared in advance, the government is often obliged to embark on a series of concessions or to accept that it is beaten.

During the debate on the budget for 1972, for example, the National Assembly was able by these means to alter the course of 400–500 million francs of revenues and to increase expenditure by about 150 million francs. Some will think this a small achievement, while others will disagree. In any case it would be the opposite of the truth to maintain that the French parliament is no more than a register for budgetary decisions. Constructively or otherwise, voting on the budget gives parliament an opportunity to make its mark.

This analysis, which at several points rejects generally accepted ideas, and which can certainly be disputed as a whole, leads to some varied conclusions.

On the two levels of budgetary information and budgetary decision-making, the French parliament can and must extract itself from a superficial crisis which has arisen from its failure to adapt to political changes and new techniques. The belief that it has lost the means of controlling and sanctioning the budget arises from an inadequate knowledge of existing mechanisms. The assemblies may not always use their prerogatives to the full, a fact which can hardly be denied, but the means do exist, which is the essential thing.

However, this situation can be expected to change fairly quickly. In a country in which it is customary to call for a reform of institutions whenever there is a change in habits, the severe judgement with which a large part of public opinion and also many political experts view parliament's budgetary powers does open considerable prospects for proposals for reform. It must be hoped that these reformers will know how to preserve what has already been achieved. Progress in the supply of information, and the use of new techniques of rationalising budgetary choices, will moreover sooner or later involve a revision of parliamentary method and procedure.

Nevertheless, the defenders of democratic institutions should not be daunted by the growing technicalities of modern budgets. Technology does not abolish decision-making, but rather the reverse. From this point of view, parliament and government have the same interests. The participation of the elected representatives in the big choices of financial policy is necessary to avoid creating a new administrative power which would involve a depreciation in the powers of both government and parliament.

The debate on the budget is an opportunity both for the opposition to criticise each aspect of government policy, although without hope, it is true, of altering it, and for the majority to justify itself. All this is ultimately subject to public opinion. The decisions are not taken within office walls but are exposed to the full light of day, and the publicity given at this time to affairs of State is one of the essential conditions of democracy.

Parliamentary intervention is moreover not entirely without effectiveness. It is not only that there are real possibilities of making changes, but also the fact that parliamentary supervision alters the situation simply by existing. Some budget proposals would be very different if they had not been subject to parliament's control, or if that control had been feebler. In addition to this, the oral and written opinions presented in the course of a budgetary debate necessarily influence the preparation of the next budget.

The task of parliament in this respect is to humanise certain rigid technocratic ideas, to remind public services of the authority of the State, and to make sure that the good sense of the representatives of the people triumphs over cold and abstract theory. To play such a role, parliamentary control does not need to be transformed by spectacular reforms; it only needs to remain firm and watchful.

CHAPTER 7

PARLIAMENTARY CONTROL OF THE BUDGET IN FRANCE

Pierre Lalumière

The classical budgetary theory as enunciated in the nineteenth century broke the budgetary process down into four stages: preparation, approval, execution, audit. The first and the third stages were meant to be the responsibility of the government; the second and fourth fell within the competence of parliament. Consequently the elected assemblies were called upon, first of all, to vote the law containing the budget (known as the '*loi de finances*)' and then, after this was implemented, to examine the operations involved in executing the law and to proceed to close the budgetary exercise by approving a final law (known as the '*loi de règlement*').

This traditional presentation of the State's financial activity rests explicitly on the premise that the power of decision in budgetary matters belongs to parliament. Therefore we must elucidate the use of the term 'control' to describe parliament's intervention, both when the budget is approved and at the stage of audit, for this usage conceals differences between the two stages. When parliament votes the budget, it takes decisions which bind the government and direct its activity for the ensuing twelve months. When parliament audits the execution of the budget, on the contrary, it compares the decisions taken by the government in its financial operations with the instructions which parliament gave initially in voting the budget. Here parliament can do no more than to carry out an audit and, if this reveals irregularities, to pronounce sanctions. The present study will be limited to examining the role of parliament during the discussion and approval of the budget proposal prepared by the government; the other stages of the budgetary process will be deliberately ignored, although parliament does intervene in them. This is not an arbitrary choice. There is a widespread conviction among parliamentarians that it is only at the stage examined here that they have real opportunity to influence the content of any of the major budgetary decisions, and these psychological considerations have led us to make our choice.

The current official doctrine still rests on the classical budgetary theory regarding the respective roles of parliament and government in the budgetary process. We might well wonder at this resistance to the pressure of time, since the theory is still but a systematisation of rules which were evolved in the historical context of the parliamentary regime of the Third Republic (typified by parliament's possession of a political strength which was formally condemned and abandoned in 1958). It would be possible with a stretch of the imagination to claim that this classical theory was still in harmony with the provisions of the Constitution of 4 October 1958, which reaffirms parliament's power of decision in budgetary matters while multiplying the legal restrictions on exercising this power. Each year, however, in actual budgetary practice the debates in parliament reveal how outdated this theory is; its survival as an official doctrine can only be the result of intellectual laziness. In fact the actual working of the budgetary institutions betrays an important decline in parliamentary influence.

In analysing the budgetary powers of parliament it is necessary to make constant reference to the original political experience which the Fifth Republic represents. Since 1962 the French political system has been an 'imperfect' presidential system; the President of the Republic is now elected by direct universal suffrage, but the government appointed by the President of the Republic is still politically responsible to one of the houses of parliament (the National Assembly). This system was set up as a reaction to the excesses of government-by-assembly experienced in the Fourth Republic. Although the constitutional texts leave parliament with important powers to exercise, the political practice of the last twelve years has demonstrated an intention to weaken the authority of the assemblies in the interests of the executive branch. The application of provisions governing parliamentary control of the budget must be put into this new political context. If we adopt a sociological point of view and analyse the actual working of the institutions, we shall become aware of the diminished role which parliament has in budgetary affairs.

TWO MODELS OF FINANCIAL POWER

It is possible to summarise the evolution over the last 100 years of parliament's financial power in relation to the State budget by two successive models, each with its own characteristics. The first model, which for simplicity's sake may be labelled the 'Third Republic model', endowed parliament with very real powers enabling it to influence the contents of the budget and by that means to determine the activity of government. The second or 'Fifth Republic model' considerably restricts the powers of decision which parliament can exercise in relation to the budget. A transition from the first to the second model took place gradually during the Fourth Republic (1946–58).

In both cases the changes in parliament's prerogatives flowed directly from constitutional provisions. The parliamentary regime of the Third Republic depended on constitutional laws which granted wide powers to the assemblies; the Constitution of the Fifth Republic was born of an anti-parliamentary reaction, which especially in its presidential interpretation of 1962 aimed at bringing the activity of the elected assemblies under lock and key. However these constitutional provisions took on their full significance only in a certain political context. Day-by-day political activity has given an individual interpretation to the theoretical provisions of the Constitution. The analysis of each of these two models will be based on law as corrected by practice, which will enable their essential nature to be determined.

The Third Republic Model

Historically speaking, French budgetary law evolved during the same period as the establishment of a parliamentary system. In fact the foundations were laid during the Restoration (1814–30) in imitation of and often in an attempt to systemise the texts and practices then applied in England. Budgetary law, then, is an importation like the parliamentary system fashioned in the same period.

The law was applied as a result of historical accident. It was in the period 1814–48 that parliament gained acceptance for a set of legally binding rules (the rules of annuality, the rule for examining the budget chapter by chapter, and so on) which gave it the right of tight supervision over government activity. This unexpected implementation of budgetary law was a consequence of political conflict.

Antagonism between aristocracy and bourgeoisie was characteristic of the Restoration and the July Monarchy (1841–8). As these two social classes had almost equivalent political influence, the parliamentary system seemed to be the only possible constitutional formula; between the sovereign, representing the aristocracy, and parliament (in particular the lower chamber) expressing the claims of the bourgeoisie, the ministerial cabinet struggled to make awkward compromises.

In the game of politics conservative social forces had the advantages of controlling the machinery of State, using the sovereign as intermediary, and of supplying the personnel of the higher civil service, which was recruited according to criteria of wealth and social prestige. Faced with this situation bourgeois circles sought to obtain (by means of parliament) the right to scrutinise ('*droit de regard*') the organisation of government; they decided that financial instruments constituted an excellent means of scrutinising the administration. Thus each improvement of the budgetary procedure marked a tightening of the hold of bourgeois circles over the government machine. These advances were supported in the name of the sovereignty of parliament; each success recorded a political victory for liberal bourgeois circles. In nineteenth-century France budgetary law played a political role.

The full blossoming of parliamentary control of the budget came during the Third Republic (1875–1940). The political context was favourable; characteristic of the Third Republican political system was the omnipotence of parliament, which provoked a chronic instability of governments. Each year discussion of the proposed budgetary law allowed the chambers to obtain extensive information about the policies of the government, to carry out a detailed scrutiny of its budgetary or fiscal policy, and to direct its activities according to the wishes of the nation's representatives. This discussion passed far beyond its financial objective and it was possible to touch on every aspect of government policy (agricultural, diplomatic, military, and so on). Disagreement over a budgetary provision often manifested lack of confidence in the general policy of the government; budgetary debates were the source of numerous political crises.

While examining the proposed budgetary law each member of parliament enjoyed a right of amendment allowing him to alter, downwards or upwards, an item of expenditure or of revenue proposed by the government. Now this right of amendment was not subject to limitations. The natural consequences of the abuse of this power were the disruption of each budgetary proposal and as a result, rises in expenditure. It was noticeable that the expenditure voted by parliament was almost always greater than that requested by the government.

The investment of the assemblies with complete political power had in fact altered the mentality of members of parliament. Previously, under the July Monarchy, the chambers sought in a mood of saving candle-ends to limit the expenses of an executive which was extraneous to them. Having taken power into their own hands they lost their interest in economy and sought to please their electors by bestowing various benefits on them.[1] These abuses, however, brought about the first limitations on the right of amendment of parliamentarians, which appeared in the standing orders (*règlement intérieur*) of both assemblies. Within each chamber the finance committee (*commission des finances*) played a role of prime importance in budgetary discussions. This permanent working group, composed of a fixed number of important politicians, often upset the whole of the proposed financial law presented to it. The debates in the committee were as important as those which took place eventually in the full assembly; sometimes they resulted in bringing the political responsibility of the government into question and in the resignation of the ministry. The finance committees were virtual 'alternative governments'. Thanks to their financial role they took on a policy function.

From a sociological point of view, under the Third Republic power belonged to a political class which was essentially a parliamentary class. The principal decisions were taken within a group of about 100 politicians who had occupied government posts (former prime ministers, former ministers and so on). These decisions were the result of laborious compromise intended to balance the contrary interests which were expressed within this directing group. Political life was made up of the conflicts which broke out between the principal leaders and of the solutions which were evolved.

It was the tradition that these politicians had access to all official papers or were informed about all important questions, whether they belonged to the government side or not. There was, then, only a very partial distinction between parliament and government, for the circuit of effective power ran through both of them simultaneously. Budgetary debates were the main annual event at which the rivalries within this directing group could be expressed. In parliament, however, there were politicians who were extremely well informed and who were capable of controlling government policy in detail. This explains the important role played by the finance committees, which brought together the leading politicians.

Although this model of control vested parliament with effective influence over the budget, there were unfortunate consequences for budgetary procedure from a strictly technical point of view.

---

[1] For the budget for the year 1884, which scarcely exceeded 3 thousand million francs, parliament proposed 46 million francs of new expenditure and 310 million francs of tax reductions.

Experience showed that parliamentary initiatives led to delay in adopting the budget or, more seriously, regularly compromised the balance of revenue and expenditure. It was possible to state that 'the assemblies were wasteful, incompetent and irresponsible' (G. Jèze). The crisis which the French parliamentary system experienced during the years preceding the Second World War showed how ill-adapted was this model of control: the scope of the problems presented by monetary difficulties or by State intervention in economic affairs made it indispensable to find a new formula for parliamentary control over the financial affairs of the State.

The Fifth Republic Model

Since the advent of the Fifth Republic the fundamental economic and financial choices have been made by the government and presented by the latter in its proposal for the *loi de finances* (or budget proposal) submitted each year for parliamentary examination. Budgetary debates no longer provide the parliamentary assemblies with an opportunity to exercise real influence over the choices proposed and thereby over government activity. The majority of observers now admit that the institution of parliament has been effaced in this way and there is a running debate on the search for means of restoring parliamentary authority.

This decline in parliament's financial role arises basically from the provisions of the 1958 Constitution and the 'organic' *ordonnance* of 2 January 1959. It is true that Article 34 of the Constitution reaffirms the power of parliament in budgetary affairs by entrusting it with the 'determination of the income and expenditure of the State'. But the *ordonnance*, in implementing certain constitutional provisions, lays down a procedure of discussion for the parliamentary examination of the budget which differs from that followed for ordinary laws. The aim is to organise the discussion in each assembly so as to prevent any disorder upsetting the course of the debate. In practice this 'rationalisation' of procedure places very severe limits on the opportunities for deputies to intervene.

Just as injurious to the privileges of parliament are the restrictions on the right of amendment of parliamentarians arising from Article 40 of the Constitution, the compulsory delays placed on the continuation of discussion, the employment by the government of the '*vote bloqué*' and the need to vote expenditure in bulk, aiming as they do to force parliament to concentrate its attention on the fundamental and overall choices proposed by the government in the economic and financial sphere. The intention of the procedure laid

E

down by the 1959 *ordonnance* is to press parliament into accepting or rejecting the budget proposal as a whole without ever getting down to a detailed examination of its provisions. Since it is technically and politically 'unthinkable' to reject the budget, this procedure forces parliament to accept the budget proposal prepared by the government without important modification. By forcing the assemblies to make a choice between 'all or nothing', the constitutional provisions deprive them of real powers of political control, limited as these powers now are to a choice between two extreme possibilities. Commenting in 1959 on the intentions of the authors of the constitution, M. Giscard d'Estaing gave an inkling of the inevitable evolution of the financial powers of parliament:

> the first objective was to make the voting of the budget as synthetic as possible in character. Parliament was to pronounce on the main block of expenditure by an examination which, while going into some detail, should not seek to pick the bones of each chapter or to initiate votes of too small a dimension thereby reducing attention and preventing an overall view of budgetary policy. The other objective was to provide the opportunity for minute control of government activity in financial affairs. The two objectives are quite contradictory.[1]

However, the provisions of the Constitution and of the *ordonnance* have been applied by the government in the most restrictive way. If parliamentarians had wanted to exploit all their potential, they could have been interpreted a lot more flexibly, in spite of their draconian nature. But the former, after some attempt at resistance, finally accepted the government's interpretation. This is indeed a paradox; under the government's influence the texts have been applied in practice in the least favourable sense for the privileges of parliament, but this has also been with the more or less resigned concurrence of parliamentarians themselves. The significance thus given these constitutional provisions in political practice has not been understood by political commentators, who have been prevented by a narrow legal formalism from recognising the facts as they are. One contribution to this book is devoted to a theoretical exposition (that is to say from the point of view of the constitutional provisions alone) of the means of information and of the privileges of parliament.[2] The author of this contribution shows that the decision-making powers of the assemblies are subject to important

[1] Official Journal, Debates of the National Assembly 1959, p. 2328.
[2] See Chapter 6.

restrictions in terms of the texts; but he also shows that, even within the confines of a legal interpretation, parliament could have derived more benefit from the privileges granted to it, however limited these may be. At the same time he constructs in hypothesis certain subtle measures by which parliamentarians could increase their powers of intervention. Some of these are akin to legal acrobatics and cannot be taken as more than academic conjecture (*hypothèses d'école*) without any chance of practical application (in particular the suggestion that standing charges in '*services votés*' could be abolished in their entirety by passing negative allocations as '*mesures nouvelles*' of the same amount). Nevertheless it is true that, from the strictly legal point of view, opportunities exist for parliament.

The brutal fact is that none of these opportunities has been used. When they are drafted, constitutional provisions are valuable and sometimes conceal several possible meanings; but at a given moment they become fixed by a single interpretation imposed by the political context. Those who are constrained by a too literal examination of constitutional texts may fail to realise this fact, but its existence cannot be denied.

Responsibility for this strict interpretation of the constitutional provisions rests with the present political institutions. The centre of gravity has in fact shifted towards the presidency of the Republic. The appointment of the head of State by universal suffrage makes the presidency the keystone of the political system. The logic of the system, and thus also its efficient operation, demands agreement between president and parliament (at least, that is, the National Assembly to which the government appointed by the president is politically responsible). Thus at each election to the legislature the President asks the electors to send to parliament a majority committed to support his actions. So far this appeal has been heard and a political majority has been regularly returned to the National Assembly to support the actions of the President; it is precisely for this reason that the Assembly finds itself politically subordinate to the President. The essential purpose of this majority is to lend its support faithfully to the government appointed by the President. The whole of the French political system as it has functioned since 1958 makes the President the pole of attraction and the origin of all 'power circuits'.

Thus the underlying political accord, which binds the National Assembly and the government, means that budgetary discussions are first and foremost a manifestation of this solidarity. The voting of the *loi de finances* is presented as a political act by means of which parliament agrees to support the major options of government policy. However this act of confidence inevitably leads the National Assembly to behave like a simple '*chambre d'enregistrement*'.

Parliamentarians certainly still try every year to wring some concessions from the government; but these are minor and never threaten the broad outline of the budget proposal. Since parliament's approval is established as soon as the debates begin, it has come to be assumed in government circles that the budget debates are confined to informing members of parliament of decisions already taken by the executive. The National Assembly, or at least the majority within this assembly, have for several years come to accept this conception implicitly.

It is common to justify the decline in parliamentary influence by the technical complexity of budgetary problems. Now that it has become an instrument of economic policy the State budget can no longer be approached in the simplistic terms of good house-keeping. Members of parliament do not generally possess the technical competence which its handling demands. The inferiority of the assemblies is revealed first where information is concerned. The activities of the State have developed by creating an enormous bureaucracy, the financial supervision of which calls for a precise knowledge of its mechanics and of the scope of its needs. Every source of information belongs either to the ministry concerned or to a specialised inspectorate. Since parliament does not have its own means of information, it is in the end the controlled who inform the controller.

The loss of power by members of parliament has also been caused by the spread of methods designed to ensure that future budgetary decisions are prepared rationally. In fact the fundamental indicators of the budget are determined on the basis of economic models whose application demands highly specialised techniques. Each year two models of reference are used: on the one hand, the chief economic measures of a contingent nature are settled on the basis of an economic budget (established by the Commission des Comptes et Budgets de la Nation), which constitutes a forecast for the coming year of the economic activity of the nation as a whole: on the other hand, the expenditure forecasts of each budget (in particular the investment expenditure) must take account of the recommendations formulated in the plan, which is a model of economic growth established for a multi-annual period. The State budget may be seen therefore simply as an instrument for executing policies formulated separately; to a large extent its content is pre-determined and can no longer be subject to any control.

The economic models which are used as a reference for preparing the budget are forecasts drawn up on the basis of coherent relationships in the development of the crucial national economic indicators (investment, consumption, and so on). Parliamentarians lack technical competence for discussing the hypotheses based on these models: even if they make only limited requests for alteration, inevitably they threaten the coherence of the calculations made. When the Economic Plan is approved, the government asks for a general vote on the proposal as a whole and refuses all parliamentary amendments. The enormous progress made with economic quantification places parliament, therefore, in a position of inferiority compared with the government and its specialist agencies.

In recent years a particularly important effort has been made to rationalise the content of the budget. In order to maximise the coherence with which the indicators of the budget are fixed from an economic point of view, economic models like the economic budget or the plan have been continually perfected. More recently still the search for greater efficiency in the use of resources and in the management of departments has given rise to the adoption of a system called *rationalisation des choix budgétaires* (RCB), which thanks to the employment of techniques of quantification and analysis allows for a better formulation and execution of administrative decisions.

But to a large extent this attempt to rationalise the content of the budget explains the neglect of the traditional function of political control. By airing the grievances of various social groups the parliamentary assemblies bring into question all the figures which have been so scientifically established. The invariably disparate amendments of parliament can sometimes alter, sometimes even destroy, the finely balanced arrangements which have been carefully prepared by government departments; they are sources of disturbance to the internal coherence of the whole system. Thus government circles tend to contrast the rationality of the executive's proposals with the irrationality of the requests formulated by members of parliament. The unavoidable conclusion is that in order to keep the budget proposal as effective as possible, intervention by the assemblies has to be limited as much as possible, if not completely suppressed.

In the economic and financial field, work must now be done mainly by experts, in view of the complexity of the decisions taken and the difficulties related to their formulation. It has been maintained that the phenomenon of 'technostructure' described by Galbraith in large economic organisations reappears in the administration of the modern State and most particularly in French government organisation. Obviously the results achieved by teams of experts working together cannot be impugned by the personal and, therefore, arbitrary intervention of members of parliament. So there has emerged a system of decision-making which is naturally superior in view of the efficiency of its techniques, and to which parliament seems to be extraneous and foreign.

Without underestimating the technical upheavals which have affected budgetary data over fourteen years, there is also a political explanation for the effacement of parliamentary assemblies. Traditionally the political behaviour of parliamentarians hardly predisposes them for the economic and financial choices which they are asked to make when voting the budget. They consider their role as essentially to limit the government's demands and to defend the interests of their electors; theirs is a power of criticism and not of initiative. There is a 'whig' tradition in French parliamentarianism which is distinguished by an attitude of opposition to authority (*resistance au pouvoir*); the people's representatives are not called upon to determine financial and economic policy, but only to say what is and what is not acceptable in proposals put before them.

Parliament is conceived to be a counterweight to the actions of the government and so perpetually finds itself in a defensive position with regard to the latter. This political behaviour, which is expressed by exercising a power of veto, puts the assemblies in an inferior position in budgetary debates. In this highly technical field the institution which has the right to initiate proposals holds a decisive advantage because it can prepare carefully, in advance, the proposals on which the confrontation will take place. Parliament's traditional power of criticism, therefore, is paralysed by the technical complexity of the measures under discussion. There has been no success so far for proposals which have been repeatedly made for associating deputies with decision-making within the government machine; this could have the result of altering the traditional attitude of parliament.

Moreover the development since the Fourth Republic of an economic democracy has encouraged governments to negotiate directly on the formulation of every major decision with the organisations representing social and professional groups. As long as legitimacy is seen as flowing from the full expression of all interests, the best decisions can only be those on which the largest consensus of social and professional forces is achieved. In the same way parliament no longer has a monopoly in representing interests, and is in competition with pressure groups (although under the Fourth Republic the activities of the latter did not devalue the function of parliament which, as the essential source of power, continued to be the final arbiter in all fields).

This co-operation between government and interest groups has met with mixed results in the Fifth Republic. It could not have taken more varied forms, ranging from the definition of policy in agreement with the representative organisations of a sector (as has happened with agricultural policy), to the laying down of the *Plan d'équipement* by use of consultative organisations of an economic nature (the *commissions de modernisation*), where the main economic groups are represented. This policy of co-operation always ends with parliament being 'short-circuited', since in so far as it is later consulted at all, parliament can do no more than approve agreements already made.[1] Implicitly the behaviour of the government and of socio-professional groups betrays a widespread feeling that the elected assemblies, and more particularly the National Assembly, no longer ensure a sufficiently accurate representation of the various economic and social forces of the country. The existence of a parliamentary majority which, with the exception of unusual and short periods, had never existed before 1958, has undoubtedly led to a distortion of the representative process at a national level. The majority parties draw their electoral support from certain social groups whose claims are accurately expressed; in contrast, because of the 'dictatorial' attitude of the majority, the socio-professional groups whose interests are defended mainly by the opposition have lost confidence in parliamentary machinery and prefer to employ direct pressure on the government. It is even possible to say that relatively well-represented social groups are not always free to express their point of view because of the tight political subordination in which the majority of the National Assembly is placed by the government. Since parliament no longer ensures an accurate expression of interests, that function has been replaced by substitutory mechanisms. This development has come to the notice of members of parliament and in a letter made public in July 1971 some deputies belonging to the political majority of the National

[1] From the many examples one can quote the agreement on incomes reached in November 1971 between the government and the main civil service trade unions on the developments for the year 1972 in salaries for employees of the public administration. In principle parliament fixes the expenditure on civil service personnel but was not associated with these negotiations or with this agreement. However it simply ratified it when the budget for the year 1972 was voted.

Assembly denounced the privileged nature of the ties between the government and interest groups:

> Political life in the Fourth Republic was dominated by parties whose monopoly led the regime to its ruin. Today there seems to be a danger of an excessive reaction in the opposite direction and of a regime dominated by parties giving way little by little to a regime of pressure groups.
>
> The leaders of these bodies, appointed sometimes with partial secrecy and little democracy, have shown on more than one occasion that they had not the means or the will to keep their promises. While on the one hand it encourages them to overbid, the uncertainty which surrounds their representativeness can with good reason raise doubts about the value of their commitment. The hearing they get from the public authorities is disproportionate to their public support.
>
> Genuine undertakings by the State can be pledged only with the co-operation of the nation's representatives elected by universal suffrage, whose own responsibility is in no way absolved by the signing of agreements reached at the level of pressure groups.[1]

The development of an ever-closer relationship between the government and interest groups also shows how unsuitable are the decision-making procedures employed by parliament in the economic and financial field. It is now accepted that all socio-professional groups who are affected must be associated with the discussion of any proposal. Therefore the decision-making process first considers the demands made by these groups, then acknowledges that disagreements should be gradually reduced so that, after numerous confrontations, a decision emerges from a set of compromises accepted by every group. The formulation of the *Plan d'équipement* is a perfect illustration of this decision-model. In fact it is carried out over a period of about two years by the *commissions de modernisation* which bring together representatives of the trade unions, employers, farmers and so on, alongside senior civil servants. The work of preparing the plan consists of collecting information, getting opinions, adapting the groups' demands to the social priorities defined by the government, and finally laying down

[1] Letter from the chairmen of the committees of finance, law, national defence, cultural affairs, production and commerce to the President of the National Assembly, *Le Monde*, 14 July 1971.

programmes which satisfy the different economic and social protagonists.

The sovereign power of decision-making, which according to the classical theory of political representation is bestowed on parliament, finds it hard to co-exist, especially in its French form, with these modern procedures for formulating the major financial or economic decisions. Parliament, the embodiment of national sovereignty, cannot make more than rough choices. In the economic and financial field, however, choices are never presented *a priori*, but emerge by an elaborate process out of the multifarious opinions given by socio-professional groups and out of the conflicts between them. This lengthy work of preparation is beyond the capacity of parliamentary procedure and has to be left to other forms of representation of social groups.

In the same way parliament is restricted by its own unwieldy powers; parliament can work only by making choices, so that in the economic field it is reduced to ratifying choices which have been made by the representation of socio-professional groups following procedures which complement its own. Faced with laboriously reached agreements between government representatives and professional groups it can challenge these neither technically nor politically; it is reduced to giving official sanction to settlements reached elsewhere.

THE APPLICATION OF BUDGETARY PROCEDURE IN PARLIAMENT

We shall be able to assess the limits within which members of parliament are called upon to exercise their responsibilities by studying the rules of procedure, written or conventional, which are applied during the annual, formal examination of the budget. Discussion of the budget in the assemblies takes place according to a procedure governed by an organic law (the *ordonnance* of 2 January 1959) which is different from the ordinary legislative procedure. The *ordonnance* of 2 January 1959 lists the different restrictions laid on the powers of parliament, the object of which is to avoid a return to the deplorable practices of budgetary debates in the previous Republics. The consequence of this rationalisation of procedure is to take away from parliament the means of exercising the privileges it has inherited.

The Government's Dominant Role in the Application of Budgetary Procedure

We do not need to take up here the constitutional provisions and the organic *ordonnance* relating to the budgetary powers of parliament, which are dealt with as a whole in another contribution to this book.[1] It will be more interesting to direct attention to the practical application of these provisions. It will not be possible in this article to describe budgetary proceedings in their more mundane aspects. We shall confine ourselves to some examples which show that the counterpart of the restrictions placed on the powers of members of parliament has been an extension of the authority of the government which manages the debates in parliament.

The first practical example of a limitation in the assemblies' exercise of their powers is the regulation concerning the content of the budget. According to the organic *ordonnance* it is forbidden to include in it provisions which are not of a strictly financial nature. With this exception the government has a free hand in determining the contents of the budget and need not necessarily include in it every financial provision which is likely to be of interest to the State and consequently to parliament. In fact since 1963 the government has undertaken a policy of 'de-budgetisation', which has meant putting some expenditure outside the budgetary document (in particular public lending of an economic and social nature), and transferring the duty of financing these items to bodies which are autonomous in relation to the State, (for example, the Caisse des Dépots et Consignations, Crédit Foncier, Securité Sociale, etc). Since this practice has gone on for several years, it is difficult to assess the amount of expenditure which has been 'de-budgetised'. The highest estimates put it in the order of between 12 and 13 thousand million francs. This apparent tidying up of accounts has the obvious result of releasing expenditure altogether from the need for approval by parliament.

It is no longer possible for the assemblies to control this expenditure, either through the State budget (from which it has been withdrawn), or through the autonomous bodies themselves (where it now appears). In fact parliament is not called upon to pronounce on the accounts of these bodies which are the sole responsibility of the Ministry of Finance.

The accounts of the great public enterprises are moreover not submitted for examination by the assemblies. All parliament receives is information on the financial and economic performance of these enterprises; the *rapporteurs généraux* of the finance committees devote part of their reports to this subject each year. However the assemblies are never called upon to approve the budget of these undertakings. The official reason given for this is a simple

[1] See Chapter 6.

one: the undertakings have a legal personality which is separate from that of the State, which cannot therefore determine their financial activities. In fact government control of public enterprises takes the form of a technical and financial 'sponsorship' (*tutelle*) exercised beforehand; control is also exercised *a posteriori* by the intervention of a '*commission de verification des comptes*' which is responsible to the Cour des Comptes. In the Fourth Republic the accounts of public enterprises were examined by a specialised sub-committee from each chamber, selected from the members of the Finance Committee. This practice was abandoned in 1959, and the Finance Committee's members are left only with an opportunity to inquire into the management of these enterprises. Since the same date, the National Assembly and the Senate have been able to set up *ad hoc* committees to examine specially designated public enterprises, but this opportunity has been used only twice in twelve years. In fact there are a number of obstacles to parliamentary control of public enterprises: the number of the enterprises (about 600) and the complexity of their legal structure (proliferation of subsidiaries in France and abroad, creation of holdings), the inordinate taste for secrecy in the conduct of their management (for fear of competition from private enterprises), and the lack of interest of members of parliament in highly technical questions. In conclusion public enterprises are sheltered from parliamentary control; the government has never encouraged its development and has sometimes even resisted efforts made in this direction.

The illustration most often quoted of the limited budgetary powers of parliament is the exercise of the right of amendment. In this respect the powers bestowed on parliament are considerably restricted by Article 40 of the 1958 Constitution, by which members may not present proposals or amendments leading to the creation or increase of a public expenditure, or to a reduction of revenue. This article of the Constitution has been subject to a very strict interpretation, particularly concerning public expenditure, where many parliamentary initiatives have been ruled out of order and have not been discussed. It is in the National Assembly above all that the government has managed to get this article applied most rigorously.[1]

Amendments put down to the government's proposals have been treated most ruthlessly. First of all the government, supported by the Constitutional Council, has had ruled out of order amendments which, while increasing public expenditure, compensate this increase either by reducing another item of expenditure or by creat-

---

[1] The Senate has adopted a more liberal attitude to parliamentary amendments.

ing new revenue. Again, because of the harsh conditions governing admissibility which have been applied to them, amendments relating to public expenditure put down by deputies during the debate remain very limited in number. Furthermore it must be emphasised that even with amendments which have succeeded in passing the procedural barriers the government does not hesitate to put pressure on the majority to ensure that most of them are not adopted. In contrast the government sometimes puts down in its own name a small number of amendments increasing public expenditure which are generally adopted by the National Assembly.

Summing up the parliamentary debates of the year 1970 the finance committee's *rapporteur général* wrote that:

> As far as credits are concerned [that is to say expenditure], 25 amendments were discussed when the budget for 1970 was before the National Assembly. Twenty originated in parliament and proposed reducing the following allocations: ordinary civil expenditure, 1,623 million; capital civil expenditure, 43 million; capital defence expenditure, 1,665 million.
>
> After the Assembly and the Senate had voted, ordinary civil expenditure had increased by 17 million, capital civil expenditure fallen by 3 million, and the level of defence expenditure remained the same. Essentially therefore one can say that amendments originating in parliament have not been retained when they have involved a noticeable variation in the allocations proposed.[1]

The evidence of the budgetary debates in the years before 1970 justifies the same conclusion: parliament's power of amendment makes only a faint difference to the level of expenditure requested by the government. In 1965 public expenditure finally approved was no more than 33 million francs lower than that provided in the budget proposal (out of a total of 125 thousand million francs); it was on the other hand 135 million francs higher in 1966 (out of a total of 135 thousand million francs), 70 million francs higher in 1967 (out of a total of 148 thousand million francs), 142 million francs higher in 1968 (out of a total of 163 thousand million francs). Unless there are exceptional circumstances obliging the government itself to make a fundamental alteration in the proposal initially presented (as happened in 1969), alterations made by parliamentary amendments (which include amendments put down by the government) are less than or at most equal to 0·1 per cent of the total of

[1] 'Rivain Report' on the proposed *loi de finances* 1971 (National Assembly), pp. 90–1.

public expenditure. Thus the committee's *rapporteur général* could in 1970 express his disillusionment in the following conclusion:

Consequently the control over public expenditure exercised by the assemblies results in no real action [*aucune véritable mise en cause*]. The effects of discussion are only marginal. All too often badly managed departments view the control exercised by the nation's representatives by means of the budget vote without too much apprehension.[1]

On the other hand the deputies' and senators' powers of revision have more scope where public revenues are concerned. A liberal interpretation has been given to Article 40 of the Constitution and, according to this, although the overall level of revenue cannot be subject to any reduction, particular items of revenue can be altered. Consequently amendments can be made to financial provisions when, although they lead to a reduction in revenue, they also allow for compensation in the form of an increase or the creation of another public source of revenue.

However, in spite of this interpretation, parliament's power of revision is limited. First of all it is accepted that members of parliament cannot threaten the broad lines of fiscal provisions, but only alter points of detail. Faced with the government's power to initiate and conceive the draft law, they have to defend the taxpayers' interests by making improvements to that law. Secondly, however, the assemblies' power of amendment is exercised mainly by means of the Finance Committee and its *rapporteur général*.

Table 7.1 dealing with the discussion of fiscal provisions contained in the budget proposal for the year 1965 illustrates the limitations of parliament's power of revision. Several conclusions emerge:

1 While the number of amendments put down was high, only one-third were adopted;
2 Most of the amendments were proposed originally by members of parliament and it is these which comprised the highest percentage of failures;
3 A very large majority of the amendments put down or supported by the Finance Committee were adopted;
4 Finally, particularly in the National Assembly, the amendments put down and supported by the government included a high percentage of successes.

[1] ibid.

Table 7.1 *Amendments Tabled and Voted on During the Debates in the National Assembly and the Senate on the Fiscal Provisions of the Budget Proposals for 1965*

Originating from	Number	Supported by the Finance Committee	Accepted by the government	Withdrawn	Declared unconstitutional	Voted on Rejected	Voted on Passed
National Assembly							
Government	32	19	32	2		0	30
Finance Committee	21	21	1	6		9	6
Other committees	10	1	1	7	1	0	2
Members	69	13	8	18	5	34	12
Total	132	54	42	33	6	43	50
Senate							
Government	6	1	6	2		2	2
Finance Committee	17	17	0	4		2	11
Other committees	9	0	2	5		1	3
Members	72	8	4	10	9	36	17
Total	104	26	12	21	9	41	33

In conclusion parliament can make some alterations to the fiscal provisions submitted to it; this show of tolerance to parliamentary activity in the field of public revenue is doubtless a survival of the old prerogative traditionally granted to parliament to consent to taxation. However the government sees to it that this power of criticism never goes so far as to threaten the content of the proposals put forward.

Since the Third Republic the financial powers of the second chamber (the Senate) have been much less than those of the chamber elected by direct universal suffrage. This inequality is still marked in the Fourth and Fifth Republics. According to the 1968 Constitution the proposed budgetary law is first dealt with by the National Assembly and is then sent to the Senate.

In the case of disagreement between the two assemblies the Constitution gives the National Assembly the right to settle the difference under certain conditions, the incidence of which depends completely on the will of the government. In fact the rules laid down by the Constitution organising the relations between the two chambers have benefited the government, which can easily avoid the criticisms of the Senate by reducing the budgetary debate to a *tête-à-tête* with the National Assembly.

In practice the Senate's control over the budget has actually been a lot more thorough than that achieved by the National Assembly. In fact the government is not able to bring into play the factor of political responsibility as a means of pressure where the Senate is concerned; the ties of dependence which in the present system bind the majority of the National Assembly to the government do not exist at the level of the Senate. Moreover from 1962 a severe political conflict put the Senate in opposition to the President of the Republic and to the government.[1] Thus the Senate has not spared its criticisms where government actions are concerned. However this attitude of the Senate does not worry the government; the latter disposes of legal means which enable it to evade senatorial control.

The relations between the National Assembly and the Senate are organised in such a way that in practice the government determines the procedure and imposes its point of view. After a first reading before the National Assembly, it is the turn of the Senate to reject, or more often alter, the text adopted by the deputies. The government, whose role is fundamental, intervenes at this point in the procedure. The extraordinary procedure (*procédure d'urgence*) is invoked and a joint committee (*commission mixte paritaire*), composed of seven deputies and seven senators, is convoked by the

[1] This conflict came to an end in 1969.

government and is charged with finding a compromise between the two assemblies.

If this joint committee does not formulate a compromise, the government is authorised to ask the National Assembly to rule definitively on the disagreement between the two chambers.

However the discipline of the majority groups in the National Assembly enables the government to get the text of its choice adopted (and to evade the Senate's amendments).

If the joint committee finds a compromise solution, the government sends it to each assembly. But it has the sole right to propose amendments to the text adopted by the committee; amendments put down by parliamentarians are inadmissible.

If the two assemblies adopt the text amended by the government, the latter gets final satisfaction. If on the contrary the Senate rejects this modified text, the government asks the National Assembly to give a decision as a last resort and can count on the disciplined support of its parliamentary majority.

Finally, to break the Senate's resistance the government need only bring about the intervention of the National Assembly for a last reading and, under the pretext of terminating conflict with the second chamber, can oblige it to adopt the government's proposal. It must be stressed that, although supported by a solid majority, the government is often prevented in the National Assembly from using procedural means to ensure the discipline of the majority groups. The best known of these means is the '*vote bloqué*', by which the government requests the Assembly to give its decision by a single vote on the whole, or part, of the budgetary proposal modified by amendments put down or accepted by the government. To avoid rejecting a part, or the whole, of the text containing provisions which they support, members of parliament resign themselves to voting government amendments of which they disapprove. Thus the *vote bloqué* is a means of forcing the hands of deputies belonging to the majority. Its systematic employment over the last twelve years shows the government's will to impose its views on parliament.

The Application of Conventions (règles coutumières) *in the National Assembly*

Over the years there has been a crystallising of practices in the National Assembly which if examined provides a measure of the decline of parliament's powers. Unwritten rules, which are not derived from the Constitution, have been increasingly accepted as a

basis of the dialogue between government and deputies. Two fundamental rules are respected during each annual budgetary debate.

1 On the one hand the government is prepared to negotiate only
with groups from the parliamentary majority and does not take into
consideration demands coming from the Opposition.

2 On the other hand individual parliamentary initiatives can be
considered only if they are supported by the Finance Committee
and by the member's political group.

Only parties belonging to the majority are called upon to play a
role during budgetary debates in the National Assembly. During the
first reading the Finance Committee (composed of a majority of
deputies favourable to the government), to which the budgetary
proposal is referred before the opening of the debates, proposes a
certain number of amendments; it can also take into account certain
modifications presented by deputies individually. These demands,
which are usually of rather modest significance, can be displeasing
to the government. At this point the same 'scenario' is played out
each year. In order to break down opposition, the government calls
the deputies belonging to the groups of the majority to a plenary
meeting in the Salle Colbert (that is to say, away from the ordinary
venue for parliamentary sessions). The real negotiations on the
budget take place during this meeting to which neither the public
nor the Press are admitted. With dire warnings the Prime Minister
and the Minister of Economics and Finance ask members of
parliament to accept the government's proposal loyally (*avec
discipline*); however to appease certain anxieties (especially
electoral ones) of the deputies of the majority, the government
agrees to accept some compromise solutions on minor points. When
discussion is taken up again in public session, the compromise
reached is presented by the government and comfortably obtains the
support of the majority, because of the minor concessions which
have been granted. There are different stages of the budgetary
'marathon' at which this ceremony can be held; it always results in
the government's point of view prevailing.

In practice parliament does not employ the panoply of means
legally at its disposal. The explanation of this anomaly lies in the
individual deputy's attitude; he resigns himself to playing no role.
His initiatives are condemned to failure if they are not supported,
first by his political group, and then by the committees. Time and
again he must scale the procedural barriers, break down the resistance of his own group's leaders and win over the leading lights of
the Finance Committee. The greatest proportion of defeats in
division, voluntary withdrawals or application of Article 40 of the

Constitution affect amendments put down by these members. Out of exhaustion the latter resign themselves to doing nothing more. This is why the great mass of deputies are intensely disaffected towards budgetary debates. In fact the whole of the work of parliament is dominated by what one minister (M. Edgar Faure) calls a 'class' of parliamentary bureaucrats (*classe bureaucratique parlementaire*), in other words, by all those deputies who hold responsible positions at the level of groups and parliamentary committees. Composed as it is of deputies belonging to groups of the majority, this 'class' acts as a screen between the government and the mass of deputies; in the dialogue between government and parliament it is used as an intermediary. This dominant group within the National Assembly is aware of the minor place occupied by parliament as an institution in the present political system. Besides, it is very close to government circles, whose ideas on the normal functioning of institutions it is led to share. In the government/National Assembly relationship this bureaucratic 'class' is apprised of the limits within which the government wants to keep parliament's exercise of its prerogatives, and seeks to get these limits respected by the mass of deputies.

In effect its view is that, in a political system which was created as a reaction against the excessive parliamentarianism of the preceding regime, parliamentary privileges can be safeguarded only if they are exercised with discretion.

The essential obstacle, therefore, arises from the collusion which is practised by the government and a small number of deputies making up the hierarchy of groups and committees. A prolonged exercise of power by the same majority has in this way led to the creation of a caste system and a concentration of power in the interest of a limited number of people. Thus the conventional practices gradually established in the course of budgetary debates have a solid sociological and political basis.

In 1971 a group of influential parliamentarians could write: 'Everything happens as if certain technocratic influences intended to confine parliament within a simple function of registration [*enregistrement*], paring down its initiative, its time for reflection and, therefore, its possibilities of representing the national will.'[1]

This diagnosis, which was made on the basis of the legislative activity of parliament, applies *a fortiori* to budgetary activity. It reveals the extent of the malaise of French financial institutions. The state budget cannot simply be a set of coherent and logical measures; it is also a means of communication between the country

[1] Letter to the President of the National Assembly of 12 July 1971, op. cit. (note 5).

and political authority. If the intervention of the nation's representatives is still considered indispensable, it must go further than a mere global political agreement given at the end of debates, an agreement which is more an act of resignation than a statement of confidence. It must have the possibility of really influencing the content of each of the great budgetary decisions; it is on this condition that members of parliament win the confidence of their electors and make their actions credible.

In the absence of a real dialogue between government and national representatives, in the French context the budget is reduced to nothing more than a technical and bureaucratic document. An instrument of the internal work of departments, it has the authority which the latter are pleased to give to it. Experience shows that the departments tend to consider the budget as a 'scrap of paper', and that in the course of the year, under the cover of official – or quasi-official – procedures, budgetary provisions, especially where expenditure is concerned, can be substantially modified as a result of the relationship between forces within the state apparatus. There is a patent crisis in French budgetary institutions; no one can say what solutions will be offered to it in the future.

CHAPTER 8

THE INFLUENCE OF RCB ON PARLIAMENT'S ROLE IN BUDGETARY AFFAIRS

Jean-Claude Ducros

INTRODUCTION

So far only the senior officials who have introduced and begun to practise it have been able to define *rationalisation des choix budgét-aires*, or RCB, with any precision. Even these have refrained from preparing a 'little red book' of RCB.[1] RCB is still emerging as a subject, and will take another five to ten years to do so. For the time being, therefore, *rationalisation* leaves room for empiricism, and while definitions of RCB are not lacking, each one illuminates a different aspect of the new system.

Among the main definitions which have been offered, the Ministry of Economics and Finance sees RCB as a 'fundamental and long-term modernisation of methods and structures, with the objective of endowing the budgetary resources of the State with increased efficiency in the accomplishment of the State's redefined tasks.' The *chef de mission* of RCB has defined it as 'methodical research, applied to public affairs, which by using all available mathematical and analytical techniques, as well as those of fore-casting, organisation and management, seeks to ensure the efficient and accurate realisation of policy.' The director of the budget thinks that RCB is 'to do more and better with less money, since money is always in short supply'. The *rapporteur* of the Economic and Social Council defines RCB as 'analytical methods which allow objectives to be defined, their costs to be calculated and their execution to be monitored'.

The Minister of Economics and Finance has provided the simplest and the most political definition as 'the better employment of every penny of public money in order to ensure greater satis-

[1] J. J. Carre, 'L'analyse de système', *Bulletin de l'Economie et des Finances* (May/June 1969), p. 114. cf. also *Statistiques et Etudes Financières* (November 1969), p. 31.

faction of public needs and a higher standard of living for the French people.' Finally an author from outside the administration writes that 'RCB consists in making explicit the objectives proposed by the different public decision-making bodies, in defining the means of attaining these ends, and in choosing the most efficient among these means.'[1]

To summarise these definitions as simply as possible, RCB is a new system of research which makes the objectives pursued by public authorities more explicit, itemises and compares the means of achieving them, and measures the results, using all significant indicators.[2] It is a system which has made its appearance in several wealthy countries, such as the United States, France, Britain, Sweden and Canada, in recent years. It is also used in certain international organisations: the ILO practises it and the EEC is showing considerable interest. It is essentially the product of developed, liberal economies; in developing countries, public objectives[3] are often only too clear, while in socialist countries the annual budget is largely a faithful reflection of the longer term plan. The constant growth of public expenditure in wealthy developed countries in recent years has made RCB indispensable to them. To give France as an example; taking 1959 as the base year, the index of gross national product was up to 255 in 1969, but the index of government current expenditure was up to 307 with capital expenditure at 292 and transfer payments at 282. Budgetary choices have always existed for these countries; their rationalisation is now essential.

It is therefore interesting to try to assess the influence of RCB on the role of parliament in budgetary affairs in a liberal country, in this case France. This role is no longer a decisive one,[4] and it is difficult to see whether RCB is likely to favour its recovery or contribute to its decline. The new system was in fact originally conceived by and for the executive alone. In the United States, for example, 'PPBS came into being to strengthen the executive.

[1] For these definitions see, in order, *Bulletin Interministériel pour la RBC* (subsequently referred to as *RBC Bulletin*), no. spécial 1971, p. 32; Ph. Huet, 20 September 1971, no. 3815–16, *La Documentation Française*, p. 6; *RCB Bulletin* (March 1971), p. 35; *Avis et Rapports du Conseil Economique et Social*, 20 November 1970, p. 648; *RCB Bulletin*, no. spécial 1971, p. 12; L. Leretaille, 'Les choix budgetaires', *Dossiers Thémis*, PUF 1972, p. 53.

[2] J. C. Ducros, 'La RCB', *Revue de Science Financière* (July–September 1969), pp. 617–63.

[3] It is true that certain South American countries are imitating PPBS, but this is at US instigation. Similarly Morocco has asked France for information on RCB.

[4] See Chapter 7 by Professor Lalumière.

Thenceforth Congress was not going to encourage the system. It would have risked losing the power it still had.'[1] In France the *rapporteur* of the *commission des finances* of the National Assembly wrote recently that 'up to now parliament's place does not seem to have been provided for'.[2] Just as with the economic plans, there has been no provision in the original texts for the role of parliament.[3] This role will doubtless take shape from experience; which is the starting point of the present study.

Nevertheless, our experience of RCB is very short. It was introduced officially only at the beginning of 1968.[4] Moreover, although it has begun to be part of parliamentary language,[5] RCB has not yet made an impression on the law or on budgetary procedure. Parliament has certainly had to acquaint itself with RCB, ever since the financial law for 1969, when an unusually lively debate revealed much interest in the RCB allocations in chapters 37–93. Certain RCB exercises (in particular those on road safety and perinatal care) were included by new authorisations in the 1970, 1971 and 1972 budgets.

Yet even in the USA, where the new system was first applied in 1965 under the name 'Planning–Programming–Budgeting–System', only some 5 to 10 per cent of total allocations are debated in Congress in terms of objectives and alternative programmes. PPBS has been confined to improving the way new sums are allocated. It has done scarcely anything to alter expenditure on projects previously approved and up to now its impact has been marginal.[6] If RCB is adopted in the same limited fashion in France, only new budgetary measures (*mesures nouvelles*) will be affected and normal departmental activities (*services votés*) will be untouched.

The Minister of Economics and Finance has promised an RCB

[1] M. L. Morissens, '*L'Expérience Américaine du PPBS*', *Notes et Etudes Documentaires*, 20 September 1971, no. 3815–16, *La Documentation Française*, p. 43.

[2] 'Rapport sur le budget 1971', *RCB Bulletin* (March 1971), p. 41.

[3] The Decree of 8 January 1946, which established the *Commissari géneral* of the plan, makes no mention of parliament.

[4] By a decision of the Council of Ministers of 4 January 1968.

[5] In addressing the National Assembly on 17 November 1971 during the debate on the budget of the finance departments, the Minister of Economy and Finance mentioned 'adapting the tasks (*missions*) of economic administration' and the 'better utilisation of means [*moyens*]'. These are RCB terms.

[6] The report by Senator Proxmire, Washington 1969, is very pessimistic on this point. It suggests that the nature of the budgetary debate in the US Congress has hardly been affected by PPBS, although 'economic analysis should be designed in response to the needs of members'. Wildavsky, *RCB Bulletin* (September 1970), p. 51.

budget for 1974, which would be multi-annual (covering two years to begin with) and which would make it possible to tie the short term – the present 'resource budget' – to the medium term – the five-year plan.[1] However, this same promise has been made annually since 1971, and what seems most likely to happen is that the two budgets will continue to be presented alongside each other, the traditional budget being accompanied by the new one stated in terms of objectives and on a multi-annual basis. A key for relating them to each other could be provided for the use of parliamentarians, enabling them to move easily from one document to the other. It seems probable however that while the RCB presentation will be used to clarify problems, the traditional presentation is the one which will remain legally valid. For this and other reasons, a permanent juxtaposition of the scientific and the democratic approach to public finance would seem undesirable.

It will be clear from what has been said that an attempt to study the influence of RCB on the role of parliament in budgetary affairs is still largely premature. RCB has undoubtedly already had an effect on administrative structures. Task forces (*administrations de mission*) have been set up and ministries have been reorganised, notably the Ministry of National Education.[2] But the budgetary consequences of RCB have only begun to appear, while its political consequences still belong to the future.

These reservations having been made, it should be observed that RCB has made its appearance at a time when the decline of parliaments, especially in the budgetary sphere, appears to be a universal phenomenon. It is possible to put forward three hypotheses about the impact on parliament of the new system.

In the first place, it is possible to argue that the decline of parliament will be intensified and accelerated by RCB. Generally speaking any undertaking dubbed as rational seems bad for parliament. Thus the rationalisation of parliament seems since 1958 to have led to the diminution of parliament. 'In the nineteenth century politics took possession of science, but today is it not science which little by little takes over from politics?'[3] RCB can be seen as a 'tool of a militant technocracy'.[4] Under this heading it will dispossess the politician, the 'amateur', in the interest of the specialists and above all, the analysts, who will become technocrats. This pessimistic

[1] cf. *Le Monde*, 6 January 1972.

[2] The Decree of 19 March 1970 and the *Arrêté* of the same date set up offices concerned with objectives and resources (*moyens*) within this ministry.

[3] Nivollet, Introduction, *Notes et Etudes Documentaires*, op. cit., p. 1.

[4] cf. *Rapport du Conseil Economique et Social*, op. cit. The esoteric vocabulary used by RCB tends to contribute to this impression.

hypothesis is frequently put forward by parliamentarians. Thus the Senator M. Pellenc has predicted 'a new reduction in the powers of parliament'; 'Political power,' he writes, 'is itself compromised by this diabolical invention.'[1] Some observers go even further: after the reign of the technocrats, they see RCB leading unmistakably to that of the robots (computers).

A second hypothesis, quite opposed to the first, is that RCB[2] will lead to the restoration of the role of parliament. First, it has been introduced and practised in France only following PPBS in the United States. Account can be taken, therefore, of the experience of the latter, in particular the disappointments PPBS has involved in the parliamentary sphere. RCB will not in any case substitute economic rationality for political rationality. Moreover, if the new technique clarifies the government's choices, it cannot fail to clarify parliament's to the same degree. RCB might even strengthen the budgetary powers of parliament. They seem weak enough today, for, although at a stretch of the imagination it is possible to say that the budget proposal presented to parliament by the government can be accepted or rejected, the alternative is an artificial one, because the budget proposal is normally accepted. It is conceivable that RCB 'programmes' will be real alternatives and certainly they will be no more difficult to amend than the budget proposal based on resources. In fact up to now 'parliamentary procedure in budgetary matters has been a classic example of a bad decision-making process', in the United States as in France. RCB can only improve this process.[3]

Rather than accept either of these extreme hypotheses, it is possible to adopt a more moderate view.[4] RCB will undoubtedly initiate

[1] *Rapport de la Commission des Finances du Dénat sur le Budget pour 1971.* cf. *RCB Bulletin* (March 1971), p. 41.

[2] The clearest statements have come from those concerned with defence. 'The system of 3PB is not designed to dictate decisions, but to provide those responsible for them with information on the consequences following from these decisions.' (H. de L'Estoile and P. Quentin, *Bulletin Le 3PB aux Armées* (September 1970). The Minister of Defence has himself stated that RCB can 'in no situation make the decision itself'. (id., p. 8).

[3] Or so parliament believed in debating the RCB credits of chapters 37–93 for the first time. (cf. *J.O.Ass.Nat.*, 22 November 1969, p. 4313.) Some deputies admittedly saw in RCB a new manifestation of the perennial conflict between legislative and executive. But this was a question of the generation gap.

[4] But it could also turn out that RCB will only affect the drawing up of the budget, while its presentation, debate and vote remain unchanged. This however seems unlikely. RCB will no doubt initially be applied to minor problems but in the longer run it will probably become 'parliamentarised'. In that case it will cease to be concerned exclusively with budgetary choices, but will also become

an important change in the theoretical position of parliament, which oddly enough has altered very little for several decades. More precisely, it could be that parliament will regain powers of control[1] at the same time as it risks losing powers of decision.

THE REDUCTION OF PARLIAMENT'S POWERS OF DECISION

RCB is designed to replace a poor decision-making process with a better one, and this at a time when parliament's powers of decision-making have been looking distinctly sickly for nearly a generation. Its role is however a complex one; while it should improve parliament's choice of ends, it is undeniably likely to reduce its choice of means.

The Improvement in the Choice of Ends

RCB is concerned essentially with the choice of means, to which cost-benefit analysis can be applied. But it cannot choose ends, which remain the exclusive province of politicians. At present RCB is notoriously impracticable for choices cutting across sectors. For example it is not for RCB to determine the respective proportions of resources allocated to traffic safety and to public health, even though both cases are concerned with saving human lives. It would be very difficult for science to replace political decisions at this sort of level. As M. Breaud has observed:

> There is no question of supplying some 'objective' illumination of the great political options.... No technique will enable us to avoid the unescapable need to decide between competing or incompatible objectives. The contribution of RCB is a better presentation of well defined alternatives, and a more accurate and consistent translation of the options given into daily action.[2]

RCB does not imply the substitution of the analyst for the decision-maker, but simply better information for the latter on the conditions and consequences of his decisions. Employing as it does almost exclusively micro-economic concepts and techniques, it is hardly in a position to play a more important part.

involved with political choice. Its title may perhaps change eventually from RCB to RCP (*rationalisation des choix politiques*).

[1] 'Control' is used here in the French sense of supervision and inspection. (See below, p. 157).

[2] P. Breaud, 'Qu'est-ce que la RCB?', *RCB Bulletin* (September 1970), p. 16.

RCB studies should then be confined to clarifying choices within the same sector; choosing, for example, in the transport sector between road or rail, or in the energy sector between hydro-electric and thermal generation. The new technique should aim to present parliament with a complete set of alternative programmes. It would fall to parliamentarians to choose between these programmes, then between different precise objectives. Thus the technician would propose and the politician dispose. There also seems no reason why the latter should not exercise some powers of initiative.

A restoration of the parliamentary function should follow. Parliament would indeed have full powers to define strategy. It might do this by means of a debate on budgetary objectives; this has already been proposed by the President of the National Assembly, who would like to see members expressing their views before the budget proposal is drawn up.[1] This would however be at the price of abandoning tactics, and considerable reservations can be expected from parliament for this reason. From the strictly electoral point of view tactics seem more rewarding than strategy; besides it can be awkward to have to define objectives, which it may be in parliament's interest to leave vague. In fact it is possible that parliament sees itself more as a critic and a petitioner than as a decision-maker; deciding objectives does not imply any power to ask for the means to carry them out.

The Reduction in the Choice of Means
The determination of objectives is the first step, and as has been argued this will continue to be the province of the politician, either in parliament or government, who will propose and select among proposals. The analyst may on occasion be employed but only to make the objective 'sensed' by the politician more explicit. The second step however consists of the formulation of alternative programmes, or of the means necessary to achieve these objectives, and here the situation will have changed, giving pride of place to the analyst.

The politician will certainly be able to intervene, by suggesting a particular means overlooked by the analyst, but at the present time he does not have the knowledge, the staff or the equipment to review and select suitable means. In a third step, it is true, it will still be he who chooses the programme or programmes which seem to him the most appropriate for reaching the objective which he has set, but at this stage the politician's choice will be largely predetermined.

In short, one consequence of RCB will be at least to reduce the

[1] *Le Monde*, 22 December 1971.

choice of means made by parliament. As this choice becomes a matter for quantitative expertise it will be the business of specialists and will cease to be the subjective affair of generalists such as parliamentarians. Of course the scientific illusion of the nineteenth century will have to be avoided, and the new system could never be used to sanctify all the executive's decisions. But one result of RCB will undoubtedly be that the choice of means, now the source of animated parliamentary debate, will be conferred on the departments of the executive. It will not escape political criticism, but it will find scientific justification. Some parliamentarians do foresee this evolution, like M. Rivain, author of the report by the National Assembly's *commission des finances* on the financial law for 1969.

Parliamentarians will be dispossessed all the more in that RCB considerably widens the choice of means. The 'resource budget' takes into consideration only budgetary means, which are by definition the resources available to the State. The 'programme budget' will naturally take account of these means and they will even continue to receive privileged treatment, but means at the disposal of the private individuals, which the analysts call 'private resources', will also appear in the programmes. Thus, if the aim is to secure or to improve road safety, 'public resources' will be used to widen the roads, abolish level crossings, and so on. The work will be undertaken by the State and will be itemised in the State's budget. Cost-benefit analysis has however shown that the wearing of safety-belts can lead to a significant reduction in the seriousness of road accidents. So the State has decided, as a start, to make installation of safety-belts in new vehicles compulsory; it is a means of realising an objective, but a means used at the expense of the manufacturers and users of cars; it is a 'private resource'. All the same it will appear in the programme budget. The latter will not be simply the budget of the State and will be presented as the budget of the whole community, the nation's budget. Parliament will undergo a loss of power over the choice of means as this expansion takes place.

Two reservations should, however, be made here. The analysts' choice of means can sometimes lack scientific certainty. There is a problem in cost-benefit analysis with quantifying costs and benefits and this can be solved in different ways. Some benefits and costs are considered non-quantifiable. Thus in the USA the State Department, responsible for foreign affairs, is gratified to have achieved its implicit objective – avoiding a third world war; but the question is how to quantify the immeasurable benefit of such a policy. How are human life, health, time, leisure, the environment, historical monuments, etc, to be quantified? At this point the initiative is passed back to the politician. For similar reasons, the price indices drawn up by the Institut National de la Statistique et des Etudes Economiques (INSEE) have not always escaped critical examination by politicians, usually from the government side, and some of these critics have been successful; in the measurement of the immeasurable, politics reclaims its ground. Moreover some of the commentators on the American PPBS have found some of its analyses descriptive and shallow, and there seems no reason why things should be different in France.[1] The analysts have been described as 'myopic' in psychological and sociological matters.[2] This myopia could be mitigated to good effect by the vision of politicians, possibly foggy but sometimes prophetic.

Parliamentary debate is moreover far from being deprived of all influence. 'Debate being open to all talents ... it is often unexpected how an assembly can embrace more aspects of a problem than the most learned meeting of technical men', remarks Professor Vedel.[3] There can be no question that, in spite of its ignorance of the scientific facts, parliament often exhibits concrete and direct acquaintance with a problem. It enriches discussion by adding the view of the consumer, the subject (*administré*) and the citizen. Moreover analysis takes time, so that parliament should be able to retain the power to make decisions relating to urgent problems and the choice of means for solving them. It might also be possible to consider making parliamentarians into analysts by providing them with the necessary training, or alternatively of making analysts into parliamentarians, by submitting them to election. This is clearly a theoretical solution, but it would be interesting to know how far and in what way the nature of parliamentary debate might be altered.

A second reservation concerns the practicality of analysts in government service monopolising the choice of means, for such a thing would be legally impossible in the present state of the law. It is true that parliament's right of amendment is severely restricted, but it has not been completely abolished. In theory it could wreck the internal coherence of a programme. Indeed, while not going as far as that, parliament revived its right of amendment by modifying in April 1970, despite the analysts' opinion, the bill on driving under the influence of alcohol, which was presented on the basis of the RCB operation, 'road safety'. It is conceivable that the introduction of programmes (sets of means designed to achieve an

[1] M. L. Morissens, 'L'Experience Américaine du PPBS', *Notes et Etudes Documentaires*, op. cit., p. 39.
[2] Ph. d'Iribarne, *La Science et le Prince* (Paris, Denoël, 1970), p. 141.
[3] ibid., p. 180.

objective) will lead to a development of the system of *vote bloqué* (Article 44 of the 1958 Constitution). In other words parlament will be able to choose between programmes, or between objectives, but the programme will have to be chosen more or less without amendment, the means being given. In this situation it will be difficult, if not impossible, to compromise. Yet, although from a scientific point of view compromise is irrational, from a political point of view it often seems to be the only rational solution, and here there is a partial justification for parliament. In future, parliament will have to choose between alternative programmes for attaining an objective it will have set itself; it will have to choose between black and white, but will be unable to get everyone to agree on grey. But it is already more or less in this position.[1]

Thus parliament's choice of means will be lost only if the law, above all constitutional law, is altered.[2] This could be accompanied by an alteration in parliamentary control.

THE INCREASE IN PARLIAMENT'S POWERS OF CONTROL

The word 'control' is used here in its French sense. In other words, when we say that parliament controls a government department, we do not mean that it has a ruling power, but that it is in a position to carry out a check on administration. In this sense it seems that the resources and powers at the disposal of parliament are very important, and even superabundant. However, parliamentary control is exercised essentially over the administrative and financial implementation of the 'resource budget'; it is essentially a 'simple' control of regularity, not of efficiency. It is applied less to the actual activities of the administration than to their budgetary aspects. It tends to seem indirect, superficial and mistimed; hence the lack of interest in this field shown by members of parliament, who are often aware of this. It should be noted here that RCB will make it necessary to strengthen parliamentary control. RCB is potentially scientific power, which could be used for absolute power; parliamentary control consequently becomes more necessary than before, whether used in the formulation of the budget or simply in its execution.

CONTROLLING THE FORMULATION OF THE PROGRAMME BUDGET

Parliament has never controlled the budget's preparation, except

[1] 'In the end, parliament will be able to do no more than accept or reject *en bloc* the budgetary choices "rationally" proposed by the executive'. Leretaille, op. cit., p. 92.
[2] In particular Article 44 of the Constitution and Article 41 of the Ordinance of 2 January 1959, concerning the organic law relating to the finance law.

during the Third Republic,[1] and this task has almost always been seen as belonging naturally to the executive power. Moreover, the budget always makes its appearance in the form of a bill introduced by the government and never in that of a proposed financial law, which would need a parliamentary initiative. Certain writers (especially parliamentarians) hope for a change with the introduction of RCB. Parliamentary control should be extended to the formulation of the programme-budget introduced under the new system. By this means the executive could be deprived of the one means it possesses of presenting its programmes as perfect and sacrosanct. Since a great part of the decision is effectively made well before the decision is nominally taken, democratic procedures must also come into play in advance, or fail to operate.[2] So it is desirable to revive parliamentary control, although this will be difficult to do in the face of both political and technical obstacles.

Control depends on information, and while parliament is not completely deprived of this, its services – such as the library and the division for parliamentary and administrative information (created in 1963) – are inadequate.

There is nothing in France to compare with the 'supreme chamber of control' in Poland, which was established by parliament and is endowed with important resources for carrying out its task of controlling the administrative, economic and financial activity of all departments. This supreme chamber even has the right, in order to have access to wider information, to attend meetings of the council of ministers.

On this point the government has made a promise. 'I am pleased to give this undertaking,' said the executive's spokesman, 'that for all RCB work, not only will the *commission des finances* be informed, as *M. le Rapporteur* wished, but it will also be associated with the work in ways to be settled between Government and Assembly.'[3] This is an interesting promise, but a rather imprecise one. There are two possible solutions as to how parliament could be given control over the formulation of the programme-budget. In the first place the research services could be duplicated so that parliament had the same services at its disposal as the government. However there are few supporters of this solution. Besides its expense and the fact that it would doubtless encourage duplication of jobs, it

---

[1] Under the Third Republic parliamentary debate took place on the budget proposal as amended by the Finance Committee.

[2] D'Iribarne, op. cit., p. 314.

[3] Report of the Finance Committee of the National Assembly on the Budget for 1971, Ph. Rivain, *RCB Bulletin* (March 1971), p. 42.

could lead either to a frustrating rivalry between the two sets of services or to a mutually accepted inaction.

Both outcomes – a government monopoly of research services and the duplication of the same type of body – could be avoided by concentrating these services in an 'independent magistracy'. This could be entitled the '*magistrature du chiffre*' or more generally the '*magistrature de l'analyse économique*'. It would formulate a language common to both executive and legislature, and the solely scientific, and therefore objective, nature of its work would be guaranteed. A deputy, M. Chandernagor, has proposed calling such a body '*la magistrature de l'information économique*'.[1] INSEE, the Directorate of Forecasting, and the economic sections of departments other than that of Economics and Finance, could be regrouped under its aegis. While it is possible to envisage the creation of such a '*magistrature*', there would in addition to its costliness be a risk of creating among the services of the State a sort of rivalry to achieve the status of '*magistrature*', that is, fundamentally, to escape from submission to parliamentary authority. Perhaps it would be enough to give parliament the same right of access as the government to the technical bodies already listed.

There is also a political obstacle to parliamentary control of the formulation of the budget, in that it affects the principle of the separation of powers. This separation has been clear in budgetary matters for a very long time; the executive has had exclusive power in the preparation of the budget, even though parliament has retained the power to make the budget into law (in other words the power of budgetary decision). In some respects certainly this separation has been qualified, but it would possibly be as well to ensure that it was preserved in budgetary matters. Parliament could safely confine itself to controlling the execution of the budget.

CONTROLLING THE EXECUTION OF THE BUDGET

The first effect of RCB will probably be a decline in the classical form of control, which rests essentially on the traditional budgetary principles. RCB will threaten these principles and some of them may not survive.[2] It is not easy to predict what will become of the budget's unity and universality which probably will still be

---

[1] A. Chandernagor, *Un Parlement Pour Quoi Faire?* (Paris, Gallinard, 1967), p. 131. M. C. Gruson, in *Renaissance du Plan* (Paris, Seuil, 1971), advocates the setting up of a 'Supreme Economic Court' which would play a similar role.

[2] Such as the distinction between *services votés* and *mesures nouvelles*. Its disappearance would have no direct consequence for parliamentary control.

respected in all essentials. But the specificity of the budget as it is now conceived will undergo modification. Instead of being granted by chapters (*chapitres*), allocations (*crédits*) will be made by programmes. Above all there will have to be a complete revision of the principle of annuality, because a programme does not cover one year but several years. In the end annuality could be no more than the exception.

The question then arises: 'Will the generalisation of economic calculation, and the adoption of new procedures in formulating and adopting the budget, result in rendering obsolete parliamentary control of the budget, the heritage of a long democratic tradition?'[1]

Control of the classical type will have to be modified. Only experience will show what form the new control of the execution of the programme-budget will take:

> As an adjunct to control through respect for the classical budgetary and accounting rules, the department responsible for the programme will be controlled by means of a scrutiny of the extent to which objectives have been achieved and the cost of the means allocated to them. . . . Thus existing *a priori* controls will be usefully complemented.[2]

In Sweden the arrival of PPBS has given birth to controls over efficiency and productivity which compare products and services provided on the one hand with expenditure committed on the other, establishing an exact relationship between the two.[3] The form of control which is emerging in France is known as 'management control' (*contrôle de gestion*). Brought over from the private sector it is based on a complex system of accountability: general accountability and accountability by department and by activity. Thus 'management control' has as its 'logistic basis' accounting information supplemented by statistical information, and involves in particular decentralisation in favour of those responsible for achieving objectives.[4] The 'objective manager' (*chef d'objectif*) must be free to employ supplementary staff, to decide current expenditure and to have recourse to the methods which he considers adequate.

A priori control of the resources used will need, therefore, to give way gradually to *a posteriori* control of the results obtained. There will be a change of terminology; the 'spending ministry' will become

---

[1] Nivolet, Introduction, *Notes et Etudes Documentaires*, op. cit., p. 1.
[2] 'Les Programmes Finalisés', *RCB Bulletin* (December 1971), p. 14.
[3] *RCB Bulletin* (December 1970), p. 36.
[4] *RCB Bulletin* (September 1971), p. 7.

the 'production ministry' (*ministère realisateur*). More precisely control of administration will be physical and financial, more qualitative than quantitative and very selective; and it will be concomitant. (For example the control of administration which is provided for the PPT (posts and telecommunications) will take place at quarterly intervals.)[1] This control will be directed at administrative efficiency rather than at administrative regularity and will carry useful sanctions, abandoning the 'punishments' inflicted up to now on those responsible for budgetary irregularities. Furthermore parliament must be given the possibility to set up 'programme committees' (*commissions de programmes*), in other words very small committees, often consisting of only one member, and specialised according to programmes and not according to departments or groups of departments.

Finally the scope of parliamentary control is likely to be extended, in so far as 'hived-off' activities (*démembrements*) are included in programmes and thus 'reintegrated' in the state. 'Hiving-off' is common in economic policy, particularly in agricultural policy (for example, the Funds for the Organisation and Regularisation of Agricultural Markets (FORMA), the National Interprofessional Office for Cereals (ONIC), and so on). At present these public bodies are essentially free from parliamentary control, but they could be 'recovered' by the central administration in the context of executing one or more programmes. RCB is certainly not inimical to deconcentration, allowing departments the 'necessary latitude in decision-making for reaching the objectives set',[2] but it tends to be opposed to any excessive decentralisation of functions. If the 'resource budget' was the State's budget perhaps the 'programme budget' will be the nation's budget, for it will concern in the end all public agents and even some private ones, so that it is conceivable that parliament could find a new domain for the exercise of control.

CONCLUSION

The expression 'RCB' has sometimes been criticised. The Ministry of Economics and Finance would have preferred the expression 'ODP' (*Optimisation des dépenses publiques*). For its part the Ministry of National Defence uses the expression 3PB (*planification, programmation et préparation du budget*). This is a matter for specialists; RCB concerns 'the budgetary act', the symbol and

---

[1] *RCB Bulletin* (September 1971), p. 11.
[2] *RCB Bulletin* (September 1971), p. 8.

F

summit of the system of public decision-making',[1] so perhaps the term 'RCP' would be best, meaning *rationalisation des choix publics, politiques, notamment parlementaires*.

Whatever term is used for it, the new system represents the tomb of demagogy, unseen pressures and corruption. Choices will have to be clarified, articulated and published. Since they will be rational, they should be easy to justify. So political life should be 'moralised'.

Rationalisation should not be confined, however, to public choices. It should be extended to the choices of private individuals, of the citizen and the subject. Is it too idealistic or perfectionist to hope for a 'rationalisation' of the claims of the contributors and recipients of public funds, in other words, the voters?

In any event the effects of RCB will be felt in the long term. In the short and medium term it will be no more than a make-shift technique. It is still very far from dealing with all choices and in France, the USA and other countries practising it its main effect has been a general strengthening of the central financial administration.

We shall have to wait for another generation. If RCB does no more than maintain parliament's choice of revenues, in particular of taxation, while (as some parliamentarians fear) conjuring away parliament's choice of expenditure,[2] it will be considered a reactionary system, because it will have brought about a return to the past.

So it would be optimistic to say that its object was less to replace than to realise democracy.[3] As the former general commissioner of the plan, M. Pierre Massé, asks: 'Shall we have enough imagination and will-power to find and to establish a form of democracy which responds to the demands of the century?'[4]

---

[1] P. Huet, 'Présentation de la Rationalisations des Choix Budgétaires en France', *Notes et Etudes Documentaires*, op. cit., p. 5.

[2] cf. The reports by M. Pellenc on finance law proposals since 1969. (Reports by the Finance Committee of the Senate).

[3] cf. P. M. Gaudemet and M. Chemillier-Gendreau, 'Nouveau Guide des Exercices Practiques', *Finances Publiques* (Paris, Montchrestien, 1971), p. 121.

[4] P. Massé, *Le Plan ou l'Anti-Hasard*, p. 13.

CHAPTER 9

PARLIAMENT'S FINANCIAL POWERS: A COMPARISON BETWEEN FRANCE AND BRITAIN

Joel Molinier

At first sight, British and French budgetary procedures appear utterly different, just as much in their historical origins as in their present essentials.

British budgetary procedure is remarkable for its antiquity. It can be seen as the result of a gradual process of sedimentation from the Middle Ages up to the 1860s. This process, moreover, has consisted of the translation into the sphere of public finance of the evolution of the powers of parliament over policy in general. In fact it is striking how all the great political problems of Britain have been associated with financial questions, and how the majority of them have been resolved by dealing with their financial aspect. Furthermore the country's main phases of political and financial history have been marked by the same events. The revolution of 1688 confirms this rule by its demarcation of two great periods on both the financial and the political planes. The first period is that of parliament's struggle from the Middle Ages to the end of the seventeenth century to establish effective financial powers for itself; the second is that of the construction of the British budgetary system, which took place essentially in the eighteenth and nineteenth centuries.

By comparison with this gradual evolution over six centuries, French budgetary procedure is of relatively recent origin. It was only during the first half of the nineteenth century (under the Restoration and then under the July Monarchy) that genuine budgetary rights were developed in France, parallel to the inauguration of the parliamentary régime. French budgetary procedure was in fact not fixed in its present form until the Ordinance of 2 January 1959, at the time of the establishment of the Fifth Republic.

In this respect it is notable that while budgetary procedure in France has been the subject of a certain number of assimilating texts, in Britain by contrast there exists no text bearing general significance comparable to the Ordinance of 2 January 1959. All one can refer to is the Exchequer and Audit Departments Act, the law on public accountability and control of the execution of the budget voted in 1866 and modified in 1921, and a dozen or so Standing Orders of the House of Commons, the most important of which were adopted at the beginning of the eighteenth century.[1] (In addition there are a few provisions of more limited scope.[2]) The British budgetary system is therefore based essentially on secular traditions, written sources being rare and often providing only an imperfect expression of modern practice.

It follows that the very notion of 'budget' is very much more difficult to define in Britain than in France. It is significant that no British official document gives a definition of the budget, while in France three great texts have successively done so:

1 The decree of 31 May 1862 generally regulating public accountability in its Article 5: 'the budget is the act by which the annual receipts and expenditure of the State or other services subjected by law to the same rules are provided and authorised.'

2 The decree of 19 June 1956, regulating the method of presenting the budget, in its first article: 'the State budget provides and authorises in legislative form the expenses [*charges*] and the income [*resources*] of the State.'

3 The Ordinance of 2 January 1959 stating an organic law relating to the financial laws in its Article 16: 'the budget comprises the set of accounts describing for one civil year all the income and all the permanent expenses of the State.'

We have, then, to examine the significance accorded in Britain to the word 'budget' without the aid of similar texts.

Historically the British indicate by the term 'budget' only the proposals for receipts presented by the Chancellor of the Exchequer to Parliament. This limited conception, which is inherited from an age when parliament sought only to approve taxes and did not yet aspire to control State expenditure, still considered as belonging to the King's domain, remains apparent today. The most recent works

---

[1] Unlike the French National Assembly the House of Commons does not possess a single set of rules of procedure. A larger number of special resolutions, about 120 in all, have been added over the years and have gradually shaped the organisation and working of the House. Frequently very old, they have been drafted in antiquated language which contrasts with the modern political and economic context. They express only strongly established practices.

[2] Such as those contained in the Public Accounts and Charges Act 1891, the Parliament Act 1911, the Provisional Collection of Taxes Act 1968 and the National Loans Act 1968.

on public finance allude to it. Thus Professor Ursula K. Hicks in the latest edition of her book *Public Finance* writes: 'the budget properly so called consists in detail of those revenues of which the recovery is proposed during the year.'[1] However even in Britain the budget is sometimes understood in the wide sense of a 'statement of probable receipts and expenditure for the coming year with corresponding financial proposals, submitted annually by the Chancellor of the Exchequer for the approval of the House of Commons.'[2]

This 'statement' does not consist of a written document. The Chancellor of the Exchequer's speech given on Budget Day is accompanied by the publication of a document of about forty pages, but the Financial Statement and Budget Report, which records the whole of the expenses and the whole of the income of the State, is only an estimate distributed to parliamentarians for information. It does not provide the basis of the budget debate and does not in itself possess any legal value.

Thus the British budget has meaning only in the material and not in the formal sense of the term. All the same instead of a 'formal budget' there are a certain number of legislative acts in Britain which authorise the revenue and expenditure of the State. These laws can be compared with *lois de finances* (financial laws) in France, as these are defined by the aforementioned Ordinance of 2 January 1959 in its first article: 'financial laws fix the nature, the quantity and the allocation of the income and expenses of the State, taking account of an economic and financial equilibrium which they define.'

Several kinds of financial law are recognised in the budgetary law of the two countries, but these different categories are not identical on both sides of the Channel. One of them is peculiar to France: *lois de règlement* (regulatory laws), in voting which parliament has a means of exercising *a posteriori* control of the execution of the budget. No such procedure is known in Britain. On the other hand the British budgetary system, like the French budgetary system, includes supplementary financial laws voted in the current financial year. This leaves the annual financial laws themselves, and if we analyse this category we shall be able to perceive the relevant differences between the British and French conceptions of the budget.

The aforementioned Ordinance of 2 January 1959 provides in its Article 2 that 'the annual financial law provides and authorises for each civil year the whole of the income and expenses of the State'. Is this definition applicable to the British budget?

[1] Ursula K. Hicks, *Public Finance* (Welwyn Garden City, Nisbet, 1951), p. 42.
[2] Definition of the word 'budget' given in the *Oxford Dictionary*.

The answer to this is no, for three essential reasons which under-line the uniqueness of the British budget. The first of these is that in Britain there is not one annual financial law but several. There are different laws providing for and authorising the expenses and income of the State. A financial law is voted regarding revenue: this is the Finance Act; another is voted regarding expenditure: this is the Appropriation Act. Added to these two principal financial laws are the Consolidated Fund Acts: in effect the debate of the budget by Parliament takes place when the financial year has already begun, so that it is necessary to pass one or two laws enabling provisional funds to be raised to permit the public services to func-tion while the final passing of the budget is awaited.[1] So the French principle of the unity of the budget contrasts with a plurality of budgetary acts in Britain: authorisations of expenses and authoris-ations of receipts are debated separately and are never grouped in a single document.

Even when seen as a whole, the British financial laws, contrary to the annual financial laws in France, do not cover 'the sum of the income and expenses of the State'. A part of State expenditure is approved permanently by parliament and does not come up for discussion every year. This comprises essentially expenditure relat-ing to the national debt and to loans made by the State to national-ised industries and to local authorities. Consequently the estimates corresponding to this expenditure do not appear in the Appro-priation Act and the expenditure is made regularly without parlia-ment voting annually until, if a fixed term is provided, the laws authorising the expenditure come to the end of this term or other-wise are repealed. As for revenue, only income tax is subject to an annual vote; other revenues do not appear in the Finance Act unless new revenues are being created or existing taxes are being modified. In fact the principle is that no public revenue can be laid down or modified without the approval of Parliament, but the majority of taxes are authorised permanently, that is until the House of Commons decides otherwise. So budgetary authorisation of expen-diture and revenue is spread not only over three or four annual financial laws but also over various laws of previous years.

Hence the principle of the annuality of the budget is given less significance in Britain than in France, although it was English parliamentarians who established this principle at the end of the seventeenth century. In fact this principle can be applied only to a part of the estimates and part of revenue; more precisely, in 1972–3, 24 per cent of expenditure and 59 per cent of revenue was author-

[1] The Consolidated Fund Acts also serve as supplementary financial laws.

ised permanently, subject to later modification or repeal, and so escaped the rule of the annuality of the budget.[1] Moreover expenses and income of an annual nature are not provided and authorised as in France 'for each civil year'. Their framework is a special year beginning on 1 April and ending on 31 March. This has been the case since 1855; the adoption by the British of a financial year which is different from the civil year did not result from *a priori* principles but simply from slow historical evolution based upon the needs of the time.[2]

In contrast to French budgetary procedure, British budgetary procedure is not based on any rational conception and its essential characteristics are empiricism and pragmatism. Like other British institutions, it is not founded on the Cartesian principle of *tabula rasa*. In this sense British budgetary law faithfully reflects the British mentality: the idea of system is alien to it.

Having thus identified the various elements which enable one to understand how the British and French conceptions of the budget differ from one another, we can now analyse in the perspective of parliamentary control the two phases of all budgetary procedure, namely the determination of the budget and its execution.

THE ROLE OF PARLIAMENT IN THE DETERMINATION OF THE BUDGET

The phase of determining the budget includes not only the establishment of budget proposals by the government but also the discussion and voting of these proposals by various parliamentary organs. This first phase of the budgetary process ends with the promulgation of financial laws, in France by the President of the Republic, and in Britain by the Queen.

In the past vital political conflicts have centred on the determination of the budget. Thus in Britain parliament has contrived progressively to gain control of all national affairs, thanks to the ingenious and effective employment of financial techniques. In this respect certainly the best example is the link established early on by both Houses between, on the one hand, the right given them to approve taxes and, on the other, the opportunity open to them to present petitions. By making the sovereign's adoption of petitions presented by parliament a condition of the voting of new taxes, parliament participated more and more significantly in the preparation of the laws of the kingdom. It was therefore above all the

[1] *Financial Statement and Budget Report 1972-3* (London, HMSO).
[2] On the historical origins of the financial year in Britain, see Bridges, *The Treasury* (London, George Allen & Unwin, 1966), pp. 188-9.

need to obtain the House of Commons' consent to taxes which led the monarchy to develop representative government. The right to raise revenue implied at once the representation of tax-payers and the consent of their representatives; these two demands, representation and consent, after having formed the basis of the financial powers of the House of Commons, served as the basis of its powers over policy.

In general it seems that the evolution of the British parliament's powers over policy and also of its financial powers have been so closely involved that in practice it is possible to see them as two aspects of the same process. This evolution, after appearing as a growth in the powers of parliament, led into the major transformation undergone by the political system of Britain from the time of Gladstone. The emergence of two large mass, coherent and disciplined parties, with national support and alternating in power, led in effect to a transfer to the Cabinet of what was essential in the financial and other powers exercised previously by the House of Commons. Having stripped the monarchy of its financial prerogatives, parliament was in turn stripped of its financial competences by the Cabinet. Taking advantage of party discipline[1] the Prime Minister and the Treasury ministers (above all the Chancellor of the Exchequer) concentrated in their hands the power to approve the budget.

Today the House of Commons is hardly able to participate effectively in the determination of the budget. In the first place the primacy of the executive in the preparation of the budget proposal is total in Britain; it has never been weakened by the prior intervention of a specialised parliamentary committee like the Commission des Finances of the Chamber of Deputies in the French Third Republic, which before their actual presentation to parliament carried out a detailed examination of budgetary documents, with all the opportunities implied by this examination for modifying and even recasting more or less completely the government's texts. In this respect, as Professor Lalumière has described, French practice is nowadays very close to British practice, Article 42 of the 1958 Constitution providing that the debate of bills should take place on the text presented by the government and no longer on the text amended by committee.

Furthermore this domination by the executive extends beyond the

---

[1] See for example the disillusioned words of a British author: 'in the eighteenth century the executive could control the Commons by means of corruption. In the twentieth century the same result was achieved thanks to party discipline.' Paul Einzig, *The Control of the Purse* (London, Secker & Warburg, 1959), p. 210.

stage of the preparation of the budget proposal to the budgetary debates which take place each year in parliament. These debates are certainly not of the same nature in the two countries; in contrast to France there does not exist in Britain any homogeneous process for dealing with the budget. In effect the proposals for expenditure and for revenue are not sent to the House of Commons at the same time[1] and are the subject of separate consideration; after having been debated separately they are inserted in many different financial laws, as we have seen. But these are only formal differences; budgetary debates in both the British and the French parliaments have the same main feature, the preponderance of the government.

In the first place, following one of the internal rules of the House of Commons,[2] parliamentarians may neither propose new expenditure and revenue nor increase expenditure and revenue provided for. Legally they only have the possibility of rejecting the financial proposals submitted to them and of reducing the level of expenditure or the level of revenue which they have to vote. The restrictions on the right of financial initiative and amendment of British parliamentarians do not then coincide exactly with the French provisions on this subject, as these have resulted from the constitution of 1958 and from the Ordinance of 2 January 1959.[3] In the field of expenditure the powers of British and French parliamentarians are the same. Members have the opportunity to reduce public spending, and face the same restriction: they are forbidden to increase public spending. By contrast British parliamentarians have certain powers which French parliamentarians do not have in the field of revenue, and vice versa. British parliamentarians may reduce public revenue: thus they are free to propose reductions in taxation; but they may not increase revenue. Inversely French parliamentarians may increase public revenues but they may not reduce them. Finally British and French parliamentarians enjoy a power of last resort in

[1] Proposals for expenditure are sent to the House of Commons beginning in February, and proposals for revenue at the end of March or the beginning of April.

[2] Standing Order No. 89 adopted in 1713 and amended in 1852 and 1866 to achieve greater rigour. This procedure was confirmed only by a long-established practice.

[3] Article 40 of the 1958 Constitution: 'proposals and amendments formulated by members of parliament are not acceptable when their adoption would have the consequence either of reducing public revenues or of creating or increasing public expenditure.' Article 42 of the Ordinance of 2 January 1959 making an organic law relating to financial laws: 'no additional article and no amendment to a proposal for a financial law may be presented unless it intends to remove or effectively reduce an expenditure, create or increase a receipt or ensure the control of public expenditure.'

both fields, that of rejecting the proposals for expenditure and revenue submitted to them by the government. The British rules have the advantage of giving parliament the opportunity to pass fiscal reductions and in this way to play a positive role as protector of the tax-payers, a role which the French parliament can assume only in a negative manner, by refusing to pass increases in taxes. Rules like these are favourable to parliament, which has tradition-ally shown more interest in reducing taxes than in increasing them. On the other hand the French system protects the financial equilib-rium fixed by the government against any later attack by members of parliament in a very effective way.

All the same this theoretical analysis does not take complete account of the residual character of the powers of parliament both in France and in Britain during the phase of determining the budget. In France parliament is granted a total period of seventy days[1] to give its views on the proposed annual financial law, whereas in Britain members of the House of Commons have only twenty-nine days to examine the whole of the estimates. It is evident from the start that a complete and detailed discussion of State expenditure is impossible. Since the beginning of the twentieth century the government and the Commons have observed a tacit agreement permitting the Opposition to decide which chapters of the budget will be submitted to parliament for debate; the other chapters are adopted without debate or are voted together. In fact the chapters designated by the Opposition are used only as an excuse for holding some general plenary debates on general policy, at the end of which State expenditure is approved automatically and millions of pounds of estimates are voted without any modification, however minor. Indeed one author has claimed that 'as far as the control of the estimates is concerned the government of Britain is a constitutional dictatorship'.[2]

On the other hand, as might seem logical since the power to approve taxes is the basis of its power, the House of Commons retains some opportunity of amending the government's proposals where revenue is concerned, and so contributing to the formulation of fiscal policy. Indeed in this field members of parliament are not willing to accept much limitation on the length of their proceedings; the Cabinet does not have a procedure available to shorten the

[1] This delay consists of forty days for the National Assembly, twenty days for the Senate and ten days for eventually finding a negotiated solution between the two assemblies with the meeting when necessary of a joint committee charged with drawing up a compromise. (See Chapter 6.)

[2] Einzig, op. cit., p. 13.

debates like that of the twenty-nine days devoted to the examination of proposals for expenditure, and by tradition the Chancellor of the Exchequer must show flexibility and good will on certain points. So the Opposition is in a position to extract some concessions from the government, notably fiscal reductions, but on the condition that it does not threaten the budgetary policy of the Chancellor of the Exchequer.

Even if the House of Commons seems to have the power of amendment where revenue is concerned (while over expenditure it only takes note of decisions already made), its powers in this field should not be exaggerated. Budget debates in the Commons do certainly provide the opportunity for a confrontation between the Cabinet and the Opposition on current problems; they enable the Opposition to get the government to be clearer and more precise for the benefit of parliament as a whole and thereby for that of the whole country; but for all that they rarely have any effective result.

As for the House of Lords, its financial powers are almost non-existent, unlike those of the French Senate which do survive, however limited they may be. As a result of the Parliament Act of 1911 the Lords are given a period of one month to examine financial bills, which are sent to them after having been finally voted by the House of Commons. But it is of little importance whether in this period the Lords approve, reject or even do not discuss these texts; when a month passes the financial bills are sent to the sovereign to be promulgated.

The phase of determining the budget of the State is then entirely dominated by the government, even more in Britain than in France. However this is only the first phase of budgetary procedure; in the second phase, of the execution of the budget, the characteristics of procedure differ considerably in the two countries.

PARLIAMENTARY CONTROL OF THE EXECUTION OF THE BUDGET

Entrusting control of a parliamentary organ is only one of the ways of controlling the execution of the budget; this task can also be confided to a judicial organ or even to an administrative one. These different means of control co-exist in France where:

1 Judicial control is exercised by two tribunals: (a) the Cour des Comptes (Court of Accounts), which by means of decrees reports each year on the correctness of the accounts made by publicly accountable bodies, that is to say, by the officials charged with collecting revenues and making expenditures; (b) the Cour de Disci-

pline Budgétaire et Financière (Court of Budgetary and Financial Discipline), before which any official participating in the execution of the budget who has committed an irregularity subject to punishment may be brought.

2 Administrative control is given to three kinds of officials: (a) the controleurs financiers (financial controllers) placed in each ministry but belonging to the Minister of Economics and Finance, who exercise an a priori control on which the performance of acts of spending depends; (b) the comptables publics (public accountants) who are obliged to check the regularity of the expenditure which they themselves make; (c) the members of the inspection générale des finances (general financial inspectorate), a 'corps' directly attached to the Minister of Economics and Finance and charged especially with controlling public accounts. It is worth adding that the magistrates of the Cour des Comptes, alongside the traditional judicial control, use non-judicial techniques, like the preparation and publication of an annual report to the President of the Republic, to control the management of departments.

3 Finally parliamentary control rests with the National Assembly, the Senate and the finance committees of these two assemblies.

Thus control by parliament in France is only one element in an extremely diversified system of control, and there can be no doubt that it is the least important element. The most effective instruments for controlling the execution of the budget are the judicial controls and above all the various administrative controls. The essential reason for this is the lack of interest shown by French parliamentarians in the technical control of the execution of financial laws, not the inadequacy of the means of control at their disposal.[1] The situation is very different in Britain. For one thing there is no longer any judicial control over the execution of the budget in that country. The Court of the Exchequer, which from the Middle Ages exercised a judicial control over everyone handling public money, fell into disuse in the eighteenth century and was finally abolished in 1880. Moreover there is no specialised body of administrative control of the execution of the budget in Britain like the inspection générale des finances or the controleurs financiers in France. There is no equivalent in Britain to the French principle of distinguishing ordinary administrators (ordonnateurs) from accountants (comptables), the latter exercising control over the regularity of the orders for payment sent to them by the former and refusing payment in the case of irregularity. In Britain the accountants do not form a

[1] For detailed discussion of this point, see Chapter 6.

'corps', being simply cashiers under the authority of the ordinary administrators. In the absence of a specialised 'corps' within administrative control – the Exchequer and Audit Department being essentially an instrument of parliamentary control, as we shall see – the task of supervising the regularity of all public financial operations from inside the administration falls to the Treasury. The role of the Treasury in the execution of financial bills is extremely important. In the last resort only the Treasury, as ministry of economics and finance, can ensure that the budget is executed with respect for the law, that budgetary authorisations are respected and that the financial administration of the State is sound. The reason for the extensive powers and the influence of the Treasury is the confidence shown in it traditionally by parliament. Every history of the Treasury tends in fact to represent this institution not as one ministry among others, but to a certain extent as a sort of intermediary between government, administration and parliament and as combining both executive and legislative responsibilities.

In the absence of judicial control and of a body specialised in administrative control, and in view of the general nature of the supervision of State financial activities entrusted to the Treasury, the control of the execution of financial bills belongs principally to parliament. The British parliament was able to exercise real control only from the second half of the nineteenth century. It was in the 1860s that parliament created the means for this; in 1861 the House of Commons set up a select committee, the Public Accounts Committee, while in 1866 the Exchequer and Audit Departments Act was passed creating the office of Comptroller and Auditor General. In the words of Gladstone the 'circle of control' was closed.

In the twentieth century, however, the need arose for parliament to extend the scope of its control. Rather than increase the powers of the Public Accounts Committee, the House of Commons chose to set up a new select committee. Thus in 1912 an Estimates Committee met for the first time. This committee eventually gave way in 1970 to the present Expenditure Committee.[1] While discussion of the budget takes place traditionally in the House as a whole, control of the execution of the budget is characterised by the work of select committees which are better suited to carry out specialist inquiries and to study technical problems.

Of the two select committees the Committee of Public Accounts comes nearest to what one would expect from a parliamentary organ for controlling the execution of financial laws. As for the Expenditure Committee, its terms of reference go well beyond this

[1] On the Select Committee of Expenditure see Chapter 10.

to cover all aspects of government relating to public expenditure, including long-term forecasting. It would not perhaps be going too far to compare its activities to those of a committee of enquiry into the costs and output of public services.[1] The functions of the Public Accounts Committee coincide with those of the Comptroller and Auditor General. It is no accident that this fundamental office of British budgetary procedure appeared five years before the creation of the Public Accounts Committee. Indeed it was already evident at that time that the committee could not hope to exercise effective control on its own without permanent and qualified assistance. That is why the role of the Comptroller and Auditor General has been conceived from the beginning as that of a 'parliamentary officer', charged with assisting the House of Commons in controlling the execution of the budget by checking or 'auditing' the public accounts. For this task the Comptroller is placed at the head of a small department, the Exchequer and Audit Department, which comprises about five hundred auditors recruited in the same way as the members of the Civil Service. The Comptroller is himself a civil servant but he enjoys a statutory position as an independent and impartial arbiter. Appointed by the Crown – in practice by the Prime Minister – he can be dismissed only following an address of both Houses; he is not appointed for a fixed period and in principle remains in office until he has reached the age of retirement. Almost all the auditors are dispersed among the majority of government departments so that in each important department there are one or more representatives of the Comptroller and Auditor General. So the Exchequer and Audit Department is a headquarters, the source of multiple branches across the whole government machine and the destination of numerous observations collected by the auditors.[2]

This permanent financial control conducted throughout the year within the administration by the auditors of the Exchequer and Audit Department enables the Comptroller, when he comes to review the public accounts after the end of the financial year, to take advantage of a mass of information facilitating his inquiries and

[1] The French *Comité Central d'Enquêtes sur le Coût et le Rendement des Services Publics*, created in 1946, is not a parliamentary body; it does include members of the finance committees of both assemblies, but it also includes senior State officials belonging to the *grands corps*.

[2] The auditors exercise only a *posteriori* control. They cannot therefore block an irregular payment, and must limit themselves to bringing the irregularities or administrative shortcomings of which they are aware to the Comptroller's attention. In France on the other hand the judicial controllers and public accountants can block, at least temporarily, a spending operation which they consider irregular.

speeding them up. In fact at the end of each financial year all the public accounts are submitted to the Comptroller and Auditor General, who must check first of all that the accounts submitted to him are numerically exact and must then proceed to compare them with the budgetary allocations voted by parliament, in order to ensure that the quantity and the allocation of the estimates has been respected. He will look into any differences between the figures of estimates granted and the figures of expenditure actually realised; this is then a control of the budgetary regularity of the financial activities of the administration. In addition to this control, there is today an audit of a wider significance, intended to promote the rationality and profitability of the financial activities of the State and revealing faults in management. This control over the effectiveness of the financial activity of the State – or 'efficiency audit' – provides a useful finishing touch to the classical audit.

The outcome of these inquiries, the extent of which is determined at the Comptroller's own discretion, are the Comptroller's reports and his certification of the authenticity of the accounts submitted to him. These accounts and reports are eventually submitted to parliament and form the basis of the work of the Public Accounts Committee. This committee consists of fifteen members selected proportionally to the composition of the House and chaired traditionally by a member of the Opposition. Its sessions are normally engaged in hearing witnesses. In practice the committee is empowered to call on any person whom it considers likely to assist its deliberations to appear before it. As a general rule the committee chooses to cross-examine the senior civil servants in each government department who are responsible for financial operations: the accounting officers. Although it is not a judicial organ, the committee proceeds in a judicial manner: in a way the accounting officer is put in the position of a defendant. The quasi-judicial nature of its proceedings is emphasised by the possibility which is open to the committee to invoke the personal responsibility of an accounting officer. This senior civil servant is in fact responsible in his own right for the regularity of the financial operations of his department – just like the *comptable public* in France – and the committee can make him personally responsible for any irregular expenditure. It is possible to say, then, that although judicial control over the execution of the budget disappeared with the Court of the Exchequer in 1880, certain characteristics of this form of control survive in Britain in the powers of the Public Accounts Committee. All the same the personal responsibility of an accounting officer is rarely invoked in the proceedings of the committee. The committee prefers to function in a more informal, but nevertheless effective, way: making recommendations to the Treasury. These recommendations, made in the committee's annual report, do not have any legal force, but by custom the Treasury accepts the obligation to see that the other departments comply with them. In agreeing to act in this way, the Treasury pays in some sense for the predominance over other departments which parliament has given it. Once the committee has reported, it falls to the Treasury to communicate with the departments concerned and to use all its influence to ensure that the committee's recommendations are put into force and to see that any irregular practices are stopped and any faults in administration discontinued. The Treasury informs the committee within one year after the publication of its report of the instructions which it has given to departments and of the measures which the latter have taken to put parliament's recommendations into effect. The Public Accounts Committee's recommendations are really endowed with the force of decisions by this procedure, founded essentially on custom and depending on the coincidence of views between the committee and the Treasury. These decisions affect the financial conduct of departments in a fairly short term because there are only sixteen months between the end of the financial year and the publication of the committee's report. The committee's control may be *a posteriori*, but it is not simply 'posthumous'.

CONCLUSIONS

In the light of this study it is obvious that the budgetary procedures of Britain and France rest, in short, on traditional conceptions which are opposed to one another.

French parliamentary tradition favours active participation by deputies and senators in discussion of the budget. On the other hand, once the budget is passed, the same parliamentarians lose interest in its execution, as is shown in particular by the conditions in which the *lois de règlement* are approved.[1] Parliamentary control, in so far as it can be exercised, takes place essentially at the time when the budget is being voted.

In Britain, on the other hand, the members of the House of Commons cannot pretend to play a preponderant role in the budget

[1] The draft regulatory law (*projet de loi de règlement*), which sets down the final results of the execution of the budget, is placed before parliament less than a year after the end of the financial year in question, but it often waits several months, if not more, before the members of parliament bother to discuss it or vote on it. The debate takes place amidst almost general indifference and with a very low attendance.

discussion, on account of strict party discipline. Certainly their formal powers seem more limited than those of French parliamentarians, in spite of the restrictions imposed on the latter by the 1958 Constitution and the Ordinance of 2 January 1959. However, constrained as they are to adopt the government's policy, British parliamentarians are familiar with means of controlling its application and checking its results; the relative weakness of control at the earlier stage is in fact balanced by a strengthening in *a posteriori* control. So the initial freedom which the government enjoys in formulating the budget, a freedom which stems from the mutual trust between the parliamentary majority and the Cabinet, is compensated for by a particularly rigorous and demanding control of administrative activity by the House of Commons.[1]

This parliamentary control does however require certain conditions for its efficient functioning. The influence of the Public Accounts Committee, which is the essential organ of the House of Commons' control over the execution of the budget, depends wholly on two factors:

1 The invaluable assistance which is given to it by the Comptroller and Auditor General and his department, by means of the audit which they perform during the financial year and after it. Without the mass of information which the Comptroller provides for it, the committee's control would be a pure fiction.

2 The agreement and understanding with the Treasury, which has not been belied for more than a century. Without the close collaboration established between the Treasury and the committee the latter's recommendation would have no greater consequence than the observations contained in the public report of the French Cour des Comptes.[2]

Moreover the Committee's power to invoke directly the personal responsibility of senior civil servants, and so to act in some ways like a judicial body, should not be overlooked, for, even if it is rarely employed, it has a deterrent effect.

Finally it should be noted that both financial committees are

---

[1] (Editor's comment) Not all British members of parliament or officials and students of parliament would share M. Molinier's generous view of the effectiveness of the Commons in administrative matters! See pp. 213–214 below.

[2] In its annual report to the President of the Republic the Cour des Comptes condemns irregularities and administrative failings which it has uncovered, makes criticisms and observations to which government departments reply. This document is of interest for the information it contains, but it has few practical effects.

required to avoid as far as possible getting involved in controversies about policy; discussion of policy is really the domain of the whole House and not of select committees. Far from harming the financial committees this limitation may be considered one of the sources of their success. The fact that their members have abstained from controversy of a party political nature during their work has increased the authority enjoyed by the Public Accounts Committee and the Estimates Committee. Indeed parliamentary committees concerned with financial control are among the few organs in the British constitutional system in which the relations between majority and opposition are blurred, thus enabling a genuine confrontation to take place between the House of Commons, without distinction of parties, on the one hand, and the government, on the other.

The coincidence of these various circumstances makes parliamentary control the keystone of the British system for controlling the execution of the budget, while in France, as we have seen, parliamentary control emerges at this level only as a secondary element in a predominantly administrative and judicial system.

CHAPTER 10

PARLIAMENTARY CONTROL OF PUBLIC EXPENDITURE IN BRITAIN

Stuart Walkland

1 The historical association of the House of Commons with the processes of public expenditure has been analysed by numerous authorities, and needs no stressing in this essay.[1] From a situation in which the government's finances acted as the main lever of constitutional development in the struggle between the executive and parliament, there has emerged over the last century or so a close and mutually supportive relationship between the executive and the House of Commons, through which the procedures of the House in this field have faithfully mirrored, with some leads and lags, the state of the budgetary art in central government. As in other national systems, the development of budgetary control[2] in Britain falls into a number of fairly well-defined periods, each of which corresponds to developments in the general theory and practice of politics and public administration. Whilst perhaps not so definable as the later but similar progression in the USA, nor as explicitly analysed by British commentators (British political and administrative science has no counterpart to the systematic study of budgetary theory which has played such a role in public service reform in the USA), the various stages of development can be separated and the parliamentary contribution to each analysed, in a way which puts recent parliamentary changes in this field in perspective.

[1] For a fairly dramatised and simplified account, see P. Einzig, *The Control of the Purse* (London, Secker & Warburg, 1959).

[2] The term 'budget' and its derivatives have a variety of connotations, not least in British practice. Popularly used, 'budget' describes the annual tax proposals of the government, and is restricted to public revenues. Some authorities use the term 'budgetary system' to comprehend all elements of public finance, including revenue and expenditure—as for example Sir Herbert Brittain, *The British Budgetary System*. As used in this essay the term follows American practice, whereby budget is synonymous with expenditure—'a process for systematically relating the expenditure of funds to the accomplishment of planned objectives'. See F. J. Lyden and E. G. Miller (eds), *Planning, Programming, Budgeting: A Systems Approach to Management* (Chicago, 1968), p. 27.

The process of government budgeting has a number of aspects. It relates to at least three principal administrative processes – the operational control of expenditure in terms of legality and regularity, largely directed to the avoidance of misfeasance by officials; the control of expenditure in terms of its effective management; and the strategic planning of expenditure for the realisation of government aims. The processes are given in this order since in most governmental systems this is the order in which they have developed. The control of expenditure and the management of spending activities have normally been given priority over the planning function, although some elements of all three functions have usually been present at all times. Historically all systems have given priority to operational control of spending, which entails the establishment of procedures for the regular disbursement of funds on a basis of strict appropriation, and for the annual compilation and central review of financial estimates. The establishment of such procedures in Britain in the last half of the nineteenth century was associated with other developments in public administration: centralised Treasury control over costing and contracts, uniform accounting procedures, civil service reform and the techniques of expenditure audits. The process of reform was a comparatively slow one. The establishment of central Treasury control over departmental estimating, the creation of an effective State audit system, the development of institutionalised responsibility in departments for the regular handling of funds on a strict basis of legality, extended roughly in Britain from 1850 to 1900, and engaged the House of Commons in the details of the budgetary process to an extent which it has never since attained. A coherent system of appropriation and audit involved the House in a criticism of annual government estimates, and in the supervision of a post-expenditure audit which was a statutory function of the State after 1866. The main parliamentary agency through which the expenditure audit was supervised was the Public Accounts Committee of the House of Commons, founded in 1861. This historic partnership between successive Committees on Public Accounts and the Treasury in the last forty years of the nineteenth century, through which the accounting procedures and spending routines of departments were brought under orderly Treasury supervision, has been charted in detail by a number of authorities[1] and needs no repetition here. By 1914 this Gladstonian system had accreted a large body of case-law, composed of

[1] See Basil Chubb, *The Control of Public Expenditure* (Oxford, 1952), chs. III and IV. Also E. L. Normanton, *The Accountability and Audit of Governments* (Manchester, 1966), ch. V.

Treasury regulations and Public Accounts Committee rulings, which together formed a comprehensive if elementary system of budgetary control of public expenditure.[1] It is with attempts to extend this system, and to inject other considerations, that the process of budgetary reform in Britain has been concerned in the last half-century.

In no way does the essential control orientation of the budgetary process in Britain appear as clearly as in the form in which departmental expenditure is classified and assembled. With varying degrees of itemisation, the expenditure classifications established through the parliamentary estimates have been based on inputs, with detailed tabulations of the items needed to operate administrative units in departments: salaries and wages, personnel, office supplies and other inputs. On these line itemisations, which lend themselves to annual incremental budgeting, are built the technical routines both for the disbursement of funds and the annual compilation and Treasury review of estimates. The parliamentary estimates are strict cash budgets, with the simple administrative function of representing the cash sums required by departments in the course of a financial year, set out in forms which facilitate departmental administration and Treasury control. An output orientation has seldom been included, and the statements on the whole do not exhibit precise analyses of departmental functions and costs. The accounting basis adopted for the departmental accounts by the Exchequer and Audit Departments Act of 1866 successfully inhibits the annual estimates and appropriation accounts from displaying information in this form. The Act adopted simple cash accounting to enable an accurate audit to be made of expenditure, and the basis for any system of management accounting is not present in the usual appropriation statements. Since on a cash basis the full resource cost of operations cannot be given, the Treasury has felt free to refuse to compile the estimates generally in functional operational terms, and instead to follow consistently a detailed layout which suits routine administrative needs, with a subhead division broadly devised to correspond with administrative divisions in departments, which usually deal with generic categories of similar charges, or in terms of totals which facilitate Treasury control.[2] The system has successfully withstood the intermittent

[1] See A. J. V. Durrell, *The Principles and Practice of the System of Control over Parliamentary Grants* (London, 1917).

[2] See S. A. Walkland, 'The Form of the Parliamentary Estimates', *Yorkshire Bulletin of Economic and Social Research*, vol. 14, no. 2 (November 1962). Also E. A. Collins, 'The Functional Approach to Public Expenditure', *Public Administration* (Autumn 1966).

pressures for more functionally orientated estimates and appropriation accounts. It is unlikely that the current vogue for output budgeting and accountable management in departments will react on the traditional formal presentation of expenditure to parliament in input categories.

2 By 1918 the British budgetary system had lost its preoccupation with simple operational control, and had taken on a management orientation. Gradual changes had prepared the way for such a development by as early as the turn of the century. Many of the administrative abuses which had given rise to the object controls incorporated in the budgetary system had been curbed by Treasury regulations and PAC precepts, by a general development of the career civil service and by the installation of reliable accounting systems by departmental finance branches and accounting officers. The Treasury and the PAC were in this fashion relieved of some of the routine preoccupations of the previous thirty years. The marked increase in government expenditure of the first decade of the twentieth century also signalled radical changes in the role of the budget system. As long as government had been considered a necessary evil, and there was little recognition of the social value of public expenditure, the main function of budgeting had been to keep public spending in check. As the operations of government came to be regarded as beneficial, the task of budgeting to some extent became redefined as the organisation of financial and administrative resources for the effective attainment of results. This fresh orientation focused attention on problems of management. All these factors converged in Britain in the period 1900–18. Management science became a subject of study, and management became a partial pre-occupation of the Treasury and the larger departments after the First World War. A small investigating section concerned with O & M was set up in the Treasury in 1919, concerned largely with the improvement of departmental procedures. The importance of this work only slowly gained recognition. An O & M section was not established under this title in the Treasury until 1941, and by 1959 the staff of the section numbered only sixty. By that year fifteen of the major departments also had their own inhouse O & M sections, with the Treasury providing a general consultancy service. Management became largely the responsibility of the new Civil Service Department after 1968, and work has been expanded considerably in the post-Fulton period, largely in co-operation with outside management consultants.

It is not surprising that, given the slow development of managerial services in central government in Britain in the period under review, the management emphasis has so far not been built into the main budgetary process, apart from an experiment with comprehensive functional costing in the Army in the early 1920s, which briefly introduced an early approach to a PPB/management accounting system for the planning and management of Army expenditure.[1] Except for this, the classification of government expenditure in the estimates and accounts has retained the traditional input orientation, although the primary control function which this incorporates has receded in importance. There has been no British equivalent to the Hoover Commission's recommendations on performance budgeting of 1948, which refashioned the US budget by adopting classifications which stressed functions, activities and projects. In fact the reverse had been the case in Britain. The major review of government accounting undertaken in 1947 by the Crick Committee[2] endorsed the simple cash basis of the parliamentary estimates and accounts, and by implication approved the input or subjective basis of the expenditure classifications. In 1961 this opinion was confirmed by the Plowden Committee on the Control of Public Expenditure. The Plowden group recommended a simplification of the estimates and appropriation accounts which did not extend to their basic form, and approved the new input classification which the Treasury and Defence Department introduced in 1962. The deficiencies of such a classification for the effective management of expenditure have often been analysed.[3] The Estimates Committee of the House of Commons, which until 1970 was the main parliamentary agency for reviewing the effective management of government programmes, often commented on its difficulties in obtaining functional costings. The committee has been generally interested in 'outputs' rather than 'inputs', and its investigations have often cut across a number of parliamentary votes. Despite the *ad hoc* costing of programmes which is now a part of some departmental systems, and the work of the Management Accounting Unit of the Treasury, the committee has often been suspicious of the costing deficiencies in departments which its enquiries occasionally revealed.

It was through the work of its two financial select committees – the Public Accounts and Estimates Committees – that the House of Commons in the period since 1918 registered the need for effective management of government operations, and attempted some critical

---

[1] See S. A. Walkland and I. Hicks, 'Cost Accounting in British Government' *Public Administration* (spring 1960).

[2] *Report of the Committee on the Form of Government Accounts*, 1950, Cmnd. 7969.

[3] See, for example, Collins, op. cit.

scrutiny of management performance. This orientation was discernible in the work of the Public Accounts Committee from about 1900 onwards. A number of authorities[1] have described how this committee of the Commons abandoned regularity audits in favour of managerial considerations in its examination of government transactions, a development which was extended by the House of Commons' Select Committee on National Expenditure during the First World War. The main agency of the House in this area after 1918, however, was the Select Committee on Estimates, first established as an economy committee in 1912, with the task of reviewing the details of the parliamentary estimates presented annually to the House of Commons by the government. During the inter-war years the Estimates Committee gradually lost its connection with current expenditure and abandoned the practice of searching for specific economies in the annual estimates in favour of broader, more speculative enquiries into the effectiveness of the administrative organisation of particular government functions. It operated after 1945 predominantly through sub-committees, which greatly extended the area of government operations which it could cover in any one year, and in this broad *ad hoc* fashion the House of Commons gained that orientation towards post- (instead of pre-) expenditure control which distinguishes it from other parliamentary systems. Pre-expenditure control disappeared entirely from its annual procedures for approving government estimates. Estimates received little effective scrutiny by the House sitting as a Committee of Supply, and parliamentary appropriation procedures became entirely formalised, effective scrutiny of the operation of the budgetary process being confined to the unco-ordinated and somewhat sporadic post-expenditure investigations of the parliamentary select committees.

In the last two years of its existence the Estimates Committee had no opportunity for registering the emphasis on management and mangerial performance which was the *leit-motif* of the 1968 Fulton Committee Report on the Civil Service, and in particular the stress on accountable management which reflected a real interest on the part of the Fulton Committee in managerial skills and their proper organisation. The committee's recommendations made management the most single important element in administrative training. In addition it wanted to restructure departmental organisation to give more weight to managerial efficiency – 'a structure in which units and individual members have authority that is clearly defined and responsibilities for which they can be held accountable ... [and there are] recognised methods of assessing their success in achieving

[1] See Chubb, op. cit., and Normanton, op. cit.

specified objectives.'[1] Apart from the 'hiving-off' of particular activities in autonomous agencies to avoid the constraints of parliamentary accountability on administration, the main recommendation of the committee was for the establishment of clearer lines of authority within departments and a stress on managerial achievement by units or individual officials. This emphasis on accountable management, a recognised private sector concept, can be traced to the influence of the committee's management consultants. By accountable management was meant 'identifying or establishing accountable units within government departments – units where output can be measured against costs or other criteria and where individuals can be held personally responsible for their performance.'[2]

An important aspect of accountability in this sense is, again, the identification of the cost of an activity, which is not provided by the normal subhead structure of the departmental budget. Some activities are specifically costed for internal control purposes, but the practice is not widespread. Accountable management depends on a system of functional control, and it is not surprising that two of the early experiments in this area have both been in the field of defence. Since the Fulton Report a cautious note appears to have crept into official or semi-official pronouncements on accountable management,[3] which stresses its limitations rather than its potential. Apart from the appropriation structure, which injects its own rigidities into departmental administration, the centralisation of personnel and finance introduces its own constraints on the authority of line managers, of a type which has little counterpart in business and industry. Nevertheless the Civil Service Department now appears to be working on a process of 'job-enrichment' in the public service – the restructuring of activities to produce a sense of managerial responsibility at the lower levels of organisations, and attempts to find adequate measures of performance.

3 It was not until the early 1960s that a distinct and self-conscious planning orientation was built into the British budgetary system, as a result of the recommendations of the Plowden Committee on the Control of Public Expenditure. Before the 1960s the planning process and the budgetary process were largely synonymous. The main stages of co-ordination and direction of departmental spending were the annual estimates review by the Treasury

1 *Fulton Report*, vol. 1, para. 145.
2 ibid., para. 150.
3 And the writings of recent authorities – see R. G. S. Brown, *The Administrative Process in Britain*, pp. 227 et seq.

and the requirement of prior Treasury approval of new expenditure. Some elements of public spending escaped this system – capital programmes and defence spending, for example. But until comparatively recently the estimates provided the main mechanism for the forward control of expenditure. Demand management calculations, however, required some advance assessment of the demands of public spending on total national resources, the mechanism for which was an unofficial Treasury review of probable department requirements two years in advance of actual budgeting. Such forecasts were a guide to how the financial costs of existing policies were working out, to the total of expenditure in the years immediately ahead and the demands likely to be made on national resources. Such planning process was largely incremental. With a one or two years' perspective most options have been foreclosed by previous commitments. The recommendations of the Plowden Committee achieved a longer time-span, opening more options and providing the basis for micro-economic analysis to determine the courses of action to pursue.

The achievements of the Plowden reforms are well known, and need little elaboration here. Expenditure surveys up to five years ahead have now become a regular part of the government's annual planning procedures. Each year the Public Expenditure Survey Committee of the Treasury identifies departmental views on present policies and the financial and statistical assumptions on which they are based, and agrees the probable cost of continuing them. The exercise is underpinned by an annual medium-term assessment of prospective movements in the economy. A draft report is considered by the PESC, and both a report on the medium-term economic assessment and on the future probable course of public expenditure are submitted to ministers, who then take, in Cabinet committee, decisions on the aggregate of public expenditure and its broad allocation to major functional heads. Since 1961 the sophistication of the process has increased, and the operation has become more systematic. Analyses of expenditure are now made not only by function and economic category but also by spending authority; an analysis of gross domestic fixed capital formation by type of asset is obtained, and new construction is also analysed by region. In addition information is obtained about the manpower implications of the expenditure forecasts. On the other hand, the surveys do not provide a complete guidance system for the allocation of resources to particular programmes within departments. Although the expenditure survey should be the basis on which a department's planning is founded, it is largely the end-result of policies already laid down. Departmental estimates are prepared in the light of the wider decisions which have been taken each year on the overall public sector expenditure figures, but the effect of the reviews on departmental programmes and estimates are marginal only. Micro-economic techniques are still needed to articulate departmental programmes with the relevant categories of the expenditure surveys, and to break down departmental expenditure in a manner which makes it possible to get more relevant strategic expenditure commitments.

One such technique is output budgeting, to use a British term for a simplified version of PPBS. Output budgeting can be used as a planning instrument to help in the allocation of resources within the main functional blocks of the expenditure surveys, and to reconcile an estimates structure drawn up on one organisational basis with the functional classifications of the survey. PPBS is a late arrival on the British scene, and it cannot be said that so far there is whole-hearted commitment to its techniques. There has been no general directive concerning its use in departments as in the USA and Canada, and apart from a well-established scheme in the Ministry of Defence developments so far have been largely restricted to feasibility studies of its application in a number of the larger departments of State. The concepts common to all PPB systems are the setting of specific objectives: systematic analysis to clarify objectives and to assess alternative strategies; the formulation of plans year by year for each programme; the projection of costs of programmes a number of years into the future; the framing of budgetary proposals in terms of such programmes; and the monitoring of performance. The only British department in which such procedures are common is the Ministry of Defence. This Ministry decided in 1964 to adopt a system modelled on the PPB system used in the United States Department of Defense. In the British model defence expenditure is allocated to fourteen major functional programmes, which are broken down into 700 minor programme elements. Functional costing is an annual exercise; an attempt is made to forecast the cost of the defence programme year by year over a period of ten years, based on assumptions which are capable of qualifications. Where alternative assumptions can be made, the alternatives are costed, producing information for different policy options.[1] Programme costings provide data for inclusion in the annual PESC report. Elsewhere in the civil programmes of the United Kingdom government, PPBS systems have since 1966 been the subject of feasibility studies by the Management Accounting Unit of the Treasury in the Home Office and the Education and Science, Trans-

[1] See *1st Report of the Select Committee on Procedure*, 1968–69, pp. 59–60.

port and Health Departments.[1] As a result of these studies the Treasury has concluded that the main potential for the application of output budgeting is in allocating resources within each of the twenty or so functional blocks used in the public expenditure surveys. All the output budgeting systems which the Treasury have so far considered broadly related to one of the PESC categories. The model programme budgets have also been devised to cover at least the five-year period of the PESC surveys, and the defence budget has an even longer time horizon.

It is apparent, however, that the Treasury is not moving quickly in the development of output budgeting in British central government. It has put forward two factors to excuse a lack of urgency: the existence of the system of broad multiple-year expenditure planning which has no counterpart elsewhere, and the relatively homogeneous departmental structure of British central government, in which programmes are not fragmented amongst a multiplicity of agencies as in the federal government of the USA. On the other hand, the executive has seen some need to proceed to a more specified articulation of departmental programmes with the PESC survey by techniques which fall some way short of full programme budgeting. The White Paper on the Reorganisation of Central Government which was published in October 1970 specifically admitted that the annual public expenditure surveys do not call for explicit statements of the objectives of departmental expenditure in a way which enables a department's plans to be tested against general government expenditure strategy; nor does the system embody detailed analysis of existing programmes and of major policy options on them. The White Paper publicised the work of a team of businessmen based on the Civil Service Department in developing a system for regular reviews which would provide more information on departmental programmes, and which would involve 'a greater emphasis on the definition of objectives and the expressing of programmes so far as possible in output terms... [in which] the pressentation and examination of alternative programmes will be of great importance.'[2] Subsequently this work has been systemised as Programme Analysis and Review (PAR) under the direction of a

---

[1] See Peter Else, *Public Expenditure, Parliament and PPB* (London, 1970). Also the *Memorandum on Output Budgeting* submitted by the Treasury to the Select Committee on Procedure of 1968–9, and *Output Budgeting for the Department of Education and Science: Planning Paper No. 1* (HMSO, 1970). For the current state of output budgeting in the DES see the *Second Report from the Expenditure Committee*, 1970–1, Memorandum by the Department of Education and Science: *Programme Budgeting in the D.E.S.*, and Evidence, pp. 95 et seq.

[2] Cmnd 4506, paras 49–52.

former businessman, Mr Ronald East, who reports directly to the head of the Home Civil Service. It is hoped by the Civil Service Department that PAR will provide ministers with a wider perspective against which to make strategic judgements about the allocation of resources in the context of the PESC reviews.

4 This long introduction has been necessary to describe the developing environment of new processes of resources allocation and expenditure management to which the British parliament has had to adapt its procedures in the decade of the 1960s. The process of adaptation has not been straightforward. Procedural developments in the House of Commons have been a reaction to a complex of considerations, not all of them linked to public expenditure; some of them have been both premature and immature, and have raised questions concerning the operation of the parliamentary system in Britain which have been hotly argued. Nor can it yet be said that the full implications and potentialities of recent procedural advances have been fully grasped by all MPs. This is not the place to describe the complex movement for parliamentary reform of the last ten years, with its pressures for increasing professionalism and specialisation within the parliamentary context. Suffice it to say that at the outset of the 1960s the House of Commons was at the same informational and organisational disadvantage in the field of public expenditure as in other areas of government activity. With parliamentary estimates whose form is in any case deficient for parliamentary purposes becoming devices for putting funds at the disposal of the executive in respect of long-term programmes and projects to which government was committed, with a welter of information from sporadic White Papers and the reports of its financial select committees, the existing organisation of the House became increasingly deficient for the collation of information on government spending activities and as a centre of the application of pressure and influence. Traditional forms and procedures were losing significance, yet retaining sufficient force to prevent the adoption of necessary innovations. Regular information concerning the executive's multiple year programmes was not available to the Commons until 1969. The Plowden Committee itself had opposed publication of the expenditure reviews on the grounds that existing parliamentary machinery was not adequate to evaluate them effectively. Despite this, the government published its reviews on a number of occasions before 1969, but regular annual publication had to wait for the Procedure Committee enquiry into the control of public expenditure and administration of that year. Similarly the House of Commons has not been provided with the full programme budgets of the Ministry of Defence, the statement on the

defence estimates which is presented to the House annually containing a brief summary of the functional defence costings for the estimates year only.[1]

The need for the House of Commons to extend its specialist organisation in the field of expenditure planning and management was recognised to some extent by the Procedure Committee of the House in the Session 1964–5, which heard evidence on this subject from a variety of individuals and organisations. Its recommendations, whilst concentrating on the need for a functional committee organisation within the House of Commons, recognised, although not clear-sightedly, a need for a more systematic scrutiny by the Commons of management processes in the public service. The report, which urged an enlargement and strengthening of the Estimates Committee, was somewhat premature, being pre-Fulton, and was not accepted by the government. Partly as a result of the report, however, the Estimates Committee's sub-committees were allowed to specialise by function from 1965 onwards, and in addition the government announced in 1966 that it would experiment with specialist committees of the House of Commons with wide terms of reference, but without the firm orientation towards scrutiny of administration and expenditure which had been envisaged by the Procedure Committee. Subsequently seven specialist committees were set up in the 1966–70 parliament, although their connection with budgetary processes was minimal. This is not the place to rehearse the confused history of this experiment, which aroused partisan attitudes out of scale with its importance, and which saw one committee disbanded and a firm refusal by the government to extend the system in the 1966–70 parliament. Criticism focused on the lack of firm orientation of the committees, whilst the difficulty experienced in staffing the extended system resulted in a run-down of the experienced Estimates Committee, whose membership was reduced and whose sub-committees were forced to discontinue the overt specialisation which had contributed to its effectiveness in the period 1965–7.

In 1968 the Procedure Committee of the House of Commons returned to the problem of expenditure control, and announced a decision 'to make further enquiries into the methods of examination and control by the House of Commons of public expenditure and the choice of priorities in the planning of it.' In the following year it published its major Report on *The Scrutiny of Public Expenditure and Administration*.[1] Its motivations were complex. Primarily it was concerned to register for the House of Commons the impli-

[1] *First Report from the Select Committee on Procedure*, 1968–9, HC 410.

cations of the 1961 Plowden Committee and the 1968 Fulton Committee on methods of planning and managing public spending. But in addition the committee was anxious to rescue the specialist committee concept from the deliberate de-emphasis and downgrading which it was experiencing at the hands of the Labour government, by linking such activity to the traditional and legitimate concerns of the House of Commons with the budgetary process. In this it has largely succeeded, and the implementation of its main recommendations have not been accompanied by the controversy which was aroused by the earlier specialist committee experiments.

The Procedure Committee enquiry was exceptional in the range and quality of evidence which it heard. Memoranda were submitted by the Treasury on the PESC mechanisms, on the conduct of the medium-term economic assessment, and on techniques of output budgeting and accountable management. Professional economists put in papers on the macro-economic significance of public expenditure, and the Ministry of Defence described its PPB system in some detail. Evidence on micro-economic techniques of expenditure planning was taken from the Fulton Committee's management consultants, and the committee's specialist adviser conceptualised and ordered the evidence in a number of papers for the committee. The committee clerk visited the USA to report on the US Defense Department's PPB system. The chairmen of the financial select committees of the House of Commons, members of the Clerk's Department and the Comptroller and Auditor General gave evidence on the present state of expenditure accountability to parliament. In general the committee was fully informed by the government on the state of the innovations in planning and management which were in the process of development. The Treasury was particularly co-operative. In evidence to the committee, published as an official Green Paper, it announced its intentions to publish annually a White Paper on projected expenditure over five years, incorporating the details of the PESC exercise, and the committee in its report was able to advise on details of its presentation.

The Report itself is clear and unambiguous. In effect the committee located the House of Commons in a new environment by recommending a reordering of the stages of parliamentary financial control. The committee envisaged three new stages: first, the annual evaluation of the government's multiple-year expenditure budget by the House, through committee investigation followed by full-scale debate; second, 'examination of the means (including new methods of management) being adopted to implement strategy and to execute policies'; and third, 'retrospective scrutiny of the results achieved and the value for money obtained, on the basis of the annual accounts and related information'.

The procedure Committee's principal recommendation was for a new, permanent and specialised Expenditure Committee of the House of Commons, to supersede the existing Estimates Committee, with functions related to all three projected stages of parliamentary supervision. It was proposed that the new agency should work through eight functional sub-committees, each corresponding to a major expenditure category, with a ninth sub-committee to rationalise the conclusions of the investigating committees and to deal with the government and Opposition about opportunities for debate. In relation to the expenditure White Paper, the House was to have annual opportunity to debate this on two days, with prior analysis and evaluation by a sub-committee of the Expenditure Committee. In relation to the detailed planning and management of departmental programmes, the sub-committees were seen as the agents of a major incursion into existing patterns of expenditure control and administration in departments, exerting pressures for the reorganisation of departmental budgeting on an output basis and the adoption of best managerial practice. As Mr David Howell, who as a member of the Procedure Committee later had the opportunity as Parliamentary Secretary to the Civil Service Department to see his ideas develop, remarked, 'output budgeting is by its nature the enemy of organisational permanence and enduring bureaucratic empires' and it is evident that some members of the Procedure Committee saw considerable reorganisation of departmental administration as a result of the joint pressures of the Civil Service Department teams and the Expenditure Committee sub-committees. As for the third stage of retrospective scrutiny of managerial performance, the committee was more reticent on how this would be organised, the implication being that it would fall to the Commons' Public Accounts Committee on the usual basis of audit department investigation.

The Procedure Committee designed its report to be a factor in the reassessment of the committee structure of the House of Commons which the Labour government had promised for the end of the 1966–70 parliament. The new Conservative administration inherited this task, and in October 1970 produced a Green Paper[1] in which it made various recommendations for reform, which were subsequently debated and endorsed by the House. A compromise was reached between advocates of *ad hoc* specialist committees of the House and those who wanted the full implementation of the Pro-

[1] *Select Committees of the House of Commons*, Cmnd. 4507.

cedure Committee's report. Three specialist committees were retained, and a new Expenditure Committee was approved, but smaller and with fewer sub-committees than originally envisaged. As incorporated into the Standing Orders of the Commons early in 1971 the Expenditure Committee has forty-nine members as opposed to the proposed eighty, with the usual government majority and chairman. It has appointed six sub-committees of eight MPs, each with mixed Labour and Conservative chairmen. These are:

1 Public Expenditure (General)
2 Defence and External Affairs
3 Trade and Industry
4 Education and Arts
5 Employment and Social Services
6 Environment and the Home Office

As the committee themselves remarked in their First Special Report of February 1971, the titles are not intended to be restrictive, but are indicative of the general area of administration assigned to each sub-committee. The areas of responsibility are very wide, a fact which the committee regretted but found necessary given the reduction in its size from what had originally been recommended. The committee has also set up a steering sub-committee, which is likely to be transitory since, unlike the former Estimates Committee, the sub-committees themselves decide their strategy within their respective fields. Initially, as the report remarks, all the sub-committees need to acquaint themselves with the general practices of financial control and budgeting which are current in the various departments of State, and major reports are not likely to be issued for some time. The committee has the power which was first granted to select committees of the House in the 1960s to appoint specialist advisers, and a number of sub-committees have recently made such appointments.

The Public Expenditure (General) sub-committee has a different role from that of the other five. It is not confined to a precise sector of public administration, but will concern itself mainly 'with studying the central area of government financial control, at Treasury and Cabinet levels and within the Civil Service Department.' As a corollary of this assignment the sub-committee will 'take note of financial techniques employed outside government and outside the United Kingdom.'

It is difficult, and somewhat hazardous at this stage, to predict the future development and ultimate role of the new committee. So far

G

as the five 'policy' sub-committees are concerned, these are programme rather than department based, and the sphere of responsibility of each is so wide as to deny them the opportunity for intense
specialisation which some reformers wished to secure. Some considerable selection of subjects within their sphere is likely, with the
sub-committee singling out both on-going programmes which have
escaped attention or major policy options which are pressing for
decision. The government itself, through its recent adoption of
selective programme analysis and review, has recognised the im-
possibility of frequent reassessment of departmental programmes
across the board of government activity. PAR might ultimately
release considerable information for the sub-committees, with scope
for a joint appreciation by MPs and officials of expenditure alternatives in selected areas. In this process it is reasonable to expect the
policy sub-committees to become the forum in which interested
groups and lobbies conduct a dialogue with appropriate officials
and politicians, of a sort which was a feature of the operation of
specialist select committees in the 1966–70 parliament.

    That this is likely to be the pattern of sub-committee investi-
gation is supported by the only policy sub-committee report issued
at the time of writing: the Education and Arts sub-committee under
the chairmanship of Mr Neil Marten,[1] which devoted the 1970–1
session to a preliminary reconnaissance of its area before embarking
on a specific enquiry. This initial survey covered the educational
component of the public expenditure survey, and in particular the
local authority contribution; the broad relationships between local
authorities and the Department of Education and Science in the
financing of all levels of education; the present status of programme
budgeting in the DES; and the broad pattern of public expenditure
in a number of areas within the committee's ambit, including higher
education, grants to universities, educational research, etc. It took
evidence of a very general and exploratory type largely from the
Treasury and the DES, and also from the main spokesman groups
for local authorities, including the Association of Municipal
Corporations and the County Councils Association. The AMC and
the CCA had considerable criticism to make of the mode of presentation of the educational component of the public expenditure
survey, and obviously appreciated the opportunity the committee
afforded for the communication of their views. Although the committee made no recommendations, it is possible that some improvement of the expenditure survey could result from the sectoral
investigations of the policy sub-committees of the Expenditure

[1] *Second Report from the Expenditure Committee*, 1970–1, HC 545.

Committee, in addition to the work of the Expenditure (General) sub-committee, whose sphere of interest is the surveys. Perhaps the most interesting evidence was that taken on the status of programme budgeting in the DES, which frankly revealed the difficulties the department was experiencing in producing an operational programme budget which did something to offset the over-optimistic enthusiasm for PPB which was a feature of the Procedure Committee Report of 1968–9. As for the future, the sub-committee obviously sees the need to be selective in its investigations, and to take up issues with considerable financial implications on which decisions are pressing. It proposes an enquiry, in stages, into the financing and administration of further and higher education in Britain. Within the near future the government is faced with the need to make major decisions affecting medium-term and long-term developments in this sector. A major review of national policy is in progress, to which the committee expects to contribute authoritatively.

So far the only other major report of the expenditure committee has been produced by the Expenditure (General) sub-committee,[1] in accordance with the section of the committee's order of reference which directs it to 'consider any papers on public expenditure presented to the House'. In this rather hurried study the sub-committee has analysed the presentation by the government of the annual expenditure surveys on the basis of an examination of the White Papers for the last two years. The report is a highly technical critique of the format of the presentations, and was produced largely as the result of what was virtually a dialogue between the Treasury and the sub-committee's official adviser, Mr W. A. H. Godley, the Director of the Department of Applied Economics of the University of Cambridge. The recommendations covered the comparability of one year's presentation with another; the desirability of publishing for parliament both the economic assessments and figures for receipts relevant to the expenditure projections; the need for the surveys to provide for a comparison of estimates and out-turn; and other technicalities of presentation which affect the usefulness of the surveys for the House of Commons. This type of review is likely to be an intermittent interest of the General sub-committee, which otherwise will be presumably concerned with clarifying for the House of Commons the decisional basis of the surveys. The sub-committee itself is to some extent unsure about its substantive future functions; as it remarked, 'It is

[1] *Third Report from the Expenditure Committee*, 1970–1: Command Papers on Public Expenditure, Cmnd. 549.

no easy task to spell out a new form of parliamentary control which might logically develop side by side with the new form of government control over public expenditure. . . .' So far the Commons' debates on the last two years' White Papers, which were held without prior committee analysis, cannot be said to have been particularly epoch-making, although hailed as a constitutional breakthrough by some authorities. They were 'take-note' debates only, and the Opposition did not divide the House. Largely because of this, attendance was poor. On the other hand the General sub-committee cannot envisage fundamentally different proceedings, although its own analyses might improve the occasions considerably:

> We think that for the immediate future what the House should seek to debate, so far as the Command Papers are concerned, is the realities upon which the figures are based – that is the programmes themselves – for example, what they are estimated to cost, what their objectives are and whether alternative programmes would or would not represent a better allocation of available resources and money; and we are concerned to see that adequate information is provided for this purpose. . . . We hope that both members themselves and those outside the House who are interested in the size of particular programmes will do more than simply argue that more money or more resources should be devoted to their favourite proposals. They should also see the issue in terms of other benefits foregone (whether in the public or private sector).

If the work of the General sub-committee succeeds in educating MPs both in the constraints in the planning of the total of public expenditure and in the opportunity costs of specific programmes it will more than justify its existence.

The Expenditure Committee has begun work at a time when House of Commons opinion is more favourable to the extension of specialist select committee work than it was in the early 1960s, and when most MPs, even if not themselves members of these bodies, appreciate the contribution which specialist committees can make to the process of scrutiny of government policy and administration. With more direct responsibility over expenditure policy than the Estimates Committee which it supersedes, the committee's reports are likely to be of more direct and immediate concern to the House as a whole, and will engage the attention of members to a greater extent than the work of its traditional financial committees, to which the House often appeared to have surrendered rather than committed its interest in this sector.

The committee's success is likely to depend more on its relationship with the executive than with its parent body, and here a number of factors are relevant. The committee started off on a better footing than some of the specialist select committees of the previous parliament. A government which had an interest in reducing public expenditure and in the efficient planning and administration of the rest found little difficulty in accepting, in general, the idea of a Commons committee whose interests were likely to match its own. This does not preclude the possibility of localised friction, and with the committee dependent on the executive for much of its raw material of information, it will at times have to tread warily. But both the Treasury and the departments responded well to the new committee. The chairman of the General sub-committee, for example, regarded its work as a 'co-operative venture' with the Treasury in the improvement of expenditure planning, a description from which the Treasury did not dissent.

On the other hand, the amount of fresh information which will be available to the Expenditure Committee's policy sub-committees as a result of new methods of expenditure planning should not be exaggerated. The Procedure Committee of 1968–9, anxious to produce a new conceptualised model of parliamentary expenditure scrutiny, overstated the progress being made in output budgeting and programme review. British government is far from developing a system which would enable it to analyse and define in quantitative terms the objectives and outputs of its programmes. The rationality of the decision-making process in these terms is still highly deficient, and will remain so for some considerable time. But if initially the emphasis by the executive is on the analysis of particular policy issues rather than on an attempt to instal larger systems of programme budgeting, this is a process to which the work of the policy sub-committees of the Expenditure Committee might make a useful if limited contribution. Over a period, however, the reports of the committee are likely to resemble those of its predecessor rather than to represent a new approach to expenditure analysis and review. In this sense the recent Commons reforms are no instant formula; they are an attempt to define and make operational the major concepts on which parliamentary control of expenditure should rest for a generation.

CHAPTER 11

PARLIAMENTARY CONTROL OF TAXATION IN BRITAIN

David Millar

1 In common with many other aspects of freedom and justice in the United Kingdom, the concept of parliamentary control of taxation received one of its earliest expressions in Magna Carta. In 1215 the nobles obliged the King to agree to 'no taxation without the consent of parliament', and one of the cornerstones of the power of the purse exercised by the English (and later British) parliament was laid. The story of parliament's long struggle to assert its claim to this power and subsequently to wield it and buttress it against the hostile policies of successive monarchs forms a major part of the history of parliament in Great Britain. The watchwords in the centuries of struggle which culminated in the Civil War and parliamentary victory of the seventeenth century were 'No taxation without representation' and 'Redress before supply', that is to say, taxpayers shall be represented in parliament, and grievances should be remedied by the Crown before money was granted.

Historically, then, the House of Commons laid claim to change policy or to veto any financial proposal put to it by the Crown. From the earliest times it was recognised that the consent of the 'knights of the shires' and 'burgesses' (the country squires and the town merchants) was required before taxes could be levied, as they and their workpeople would bear much of the burden. The knights and burgesses, thus summoned to parliament, became the House of Commons; the King's Great Council developed into the House of Lords, but the power of the purse remained with the Commons. By the late fourteenth century, authorisation came to be given to taxation and expenditure by Bill instead of by resolution. The importance of this development was that it offered the Commons considerably greater opportunities for control over finance in the various stages of Bills – in the Committees of Supply and Ways and Means and in the House itself – than did the shorter proceedings on resolutions.

Financial proceedings in the Commons – whether on expenditure or taxation – thus at an early stage became legislative proceedings, and in essence so remain today. The legislative authorisation of expenditure and taxation can fairly be described as 'the fulcrum of the Commons' financial power'.[1] But the extent and exercise of that power vary as between expenditure and taxation and, according to the viewpoint taken, in their range and efficacy. The history of the Commons' attempt to control expenditure and their present exercise of their power of scrutiny is set out in the last chapter. It may be helpful, however, briefly to set out the cycle of scrutiny of expenditure, in order to point out the contrast with the Commons' scrutiny of taxation.

Three principal processes may be defined in the process of government budgeting: operational control of expenditure from the point of view of legality; control in terms of the administrative management; and control by means of long-term planning in the light of the government's economic objectives. Operational control is exercised principally through three Consolidated Fund Bills during each session. One of these Bills fulfils the added function of appropriation of supply to the classes and votes of the estimates and is known as the Appropriation Bill. But these Bills are rarely debated by the House, their stages normally being taken formally to permit general debate on topics of importance and, on certain occasions, of particular interest to backbenchers. The appropriation accounts are examined by the Public Accounts Committee, which reports to the House on irregularities. Detailed scrutiny of departmental estimates has largely been supplanted by general debates, some of topical interest; the subjects are chosen by the Opposition. To some extent, these debates afford an opportunity to discuss the government's economic objectives and possibly to influence them, but their primary purpose is to enable the Opposition to criticise the government's policies, or lack of them. The three financial select committees of the House play an important, but limited, role in scrutinising the efficiency of the government's administration and in examining the provision of expenditure made to fulfil its future objectives. Between them, however, they are able to enquire into only a very small proportion of the administration or of the forward expenditure projections.

Control of taxation[2] has traditionally been exercised by means of

---

[1] G. Reid, *The Politics of Financial Control* (1966), p. 53.

[2] 'Control of taxation' is used in this chapter as denoting the strict regulation of taxation, as opposed to oversight and general guidance, as implied by the French word *contrôler*.

the rules and practice of the House which provide that taxation is authorised by legislation or by resolutions of the House. This type of control corresponds to the operational control of expenditure referred to above. The reality of the legislative examination of proposals for taxation is, as will be discussed, much greater than the equivalent examination of expenditure. The financial committees of the House spend little time in examining the administration of the system of taxation. The debates on the budget[1] and the Finance Bill in theory afford opportunities for discussion of the economic policies of the government, but in practice, for various reasons, few members use these occasions for this purpose.

2 The financial procedure of the House is governed by general rules, which are based in turn upon practice and standing orders. Rule 1 states that a charge does not acquire full validity until authorised by legislation; it must originate in the House of Commons and, if it is a service paid for by moneys provided by parliament, must be appropriated to its purpose in the same session in which it was presented to the House.[2] The origin and development of this rule have already been considered above. Rule 2 is that 'a charge cannot be taken into consideration unless it is demanded by the Crown or recommended by the Crown'. This rule is described in Erskine May as 'a long established and strictly observed rule of procedure which expresses a principle of the highest constitutional importance'.[4] Financial initiative in the Commons is thus reserved for the Crown, and private members may only proceed with proposals which involve the imposition of taxes if they have a Crown recommendation. This rule originated in the fourteenth century, when the Commons were not slow to appreciate the obloquy which they would attract if members themselves made proposals to tax the people. Rules 3 and 4 are of considerably less importance than the first two rules, being concerned with domestic procedure of the House with the object of ensuring that special care is given to financial business.

The cycle of business under 'Ways and Means' (i.e. ways and means of levying taxation in order to provide 'Supply' money to cover expenditure) is linked to the tax financial year, from April to April.[4] The budget statement introducing the budget proposals is

[1] 'Budget' is used in this chapter as connoting the annual tax proposals of the government, being restricted to public revenues. It is used in the essay on public expenditure in a contrary sense (Chapter 10).

[2] Erskine May, *Parliamentary Practice*, 18th ed., p. 683.

[3] ibid., p. 687.

[4] A detailed description is given in the essay on parliamentary control of the budget in France and Great Britain (Chapter 9).

made between mid-March and mid-April, chiefly depending on the date of Easter and on the economic situation. Strict secrecy shrouds all the budget proposals, even those which do not involve changes in taxation. The statement includes a review by the Chancellor of the Exchequer of economic developments in the past twelve months and of the economic outlook for the next twelve months, both of which are supported by published figures. The budget statement forms no part of the formal financial procedures of the House and the reader will search the Journal of the House in vain for any mention of it. The ensuing four days of the budget debate are nevertheless the most important annual debate held in the House. It has been tentatively calculated that about one-third of the time in recent debates has been spent in discussion of taxation, the remainder of the time being spent on other factors in the economic situation.[1] Members may debate the tax changes proposed by the Chancellor, as well as existing taxes and suggestions for new taxes. Speeches may concern anything from constituency matters to the need for a new world monetary system, and the result is a disconnected and fragmented debate, to which it is difficult for ministers to give a balanced reply. At the end of the debate each taxing proposal, embodied in a Ways and Means resolution, is put individually to the House, at which stage the opposition may force a vote on each or any resolution. The Finance Bill, giving legislative embodiment to the budget proposals, is then formally introduced, and is debated about two weeks later on second reading.

The Finance Bill is usually the most important Bill of the session and progresses through the stages of second reading, committee, report and third reading. In 1968, 1969 and 1971 (the general election having curtailed proceedings in 1970), the Bill was committed in part to a standing committee.[2] This new development, first recommended in this form by the Select Committee on Procedure of session 1958–9,[3] but resisted for ten years on various grounds by the Treasury, has enabled the whole House to consider the crucial half-dozen clauses of the Bill containing the principal taxation proposals. Tax matters of less importance and administrative and technical aspects are considered in standing committee of thirty to forty members. This procedure was strongly opposed by

[1] *Second Special Report from the Procedure Committee*, session 1969–70, p. 116 (HC 302).
[2] Standing committees belie their name in that each is set up to consider the Bill committed to it, members being appointed who are concerned with that Bill. When the Bill is reported to the House, the Committee is *functus officio*.
[3] HC 92 – I, 1958–9, *Report*, para. 9.

the Conservative government in opposition, but, as it was proposed by the Conservative government in 1971, may be said to have won general acceptance in the House.

The second reading debate of the Bill permits 'a general review of national finance'[1] but tends to be orientated more towards taxation than the budget debate. Little time is spent in considering the expenditure proposals of the government to finance which the taxation is required. Proceedings in committee are governed by the rule, which applies Rule 2 on financial proceedings, that 'amendments must not exceed the scope, increase the amount or extend the incidence of any charge upon the people' defined by the Ways and Means resolutions already recommended by the Crown and agreed to by the House.[2] While few members probably wish to increase the burden of taxes falling upon their constituents, the effect of this rule is to limit severely the scope of amendments which private members can move in committee. Despite an annual resolution authorising charges incidental to a tax which arise from provisions designed to afford relief from tax, an amendment which, for example, proposed to alter the incidence of income tax as between landlord and tenant would be out of order, even if the total charge upon the people were not thereby increased. The Procedure Committee have recently recommended that amendments proposing this type of change should in future be allowed to be moved,[3] and the government are considering this recommendation.

Although it is difficult to gauge the effectiveness of committee proceedings on a Finance Bill in securing changes in that, or in a subsequent, Bill, in 1964, 1965 and 1968 major concessions and changes were introduced by the government at report stage of the Bill, following debates in committee.[4] The view has recently been expressed that 'Pressure groups, to their satisfaction, still find members of parliament capable of influencing taxation law during the parliamentary process.'[5] New points may be put forward on report stage but, as proceedings in the House of Lords other than second reading are formal, any which the government wish to adopt may have to await next year's Bill. Debate on third reading of the Bill is losing its importance year by year, but does provide an opportunity to members to comment on the effect of the Bill, includ-

[1] May, op. cit., p. 773.
[2] ibid., p. 774.
[3] *First Report from the Procedure Committee*, 1970–1, HC 276, para. 9.
[4] *Second Special Report from the Procedure Committee*, 1969–70, pp. 120, 130–1.
[5] Reid, op. cit., p. 11.

ing the amendments made. Although the committee stage of the Finance Bill has been divided into only three sessions, it may not be premature to hazard the suggestion that proceedings in standing committee have given somewhat more scope to the Opposition and to private members of all parties to press their proposals for amendment. The standing committee on the Finance Bill is not under such pressure of time as exists in proceedings on the floor of the House, a junior minister is often in sole charge, and in these circumstances persuasive arguments can be deployed more effectively in the more informal atmosphere of an upstairs committee room.

Apart from the Finance Bill, certain Bills whose main purpose is to levy taxation are introduced by the government. Recent examples have been the National Health Service Contributions Bill of 1960–1 and the Customs (Import Deposits) Bill 1968–9; one of these Bills is introduced approximately in every other session. In addition, certain Bills may contain taxation provisions incidental to their main purpose; two or three of such Bills are introduced each session. The former class of Bills offers opportunities to members to raise wide issues, for example when a new tax is proposed, its effect on the economy and alternative methods of raising the revenue could both be debated. On the latter class of Bills, debate is limited to the tax proposal involved in each Bill. The Treasury also has power, notably since the enactment in 1932 of the Import Duties Act, to make orders or regulations as delegated legislation making detailed changes in the rates and incidence of certain duties or taxes, for example the import duties on specified goods entering the country. These are not capable of amendment, debate on them is usually limited to one and a half hours, and the House can only approve or disapprove them. In 1961, further delegated powers were given to the Treasury in the Finance Act to vary excise duties and purchase tax by means of the 'regulator' powers. Thus far we have considered parliamentary scrutiny of the budget and the consequent (and other) taxing legislation in terms of the opportunities afforded to members to exercise political control over the financial policies of the government. We have seen that the government is vulnerable at every stage, from the voting on Ways and Means resolutions at the end of the Budget debate, through all the proceedings on the Finance Bill until third reading. This 'vulnerability' is, in the days of well-organised political parties and tight party discipline, often more theoretical than actual. But a government may find itself deserted by its supporters during an all-night sitting in committee on the Finance Bill, or they may deliberately engineer a defeat in

committee to warn the government of their anxiety about some of
its fiscal proposals.

The budget has importance as an instrument of the government's
control of the economy, particularly in the field of macro-economic
policy. But although members may discuss this aspect during the
budget debate, they have little information on which to base their
contributions and no opportunity, commensurate with the importance of this function of the budget, to record their opinions, for
example by putting down motions on which a vote could be forced.
Proceedings on the budget offer the House little or no opportunity to
exercise its function of overseeing the structure of the tax system
and its administration. This is primarily a select committee role,
and to some extent the Public Accounts Committee examines the
administration of the tax system, as *did* the Estimates Committee.
But the House has no body which can play the part of the Commission des Finances of the National Assembly, nor of the Appropriations and Finance Committees of the Bundestag, in their
detailed examinations of the contents of the budget and their administrative implications. This function was until the early years of the
century performed satisfactorily by the Committee of Supply, which
spent many hours on the floor of the House on such detailed work
in regard to the estimates for expenditure. Until 1939, the House did
however use its select committee system for considering proposals
for new taxes and the reform of existing taxes and the effect of
taxation in various sectors of the community. From 1900 to 1939,
seven select committees were set up, each on a government motion
which limited the committee to the consideration of a single tax but
gave it power to seek evidence from outside bodies and individuals
as well as from the Treasury and Inland Revenue Department. By
the means of these committee enquiries, the House was able to exercise some influence in the field of taxation, often before government policy had been formulated. No select committee had been set
up since 1939 to examine any aspect of taxation until in 1971 the
government published a Green Paper containing proposals for
reform of the corporation tax, and appointed a select committee to
consider the proposals and report to the House.

3 From this brief account of the history and present functioning
of the scrutiny of taxation by the House, it will be apparent that few
changes have been made in the last half-century. The first major
change was the abolition in 1966 of the Committees of Supply and
of Ways and Means, and with them went a good many complicated
procedures, described then by the deputy speaker as 'mumbo-
jumbo'. Two years later, part of the Finance Bill was committed to

a standing committee. But a member of the House in 1921 would still in 1971 find himself very much at home in the Budget and Finance Bill debates. In the world outside Westminster, however, events have forced fundamental changes in the conduct of economic policy, especially since the Second World War, and our 1921 member would be overwhelmed by the depth and scope of these changes. The extent of his *bouleversement* provides some measure of the failure of the House to adapt its financial procedures to the rapidly evolving economic situation. The principal changes which bear upon these procedures are the various new roles which fiscal policy and the system of taxation have been called upon to play, and the development and publication of forecasts of expenditure and forward economic assessments by the government as part of its management of the economy.

The purpose of taxation may be briefly summarised as primarily budgetary, and as related to economic, industrial and social policy. As Mr J. H. Robertson, specialist adviser to the Procedure Committee in 1968–9, has written: 'Decisions about public expenditure, taxation and government borrowing are interrelated; any difference between expenditure and revenue has to be met by borrowing in one form or another.'[1] Such decisions are among the principal instruments for short-term regulation of the economy and are important factors in directing its long-term development. Yet the financial debates in the House offer members few opportunities to examine government decisions on the relationships between spending, taxes and borrowing. Again, taxes and charges can be levied in various forms and by differing methods, and decisions on the 'mix' decided on by the government are a vital factor in economic management; but the House lacks both a suitable occasion to discuss these matters and the information necessary to form a basis for debate.

In the realm of economic policy, taxation is an important weapon in the hands of a government seeking to fulfil the major economic objectives of allocation of resources in the short and long term, the maintenance of internal and external stability, and the assurance of equitable distribution of resources. These objectives can of course be sought by means of regulation of expenditure as well as through the tax system in its widest sense. But we have already established the close interrelationship between expenditure, taxation and borrowing. In the industrial field, the impact of direct taxes upon industry, such as corporation tax, excise duties and selective employment tax, needs no emphasis. The system of taxation also impinges less

[1] *Second Special Report from the Procedure Committee*, 1969–70, HC 302, p. 22.

directly in many ways on industry and commerce, for example in the regulation of credit, the incidence of investment allowances, depreciation allowances, the regional employment premium and other tax incentives to industry. Income tax, capital gains tax, purchase tax and customs duties on imports also have important effects on the pattern of industry and commerce, both individually and conjointly, and their indirect effects have probably never yet been adequately assessed. These matters are of central importance to the management of the economy and the ability of the government to achieve a level of economic activity sufficient to enable it to realise its broader political, military, social and other objectives. Yet the House has no means of analysing these functions of the system of taxation, of informing itself adequately upon them and of considering them apart from other matters such as specific expenditure or taxation proposals or a situation of particular economic difficulty.

In the field of social policy taxation has during the twentieth century in Britain been used deliberately to redistribute wealth and income between certain sections of the community. This purpose of taxation is of fundamental political importance and has always aroused deep controversy in parliament and the country. Redistribution of wealth is achieved also by expenditure on services such as housing, health and education and by social security measures, but to an increasing extent these are becoming enmeshed in the tax structure in a general sense and in respect of particular arrangements, such as the 'clawback' from high income families of amounts equivalent to the family allowances granted to all families. This process has given rise to the proposal for a negative income tax, which has been raised in budget and Finance Bill debates in recent years.

The other major development which would astonish a member of the House who had occupied his seat even as recently as twenty years ago is the development and publication of the five-year forecasts of public expenditure and the formulation of the medium-term economic assessment. The relationship between these important advances and taxation was expressed in three often-quoted sentences by Sir Richard Clarke, then Second Permanent Secretary at the Treasury:

One may look at taxation as the means by which the government raise the money to pay for the public expenditure. Or one may look at taxation as the instrument by which the government restrain the growth of private consumption and private investment to the extent necessary to make room for the growth of public services on the one hand and exports on the other. But whatever one's approach, this is the strategic point to which the long-term review of public expenditure and resources is bound to lead.[1]

Sir Richard made a powerful case for complementing the forward projections of expenditure and resources by projections of the means of financing such expenditure. One might go further and argue the case for distinguishing in projections of revenue raising between the elements of the 'mix', such as taxation, borrowing, charges and contributions, and the case for making projections of alternative 'mixes'. Some of this work is already done in the Treasury, but is not now published. The first public expenditure White Paper did contain projections for three years ahead of receipts in respect of each of the major spending programmes, e.g. transport, housing, law and order.[2] But similar projections of receipts did not appear in the second expenditure White Paper on the ground that the projections were 'based on what are inevitably arbitrary and highly uncertain assumptions'.[3] In their Report on Command Papers on Public Expenditure, the Expenditure Committee comment on this change, note the opinion of outside witnesses that projections of receipts ought to be published and record their lack of conviction in the validity of the Treasury's arguments against the projection of receipts.[4] The committee preferred not to reach a conclusion, however, until an expenditure committee had reported on the relationship between economic management and public expenditure. It would seem that, in the absence of projections of receipts and of annual publication of a medium-term economic assessment, the House has little information as a basis for debating the merits of the public expenditure of which forecasts are published.

It is now possible to summarise the opportunities open to the House for debating the structure of the tax system and taxation in its widest sense, the information available to it for this purpose, and the extent to which procedures exist for detailed examination of and enquiry into these matters. Apart from the budget and Finance Bill debates, the House spends one or two days in December or January

---

1 *Management of the Public Sector of the National Economy*, Stamp Memorial Lecture, 1964.
2 *Public Expenditure 1968–69 to 1973–74*, Cmnd. 4234, 1969.
3 *Public Expenditure 1969–70 to 1974–75*, Cmnd. 4578, para. 19.
4 *Third Report*, session 1970–1, HC 549, paras. 31–42.

debating the annual public expenditure White Paper. It would seem to be difficult to devote an entire speech to taxation in this debate, but limited references to means of financing expenditure would appear to be in order. Otherwise, the House normally spends about two days per session in general economic debates, often in response to difficulties occurring in a particular aspect of the economic situation. As regards the information available, the government in February 1969 and May 1970 published medium-term economic assessments, but both contained fairly general information with little statistical support.[1] Little information on receipts is now published in the expenditure White Paper and it seems unlikely that the results of the programme analysis and review studies being conducted for the government will be published. On the other hand, the financial statement and budget report, published annually on Budget Day, does contain certain general statistics on expenditure and receipts.

The House has few procedures at present which enable it to make detailed enquiry into taxation matters. The Public Accounts and Expenditure Committees are empowered to enquire into the administration of the system of taxation, but this is only a small part of the taxation field.[2] The committee stage of the Finance Bill enables members to raise points put to them by constituents and outside bodies, but these are normally of a political or technical nature. The House has not between 1937 and 1971 had the benefit of a report from a select committee, appointed to examine a proposal for a new tax, or an existing tax, which would assist it in deciding on the desirability of any changes proposed. It has no means whatsoever of examining the structure of taxation and its complex relationship with economic, industrial and social policy.

4 The Procedure Committee in session 1969–70 embarked upon an enquiry into the procedures used by the House to consider the principles and structure of taxation. They received evidence from members of the House and outside bodies and individuals, much of which was devoted to criticising parliamentary procedures for scrutiny of taxation or the lack of them.[3] Professional bodies complained of a deterioration in the standard of fiscal legislation, largely due to the lack of time and opportunity for adequate study

[1] *The Task Ahead – Economic Assessment to 1972* (HMSO, 1969); *Economic Prospects to 1972 – a Revised Assessment* (HMSO, 1970).

[2] The nature and functions of the Expenditure Committee are fully set out in part iv of the essay on parliamentary control of public expenditure (chapter 10).

[3] *Second Special Report from the Procedure Committee*, 1969–70, HC 302; *First Report from the Procedure Committee*, 1970–1, HC 276.

of legislative proposals (principally the Finance Bill) by the public and by expert bodies and individuals. Lack of time for debate of fiscal legislation and for proper discussions in committee were also adduced as reasons for the low standard of financial legislation passed by the House, and its drafting was also criticised. The committee expressed anxiety about the shortcomings in the work of the House which they revealed, but pointed out that, until the tax year and the calendar year were made coincident, thus enabling consequent adjustment of the periods during which the House sat in each year, it would be difficult to find more time for consideration of the Finance Bill.[1] They did recommend, however, that parts of the Bill might be published earlier than at present, possibly in the form of a White Paper. The committee recorded that suggestions had been made that the Finance Bill should be examined as to its administrative implications by a select committee and that a select committee might, in addition to the normal committee stage, examine clauses which raised detailed or technical problems. These suggestions were judged by the committee to be impracticable by reason of lack of time during proceedings on the Bill.[2]

The principal proposals put by witnesses to the committee were for the appointment of a select committee either to scrutinise the economy or to enquire into more limited matters of taxation and administration. Whatever particular form of committee and scope of investigation was proposed by witnesses, almost all were united in their conviction of the need for a select committee (or subcommittee) to cover taxation matters in some form or other. Two financial journalists advocated the appointment of a select committee on economic affairs.[3] They argued that the conduct of public policy and the quality of politics altered in direct relation to the quality of public debate about it. The quality of debate in turn varied directly with the quality of information and understanding deployed by parliament. An economic affairs committee would 'make a major contribution both to the vitality of parliamentary democracy and to the conduct of economic affairs.' Its functions would be to consider a current economic assessment; the long-term economic, fiscal and financing implications of the government's annual public expenditure White Papers, including assessment of the accuracy of government forecasts of growth and resources and the desirability of the allocation of resources made by the government; and to investigate special topics of economic interest, such as

[1] HC 276, 1970–1, *Report*, paras 11, 12.
[2] HC 276, 1970–1, *Report*, para. 20.
[3] HC 302, 1969–70, pp. 40–56, 145–65.

poverty economics, international monetary reform, trade policy and multi-national companies. The committee's principal tasks would be to elicit and elucidate information, in order to inform members and the public of the issues at stake and to confront Whitehall with an effective interlocutor on economic matters. It would not in its reports be expected to judge or recommend policy as such, but would seek to clarify 'the issues with which policy has to deal'. The committee would have 'a sufficiently large membership to enable it to man up to six sub-committees' and would need, it was suggested, 'a substantial staff, including perhaps five professional economists, as well as the ability to retain consultants *ad hoc* when required.'

The case for an economic affairs committee, as envisaged by the witnesses, rested on four main points, which were briefly as follows:

1 The committee would be a necessary counterpart to the Expenditure Committee.
2 It would contribute to the better conduct of economic policy.
3 The standing of parliament demanded that it should equip itself to carry out 'its fundamental duty of scrutinising and questioning government policy in the vital area of economic affairs', rather than leave this duty to bodies such as the National Economic Development Council, which was a government body.
4 The committee would open up new areas of economic policy to public discussion, particularly before the government had formulated its policy in these fields, and serve as a focus for academic economic discussion.

Two academic witnesses proposed a different approach to the need to study the economy.[1] They emphasised the cardinal importance of the close relationship between expenditure and taxation, and the need to examine each in terms of the other. They believed that any select committee which studied taxation and expenditure should do so on the basis of three general objectives of social and economic policy, i.e. the allocation of resources and policy for investment; the maintenance of internal and external stability in the economy; *and the need for equitable distribution of access to the use of resources.* They proposed that the House should consider these matters by appointing a budget committee. This committee should concern itself 'primarily with examination of existing tax measures and the consideration of possible new measures, rather than with the short-term policy intentions of the Government.' It could operate either through three sub-committees, each being

1 ibid., pp. 93–111.

responsible for investigating one of the three broad areas of policy defined above, or through a sub-committee on expenditure and one on taxation. A further role suggested for the committee was to 'co-ordinate and disseminate information about pertinent research activities as a whole' and to undertake a considerable research pro-gramme of its own. The Procedure Committee rejected the proposal for an Economic Affairs Committee on the grounds that few mem-bers could devote sufficient time to the work of such a committee and that it would either lead to confrontations with the government or be limited to long-term, general issues. The committee found the suggestion for a budget committee to be too wide in scope and felt that the limited resources of the House for select committees as regards members' time and energies would be better spent in investigating work than in research.[1]

A variety of proposals was put to the committee urging the appointment of a select committee on taxation. These ranged from a committee with powers limited to enquiry into the operation of specific taxes in the existing structure and into anomalies and tech-nical difficulties, to a permanent select committee to report upon long-term aspects of taxation policy, including possible new taxes and changes in old ones.[2] A rather different approach was made by an independent witness who favoured the addition to the Expendi-ture Committee of a further sub-committee on economic and financial administration.[3] The sub-committee would scrutinise financial and economic administration, including the economic implications of different forms and levels of taxation; the adminis-trative arrangements for preparing new tax proposals for presen-tation to ministers and parliament; and the efficiency of tax administration.

Confronted with such a wealth of possibilities, the Procedure Committee first set out the main functions which it believed a tax-ation committee should fulfil. These would be to enquire into pro-posals for new taxes and for major alterations to the structure of existing taxes, to examine the existing system of taxation and to consider the economic implications of various forms of taxation.[4] There would also be scope for it to consider 'the general coherence of taxation policy in the light of the long-term budgetary plans of the government.' But the taxation committee should work on specific subjects, rather than conduct wide-ranging enquiries. The

1 HC 276, 1970–1, *Report*, paras 23, 26.
2 ibid., paras 27–8.
3 ibid., para. 29.
4 ibid., paras 30–3.

Procedure Committee foresaw that the committee, in the course of enquiry into the economic implications of taxation, might be led to examine wider economic issues, but believed that such a widening of the committee's field would nevertheless be of benefit to the House. There remained the question whether the taxation committee should be independent or should be appointed as a sub-committee of the Expenditure Committee. The problem perplexed the Procedure Committee, but they eventually recommended the latter course, partly to re-emphasise the importance they attached to the link between expenditure and taxation and partly to ensure the independence of the sub-committee from government interference with the course of its enquiries.

Grave objections were raised by the Treasury in 1969 and in 1970 to the proposals made to the Procedure Committee that the House should seek to improve its examination of taxation and financial matters. Although the Treasury evidence given in 1969 to the Procedure Committee was almost entirely negative, that in the succeeding year was less so in some respects. The principal objections made by the Treasury were that a select committee on taxation, if it decided upon subjects of enquiry, might well trespass on the area of political initiative properly reserved for the government.[1] Further, the taxation committee might, even if it avoided this pitfall, be drawn in the course of its work into consideration of politically controversial proposals of new taxes, or aspects of existing taxes. If these predictions proved correct, the Treasury argued, the officials summoned to give evidence to the committee would find themselves having to refuse answers to questions dealing with politically controversial matters or which covered matters on which officials gave confidential advice to ministers. The Treasury's fourth principal objection was that to service a permanent taxation committee would involve much additional work by ministers and officials, all already hard-pressed.

In the course of the budget debate, the chief secretary to the Treasury, while reiterating certain of these objections to the Procedure Committee's recommendations, nevertheless came some way to meeting a few of the recommendations.[2] He undertook to examine some of the minor proposals with a view to implementing them if practicable. Although he rejected the proposal for a permanent and independent taxation committee, he indicated the government's acceptance of the proposal for *ad hoc* select committees to investigate aspects of taxation referred to them by the government.

[1] HC 276, 1970–1, pp. 1–47.
[2] Parl. Deb. 815, col. 46–53 (5 April 1971).

A month later one such committee was appointed to consider the Green Paper on the reform of corporation tax; to some extent this marked a return to the use of select committees to examine aspects of the taxation system, a practice which had not been used since 1937. Despite their negative approach to the committee's report, the Treasury had earlier committed themselves to the view 'that it is of utmost importance that parliament should have a more effective role than at present in the control of fiscal and economic policy – as a matter of democratic principle, on the grounds that ministers and officials are not the sole repositories of fiscal and economic wisdom'; and in order to win public acceptance for unpalatable measures through parliamentary debate. They also recognised that the present system of taxation might now need review, and that procedures for undertaking this might be improved.[1]

5 Parliamentary control of taxation in Britain is less effective in practice than in theory. The House has the annual opportunity of voting against each resolution which embodies a major change in the budget, and of voting against the second and third readings of the Finance Bill. But these votes concern only the provisions of the budget for that year and do not afford the House an opportunity of voting on the government's conduct of financial, fiscal or taxation policies in general, except such of them as are covered by the budget. They act rather as a Damoclean sword which rarely threatens the government, but which is capable of inflicting dire injury upon them if wielded in earnest. On the other hand, the legislative activities of the House in considering proposals for taxation have continuing importance at a detailed level. Parliamentary control of taxation in Britain provides certain occasions for discussion of the government's economic objectives, arising largely from the fact that the budget has acquired considerable significance as a means of steering the economy. The budget debate and the second reading debate of the Finance Bill give those members who are lucky enough to catch the Speaker's eye a chance of viewing the budget as part of the macro-economic policies of the administration. But the utility of these outlets is strictly limited, and there are no procedures to match the advantages of a select committee reporting to the House, for example, on the economic effects of a tax, thus providing a base document for a debate on that and other taxes and their effects. In France and Germany, close scrutiny of the budget is made possible by the procedures followed in the Finance Committee of each parliament. No equivalent procedure exists in Britain, although enquiries may be conducted on rare occa-

[1] HC 27b, 1970–1, p. 2.

sions by the Public Accounts and Expenditure Committees into the efficiency of administration of the system of taxation or of individual taxes within it. Otherwise, the House has no opportunities within its financial procedures to carry out such enquiries.

There seems no doubt that the House should resist the suggestion that it should cease to act as a legislature in approving taxation. Members still derive influence in the country and over the government from their role as legislators in the financial and fiscal field, and to relinquish these assets would considerably weaken the House and their position in it. The House nevertheless lacks the ability to consider expenditure, taxation and borrowing as instruments of government policy on the basis of full information provided by the government and supplemented by analytical and fact-finding reports of the Expenditure Committee and of some type of permanent select committee (or sub-committee) on taxation and finance. Such a committee is essential also to inform the House of problems arising in the incidence and effect of specific taxes and, as its work developed, to examine proposals for alternative forms of taxation and also the broader economic effects of taxation. As the annual debate on the expenditure White Paper develops and the work of the Expenditure Committee progresses, it is likely that more members will become aware of the imbalance in the approach made by the House to the related fields of expenditure and taxation. Entry into the European Economic Community may, by bringing European parliamentary procedures more strongly into focus, sharpen the interest of members in their own procedures and in the differences between British and continental practice. Perhaps the most useful long-term factor working in the interest of parliament is the growing recognition by governments that the public will more readily accept distasteful measures if it is given adequate information about them and if they are fully examined and debated by its representatives in the national forum of parliament.

CHAPTER 12

THE HISTORICAL AND CONSTITUTIONAL FOUNDATIONS OF THE BUDGETARY SYSTEM IN ITALY

Valerio Onida

FUNDAMENTAL CHARACTERISTICS OF THE BUDGETARY SYSTEM

To understand the nature of the budgetary system in Italy it is necessary to bear in mind not only the principles which underly it, but also the effects of custom and practice. Here, more than in any other sphere of constitutional law, custom plays a major role and often gives rise to substantial contradictions between the apparent scope of the legal prescriptions and the actual functioning of the system. This is especially true with regard to the role of parliament in budgetary decisions and in public expenditure in general.

The current rules for public accounting arise, in large part, from the General Law on State Accounting (*Legge Generale sulla Contabilita della Stato*) and its connected Order, which date respectively from 1923 and 1924, and also from the sole legal text on the Court of Accounts (Corte dei Conti), dating from 1934. However, the core of this system reproduces the content of even older legislative provisions deriving from the first years of Italian unity. Even in recent years no major changes have been made to this system.

The organisational apparatus of public finance can be described briefly as follows. There are three ministries operating in the field of public finance in Italy today: the Ministry of Finance, the Treasury and the Ministry of the Budget. The oldest of these is the Ministry of Finance, which for long periods (until 1877 and again from 1923 to 1944, as well as for a few months in 1947) combined all the administrative functions relative to finance and to the budget. Nowadays, however, it only handles revenue and, in particular, the assessment and collection of taxes. In the Treasury, (established in 1877, suppressed in 1922, and reconstituted in 1944) are concentrated most of the functions relating to the budget and the control of State expenditure, as well as those relating to the national debt and treasury services. Of particular importance is the Ragioneria

Generale (General Accounts Office). This is an organ set up within the Treasury, but on which depend offices within individual ministries (*ragionerie centrali*) and in the peripheral administrations of the State (regional and provincial *ragionerie*).

The tasks of the Ragioneria are to estimate the budget and also to follow its day-to-day administration. It must check that every item of expenditure conforms to the rules and to the prescriptions of the budget itself, maintaining written accounts of all the financial operations of the State. In practice, the Ragioneria is the only organ which follows closely and participates actively in the whole process of funding State expenditure, including the initial drawing up of the laws authorising the expenditure (whose presentation, whatever the subject, is always made in 'harmony', i.e. with the agreement of the Treasury), the allocation of expenditure in the budget submitted to parliament, the actual commitment of funds by incurring debt, and finally the issuing of authority for expenditure. The law requires that the Ragioneria guarantees not only legal conformity but also *proficuità* (profitability or efficiency). In practice, however, its control is essentially that of ensuring legal conformity, since the control of *proficuità* has not always been precise or even practicable.

More recently, in 1947, the Ministry for the Budget was established. However, its powers have not substantially impinged upon those of the Treasury and the Ragioneria. Its limited tasks relate both to collaboration and co-ordination between the annual budget and the most important government bills involving expenditure, and more generally to the whole field of State financial activities. These tasks were extended in 1967 with the establishment of planning organs and with the first experiments in long-term economic planning. From then this ministry (which took the name of Ministerio del Bilancio e della Programmazione Economica) has been concerned with the problems and processes of planning (*programmazione*) and also with ensuring agreement between plans, budget and expenditure. Nevertheless, for various reasons, the planning machine in Italy has not yet achieved a high level of authority. There exists a certain dualism between the Ministry of the Budget and the Treasury. However the latter, and in particular the Ragioneria, is in practice the most influential body where expenditure decisions are concerned.

In spite of the substantial continuity of the rules of budgetary procedure, the functions of parliament have been repeatedly revised – in written form if not in practice. There are rigorous limitations on the executive's power to present the budget given the need for parliamentary debate, and control becomes successively more minute towards the conclusion of the budgetary process.

The budget, as prepared by the government under the all-important direction of the Treasury (and more precisely of the Ragioneria) and with the collaboration of the Ministry of the Budget, is submitted to parliament five months before the commencement of the period to which it refers. It is subdivided into an estimate of future income and into as many estimates of future expenditure as there are ministries, together with a general statement and the budgets of the semi-autonomous public bodies which are related to the State budget. The budget is ratified by an appropriate law, following, in each chamber, a process of fundamental examination analogous to that normally followed for other laws. A committee is charged with carrying out a preliminary analysis of the budget before it is referred to the plenary session.[1] For a normal Bill this preliminary examination is undertaken by a single committee (often with advice and opinions from other committees on certain preliminary or detailed aspects), but the preliminary examination of the budget is subdivided. Consideration of general aspects and the allocation of expenditure into different headings are within the competence of the budget committee (*commissione bilancio*); aspects relating to single heads of expenditure pass to the appropriate specialised committee whose report is attached to the general report finally presented to the plenary session.

Examination and approval by parliament turns not only on the articles of the budgetary law, but also on the headings of income and expenditure. The budget is highly specialised, meaning that the headings among which expenditure is allocated (in a way severely limiting the executive) are very numerous (around 3,000 today). According to the principle of the universality of the budget as sanctioned by the law of accountability, strictly speaking *all* the administrative expenses of the State should be included. However in spite of this the formation of extra-budgetary bodies of dubious constitutional legitimacy has been permitted.

[1] According to Article 72 of the Constitution any Bill is subjected to the examination of a committee (made up of representatives of the various political groupings present in the assembly according to their proportions therein). This committee discusses the Bill, submits amendments and finally submits it to the assembly which then proceeds to discuss it and to vote article by article (with possible new amendments) and on the Bill as a whole. The committee can also be required to discuss the basic law outright in place of the assembly reserving for the latter only the final vote. This latter procedure (which cannot be followed if there is opposition from a minority defined by the committee or the assembly or even the government) is, however, not applicable to certain categories of laws amongst which are those relating to the budget.

Parliament's approval is of limited significance for the income side since the figures under each heading do not restrict the power or the duty of the administration to assess and collect revenue. However parliament's approval is required before expenditure can be undertaken for any purpose during the financial year. The Italian budget is essentially 'limiting' in nature and not 'funding'; in technical language it is a *bilancio di competenza,* not a *bilancio di cassa.* Budgetary allocations represent, on the one hand, the revenues which it is envisaged will be *authorised* during the budgetary period, appearing in the accounts as credits to the State, and, on the other hand, the expenditure which it is envisaged will be *committed* during the budgetary period, appearing as debits to the State. The budget does not describe financial activity at the moment of cash flows, of the actual collection or allocation of the sums concerned. Regarding expenditure in particular, the budgetary regulations authorise and restrict the government with regard to sums which can be used, that is, debts which can be incurred under each heading throughout the period; it does not refer to payments actually made.

Transfers from one heading to another (virement) are not admissible without an appropriate law for variation of the budget, and expenditure going beyond the figures set down in the budget is possible only in explicitly determined circumstances, and in relation to fixed and obligatory expenses precisely defined by law.

There are two kinds of control over liabilities and payments, designed to preserve the limits set by budgetary allocations, and more generally to ensure conformity to the law. These are the 'internal' control carried out by the Ragioneria and, following this, the 'external' control of the Corte dei Conti.

Every act incurring liabilities or making a payment is examined by the competent office of the Ragioneria. The head of the latter, if he finds any irregularity, refuses to give his approval and refers the matter immediately to the minister responsible for the branch of administration in which the action takes place. If the minister still wants the action to go on, he must give a written order to the Ragioneria Generale. However, he cannot give this order – and therefore the action cannot proceed – if the expenditure involved exceeds what is appropriated by budgetary allocation or has been erroneously entered in the budget.

The Corte dei Conti is an organ with an ancient tradition in Italy, and it has both judicial functions (relating to the responsibility of State accountants, and to war pensions, which do not interest us here) and functions of administrative control. The Court exercises control in various ways over public bodies subsidised by the State, but in particular it examines all the most important governmental activities and all those which involve expenditure. It verifies their conformity to the law and to the provisions of the budget. When, on finding an irregularity, the Court refuses to give its approval, only the Council of Ministers can decide that the expenditure should still take place. The Court then reports on the matter fortnightly to parliament with its own opinions. If expenditure exceeds the allocations of the budgetary headings or is given erroneously in the budget, or in certain other special cases, the Court has the power to stop the activity concerned by means of the so-called 'absolute refusal of registration' which cannot be countermanded even by the Council of Ministers.

The role of the Court of Accounts is very controversial, but its historical function was to enable parliament to maintain financial control, and it tends to be seen as the instrument, the *longa manus*, which parliament uses to ensure that the government does not exceed the limits set by the law and the budget. In fact, the Court enjoys a relative independence from government control which is guaranteed by the Constitution. The *consiglieri* (counsellors) of the Court are nominated by the government (by promoting officials of the court itself or by recruiting outsiders (political appointments)), but they cannot be dismissed without the full agreement of the presidents of both chambers. Moreover, the Court, according to the Constitution, reports directly to the two chambers. For these reasons it is often maintained that even in the exercise of its controlling functions, the Court is an organisation of a judicial rather than administrative nature, or that it is a 'neutral' organ freed from government direction. So the control exercised by the Court differs from that of the Ragioneria. Although effected in the same way and with the same aims it is regarded as control external to the active administration.

Parliament even has a central role on paper in *a posteriori* control of expenditure. After the Court of Accounts has all of the accounts of expenditure and given written verification of their conformity with the estimates, the final account is submitted to the two houses of parliament which approve it by passing it as law.

In short, therefore, unless a budget is approved by parliament the government is unable to carry out activities involving expenditure. If parliament does not approve the budget before the beginning of the financial year, it must hurriedly approve a law giving provisional authorisation for expenditure to be incurred under any heading up to a sum equivalent to one-twelfth of the total, multiplied by the number of months to which the authorisation refers (the maximum is four months).

The Italian budgetary system would appear from the foregoing to be characterised by the greatest possible control by parliament over all expenditure by the executive.

Reality is very different. The vast range of formal powers gives no indication of the extent of parliamentary control in practice. On the other hand many difficulties and obstacles face the administration as a result of the intricate net of restraints which covers all public spending. Thus, a law is necessary to transfer sums from one heading in the budget to another, not to mention the fact that Treasury agreement is required to transfer sums from one subsection of a heading to another. This produces rigidity in the distribution of expenditure among the different items. It is almost completely impossible to exceed the limits of budgetary allocations, to evade the fetters of the 'twelfths' authorising provisional expenditure, or to escape the multiplicity of controls exercised by the Ragioneria Generale and the Court of Accounts. If parliament's powers of control are of very little significance, there is on the other hand little corresponding liberty of manoeuvre for the executive, or at least for the individual departments handling expenditure.

Getting parliament's approval for the budget proposal is not an obstacle to the government and notable variations in that proposal are not usually made. However, the drafting stage of the budget is becoming less significant as public expenditure becomes more rigid, so reducing the margins of choice available even to the government. The main cause is that substantial amounts of expenditure in various sectors are increasingly predetermined by earlier legislation. Not only the objects and total amount of the expenditure can be settled in this way, but also its distribution over different years. This phenomenon will be discussed more fully below. At this point it is sufficient to underline the decisive role of this factor in reducing the budget's significance as a financial and a political document – not only for parliament but also for the government.

The budgetary system is dominated by the concept of strict parliamentary control. It is designed to place tight restrictions on government expenditure and to ensure that these are respected. In reality, however, parliamentary control is emptied of all significance. The root of this apparent contradiction is most likely to be found in the fact that the type of parliamentary control for which the system is designed, and which it tends to create, is quite different from the type of control which the assemblies really want. The necessary estimatory intervention of the law, the extremely specific allocations of expenditure, the prohibition on virement or expenditure in excess of allocations, the rigorous control by the Court of Accounts, all these are symptoms of a form of budgetary discipline which makes sense if parliament is expected to intervene to limit expenditure, to decide whether and to what extent the requests of the executive should be granted, to reduce allocations regarded as excessive, and to ensure that the government does not pass the limits set by the budget through administrative action. This is of course considered to be the original and traditional role of parliament in the field of public finance (the defence of the tax-payers against the demands of the executive). But in practice the attitude of parliament is radically different; hence the tendency to foist increases in expenditure, or in certain categories of expenditure, on an executive which is more preoccupied with the exigencies of a system dedicated to saving.

It can be said that in Italy the function of containing expenditure has never been a dominant role for parliament. Whatever has been said in theory, the attitude of the assemblies even a century ago was more favourable to expansion than to limitation of expenditure.

As a result there is dichotomy between the objectives of the rigorous régime of ties and controls on the one hand, and the real attitudes and interests of those involved on the other. Although the system finds its historical and theoretical justification in the necessity for parliamentary control of public finance, in reality it serves to keep the significant powers of control, not with parliament, but with other organs such as the Ragioneria and the Court of Accounts.

The Court of Accounts, for example, professes an 'interest' in the specificity of the budget, criticising the existence of appropriations for varied or general purposes as leaving too much to administrative discretion. It also tends to describe its own theoretical position in the constitutional framework as one of 'neutrality'. The Court stands for the most rigorous interpretation of the Constitution where the budget and expenditure are concerned. In its reporting it does not hesitate to criticise the laws themselves, sometimes in effect censuring itself. It once brought allegations of unconstitutional practice relating to money laws (*leggi di spesa*) and the budget before the Constitutional Court, although without success in that the Constitutional Court held the matters raised inadmissible.[1] This clearly reveals the detachment of the Corte dei Conti from its original function as parliament's *longa manus* controlling the administration of the budget.

Parliament's lack of interest in this type of financial control, which is not only a contemporary phenomenon, nor one confined to Italy, is likely to be irreversible whatever technical and procedural innovations are made. It is manifested in the ritualism and lack of seriousness of the debate on the budget. The explanation is to be found in the type of interest group and party political demands which tend to find expression in parliament. Parliament has no interest in establishing a dialogue either with the government as a whole or with individual departments with the aim of containing expenditure, nor could this be seen as its proper role as an institution or as a part of the political system, however unorthodox this might seem in the light of traditional interpretations.

There is no doubt that the problem of public expenditure from a political or constitutional point of view is how to rationalise it in view of its purpose, and thus to avoid wastage of public money. Nevertheless this problem is above all one of impressing on the

---

[1] The body presiding over the constitutionality of laws in Italy is appropriately, the Constitutional Court. Except in cases of disagreement between State and regions it can be called in judgement only by a judge who in the course of judgement discovers that a clearly well-founded question concerning the legality of a law may be prejudicial to the outcome of the case. This prejudice or consequentiality is regarded by the Court as requisite before the question is admissible. If, however, the Court declares a law to be unconstitutional, its sentence has general effectiveness, thus causing the amendment of the illegitimate law. The Court of Accounts in 1966 and 1967 in examining the reconciliation of the final accounts of the State (an examination carried out in accord with judicial procedure) posed the Constitutional Court various questions of constitutionality relating to the budgetary estimates and to certain laws authorising expenditure. It held that they were contrary to constitutional norms concerning the prohibition of establishing new expenditure along with the budgetary law, and the obligation in laws involving new expenditure of indicating the means to meet it. But the Constitutional Court held that, for the purpose of judging the reconciliation, which was the business of the Court, no question of the application of the law cited was raised and that therefore the questions posed were irrelevant. Hence, as recorded in the text, it declared them inadmissible without examining their merits (see Constitutional Court, Sentence 30, December 1968, no. 142, in *Giurisprudenza Costituzionale* (1968) p. 2337).

What is to be underlined here is that the Court of Accounts' initiative expressed an attitude of criticism and control to the Court, in defence of the constitutional norms regulating public expenditure. In this way the original significance of the Court's control, aiming at ensuring respect for the laws, that is to say of the will of parliament on the part of the executive, was profoundly altered.

administration a greater capacity for expenditure, of reducing inertia and delay, of effecting the allocations decided in the budget as quickly and as flexibly as efficiency – not to speak of other criteria – demands. It must be recognised that the organisation of the budget in Italy does not offer parliament adequate instruments for this end. On the contrary the basic instrument at parliament's disposal – the vote on annual expenditure in the budget – seems to be completely inadequate for this purpose; there are many reasons for this and we shall mention only the chief ones. Even if it has value in placing stringent limits on the expenditure of the administration, the allocation of fixed sums under the budget headings does not have similar effectiveness in obliging or inducing the government actually to spend the sums granted. Implicit in the voting of the budget is a political directive for the government to distribute the sums indicated to their respective ends. However this directive does not constitute a precise legal obligation, and even less an effectively sanctioned one.

The most striking illustration of this fact can be seen in the growth of the *'residui passivi'*, which owes much to the fact that Italy has a *bilancio di competenza*, the mechanisms of which have been outlined above. Sums which have been authorised, but not collected and passed to the Treasury by the end of the financial year, make up *'residui attivi'* (reserve assets). Sums which have been committed, but not paid by the end of the financial year are *'residui passivi'* (reserve liabilities). Neither appear in succeeding budgets and neither are treated for administrative or accounting purposes as part of the appropriations for a given year. On the expenditure side, in addition to *'residui passivi'* properly so-called, there has been an important growth in so-called *'residui di stanziamento'* (allocated reserves). These represent sums which are allocated in the budget for investment expenditure, but which at the end of the year are not only unpaid but also uncommitted. In other words they are sums for which the State has not incurred liabilities. In spite of this it is perfectly legal to keep these sums in the reserve account from which they can be taken during later financial years without further budgetary authorisation.

The size of *residui passivi* of both types has become remarkable. At the end of 1970 they amounted to 7,845 billion lire, of which 35·6 per cent (equal to 2,790·5 billion lire) represented *residui di stanziamento*. This should be compared with a total budget in which sums appropriated came in 1970 to 14,714 billion lire.[1] Parliament

---

[1] See Chamber of Deputies, *Problems of Expenditure and Public Accounting* Rome, 1972), table on p. 381 and Table 10.

has only slight control over the administration of these reserves. They do not appear in the estimates and the form which they take, especially the *residui di stanziamento*, takes much meaning out of the data in the budget, since the budgetary allocations do not correspond to effective administrative activity using and distributing funds in any particular year.

On the other hand the controls on expenditure are very successful in impeding the administration from exceeding budgetary allocations approved by parliament. The Ragioneria and the Court of Accounts effectively prevent spending for which there is no authorisation under the relevant heading of the budget, or which has mistakenly appeared under the wrong heading. These controls are not ideal by any means for stimulating expenditure in a positive sense. Up to 1964 the expenditure accounts (from which are derived the totals of spending actually made in the preceding financial year) were presented to the chambers for examination after great delay, reducing even further the significance of *ex post* control of expenditure. Moreover, while the reports on the final balances made by the Corte dei Conti to parliament give a clear breakdown heading by heading of expenditure which, for whatever reason, has gone beyond the limits of the headings in the budget, there is only a summary account of sums committed and paid which are *less* than those allocated.

The most powerful weapon (though in practice almost always blunt) of parliament over the budget is to reject it as a whole. This summarises the relative positions of parliament and government on the subject of expenditure. Parliament can reduce supply to the government but in voting on the budget it does not possess a comparable means of compelling the government to spend more.

The procedure for voting the budget is, in short, dominated by an 'ideology of saving', which is not entirely in tune with the real attitudes of the chambers. In the field of State expenditure, parliament controls, so to speak, the brake and not the accelerator. To the fact that the budgetary system is inspired by the need to prevent over-spending and not by concern with efficient use of expenditure, it must be added that the structure and organisation of the Italian parliament are not adequate for the role which parliament itself wishes to play. For the 'power of the purse' to be exercised in the sense of encouraging, rather than containing, expenditure, there must be a public authority capable of considering analytically the annual global strategy which takes account of changing situations. Parliament is not such an organ at present, both because of its lack of fact-finding instruments, and of its methods of organising its work; and perhaps also because of the attitudes and behaviour of its members.

In practice it is of course difficult to realise aspirations of this type. It is even hard for the government itself to find structures and methods which would support a budgetary policy based on decisions fully considered in a collegial way. The tendency is for the process to be dominated by one part of government (the Treasury and the Ragioneria in particular) or by the dealings between that one part and individual ministries.

THE RULES OF THE 1948 CONSTITUTION

If, in the light of the general remarks made above, we ask how the principles of the Italian budgetary system have been changed, we are bound to say that the tendency has been if not to aggravate the crisis in parliamentary control of the budget, then certainly to do little to resolve it.

We have already noted how the most recent organic systemisation of the laws on accountability took place in 1923–4. It was within this system that the Republican Constitution of 1948 sought to impose its own discipline on budgetary questions.

In particular the Constitution made the following provisions:

1 Annual parliamentary approval of the budget and of the accounts is obligatory, but the government is responsible for introducing the necessary proposals (Article 81, sub-section 1).
2 Only the plenary session may pass the laws approving the budget and the accounts so that approval by parliamentary committees alone is impossible (Article 72, sub-section 4).
3 The law containing the budget is not subject to repeal by referendum (Article 75, sub-section 2).
4 Provisional authorisation of the budget must be approved by law and for not more than four months at a time (Article 81, sub-section 2).
5 New taxes or expenditure cannot be established by the law approving the budget (Article 81, sub-section 3).
6 Any other law which involves new or increased expenditure must indicate the means by which expenditure is to be met (Article 81, sub-section 4).

Only this last provision, which is a significant innovation, introduces new principles. Otherwise the Constitution sanctions and consolidates principles and guide-lines already enshrined in previ-

H

ous legislation and doctrine. Its effect is therefore one of continuity rather than of innovation. In essence the constituent assembly wanted to reconfirm the traditional institutional features of the budget, showing that these features were essential to the type of parliamentary régime it prescribed. The 'traditionalism' of the constituent assembly emerges clearly, for example, where it provided explicitly in accordance with tradition that the budget law cannot change existing regulations, but rather executes them from a financial point of view. In this way it upheld the prohibition of 'tacking', that is to say, mixing financial provisions of the budget with provisions governing new taxes or new expenditure (Article 81, sub-section 3). Moreover it is clear from the way in which the budget law upholds the necessity of parliamentary examination and approval that parliamentary control of the budget was considered of enduring political importance (Article 72, sub-section 4).

DISCUSSION AND REFORM OF BUDGETARY AFFAIRS FOLLOWING THE ADOPTION OF THE 1948 CONSTITUTION

Political and legal debate on budgetary matters in the period following the adoption of the Constitution focused on two main aspects: first, the structure of the budget and the parliamentary procedures for dealing with it; and secondly, the consequences for legislation involving expenditure of the implementation of the two constitutional principles according to which the budget law cannot establish new expenditure and each law involving expenditure must indicate the measures to cover it (Article 81, sub-sections 3 and 4).

The first thread of the debate is that which led, after many proposals and fruitless attempts at reform, to the law of 1 March 1964, No. 62, which laid down new principles for drawing up the budget. It should be said at the outset that even this law left unaltered the fundamental features of formal budgetary procedure, viz the system of *bilnacio di competenza*; the universality and the analytical nature of the budget; the process whereby individual allocations approved by parliaments set impassable limits to expenditure by individual departments, and the theoretically complete control and detailed scrutiny of the budget by parliament.

The law of 1964, which in parliament's own view should have been merely a first step towards more radical innovations, only introduced three modifications to what applied previously. It brought the financial year into line with the calendar year. It provided for a new system of classifying income and expenditure in the budget (based on 'economic' and 'functional' classification), to supplement the old 'administrative' classifications of departmental expenditure which was not abandoned. It united all the estimates (both of income and of expenditure), and brought them together in a single draft bill. The first of these modifications was largely technical in purpose. The second sought to clarify the economic effects of expenditure voted in the budget and to render the costs of different services more easily calculable, but has not, as it has already been remarked, affected the compartmentalism and rigidity which typify the Italian budgetary system of breaking expenditure down into narrow headings. The third and most controversial sought to make parliamentary scrutiny of the budget more flexible and less mechanical, but it has not made examination by parliament much more significant or much less formal, and it has not prevented frequent recourse to provisional authorisation.

One's impression, both from examining the preparatory work on law No. 62 of 1964 and from the debates which preceded it in the first four Republican legislatures, is that parliament still saw the proposals for modifications in the budgetary system in terms of defending the rights of parliament, even though the circumstances and the positions of the parties had changed. Thus the traditional concept of the budget as a fundamental act of State financial policy seems to have prevailed.

The unification of the estimates (each one of which was the subject of a separate draft bill before 1964) had been proposed ever since the Republican parliament came into existence. In every legislature which followed it was repeatedly proposed again but it encountered long resistance. It was opposed not only on technical grounds but also for fear of limiting both the political significance of the budget and parliament's powers of decision-making and control. Similarly, however, the supporters of change adduced amongst the principal arguments in favour that unification, far from diminishing, would increase the effective power of parliament in budgetary matters, making it easier to consider and even to pass amendments to the budget moved on parliamentary initiative.

The order in which parliament examines the various parts of the budget was also a subject of contention and discussion. When separate estimates were approved by separate bills, the Treasury's estimate, including a summary of the budget and fixing thus the overall total as well as the distribution among departments, was approved first. Now this procedure was justified on the grounds that it would be logical to determine first of all the totality of the expenditure, then the sub-division by sectors, and finally its distribution within the various sectors. The procedure would enable parliament to fix as a preliminary the general lines of budgetary policy.[1] Its opponents replied that parliament's method of examining the budget would derive from unreal global data and decisions, rather than from an analytical scrutiny of expenditure requirements. In the end the law of 1964 ordained that approval first be given to the overall total of income and expenditure, then to the individual estimates of expenditure, and finally to a summary of the general position. This was proposed as a way of reconciling the need for a preliminary fixing of the overall total of expenditure with parliament's wish to be able to amend the budget and even to modify the distribution of expenditure among departments.

In reality, however, even after the reform of 1964, during parliamentary examination of the budget it is unusual for amendments to be passed making significant changes to the proposals presented by the government in such a way as to cut into the general total of expenditure or its major subdivisions. All this confirms that the preoccupation with safeguarding the formal decision-making powers of parliament in budgetary matters is more or less remote from the reality of decision-making in public expenditure.

THE GROWTH OF LONG-TERM EXPENDITURE AND ITS EFFECT ON THE ROLE OF PARLIAMENT

The tendency of members of parliament to be interested less in restricting expenditure, and more in promoting expenditure or at least ensuring its effective distribution, helps us to understand another feature of the system of public expenditure in Italy as it has evolved in the period following the adoption of the Constitution. This is the increasing tendency for the locus of decisions regarding both the overall amount and the particular use of expenditure to move out of the annual budget altogether into the procedure for passing ordinary laws which require and provide expenditure in particular sectors for a fixed number of years, often for many years, allocating it in constant or growing annual quotas. This tendency has contributed greatly to making the budget more rigid. The latter has increasingly become – and is now almost completely – simply a summary in figures of expenditure decisions already taken outside the budget itself. Its political significance and its importance as a planning document are thus ultimately reduced.[2]

[1] See Ragioneria Generale, Notes on the 'General Summary' of the Estimatory Budget and on the Procedure Whereby it is Approved by the Legislative Assemblies (Rome, 1954), pp. 20–1.
[2] It recently happened that some appropriations provided for in long-term

An important cause of this has been a certain interpretation of the constitutional rules already noted. According to this interpretation no new article can be established in the budgetary law (Article 81, sub-section 3), and laws involving new or increased expenditure must indicate the means whereby it is to be met (Article 81, sub-section 4). The first rule has the result of intensifying the distinction, itself not entirely new, between money laws (*leggi di spesa*) and budgetary laws (*leggi di bilancio*). The former are laws which provide for certain given actions to be undertaken by the public administration, and authorise the necessary expenditure (which is eventually allocated in the current budget or in successive budgets). The latter are laws which give annual authority for the commitment and payment of expenditure provided by legislation in force. Without Article 81 (3) of the Constitution expenditure could be made on the sole basis of an appropriation in the budget and without mention in any other law. (That did in fact happen before, although it was often anomalous in terms of budgetary law.) Today every expenditure must have a double foundation: an appropriation in the budget, and a law, or more usually an order, consenting to the execution of the expenditure or of the activity which the expenditure accomplishes.

According to the most rigorous interpretations every appropriation ought to be specifically based on a *legge di spesa* prior to the budget. If this requirement was carried to its extreme conclusions, since every law involving new expenditure must indicate the means whereby it is to be met, all expenditure would have to be envisaged in laws (prior to the budget) which fixed an amount (or in the case of long-term expenditure, an annual amount) with the related financial 'cover'. At least it would be illegal to postpone the quantification of expenditure until future annual budgets. This would lead to total rigidity and at most to the futility of the annual budget, but it is not a reasonable interpretation of the Constitution. Although the Constitution lays down a distinction between *leggi di spesa* and *leggi di bilancio,* it limits itself to requiring that every expenditure appropriated in the budget should be based on a previous order (even if that order did no more than to lay down the institutional objectives of a public body). Thus it allows *leggi di spesa* to leave it to the budget to determine what sums should be spent each year on purposes envisaged. In turn the obligation to indicate the means

laws were suppressed or reduced in the budgets within which they were destined to weigh by law and put back to following years. This is, however, a strategem of dubious constitutionality and thus it has been seldom used up to now. (See Chamber of Deputies, *Problems of Expenditure*, p. 387.)

whereby new expenditure will be met is valid only if the *legge di spesa* requires that given quotas of expenditure be made in given periods.

The increased adoption of long-term money laws has been, and probably still is, a response to political necessity. There is no single and authoritative political centre for controlling public expenditure. Within the administration there is conflict between forces opposing expenditure and those favouring expenditure or at least favouring the expansion of certain sectors. At the same time there is no general framework of medium-term planning for public expenditure as a whole. Thus the formation of long-term money laws answers the need of individual departments and agencies which seek to get appropriations corresponding to sectoral programmes sanctioned once and for all and thus avoid the periodic revision and reconsideration which would take place if expenditure were fixed by the annual budget. On the other hand, the very need to ensure that new expenditure has the constitutionally required 'cover' (Article 81, sub-section 4, Constitution) sometimes means that the *leggi di spesa* include a reference to the amount of allocations, thereby 'reserving', as it were, a certain quota of the funds thought to exist for the purpose of cover.

For its part parliament can see rigid and detailed *leggi di spesa* as means of getting back some of the financial power which the right to approve the budget does not give. If parliament is interested, not so much in imposing limits on the government's expenditure as in positively influencing its actions and decisions, then the budget is less useful than long-term *leggi di spesa*. It is difficult for parliament when dealing with the budget to make more than marginal changes to the plan for allocating expenditure formulated by the government. Experience has shown that it is much easier to amend laws dealing with expenditure in particular sectors. Furthermore, in passing *leggi di spesa*, parliament is again following an analytical procedure for fixing expenditure – starting, that is, from a single sector and a single activity, whereas in the budget it is treating decisions of a 'synthetic' and global type.

The fact remains that by increasing use of long-term *leggi di spesa* parliament has reduced the significance of choices made in the budget, which are more and more predetermined.

Indeed *leggi di spesa* go only a certain way to give parliament real financial powers. In one way, the constitutional requirement of cover for new expenditure imposes a greater restriction on parliament than on the government. The latter is better placed to lay hands on additional cover (for example when there is a surplus of revenue over what was forecast) or to provide means of cover beforehand in the budget.[1] Nevertheless this constitutionality has been questioned, partly on the grounds that they lead to an evasion of the constitutional obligation of coverage, and partly because they can aggravate a budget deficit. They are certainly very useful for governments, which sometimes use them to finance new expenditure proposals of their own without needing specific budgetary approval.

Not even by means of *leggi di spesa* can parliament fully pursue its aim of exercising real financial power in conformity with its real political interest. This interest, like that of any centre of government expenditure, assumes that the following opportunities should be available: (*a*) to ensure that given sums are spent for fixed purposes; (*b*) to ensure that the sums concerned are efficiently allocated; and (*c*) to see to it that they are spent at the right time. The procedure of *leggi di spesa* provides an effective opportunity for aims of type (*a*), especially when the law allocates funds for various purposes analytically and provides, as often happens, that the relevant appropriations shall be effective even after the financial year of the budget to which they belong. In this way they fix the destination of funds to specific purposes in advance (although they increase the incidence of the so-called *residui di stanziamento* treated above). However the *leggi di spesa* do not help aims of types (*b*) and (*c*), since neither the debate on a *legge di spesa*, nor the eventual appropriation of the sums concerned in the budget, ensure that the sums will in fact be spent, and much less that they will be spent within the time indicated, as is illustrated by the phenomenon of the *residui di stanziamento* which represent expenditure debated and appropriated, but not spent and not even committed by the administration.

The growth of the long-term *leggi di spesa* of a sectoral character, but not related to an overall plan, leads undoubtedly to rigidity in sectors of public expenditure. This deprives not only parliament, but every other central organ, of the opportunity to practise effective planning of public expenditure in the medium and short terms. Not surprisingly, therefore, bodies concerned with planning have argued

[1] For this second purpose the government can use the so-called *'fondi globali'*. These 'general-purpose funds' are not provided for in financial law, but they have been introduced in practice and are constantly included in the budget. They consist of supplies of money which bear only a formal similarity to other appropriations in the budget, and they are not directly available to finance spending. The *fondi globali* are in certain respects analogous to reserve funds (like those for obligatory expenditure or for unforeseen expenditure which also appear in the Italian budget), except that withdrawals from reserve funds for use under headings of real expenditure is at the executive's discretion, while the utilisation of *fondi globali* requires a new law authorising some new expenditure.

the need for more flexible types of money law, in which only the destination of expenditure and the methods would be laid down, and it would be left to the budget, in the framework of long-term programmes and forecasts, to quantify expenditure on an annual basis even if only in relation to short-term requirements. This demand has been made for some time, but it cannot be said that up to now it has received wide support.

Not the least cause of this is the fact that even now we lack the instruments for a plan in which a general framework for public expenditure could be included, and in terms of which decisions about sectoral laws as well as annual budgetary decisions could be made.

PROPOSALS FOR THE ADOPTION OF A 'BILANCIO DI CASSA'

As early as the reform of 1964 the idea was mooted of replacing the traditional Italian system of a *bilancio di competenza* with a *bilancio di cassa*, or at least to adopt both together. This idea was fully discussed in the following years, and it can now be said that it is favoured by large sections of parliament and of the administration,[1] even though it has not been proposed in legislative form.

At first sight the *bilancio di cassa* seems to weaken the traditional function of the budget as a limit on commitments to spend, replacing this with a limitation only on payments. In other words there would be a decline in the annual importance of the process of fixing analytically the limits to possible commitments represented today by the individual headings in the budget. The only restrictions on the administration in undertaking liabilities would be *leggi di spesa* or possibly a long-term *bilancio di competenza* (as has been pro-

[1] See for example the interventions of the Ministers of the Budget (Socialists) Giolitti, in *Senate Acts*, sitting 25 February 1964, p. 5024, and Pieraccini, in *Senate Acts* afternoon sitting 28 November 1967, p. 39357. The note of senator Medici (Christian-Democrat) presented to the study committee on Article 81 of the Constitution evolved in 1966, in *Conclusive Document on the Work of the Interparliamentary Study Committee on Problems Stemming From Article 81 of the Constitution* (Rome, 1968), pp. 17–18. More recently see 'Preliminary Planning Document (Elements for the Foundation of a National Economic Plan 1971–5)', sponsored by the Ministry of the Budget and Economic Planning (Rome, 1971) in *Quarterly Review of Public Law* (1971), p. 815, and *Public Expenditure* (1972), p. 325, the outline of 'National Economic Plan 1971–75 (general part)' sponsored by the Ministry of the Budget and Economic Planning (Rome, 1972), in *Quarterly Review of Public Law* (1972), p. 499 and in *Public Expenditure* (1972), p. 345, the 'Conclusions and proposals' elaborated by the budget Committee of the Chamber of Deputies on the completion of the fact-finding survey on these subjects between 1969 and 1971, in Chamber of Deputies, *Problems of Expenditure*, p. 44.

posed by some). The authorisation of expenditure would be much
less analytical and detailed than the division of the budget headings
is today. Consequently one aspect of expenditure control would also
decline or undergo a radical change, that is, the examination of acts
undertaking liabilities to verify whether they are provided under the
relevant budgetary heading or not. As we have seen, this examination can be used by the Court of Accounts to prohibit the assumption of any liability under certain circumstances (absolute refusal of
registration).

However the preoccupation in some quarters with this possible
weakening of parliamentary control seems to overlook changes in
the perspectives and attitudes of parliament with regard to public
expenditure which have already been mentioned here. If parliament
is 'interested' not so much in imposing limits on expenditure, but
rather in ensuring an efficient allocation of given resources at the
right time, and in being able to control it, a *bilancio di cassa* seems
to be more appropriate.

This is not so much because it expresses more significant data
than the *bilancio di competenza*, but because it is more likely to
express the economic effects of public expenditure. This is because,
although given the many different technical delays which can
obstruct the process of expenditure, it is not easy with a *bilancio di
competenza* to isolate political responsibility for any discrepancy
between appropriations, liabilities and actual payments (as experience with '*residui*' shows), nevertheless with a *bilancio di cassa* it
should be somewhat easier to match the estimate with actual needs,
and also to check why there is any discrepancy in the period concerned between estimates and payments actually made. It would
moreover enable a more consistent and vigilant control by parliament over the executive's drawing of funds from the market. With a
bilancio di competenza an estimated deficit can become a balance or
a surplus (or even a larger deficit) by virtue of a discrepancy
betweem liabilities and payments, and because '*residui*' are
managed in a certain way (which does anyway largely escape
parliamentary control). With a *bilancio di cassa* it should be clear
from the outset what kind of financial operations the government
intends to complete in the year to offset any deficit as well as how
much money is involved. It should be possible also to assess how
much recourse the government has had to the money market in the
light of the actual needs of the budget, and to do this without
postponing the act of approving expenditure until the budget has
been finally approved. Today the crediting operations have to be
completed before the expenditure can be written into the budget.

Undoubtedly in the new system the budget would lose part of its traditional function of setting limits to public expenditure. The authority for expenditure would rest with long-term laws, which would not lay down the amount of expenditure to be made annually and would only express what overall sums the main sectors were intended to spend, while the annual budget (preferably in the framework of a multi-annual plan) would be given the task of defining what sums it was intended to spend on various specific purposes during the year. However the budget would acquire greater significance as an instrument for conjunctional financial planning in the short term, an instrument sanctioned by parliament and more easily controlled by it both *a priori* and *a posteriori*.

CONCLUSIONS

Political and constitutional factors are more important than technical ones in deciding whether parliament could acquire greater influence in economic and financial decisions. In this respect it is wrong to distinguish parliament and government as autonomous and separate powers, since the real political balance of forces is usually between the majority (governmental and parliamentary) and the Opposition. However this notion does not apply fully to a complex political system like the Italian one, characterised by a plurality of parties, by non-homogeneous government majorities, and by relationships between the political forces present in parliament which are not reducible to simple distinctions between majority and opposition parties. The government represents only certain parties, and sometimes only some groups within the major parties are represented. Whether a particular party or group is part of the majority, or formally in opposition but collaborating with it, it often manages to influence the content of decisions entrusted to parliament more than the decisions made by the government. Moreover, the latter is tied more than parliament to the bureaucracy of ministerial departments, and is therefore more susceptible to its influence. Moreover the organised interests which have influence in parliament sometimes differ from those with access at government level. Thus in Italy at least the division of power between parliament and government can be important for the outcome of policy and for the general functioning of the system.

In general, parliament's real power lies not so much in approving more or less binding documents and plans like the budget, as in its ability to participate in the process of formulation and modification of decisions of financial policy. This lesson emerges clearly from the experience, generally judged unsatisfactory, of the first Italian five-year plan.

When this was proposed, there was much discussion of the way in which the plan should be approved. The way chosen was that of approval by law, because it was hoped in this way to make the plan more binding. Thus parliament examined and approved in legislation a voluminous economic programme for the quinquennium 1966–70, containing a series of very heterogeneous propositions: forecasts, objectives, qualitative and quantitative targets. This was to represent 'the outline [*quadro*] of the economic, financial and social policy of the government and of all public investment' (Article 1 of the law of 27 July 1967, No. 685) and was meant to be integrated and put into effect by means of further legislative, as well as administrative, measures (Article 2 of the same law). In fact neither the activities of the private sector nor those of the public administration, including legislation, budgets and expenditure which followed the approval of the plan, were particularly affected by it, and the statements it contained made it even less binding. The plan was worth little more than the paper on which it was written. The intervention of parliament in approving the plan, therefore, has not meant significant participation by parliament in the real determination of the economic and financial policy of the country.

As a result the need for future regulation of the process of drawing up and executing the plan became clear. The methods of intervention by parliament, regions, unions, etc. in planning needed to be defined. Article 3 of the law approving the first plan provides for appropriate legislation to this end and an initiative was taken by the government in 1967. Nevertheless, to date the law on planning procedure has not been approved, and the very forces which promoted it do not know how to launch it. Neither the contents nor the status of the second five-year plan have yet been decided. It is hoped in some quarters that the next plan may be approved, not merely by passing a law, but by the truly political participation of parliament, meaning that, instead of authorising in one law the entire process of planning, the emphasis would be on the authorisation of public expenditure, and on finding a new relationship between the plan, the *leggi di spesa* and the budget, rendering the budget more flexible in nature and working and more sensitive to the objectives of the plan.[1] These ideas are based on the realisation that a real plan does not result so much from a series of documents, but from a coherent

1 See 'Preliminary Planning Document' of the Ministry of the Budget, in *Quarterly Review of Public Law* (1971), p. 803, and 'Second National Economic Plan' in *Quarterly Review of Public Law* (1972), p. 489.

and organic process of decision-making carried out over time, adhering to stated objectives and continually updated with respect to changing economic, social and political circumstances.

The problem of the financial powers of parliament as an institution is not so much one of whether or not the chambers can approve a financial document by some solemn act, as the way in which parliament, government and the various parts of the administration are related to one another in the process of making the decisions which determine public expenditure. It is also important to know what type of intervention parliament manages to achieve in this process. Finally, we must stress that fact-finding instruments and coherent formulation of decisions are as necessary to parliament as to any other institution involved in complex problems of financial and economic control.

CHAPTER 13

THE ITALIAN PARLIAMENT'S ROLE IN EXPENDITURE DECISIONS

Vittorio Mortara

THE IMPORTANCE OF THE BUREAUCRACY IN PUBLIC SPENDING

In considering the problems of public expenditure in Italy the role of the bureaucracy must be taken into account, or only formal analysis is possible. There are several reasons for this and it is useful to examine them at the beginning of this chapter. Otherwise it will not be clear why a chapter on parliament's role deals so much with administrative bodies and so little with parliamentary institutions.

First of all one has to take account of the rather peculiar relationship of Italian bureaucratic institutions to political institutions and, more particularly, to the government. Many factors have contributed to make Italian civil servants more or less independent of the ministers and secretaries of state who should be their leaders. These include an impressive number of protective regulations; a system of negative sanctions which can be put into effect only with great difficulty; the fact that promotion is based on age, or knowledge of abstract rules, rather than on job performance; and finally a method of operating which makes it impossible to apportion responsibility for errors or omissions. Instead of the usual game for two sides, which is said to characterise a parliamentary democracy on the French or British model, in Italy the game is played by three, in which the players are parliament, government *and* bureaucracy. Indeed it would be reasonable to suppose that the contestants in the game of public expenditure could multiply almost indefinitely in view of the vertical or horizontal divisions which exist within the bureaucracy (relating to both professional groups and different hierarchical levels).

Secondly there is the way in which the State's expenses are provided for in Italy. The general procedure laid down by the Italian constitution and the all-important distinction between budget legislation and other laws involving expenditure have already been dealt with.[1] We shall deal here only with the situation resulting from these provisions. Public expenditure is provided for and regulated by a very large number of self-contained laws which continue to pile up without following a general scheme. In such a situation only technicians, that is the bureaucrats, can perform with any real skill and understanding. The civil servants who manage to acquire a particularly important position are those who have the specific task of putting the disconnected and fragmentary legislation on expenditure into a single annual document, the national budget: in fact only these officials can have a general picture of the expenditure of the State as a whole. In the final analysis a certain number of *dilettanti* (politicians who are members either of parliament or of the government) find themselves confronted by professional technicians. The *dilettanti* can have their way in *certain* circumstances by exerting a considerable amount of energy, but in the long run and above all in day-to-day routine there is no doubt that specialised technical knowledge of the complex set of regulations governing the distribution of expenditure wins in the end.[2]

Finally the role of bureaucracy in the process of spending is magnified by the fact that both the expenditure laws and the national budget are merely authorisations: together they give certain broadly defined public bodies the right to spend certain sums. The actual expenditure takes place at the end of a long procedure, which can sometimes be prolonged for years, including many bureaucratic decisions which involve delay or which might nullify the decision to spend embodied in the law. In fact in this procedure there is usually a series of administrative acts (that is, self-contained but normally instrumental decisions), the formal characteristics of which are deemed more important than the material. Such acts descend as it were from top to bottom, and follow a strict order, so that if one of them is missing or gets delayed, the process is hopelessly obstructed. The lower one gets in the hierarchy of the acts, the more one finds that it is the bureaucrats, and only they, who perform and control them.

THE PROCESS OF PREPARING, PASSING AND EXECUTING LEGISLATION FOR EXPENDITURE

Now that we have justified the introduction of a third party (if not

---

[1] See Chapter 12.

[2] One should note that Italian bureaucrats can be considered 'professionals' only in the limited sense that politicians are *dilettanti* in public administration. It cannot be maintained that a 'professional ideology' is present in a structure which is dominated to such an extent by non-specialists.

more) into the account of how public expenditure is controlled, we may briefly describe the process by which the State's money is spent. It will be possible in this way to describe, explain and evaluate the roles played by the three main protagonists, and to collect data to contribute to at least a hypothetical answer to the question of who controls expenditure in Italy.

Two warnings must be given first. We shall be mainly concerned with the expenditure laws initiated by the government (as distinct from those which are presented to parliament by the other possible sources provided by the constitution: viz members of parliament, regional councils, groups of at least 50,000 citizens, and the National Council for Economy and Labour (CNEL)). We do this because government Bills on expenditure set the 'tone' of public expenditure by their importance, if not by their number. Secondly, the fact has to be taken into account that our generalisations, while having descriptive value for the first stages of the process of spending (the formulation and approval of the law), in which it is simple enough to define common characteristics and normal behaviour on the part of the main institutional actors, will give no more than a general indication of what happens in the final stages of execution. Indeed, given the lack of general pattern other than what is given by the General Law on State Accounting (*Legge Generale sulla Contabilità dello Stato*),[1] which may anyway be changed by any single law, in these later stages there is an enormous amount of variation. There are differences in the way laws are formulated and even in the kinds of expenses provided in the same law. Moreover meaningful generalisations about these later stages would have to take account of the range of offices given the task of execution, of differences in the geographical location and in the timing of expenditure and so on.

The Origin of Government Laws Involving Expenditure

One cannot be precise about the preliminary stages of the process leading to the formulation of an expenditure law, because it involves the channelling of political demands which come to the government's attention in different ways and at different times. In the past there were two main channels: one of them, passing through institutionalised pressure groups, or through the normal channels for expressing public opinion, led to the organs of the political parties charged with preparing party programmes, and eventually to the government itself when the parties were called

[1] See Chapter 12, p. 215.

upon to join it; the second channel was the bureaucracy. In most recent times this latter channel seems to have been used less and less. The bureaucracy still puts forward requests for legislation involving expenditure in the course of its normal tendency to expand its own structure and to seek easier careers for its members, but it does not seem nowadays to press for legislation on behalf of any specialised clientele of its own. The channel which seems to have achieved special relevance in recent times passes through the trade unions, which, by using their own methods of exerting pressure, have succeeded in many cases in imposing their own priorities on the parties. As a matter of fact the most important expenditure laws in the past few years (for example the laws concerning the institution of the national health system, the social security system, subsidised housing and government intervention in the economy) have been formulated by the government after *formal* bargaining with representatives of the major trade-union federations. Finally it is worth mentioning that the first five-year plan (the period which terminated in 1970) does not seem to have been of any importance as a blueprint for actual legislation. Even if they had a high priority in the national plan, ideas and proposals which were not explicitly brought forward by the above-mentioned channels have tended to be abortive.

The 'Political Phase'

That part of the process which aims at transforming an idea or a request for legislation into a formal document can be seen as having two phases, which can be called respectively (without any pretension towards rigid definitions) the 'political phase' and the 'administrative phase'. The political phase is concerned with ascertaining what the content of the law will be. In particular it is concerned with establishing the total amount of expenditure, the categories of recipients and the goals of the expenditure. Obviously the activities carried out at this stage lack a fixed procedure dictated by practice or law. Usually there are informal meetings of the secretariats of the parties which make up the government coalition (or of the experts of these parties),[1] and in some cases formal meetings are called at ministerial level, in which all the ministers concerned participate. In addition to ministers that is, the heads of the ministries who will be

[1] These are people appointed by the political parties to study social or economic questions in order to acquire documentation or technical expertise. In many cases they are university lecturers or professional people of undoubted competence, but there have been cases of 'experts' whose only title to the job derived from the need for political equilibrium within individual parties.

responsible for seeing that the substantive goals provided by the law are attained, along with the heads of the so-called financial ministries,[1] higher officials usually take part, especially those from the Ragioneria Generale (General Accounts Office),[2] as well as experts from the planning bureau. If the proposal does not raise great political and economic difficulties, this stage can be completed in a few days, and for laws on expenditure of little quantitative or political importance it can be omitted completely (as usually happens with laws benefiting small groups of people, often including members of the public administration itself). But if the issue for which the law is going to be enacted has great political importance, or if the money to be spent is expected to have an effect on the Italian economy, the political stage can be prolonged for months and endanger the government's stability, as happened recently with the laws mentioned above involving negotiations with representatives of the trade unions.

The 'Administrative Phase'

Coterminous with the activities we have just described but distinguishable from them is another set of activities which together form what we have called the 'administrative phase'. These are intended to give form to the content already agreed upon, or if, as sometimes happens, the 'political phase' is omitted, to determine form and content together. One point which is very important for the main theme of this chapter is that the administrative phase does not merely involve an automatic transcription into a formal proposal of things already decided. Among the decisions which are almost always dealt with for the first time in this phase are those regarding the allocation to different organisations of responsibility for spending, which depends on an organisation's institutional location and its place in the hierarchy of institutions, as well as decisions regarding the procedures which will be followed in the act

---

1 There are three finance ministries, the Treasury, the Ministry of Finance and the Ministry of the Budget and Economic Planning (see Chapter 12). The recent establishment of the third of these seems to be due to the double preoccupation to ensure wider political participation in the administration of expenditure and to provide an institutional home for economic programming which does not have a precise role. The search for an area within which the Ministry of the Budget and Economic Planning can act (an area which has to be partly taken away from the Treasury and in part created *ex novo*) and the resistance put up by the other ministries have been constant factors in the Italian administrative scene in the past few years.

2 See Chapter 12, p. 216, for a detailed description of the power of this dominant office.

of spending itself. Another important type of decision may be taken in this phase, which concerns the division into categories of the total sum allocated (or of various yearly instalments decided during the political phase). Such categories are for example 'expenditure on personnel', 'construction of buildings', 'purchase of equipment'. Later, when the sums are inscribed in the annual budget, each division will correspond to a particular heading of the budget.

The activities which make up the 'administrative phase' take place mainly in the operational sections of the ministries, which are theoretically responsible for drafting the legislation. However on those aspects which are more strictly financial these sections must consult with representatives of the Treasury. In reality, especially for those aspects of the law which will determine how and when the sum authorised will be spent (that is, procedures for spending, types of control, division into budgetary headings, and so on), a leading role falls to the Ragioneria Generale as the institution responsible for 'managing' the national budget. This role amounts almost to a dictatorship, although extensive negotiations with the representatives of the spending ministries are usually necessary before a decision on these issues is reached; they are, after all, from many points of view the important issues.

The role played at this point by the political institutions has already been mentioned. The particular technical requirements used to justify the choices made seem to make it impossible for ministers (with the exception perhaps of the Minister of the Treasury) to exert a direct influence. However pressures of various kinds can be exerted through those offices which are directly dependent on ministers (cabinets and private secretariats) or through politically sensitive civil servants who have been appointed to high positions as a result of political pressures. Very little is known about these areas, however, in which political and technical considerations are confused, since officially such things do not really happen.

Other Aspects of the Preparatory Activities

We can conclude here the brief summary of events which precede the presentation of the Bill to parliament. Practice and the constitution dictate other steps which usually have a merely formal value. Even the required approval by the Council of Ministers is almost always a routine matter. Cases of approval 'in copertina' are not unknown. Here approval is based on the limited information made available on the cover of a file, which inside should contain the text of the law and all the documents to justify it, but which is often empty because the text of the law is not yet ready.[1]

Parliamentary Consideration

The parliamentary stage in the process of formulating laws on expenditure merits separate treatment because of its importance and its complexity. I will therefore confine myself to examining in some detail a single problem of particular relevance in this context: the amount of influence exerted by parliament on expenditure Bills presented by the government.

The Italian constitution provides for two different ways of approving laws. If by decision of the offices of the presidents of the two chambers a Bill is assigned to the 'decentralised procedure', the Bill will be discussed only by one or more of the standing committees (each of them competent for a particular subject matter – for example, foreign affairs, agriculture, justice, etc.) which in this case are able to approve the Bill directly, if there is a majority in favour of it. If on the other hand a Bill is assigned to the 'ordinary procedure', it will be discussed and eventually approved by the assembly, subject to preliminary investigation by one or more of the standing committees. For Bills providing for expenditure of any kind, it is provided that in both houses of parliament the debate – that is, the debate by the assembly in the case of 'ordinary procedure' and the final debate by the standing committee in case of decentralised procedure' – must be preceded by an examination by the special standing committee responsible for the national budget, whose opinion is decisive for the outcome of the legislation. The purpose of this examination is to see that laws on expenditure can be covered financially, whether by drawing on existing budgetary appropriations or by other means (for example, by new taxes).

Members of parliament are provided with plenty of relevant information. Every Bill is preceded by a brief note explaining why the law and the expenditure are deemed necessary by the government; each stage of the debate is preceded by a report by a member of the majority (usually briefed by the officers of the ministry sponsoring the Bill) and by a member of the minority. Both the authors of the reports and other members of parliament can draw freely on information provided by the information offices of the chambers and (according to the most recent set of regulations) can ask for formal hearings to be held. Actually very little is known

[1] One should note that, in cases where the political phase has been omitted, approval '*in copertina*' legitimises decisions taken principally or entirely at a bureaucratic level.

about the extent to which members of parliament use the facilities available for getting information.

At first sight and on a formal level the instruments at the disposal of the Italian parliament for controlling public expenditure seem imposing. In fact, not only is every spending measure (and in many cases these are minutely detailed measures) subject to separate examination by parliament, but a minimum of four collective bodies is called upon to discuss the measure itself. If the Bill is following the 'decentralised procedure' it will be scrutinised in both chambers by two standing committees (one of them responsible for the subject matter and the other one for the financial aspects). If the bill is following the 'ordinary procedure' there will usually also be a very extensive debate in front of the full assemblies. Moreover, as we have already seen, the members of parliament can draw upon many sources of information.

If we try to leave the formal level and ascertain what is the actual behaviour of Italian parliamentarians with respect to the scrutiny of laws on expenditure proposed by the government, we find ourselves confronted by contradictory opinions, each of which can be supported by the very little data available.

It has been said that the Italian parliament limits its role to rubber-stamping decisions taken elsewhere. In fact, the first impression one gets from the data available is that very little influence is exercised by parliament on legislation proposed by the government, at least if we consider control in terms of the number of Bills selected for examination. More than 90 per cent of such legislation is approved in a relatively short time.[1] There are no available data on the percentage of draft Bills leading to expenditure laws (although these Bills make up about 60 per cent of total government Bills) but there is no reason for thinking, in spite of the slightly more complex procedure provided for, that parliament has been any more selective in dealing with them than with ordinary Bills.

A more realistic opinion is probably that a good deal of influence is in fact exerted, even if parliament does not fully utilise the power the Italian constitution gives to it. We know for example that a notable percentage of governmental Bills[2] is approved only after amendment or even after the incorporation of the contents of other legislation on the same subject presented by members of the majority parties, or less often by members of the minority parties.

[1] This fact and the following ones relating to the activity of the parliament are taken from research carried out on a sample of approximately 2,000 Bills presented to the Italian parliament from 1948 to 1968. The report on this research is awaiting publication.

[2] The exact percentage found in the course of the research mentioned earlier is 43·7 per cent.

There is no systematic data available on the content of the amendments and therefore we do not know how far the original text of the drafts is changed, or whether such changes have a bearing on the quantitative or other aspects of public expenditure. And we know for certain that in the fifth legislature (1968–72) strong opposition encountered by the government in passing expenditure laws pertaining to matters of great political interest has made some critics talk for the first time of 'government by assembly'. It is possible to mention the extensive changes forced by parliament in the law on public and subsidised housing and the defeat suffered by the government in trying to get parliamentary approval for the decree on special intervention in economic matters. Much less is known about Bills involving smaller amounts, which are generally discussed only in the secrecy of the standing committees.

On the basis of the evidence available, therefore, we may conclude that parliament, although by no means fully utilising the instruments at its disposal, is not without a say in matters pertaining to public expenditure. The problem then arises of whether we can talk about a 'parliamentary policy' on expenditure as opposed to the 'government policy'. Not enough research has been done on this and it is therefore impossible to give meaningful generalisations. The little evidence available on the content of amendments to government legislation seems to indicate that they do not result from rational, concerted decisions, but tend rather to be spasmodic and to result from partisan stances taken by some parties' representatives or by pressure groups with varying degrees of organisation. We know for example that there has been a consistent and growing pressure on the majority parties from the left-wing parties in the Opposition to modify expenditure procedures in order to increase the decision-making powers of local government (which left-wing parties control in many parts of Italy) and in general to decentralise the decision-making process. Among the pressure groups more active in the Italian parliament (and more successful in obtaining legislation and amendments to the government's drafts) are the public corporations (IRI and ENI seem to have the best lobbying organisation) and the public administration itself. On the public administration as a pressure group it is perhaps worth mentioning that its influence is used only to get career advantages or salary increases for individual officials or small groups of them; there is little evidence of the system which has been described, for example, in the United States, whereby relations between officials and members of parliament serve to increase or sustain the areas of responsibility of different services and offices.

The Execution of Laws on Expenditure

We shall now try to describe the procedure by which authorised public expenditure is implemented in Italy. Again, moving as it were from top to bottom of the process, it is more and more difficult to proceed by general statements. After the law has been approved, and before actual spending can begin, a certain number of activities have to be performed. These activities, which can be described as being 'higher administration', are instrumental to the making of appropriations (*decreti di impegno*), meaning the formal documents (signed by the competent minister) specifying the actual destination of all the sums allocated by the law. Before this crucial point in the process two formally independent sets of activities have to be performed: the 'programming' of the expenditure and its 'specification' under different headings of the budget.

Programming is the procedure which is intended to relate appropriations to actual needs, so that a rational allocation of the funds available can be made. Strange as it may seem, this generally takes place in Italy *after* expenditure laws have been passed. Depending on what provisions are contained in a particular law, the procedure can be shortened so that funds are simply allocated, according to predetermined criteria, among the various parties to which they are due (usually organs of the public administration at lower levels or other public bodies). But there may be a long and extremely formal procedure in which a score of administrative bodies at various levels are required to intervene. Such complexity has reached a peak in the programming procedure provided in some fairly recent laws (mainly in the field of public works). These laws specify that the appropriations should be made following the drawing up of a national programme for expenditure in a given sector. The national programme in its turn is compiled by amalgamating local programmes based on the decisions of communes, provinces and decentralised organs of the State; these decisions are formal ones and have to follow rather complex and lengthy procedures themselves. In these cases it is quite normal for the time set for the spending of the money granted by the law to expire even before the appropriations are made.[1]

Programming takes place in specialised offices of the various ministries and involves mainly the activity of civil servants. However, since it terminates in an appropriation which involves ministerial responsibility, and because of its political relevance (after all 'who gets what' is decided mainly at this stage), political pressures

[1] On the other hand, when a formal procedure for programming is not provided for, cases occur of ministers who appropriate in a very brief period of time sums which will not be provided in the budget except in later years.

are quite common. In practice by intervening in these programming activities ministers can get some orders made more quickly than others or can use the margins of discretion left by the law to increase the sums destined for certain categories of recipient (for example, members of their own constituency).

Very often the second operation, 'specification' into headings in the budget, is also made at this stage, if it has not already taken place before the legislation was presented to parliament. This is an important operation because the Italian budget is so inflexible that failure to take account of the real requirements of different activities may cause a sudden stoppage in spending when funds under the heading concerned fall short. It often happens that sums under other headings, although appropriated under the same law, remain unused for a long time. It is important to note that despite its very substantial relevance, the specification of funds is considered almost exclusively as a technical and legal operation. This is demonstrated by the fact that although the division into headings is formally a concern of the minister responsible, the institutions of technical, financial and administrative control (once again the Ragioneria) play a most important role in preparing for it.

The final stage, which begins with appropriation and ends with the issuing of paying orders, varies enormously depending on a series of complex factors. In some cases where direct payments are made to public bodies the procedure can be relatively simple, although various steps must be taken to see whether formal requirements are being observed and to set in motion the paying organs. In other cases, i.e. when the funds are to be paid in exchange for activities and goods necessary to the public administration, the procedure is usually very complex and involves a sequence of formal administrative acts by different organs at the central and peripheral levels.[1] This final set of activities is meant to be performed by civil servants alone. Political intervention (that is by ministers or secretaries of state, usually to speed up the procedure) is fairly common, but is deemed to be corrupt and causes resentment among the minor officials who are usually in charge of the activities to be performed at this stage.

The System of a posteriori Control

The system of *a posteriori* control on the activities of the Italian

---

[1] Obviously at this phase activities of organisations or individual recipients of expenditure can be provided for, and their concern and responsibility can exert a considerable effect on the speed with which the procedure is carried out,

administration is complex and no more than a very brief sketch can be given here. As we have already seen, the whole administrative process by which the State spends its money is composed of a series of administrative Acts. The General Law on State Accounting (which, unless a particular expenditure law provides otherwise, dictates the standard procedure for spending) provides that *each* administrative act pertaining to spending can be performed only if it has passed two different procedures of control. One of these is carried out by the Ragionerie centrali (i.e. decentralised offices of the Ragioneria Generale in each ministry) and is intended to check that the act of spending is based on the funds available in the relevant heading of the budget, and that the act is likely to perform the function intended. The other procedure of control is entrusted to the Court of Accounts (Corte dei Conti) a quasi-judicial institution which acts among other things as a parliamentary watchdog on matters pertaining to public expenditure. It deals only with the legality of the act, i.e. whether it is in accordance with the provisions of the relevant laws. Actually both procedures tend to take into consideration only the formal and legal aspects of the act and materially there is no different between them.

The control procedures of the Ragioneria and the Corte dei Conti take place, as we have already said, before the act of spending can be effected. Especially when a procedure is made up of many acts which have to be performed in strict chronological order, they can slow down the process of spending considerably.

General Remarks

Probably the criticism advanced most often against the process we have briefly described is that it is slow. The sum of money authorised by law, and even appropriated but not spent, is growing every year, while obviously the social needs which the expenditure is designed to satisfy become more and more pressing. Actually the complexity of procedures involved is only one of the factors which affect the timing of the spending process, although it is a very important one. For example, in the field of subsidised housing, the money allocated cannot be spent because there is no suitable area for building or because the money market is not able to provide the bulk of the funds to which the State's contribution will be attached (in fact in many instances the money allocated is needed for the payment of interest on loans). It is obvious that delays caused by these and similar factors could be minimised by accurate planning. However, even when this is carried out before the Bill is presented to parliament or before the appropriations are made, the length of the spending procedure makes it very difficult to match any forecast to reality.

A second point often raised by critics of the present situation is that it leaves the door open to a large amount of political 'clientism' and plain corruption. This would seem to contradict the remarks we have been making to the effect that the spending process is rather rigid and that there are influences on it at many different points. Actually the contradiction is only apparent. The complexity of procedures, and the general inability of the administrative machinery to cope effectively with this, have caused a giant backlog of work to accumulate. For the 'customers' of public expenditure, the only way to avoid extremely long delays is to try to get preferential treatment. This may involve getting a minor violation of the procedure prescribed by law, such as eliminating some parts of it, undertaking at the same time activities which according to the law should be carried out in chronological order,[1] or simply getting some cases dealt with before others which have been waiting for a longer time. There are many ways to obtain such results: one may simply bribe minor officials, or try to get a friend (or a friend of a friend) to take care of the case, or try to bring political pressure to bear on the official (by contacting a minister, a member of parliament or a powerful party official).

One can object that phenomena of this sort are part of the pathology of any bureaucratic system and do not merit mention in this brief *excursus*. Actually the systematic way in which they occur and their almost total institutionalisation in Italy mean that in the Italian public administration they constitute something that is physiological rather than pathological.

PUBLIC SPENDING IN ITALY: WHO DECIDES?

After describing the spending procedure, we can return to the original problem: who controls the expenditure? Even if we avoid the implicit ambiguity of the term 'control' by reformulating the question as 'who makes the decisions which are relevant to public spending?', we are still far from a satisfactory definition of the

[1] One should note that very often such 'violations' of the law are indispensable if that expenditure is to be carried out at all. It is not merely by chance that one of the most effective weapons which the Italian public administration has to support its own claims for better treatment consists of the so-called '*sciopero bianco*' (go-slow or literally white strike). This is a form of protest which consists of applying punctiliously and carefully standards which regulate a certain activity, and unfailingly provokes paralysis in that activity.

problem. In fact, control of expenditure can refer both to the method of determining how much of the public money should be spent and allocated among the various social categories, and to the methods of settling the timing of the expenditure. The first type of problem is of great importance, for on it depends the ability to influence the structures of society and to determine in which direction they will be able to develop. In recent years, however, the second problem has emerged more and more dramatically – at least in Italy – for on this depend the State's opportunities to control economic machinery and to intervene at the right time in order to avoid disequilibria. We shall tackle the two problems separately.

Decisions About the Amount to be Spent, its Objectives and the Social Categories which will Benefit

A large part of the national budget, consolidated in fixed expenditures or flowing from laws passed many years earlier, for practical purposes evades all control. This is well known and happens in practice in all countries so that it is not worth dwelling on here. The remaining part of the funds annually allocated by expenditure laws can be subdivided into two parts, one of which, the larger one, can be called 'planned expenditure', while the other and smaller can be called 'unplanned expenditure'.

Planned expenditure is allocated through government Bills, and by calling it 'planned' I do not mean that the department responsible for national planning plays a major decision-making role in it; there is simply an *opportunity* for forecasting and for rationalising allocations. Actually, as we have already seen, the process of drafting government legislation is a complex one in which many actors play a part. Probably the most important influence on the decisions we are discussing is exerted by the secretariats of the parties which make up the government coalition, although trade unions and other important pressure groups are also relevant in this regard. Therefore the traditional dichotomy of parliamentary control and government control over expenditure loses much of its importance; in the Italian régime there is a close link between parliament and government, and both depend considerably on the secretariats of the parties, so that disagreement between government and parliament on matters of policy is possible only when the governing coalition is very weak or when party discipline does not work.

As regards the role of the bureaucracy, one must distinguish between the officials of the spending ministries and those of the financial ministries. The former, whose role was important in the past, have lost much significance, except as regards laws of little political interest (for example those intended to alter some detail in the structure of public administration). Two hypotheses can be advanced to explain this. On the one hand it is possible that the role of civil servants is becoming less apparent because of their progressive politicisation, which makes it difficult to distinguish their position from that of the political organs. One can also put forward the hypothesis that the appearance of party 'experts', who are being employed more and more frequently, lessens the dependence of non-specialists on the bureaucrat's technical competence. But the situation is quite different with the officials of financial ministries and in particular of the Treasury. The importance of the Ragioneria Generale has not been affected; it remains an arbitrator among sectoral interests on increased spending, and also as a restraint on general tendencies toward expansion. There is a good reason why the *Ragioniere Generale* (State General Accountant), together with the Governor of the Central Bank, attends the most important meetings at cabinet level in which decisions on spending are made: doubtless he puts forward his own ideas and opinions at these meetings as well as those of his staff. Once again the reason for this can only be supposed. One might think that the considerable prestige enjoyed by officials of the Ragioneria would impress even the politicians. On the other hand, because of the detailed technical knowledge at their disposal, and in particular their knowledge of the workings and the structure of the budget (which, as has already been said in this chapter and in the other chapters of the section on Italy, is rigid and can be handled only by experts), they have become increasingly necessary as the total amount of public expenditure has increased.

We may then turn to the second part of expenditure: the 'unplanned expenditure'. This is undoubtedly of minor importance but must not be overlooked if one wants to get a complete picture of the Italian situation. The destination of these sums is decided directly by parliament, either by amendment to the government expenditure laws or by expenditure laws presented by its own members. There are scores of such 'micro-laws' and in practice the safeguard offered by Article 81 of the Constitution (which provides that no law involving expenditure can be passed which does not say where the money allocated is to come from) is very often not observed. These sums are allocated in a haphazard fashion, and there is no co-ordination or rational planning other than that exercised by the standing committee on the budget, which is not very consistent. Even the ever-present Ragioneria can do no more in this case than to take note of the legislation, and to dig around 'in the creases of the budget' for the money needed to meet the expenditure provided for. As we have already said, the total amount allocated in this way is rather small, so that its relevance for the problem of parliamentary control of expenditure is not very great.

Decisions Relevant to the Timing of Expenditure

Let us now turn to the second question, concerning who makes the decisions about when the appropriated sums will be spent, having thus a direct effect on the economic and social structure of the country. The conclusion that one would be tempted to draw is that in Italy no one controls expenditure in this sense. In fact the procedure which we have tried to describe makes it impossible to get a reliable forecast on when a sum of money which has been appropriated will in fact be spent. There are so many and such considerable influences on the timing of expenditure that the effect is almost completely random. Sums appropriated in the budget in one year can be spent in the course of that year, the next year, the next five years, or never.

However this pessimistic picture must be qualified in some way, for a certain limited amount of control seems to be possible. Among the institutions of the State capable of decisively influencing the timing of the expenditure procedure there is the Treasury and, in particular, its Ragioneria Generale. The latter can act in two different ways and at two decisive moments, one being the 'administrative phase' of the process of drafting the expenditure law and the other including in practice the whole of the spending procedure after a Bill is approved. Thus, it is the Ragioneria which decides in drafting the Bill whether the standard procedure will be adopted, (following the General Law on State Accounting; this provides for a series of decisions each having its own methods of control and its own formal requisites), or whether a different, more rapid procedure may be used which may omit preliminary controls and, for example, substitute for a set of decisions taken in succession by different bodies a single decision taken by a committee consisting of representatives of all the bodies concerned. A decision to abandon the traditional standard procedure has rarely been taken, but it does sometimes produce very good results, particularly in improving the timing of expenditure. Secondly, after the approval of the Bill, the Ragioneria, in its capacity as organ of preliminary control, can act on the actual spending procedures and, even though it cannot do much to speed them up, is in a position to slow them down almost as it pleases. Finally, there are other organs of the Treasury which are able, by means of their control of part of the money market, and of their capacity to issue payment orders, to act on some crucial point of process, speeding it up or, more often, slowing it down.

If there are opportunities to control the timing of State expenditure in Italy – and this is by no means certain – they belong without doubt to the Treasury. What is impossible to say, mainly because of the lack of relevant and systematic information, is whether and, if so, to what extent, the officials of this ministry, and in particular those of the Ragioneria, do make use of these opportunities. Obviously, it is even more difficult to say if these officials are executing their own policies or are being faithful servants of the minister of the Treasury and, through him, of the duly elected political representatives.

CONCLUSION

I have tried to give a somewhat simplified picture of the spending process of the Italian State, to give an idea of the main problems it raises and to propose some hypothetical explanations. In so doing I am perfectly aware that I have left out much which could be of great importance. Some of the things which are necessary to understand the situation and the problems related to public spending better are pointed out and explained in the other chapters which make up the section on Italy in this book. For others, it would be necessary to refer the interested reader to more detailed essays or books which unfortunately do not exist. Almost no research has been done on most of the topics we have touched upon, and, what is probably more important, no research is, as far as I know, being executed or planned.

In conclusion a warning may be necessary: some of the things which have been said here may strike a reader who has never had anything to do with the Italian spending process (or with Italian bureaucracy) as exaggerations. In fact, even if it has been necessary to write more on the negative aspects than on the positive ones, the total picture presented here is by no means exaggerated. If all is not well in the State of Italy, as the international news media in the last few years seem to indicate, then the complete incapacity of the Italian government to plan and execute a rational policy of spending has much to do with it.

CHAPTER 14

SPECIAL PROBLEMS OF BUDGETARY DECISION-MAKING IN ITALY

Sabino Cassese

THE WEAKNESSES OF PARLIAMENTARY CONTROL OF THE BUDGET

The prevailing opinion in Italy is that examination and approval of the budget by parliament is a pointless ritual. The ritual, both in committee and in plenary session, is carried out in rooms which are half deserted. It is no more than a general debate on the government's policy as a whole or on its policies for different sectors; few interventions by members of parliament refer to specific chapters of the budget, and those which do are made invariably by the same small group of members who are specialists in public finance. The debate is dominated by ministers, and those members of parliament who do intervene often get their additional information from the same government officials who advise ministers. The only material which is officially supplied to parliament by the government along with its estimates of revenue and expenditure is an 'introductory note' accompanying the general summary of the estimates, and 'introductory notes' accompanying the estimates themselves. Consequently there are few proposals for amendments and the formal limitations on parliament's power of amendment in this field mean that in any event these have to be agreed with the government before they can be introduced. Budgetary procedure has never given rise to a crisis of confidence since the Second World War, and in the history of Italy since Unification it has only once given rise to the resignation of a minister.

The causes of this weakness are complex. The first concerns the contents of the budget. In practice the budget simply registers decisions which have already been taken by parliament itself, usually in so-called *leggi di spesa* (expenditure laws), which indicate in more or less detail expenditure which is going to be undertaken over one or more years. Expenditure so indicated cannot be altered by the government, so that it has to be incorporated in the budgetary estimates for the year in which it is to be made. The only way by which parliament can alter them is by amending the *leggi di spesa* concerned, which it will not normally do. It cannot do so when voting on the budget. The inclusion of new expenditure in the budget is forbidden according to the usual interpretation of Article 81, Section III of the Constitution, which requires that expenditure be authorised only by *leggi sostanziali* (substantive laws). In recent years 88 per cent of total expenditure has arisen from decisions previous to the voting of the budget and has been included in the budget obligatorily. The inflexibility is greater in some cases than in others, as we shall see later when we consider the problem of the so-called *fondi globali*.

A second cause of the weakness is that large amounts of public expenditure are not shown in the budget at all. The most important omissions are the expenditure of certain public bodies which are financed autonomously (the regions, provinces and communes) and that of others which are in receipt of government subsidies (public utilities and public enterprises). Extra-budgetary expenditure is already as much as one-sixth of total public expenditure on capital account and almost one-half of total public expenditure on current account. If one adds to this the investment expenditure of public enterprises and of joint-stock companies in which the State has an interest, one can say that more than half of total public expenditure is excluded from the national budget.

A further cause of weakness is that a large number of budgetary provisions are simply not carried out. In recent years approximately 25 per cent of expenditure provided (most of it on capital account) has not been used during the years covered by the budget in question. The amount not spent by 1970 amounted to half of the total of expenditure provided for the financial year 1970 itself. In order to understand this one must realise that in Italy the national budget simply gives authorisation for the allocation of expenditure, and is only the first of four main stages preceding the actual payment out of public funds. Estimates of the final expenditure are made (following Article 5 of the Law of 9 December 1928), but are for internal use only.

From what has been said so far it can be seen that the Italian public administration, which is responsible for more financial activity in the country's economy than any other body (in 1969 expenditure by the State came to 27 per cent[1] of the national pro-

---

[1] According to G. Stammati, *Considerazioni Sulla Spesa Pubblica* (1971), p. 4. But it was as much as 34 per cent according to the UN figures quoted by Peter Else in Chapter 2, p. 32.

duct, compared with 15 per cent in 1910), does not produce a meaningful statement of its budget. Two aspects of this problem are worth emphasising. The first is economic, concerning the time it takes to implement expenditure and the relationship between the impact of expenditure on the economic situation and the result intended by political organs. In 1960 a study made by some sections of the Ragioneria Generale (general accounts office) showed that both general and sectoral interventions intended to deal with a crisis took place about three or four years after the first sign of the unfavourable economic trend which led to crisis in the first place. The study came to the conclusion that 'in effect such interventions are faced with a *fait accompli,* for, with the reversal of the curve of the economic cycle, a depression has already given way to a new period of expansion.'[1] Moreover one economist has observed that: 'the result is a paradox in that multi-annual programmes, sometimes justified as boosts to economic expansion, produce an initially deflationary effect, because, although by law bonds to finance the expenditure have to be floated, the administration is unwilling when the time comes to put the expenditure into effect.'[2] At other times the Ragioneria Generale determines short-term policy by postponing the collection of funds to finance expenditure because of the situation of the money market.

This brings us to the second important aspect of the problem, which is a political one concerning the real power of decision over public expenditure, and more generally over management of the economy as well. Representatives of most political parties have remarked that the failure to realise expenditure provided in the budget has invalidated many of the powers of parliament: 'Every year the Italian parliament is forced to approve a budget which is nothing more than a formal document.'

On the other hand there is a

Rude and insensitive bureaucratic power which manages to avoid complying with any provisions or measures (even extremely urgent ones) voted by parliament to deal with economic situations or unexpected events. Fundamental aspects of the country's life are determined by the Minister of the Treasury or by the General Accountant acting in agreement with the monetary authorities,

[1] *Gli Interventi Dello Stato Nell Economia: Tempi di attuazione di Algune Spese Pubbliche.* ed. cicl (1960).

[2] N. Andreatta, *Successo* (February 1971), p. 45.

who are continually trying to put into effect a policy which is concerned exclusively with the threat of inflation.[1]

Another study of these problems remarked in the same vein that:

Management of the residual balances enables complete evasion of political control by parliament, and gives the minister of the Treasury and the General Accountant the scope to exercise discretionary powers over the whole distribution of public expenditure, something which is absolutely unprecedented in any modern constitutional state.

The result of this is to make the budget 'merely an accounting fiction', which

misleads parliament and public opinion about the total amount and about the actual timing of public expenditure, both of which flow from choices which are not always wise, and are in any case divorced from any political judgement and made in an excessively arbitrary and discretionary manner by a few higher public officials, who are endowed with powers which they are not fitted to exercise.[2]

Finally, the General Accountant himself has recognised that:

When the minister of the Treasury is not required to make payments, the funds can be used for other purposes. For example, if it is a question of expenditure financed on the open market, the funds thus raised by the Treasury can be used partly or wholly to cover the deficit in the national budget, so that the Treasury can run up debts expressly for this purpose, as the budgetary law explicitly permits. Therefore, funds are not blocked but diverted.[3]

THE DECLINING IMPORTANCE OF PARLIAMENTARY CONTROL OF THE BUDGET

In Italy for various reasons ministerial control of the public administration is only indirect (meaning by this the traditional public administration organised as ministerial departments and subject to

[1] See the intervention by Sig. E. Peggio in the Chamber of Deputies' debate on the White Paper on public expenditure, reprinted in *Politica ed Economia* (June, 1971), pp. 17–18. Similar remarks were made by members of other parties.
[2] P. Armani Settante (August–September 1970), p. 10. *Nord e Sud* (December 1970), p. 104.
[3] G. Stammati, debate on public expenditure, in *Adesso* (1968), p. 45.

I

the laws governing public accountability and public employment). Although the traditional public administration is placed under the political direction of ministers and is obliged to act according to statutes passed by parliament, ministers have little to do with day-to-day decisions and are frequently changing, and the statutes rarely set clear objectives or go into the details of organisation. Moreover the personnel of the public administration are shielded from political influence by the ruling principles of administrative impartiality and neutrality, and by the nature of the laws governing public employment, which have been introduced after all under pressure from the same personnel. The personnel of the administration use the statutes governing public accountability in a ritualistic manner to lend weight to the technical aspects of administrative procedures and to the specialisation of administrative staff, and this has made the higher administration more or less autonomous with respect to politically appointed heads of departments.

This would have led to chaos if it had not been for a countervailing tendency. In practice one part of the public administration has tended to gain predominance and to assume the power of direction over the rest. This may be a tendency in all public administrations. An administrative organisation is neither monolithic nor static, so that, if it is left to function on its own, it tends to split up into many bodies with financial autonomy. Meanwhile the central direction tries to make uniform rules, but the other parts tend towards evasion and self-defence, resulting in widespread mistrust and suspicion, in delays to administrative action, in a maldistribution of funds, in inflationary demands by spending departments, and so on.

In Italy during the period of administrative growth the role of the Ragioneria Generale has been particularly important. This office has served as a co-ordinator and has assumed a general responsibility for control. The tendency of the laws prevailing since Cavour's Bill of 1852 has been to give the Ragioneria functions which are similar to those of the office of the President of the Council of Ministers. This is particularly true of the 1923 regulations providing for a single set of estimates.[1]

[1] One recent minister of the Treasury stated that the 1923 regulations went a long way to confirm that 'alongside the harmonisation and co-ordination provided by the Council of Ministers and its President at the political level, the minister responsible for controlling public expenditure performs parallel functions at the administrative level by means of the Ragioneria Generale . . .

. . What is at stake here is a delicate task of determining the economic and financial choices on which the budget itself is based.' E. Colombo in *Saggi in Onore della Ragioneria Generale dello Stato* (Rome, 1969), pp. 8, 10, and 14.

Significantly, in dealing with the bodies responsible for spending public funds, the Ragioneria has chosen to approach the rest of the administration from a concern with the expenditure of money (*il metode di spesa*). In a way it was inevitable that those with this concern should have prevailed over those concerned mainly with the fixing of goals or with planning, given the period (the third decade of this century) and given that the planners were powerless in their conflict with those who administered public funds. The latter (in practice, the Ragioneria) were also planners in so far as they were responsible for deciding how administrative action was to be financed. However, they could not assert this interest for fear of losing their own powers. Instead they had to find other excuses for planning, like the need to economise on public funds, the need for 'consistency' in public finance, and so on.

In fact the role of the Ragioneria Generale has important consequences for the powers of parliament in budgetary procedure. Not only does the Ragioneria draw up the draft budget for parliament's endorsement or approval; it also amplifies the budget by its decisions, although legally speaking it has no right to do this. This is why the budget cannot be regarded as a useful statement of economic policy or as a means of mobilising support for it. Indeed it would seem that parliament does not have real power over the budget as a whole, but only over certain aspects of it. Moreover it does not use its power deliberately to achieve positive results but defensively to protect an exclusive right. In this way parliament actually accepts the role of the Ragioneria Generale. Although sometimes it is jealous of the latter's authority as directing agency for the public administration, parliament in fact adopts the same method, that is, setting financial limits to administrative activity. The difference between the two bodies is that, while this is the only way the Ragioneria can play its role, for parliament it is no more than a poor substitute.

Control by parliament has two different effects: it makes the allocation of expenditure into different budgetary chapters less flexible, but at the same time it enables the administration to get approval for *fondi globali* (a kind of general or 'discretionary' fund voted as a sort of supplementary to the budget proper). First, then, it has a restrictive effect, because there are many budgetary chapters (about 3,000). Secondly, however, since 1949–60 parliament has allowed the insertion in the budget of *fondi globali*, which are a means of overcoming inflexibility in the allocation of expenditure. The *fondi globali* are agreed from time to time with the annual budget, and are not covered by any general legislation. They are the only important flexible component of the budget, and in 1970 accounted for 7 per cent of total estimated expenditure. Nevertheless parliament uses its authority over allocation of expenditure to fix an overall ceiling, and this has the negative effect of excluding policies which involve expenditure above the level provided. This restrictive use of power does limit the scope of later decisions.

However parliament's real influence is exercised not so much by means of the budget but rather by means of the *leggi di spesa*. It is in these expenditure laws that the basic choices are made. Since the 1950s the most important of the *leggi di spesa* have contained the State's plans for administrative sectors (that is, plans for the depressed areas of the central north, for school and university building, for the development of provincial highways, for *autostrade*, for the State railways and for the development of the telephone system) and for autonomous public bodies (that is, plans for La Cassa del Mezogiorno, for Calabria, for Sicily, for housing for farm-workers and others). This has not taken control of the budget out of parliament, but it has changed the nature of parliament's intervention, which is concerned increasingly with particular sectors. Thus the role of parliament and that of the Ragioneria are now tending to go in different directions. The first is subject increasingly to the influence of particular interests and is generally an 'advocate of expenditure'; the second tries to keep its central position as the overall controller of public finance, but in such a way as to seek to limit expenditure. However parliament's opportunity to have an aggregative influence through control of the budget is now thought to have gone, (although a new opportunity is seen in parliament's intervention in the procedure for national economic planning).

THE ROLE OF THE RAGIONERIA GENERALE

We shall now examine how the General Accounts Office is able to influence administrative activity in general by means of its budgetary powers. We are concerned with the Ragioneria's function with respect both to expenditure formally entered in the estimates of other ministries and to that entered in the Treasury's own accounts (which make up a good third of total expenditure).[1]

Before a *legge di spesa* is prepared, provisional estimates are drawn up by the relevant sections of the ministries concerned on the basis of their various requirements. These provisional estimates are

[1] The Treasury's accounts cover the *fondi globali*, expenditure on parliamentary services and on the Constitutional Court and other general or constitutional bodies.

submitted to the Ragioneria Generale through *ragionerie centrali* in the individual ministries themselves. The minister of the Budget's agreement is required if estimated expenditure amounts to more than 1,000 million lire or extends over more than one year. Otherwise the Bill can be presented by the Treasury and the department concerned without the need to obtain the approval of the minister of the Budget. Moreover the provisional estimates on which *leggi di spesa* are based are not usually detailed where the fixing of objectives or the timing of expenditure are concerned.

As the first step in the preparation of the budget itself an indication of the general lines of budgetary provisions is drawn up by the Comitato Interministeriale per la Programmazione Economica (CIPE) on the basis of a report by the minister of the Treasury. The real work begins when the Ragioneria Generale sends a draft text showing the appropriations for previous years to the *ragionerie centrali*; their ministries then hold discussions, after which the draft budget goes to the minister concerned. Since 1957 the minister has also consulted the ministry's *consiglio di amministrazione*, a board consisting of senior officials in the department and exercising responsibilities in the field of personnel administration, discipline and so on. All proposals are then sent to the Ragioneria Generale, which makes a general review and takes up again with the spending departments those requests which it considers 'inconsistent'. After agreement with the Minister of the Budget the draft budget is discussed in the Council of Ministers and presented to parliament.

After parliamentary approval there is a still more complex procedure. Surprisingly enough at this point there is a new examination of the needs on which proposals for expenditure are based. Ministers, either singly or collectively, take action following this reappraisal. If a programme for public works is involved, there are several stages: drawing up a project; drawing up a contract; and carrying out the project. The Ragioneria and Corte dei Conti intervene at each stage. Even from this superficial account we can notice some general procedural characteristics of the budget. First the Ragioneria is ever present and is the only body which can have a general idea of the available resources and of the demands on them. It intervenes in every phase both of preparation and of execution. Secondly, the assessment of resources *precedes* the choice of policies, not only when the budget is being formulated but also in the later phase. This is an important point, because it reveals that the 'normal' procedure whereby resources are allocated in relation to objectives (and, therefore, are allocated after the determination of objectives) is reversed. If expenditure is decided before an analysis of administrative functions is made, policy becomes a function of the amount of money available.

In the preparation of the budget (which is less interesting, because it ends with a document which is widely ignored), the Ragioneria decides what happens because it holds the purse-strings. If a department asks for a hundred and the Ragioneria gives only ten, it means not just a change in the size of the programme but a change in the programme itself. The examination of the draft budget in the Council of Ministers is notoriously rapid and summary.[1] We have already dealt with the parliamentary examination. Here the authorisation which is given in the budget does not give the spending ministers a free hand; it is still the Ragioneria which determines what procedure is followed after the budget is passed.

According to some people there is in fact a sort of 'blocking' of funds. Two recent episodes have confirmed that the process of distributing expenditure is anything but mechanical and is dominated by the political ideas of the Ragioneria. The Treasury Ministry has now insisted that the *ragionerie centrali* should report to individual ministers every two months on the progress of their department's expenditure, so that 'they [ministers] can see how necessary it is to show imagination in making major political decisions . . . and in spending funds assigned to individual budgets.'[2] One minister threatened to resign when it was complained that La Gestione per le Case dei Lavoratori (the agency responsible for providing houses for workers) which fell under his jurisdiction could have spent the very considerable funds available to it more quickly.

In contrast some maintain that delays in distributing expenditure are purely technical in origin. Some people blame the procedures for audit, others the budgetary procedure itself. The procedure for audit is said to be too slow and to render administration 'unable to spend'. Some have called for a reform of the regulations governing audit and accountability. Others place the emphasis on the need for reform of procedures for contracts, subsidies, expropriations, and so on. However, these criticisms and the general ideas which inspire them reflect that mechanistic outlook which considers only legal and technical aspects. In fact the ideology of the mechanistic *apparat* has its widest impact on the field of expenditure, aided as it is there by the technicality of the procedures for budgeting and accounting.

[1] See the intervention in the debate in the Chamber of Deputies on 11 December 1969, no. 230, p. 13794.

[2] Sig. M. Ferrari Aggradi, in *Il Globo*, 13 August 1971.

Neither the problem of diffusion and multiplicity of decision-making centres on the one hand nor that of the slowness of procedure on the other can be understood only in terms of legal and technical aspects. The first problem arises partly from features of the political system, like institutional pluralism or inter-organisational conflict, and partly from traditional institutional aspects, like the tendency to 'duplicate' departments in face of the persistence of existing ones. The second problem arises partly from the high turnover of political compared with administrative personnel, partly from the protests which the officials controlling expenditure make when their function is given to other parts of the administration, and partly from the centrifugal effects of setting up autonomous public bodies. In addition to this there is the influence of the 'clientele'. One need only compare the speed of decisions which have as their destination the big economic public corporations with the slowness of other expenditure.

We have already said that the General Accounts Office seems to be a bureaucracy concerned primarily with upholding an unwritten rule that the budget should balance. The description of its role in legislation and in parliamentary debates leaves no room for ambiguity, Phrases recur such as: 'to contain public expenditure within proper limits'; 'to regulate and contain expenditure'; 'to ensure economy in expenditure'; 'to reduce or avoid any burden on the budget', and so on.

The predominance of the Ragioneria's attitude has meant that political leadership was in line with administrative activity only when policy-makers were obsessed with the problems presented by the budget deficit. However the prevailing financial ideology has later got out of step with political leadership, and the policy of the officials responsible for expenditure has diverged from the attitude of the political leadership, which is now more favourable towards expenditure and towards legislative innovation. The bridling effect of the bureaucracy has now become apparent, or what some people call its 'sabotage'.

The belief in financial orthodoxy, which has been supported in Italy by officials responsible for expenditure and by wide sectors of public opinion, led to successful opposition to the Keynesian revolution, mainly because the doctrine of expansion was not held as widely or strongly in Italy as it was elsewhere. One should also add, however, that this doctrine has encountered almost insurmountable difficulties outside Italy as well. Unsuccessful attempts have been made in France (with Leon Blum in 1936, and in 1945–7 with a separate Ministry of Economic Affairs which was then slowly integrated into the Ministry of Finance) and in Britain (with the creation in 1964 of a Department of Economic Affairs, which had a crisis in 1967 and was disbanded in 1969, with the transference of its tasks to the Treasury) to create a super-ministry of the economy designed to promote development and play the role of 'advocate' of expansion and growth against the Ministry of Finance, concerned with short-term economic policy and managing the deficit (occasionally favouring development, it is true, but with the accent more on stability). The two experiences mentioned have numerous characteristics in common. They were attempts by socialist forces; they aimed at giving the accountants of the State the same position that accountants occupy in firms; they were put into effect by new personnel on contract, rather than by the bureaucrats of the Treasury; and they were attempts to introduce into the management of the economy a 'creative tension' between the economic and finance ministries.

In Italy a different road has been followed. The doctrine of expansion is not popular and leadership of the rest of the public administration remains firmly in the grasp of the machinery for controlling expenditure. The subject of national economic planning has been raised in a way which stresses the need for equilibrium. Attempts at national economic planning carried out from the 1930s onwards have all been incomplete for one reason or another.

In the discussion which takes place between the Ragioneria and other departments there seems no doubt that, in contrast to what seems to happen in the Fifth Republic, the spending ministries and parliament behave as 'advocates' of expenditure, as a result mainly of pressure by both organised and diffused interests. In its relations with the other ministries, however, the Ragioneria does not behave altogether inflexibly. It leaves them scope for action and acts as a marginally limiting factor. In this sense we must qualify what was said earlier about the Ragioneria controlling the administration.

On the other hand, this is the only kind of control which would be compatible with the existence of a number of different administrative organisations, all more or less autonomous, and all of which, if they were supervised inflexibly, would revolt at the pressures coming from the one centre for control of expenditure. To show relative flexibility is, therefore, the only way of keeping fundamental decisions on policy in the hands of the privileged members of an oligarchy. Furthermore it is the only way of coping with the amount of pressure from a diversified 'clientele' (the 'administered', interested in expenditure) whose pressure is by this means divided. For the clientele tend to exert influence on spending ministries for decisions of little importance, and the Ragioneria for decisions of great importance. If the Ragioneria were less flexible the pressure unleashed on it would be insupportable.

Some groups have privileged access to centres of decision-making in the public administration, while others prefer to bring influence to bear on particular centres. The pressure is applied in different places according to the requirements of the case. On a more general level however there is a sort of harmony between the Ragioneria's activity and that of large financial groups. It has been noted several times that the containment of expenditure favours large financial groups who have a free hand on the financial market. However, to analyse a problem like this a level of research would be needed which cannot be attempted here.

THE PROBLEM OF SEMI-AUTONOMOUS PUBLIC BODIES

The observations made up to now concern the traditional administration consisting of ministerial departments. We have noted several times that there is an important amount of expenditure in Italy which in varying degrees evades the State budget. This is the expenditure of public bodies which are autonomous of the central administration to a greater or lesser extent. Some have full political autonomy and separate finance; others have managerial autonomy but are subsidised; others are really organised as commercial enterprises.

The historical motive for this centrifugal tendency was probably dislike of the existing regulations on public accountability, to which these organisations were supposed to be subject. Although the Ragioneria succeeded in gaining predominance over ministerial departments, it seems to have realised that the new forms of administration (especially the economic ones) have evaded it and it either exerts no control or only a control of minor importance over them.

The variety of centres of expenditure which fall outside the budget and outside ministerial departments makes it difficult to provide a comprehensive analysis. (Some have recourse either mainly to the market, or mainly to the Treasury, and the relative proportion of public financing varies from time to time.) However, one should stress that, although many of these autonomous organisations have their own sources of finance in addition to the funds received from the State, in recent times they have begun to operate in fields which used to be the preserve of the ministerial departments.

CONCLUSIONS: RECENT PROPOSALS FOR REFORM

From this examination it seems that the expenditure process in Italy is not specialised; there is no division of labour, only of sectors; and the machinery of the Ragioneria predominates. The process is partly iterative: but the decisions are taken to a large extent incrementally and there is one organisation which dominates the whole process. There is some planning but only by the authority responsible essentially for supervising public expenditure.

The main decision-makers in the field of public expenditure have different fields of responsibility, in the sense that some make decisions on some expenditure, and others on other expenditure. The one exception to this rule is the domination of certain departments by the Ragioneria Generale. However, all the centres of control (Ragioneria, Corte dei Conti) try to gain access to the same paraphernalia of control instruments, in the hope of being able to fight with weapons which match those of their counterparts. On the whole the picture which one gains from the analysis carried out is that of a budget which belies the interventionist principles of most modern public expenditure. Most reform proposals seek to restore its lost influence, but they go about it in different ways.

There are those who suggest giving greater power to parliament, particularly by the introduction of what is known as a *bilancio di cassa* (a budget to approve only cash transactions). In that case parliament would take decisions about actions which were actually carried out and the executive would be forced to indicate only those sums which it intended to spend and indeed would spend.

There are those who propose tying the budget more tightly to the five-year plan. Already the law of 1967 on the organisation of the Ministry of the Budget and of Economic Planning goes some way towards this. First, the prior agreement of the minister is required for bills (*leggi di spesa*) involving more than 1,000 million lire expenditure or involving expenditure spread over several years (as we have remarked above). Secondly there has to be a decision by the Comitato Interministeriale della Programmazione Economica (CIPE) on the general lines of the departments' plans for inclusion in the budget. Thirdly the minister of the Budget and the minister of the Treasury are required to collaborate in drawing up the general lines of budget estimates, and must agree on the presentation of those estimates to parliament. This is not enough for many people. There is still the problem of formulating policies and it is necessary to emphasise the need for indications of 'end-projects' and 'objectives'. In this respect there have been proposals for introducing budgetary programming techniques and for rationalising budgetary choices.

Finally there is one set of proposals which favours the strengthening of the powers of the Ragioneria, although these find less support. The main idea here is to extend the Ragioneria's control to cover autonomous public bodies. All these proposals meet special difficulty because their realisation would involve important changes in the way the machinery of administration is managed in Italy. Our main conclusion here is that the main obstacle to radical change continues to be the important role of the Ragioneria Generale, which is in turn closely related to general features of the Italian political process.

CHAPTER 15

PARLIAMENT AND THE BUDGET: PROCEDURES AND POLITICS IN THE NETHERLANDS

Hans Daalder and Sonja Hubée-Boonzaaijer

INTRODUCTION

The development of parliamentary control of the budget in the Netherlands presents, at first sight, a curious paradox. On the one hand, there is a tendency for an extension of parliamentary control: from the days when an independent parliament was first established in 1814, its powers over estimates and expenditures have expanded and become increasingly precise. But on the other hand, parliament's role in the actual making of budgetary decisions has lost in lustre. As political parties have forged new links between the Cabinet and the parliament, as the development of the social service State has broken down the barriers between State and society, as in a cumulative and reciprocal process bureaucratic agencies and a host of special interest groups have proliferated, parliament seems to have lost its one-time image as the Great Inquest of the Nation. From its lofty pose as the Protector of the National Interest – judiciously seeking to strike a balance between the need for government expenditures on the one hand and the duty to guard the taxpayers' interest on the other – parliament seems to have become only one among many competing institutions and interests. Or more precisely, parliament seems to have become an arena for other actors rather than an independent source of effective political power. Although members of parliament have obtained increased legal powers to determine budgetary policy, they have felt less influential and effective. In a Leiden University survey held in 1968, members of the Dutch Lower House were asked to assess their degree of influence over various types of government activity. Only a relatively small minority (19·9 per cent) felt that they had too little influence on legislation. More than half the members (55·3 per cent) thought their influence on government administration too small. But a very much larger percentage (74·5 per cent including a clear majority of the members of the government parties) felt that they had too little influence on government expenditure.[1]

The contrast between increased formal powers and a sense of frustration about actual influence determines the contents of this paper. In Section I we trace the development of legal parliamentary control in the nineteenth and twentieth centuries. In Section II we give a short description of the way the budget is presented to parliament, and of the manner in which both Houses organise the budgetary debates. And in Section III we seek to analyse the role of parliament in the complex politics of the budgetary process.

I   THE DEVELOPMENT OF PARLIAMENT CONTROL IN THE NINETEENTH AND TWENTIETH CENTURIES

The power of the purse played an important role in the development of responsible parliamentary government in the Netherlands.[2] Table 15.1 seeks to compress the main constitutional changes which have occurred since 1814 when a national parliament was first established as part of an independent, centralised kingdom. From this table, one may draw the following conclusions about the development of parliamentary control.

1   Since 1814 the Principle that All Government Expenditure Needs the Prior Authorisation of Parliament has been Greatly Extended

The framers of the 1814 Constitution had orginally wanted to consolidate all normal, peacetime expenditure in one budget which parliament would grant once and for all. The chief motive for this proposal was the desire to ensure that the central government should not be dependent on the whims of the individual provinces, as the weak central governing institutions had been in the days of

---

[1] See H. Daalder and S. Hubée-Boonzaaijer, *Kamers en Kamerleden-enige resultaten van een mondelinge enquete onder de leden der Staten-Generaal gehouden in 1968* (Department of Political Science, Leiden University, 1971), pp. 18–19 and Table 20.

[2] For general analyses see for instance R. Kranengurg, *Het Nederlands Staatsrecht*, 8th ed. (Haarlem, Tjeenk Willink, 1958); P. J. Oud, *Het Constitutioneel Recht van het Koninkrijk der Nederlanden*, 2nd ed., 2 vols. (Zwolle, Tjeenk Willink, 1967—70); C. W. van der Pot and A. M. Donner, *Handboek van het Nederlandse Staatsrecht*, 9th ed. (Zwolle, Tjeenk Willink, 1972). See in addition in English, E. van Raalte, *The Parliament of the Kingdom of The Netherlands* (Parlement, Den Haag, Staatsuitgeverij, is now in its fifth edition) and Hans Daalder, 'The Netherlands: Opposition in a Segmented Society', in Robert A. Dahl (ed.), *Political Oppositions in Western Democracies* (New Haven, Yale University Press, 1966), pp. 188–236.

Table 15.1 *The Development of Parliamentary Control over the Budget Since 1814*

	1814	1815	1840	1848	1888	1917 and after
A. The development of political institutions						
1 The composition of parliament	Unicameral (Lower House: 55 members	Bicameral + 55 members from Belgium 1815–30)	Bicameral	Bicameral (Lower House: 68–82 members)	Bicameral (Lower House: 100 members)	Bicameral (Lower House: until 1956—100 members; since 1956—150 members)
2 Electoral system — Upper House		Nominated by King for life		Indirectly elected by provincial legislatures; until 1917 from richest citizens or occupants of particular high offices		
Lower House		Indirectly elected by provincial legislatures		Directly elected in districts with 1–3 members (single-member districts since 1896)		Directly elected by nationwide proportional representation after 1917
3 Suffrage requirements		System of indirect elections only		±11% of adult males over 23	1888: 26% 1896: 49% 1910: 63% of adult males over 23–25	Universal suffrage for men: 1917 for women: 1919

4	Development of ministerial responsibility	Ministers responsible to King only	First case of individual ministerial resignations after adverse parliamentary vote 1839; constitutional revision of 1840 introduces criminal responsibility of ministers for unlawful Acts of the Crown	Full ministerial responsibility to both houses established since 1848; last attempt to keep cabinet in office against the will of a Lower House majority failed in constitutional conflicts of the period 1866—8.
5	Development of general legislative powers:			
	Legislative initiative	Crown and Lower House, for budget Crown only	*idem*	*idem*
	Legislative amendment	Absent	Absent	Lower House only

Table 15.1—continued

	1814	1815	1840	1848	1888	1917 and after
Prerogative powers acts	Considerable use; reinforced by enabling				Narrowly circumscribed in court case of 1879 regulations laying penalties should invariably rest on constitutional or other explicit legal authority	Considerable increase of delegated legislation
B. The development of budgetary powers						
1 General	Parliament can only accept or reject total budget		Parliament can accept or reject individual departmental budgets	Lower House can amend budget; budget divided in individual departmental budgets which are sub-divided in separate votes		
2 Estimates	Ordinary peacetime estimates to be approved as a con-solidated grant once for all; years; extra-	Ordinary estimates to be voted as a con-solidated grant every ten years; extra-	Total budget to be voted every two years	Annual budgets		1922: constitutional revision allows bi-annual budgets; but annual budgets maintained in Accounting Act (1927)

3 Expenditures	extraordinary wartime estimates to be voted every year	ordinary estimates every year	Little control over income; general reports on government expenditures sent to parliament for information only	1841: annual reports on expenditure to be drawn up by Chamber of Accounts, and to be sent to parliament	Detailed accounts, covering all income and expenditures, to be drawn up annually chapter by chapter by the ministers concerned and to be approved by General Auditing Court; closing of accounts by Act of Parliament required from 1848–87, but only officially introduced in Accounts, and Accounting Act of 1927
4 Approximate share of government expenditures as a % of net national income	1815: 7·7%			1864: 9·3% 1890: 11·1% 1910: 8·5%	1930: 13·1% 1950: 28·5% 1960: 24·3% 1970: 28·5%

the old Dutch Confederacy before 1795. Only extraordinary expenditures, in particular those related to defence, would need annual parliamentary approval. This attempt to deprive parliament of any real control over normal government expenditure was abandoned in 1815 at the insistence of Belgian politicians who had known effective budgetary rights in their own provincial assemblies and who did not wish to see such rights get lost in the new kingdom of which the Vienna Congress made them a part. It was then decided to include all ordinary expenditure in one consolidated budget which would need parliamentary consent every ten years, while extraordinary expenditure would require annual approval.

The new system came under increasing political strain when Dutch government finances fell into a complete disarray as a result of the conflict over the Belgian secession after 1830. In 1839, the Lower House refused to pass the decennial budget, as it objected to a proposal to mortgage future colonial surpluses as a guarantee for a new government loan. The two directly responsible ministers of finance and the colonies resigned, the first instance of effective ministerial responsibility in the Netherlands.

These conflicts led to a constitutional revision in 1840. Under this revision, the split budget was replaced by a bi-annual budget in which there was no longer any distinction between ordinary and extraordinary expenditure. Separate votes were introduced for each departmental budget. As an outward token of the personal responsibility of ministers for unlawful acts of the Crown, ministers would henceforth countersign all public royal acts. The King's objection to such constitutional reform was one reason for his abdication in 1840. Parliament began to take a more detailed interest in all aspects of government finance. But really effective changes came about only in the more drastic constitutional revision of 1848. This introduced a directly elected Lower House; full recognition of the principle of ministerial responsibility; the right of the Lower House to amend legislation, including the budget which was to contain separate votes for each subsection of a department; and a large number of other democratic rights.

The principle of full parliamentary control was thus firmly recognised. Occasionally, there were still somewhat acrimonious debates on the propriety of defeating budgetary proposals for reasons which lay outside the realm of purely financial considerations. But successive parliaments increasingly used their new budgetary powers to reinforce their control over general government policy, and to consolidate the principles of individual and collective ministerial responsibility. A simple count reveals that between 1848 and 1888 parliament forced four cabinets out of office when their financial proposals did not meet with its approval. In addition, four ministers for the colonies, three ministers of foreign affairs, three ministers of finance, three ministers for the navy and two ministers of war were individually ousted from office either by the Upper House (three times), or the Lower House (twelve times).[1] In many cases, parliament rejected entire departmental budgets (the last instance occurring in 1919).

Such hard tactics tended to fall into disuse after 1888, however, when the development of political parties forged new links of trust between the Cabinet and a majority in parliament. From occasions for an ultimate showdown between the executive and the legislature, budgetary debates tended to develop more into opportunities for members of parliament to vent general views on policy or to air special wishes and individual grievances. For such a purpose the introduction of motions seemed a more appropriate weapon than the refusal or amendment of budgetary proposals. The secure establishment of the principle of prior parliamentary authorisation did not therefore in practice prevent a situation of executive dominance in budgetary policy.

2 *Parliamentary Control Over Government Income and Actual Expenditure Increased Parallel to its Growing Role in the Authorisation of the Estimates*

Under the 1814 Constitution the only body enquiring into government income and expenditures was the resurrected General Auditing Court, a venerable body which can trace its origin to the fifteenth century.[2] The King was to submit a general report on government expenditure to parliament for information only, but for years such reports were presented only irregularly. In practice, special enabling acts, independent borrowing powers, uncontrolled colonial profits, and massive private exploits allowed the activist King William I (1813–40) to escape a close scrutiny of government finances. On this point, the 1840 constitutional revision sought to tighten control, as it did on the estimates. It made annual reports on government expenditures obligatory. In 1841 a new Act of Parliament greatly increased the investigatory powers of the Auditing Court. In 1848 a new clause in the Constitution required the draw-

[1] Calculated from the list of Dutch cabinets published annually in *Parlement en Kiezer*, Den Haag, Nijhoff.
[2] See A. N. Biswas, 'Audit and Control of Efficiency in the Netherlands', *Public Administration*, 17 (1959), pp. 361–5.

ing up of annual accounts by this chamber, and the closing of the accounts by Act of Parliament. This requirement was not implemented, and the article was left out of the Constitution in 1887. But the reports of the chamber became much more detailed, so that parliament was more fully informed on all aspects of government income and expenditure. The Accounting Act of 1927 compelled ministers to draw up the accounts of their department chapter by chapter, and to seek approval from the Auditing Court. Henceforth, the accounts were to be closed by Act of Parliament. The Auditing Court could inquire under this act into both the legality and the relative efficiency of particular items of expenditure (although it was poorly staffed for the latter purpose). In 1923 the Lower House established a Standing Committee on National Expenditure which was to report to the whole House on all matters raised by the Auditing Court and in general to watch over matters of government spending.

3 *The Closer Control by Parliament Contributed to a Formal Strengthening of the Position of the Minister of Finance in Relation to Other Ministers*

For a long time, a strong tradition of individual ministerial autonomy had made each minister practically the undisputed master of his own budget, and to this day every minister remains responsible for his own budget and expenditure both to parliament and the Chamber of Accounts. But when individual ministers were inclined to accede too easily to parliamentary demands for increased government expenditure in their own particular sphere, a cabinet decision laid down emphatically in 1919:

(*a*) All drafts of bills and of other proposals which ministers intend to circulate to the Cabinet must first be sent to the Minister of Finance.

(*b*) In written or oral contacts with parliament, no commitments may be entered into which could lead to an increase in government expenditure, unless prior approval has been obtained from the Minister of Finance or the Cabinet.

(*c*) No changes which could result in increased expenditure may be made in a proposed bill, or amendments accepted on the floor of parliament, unless the Minister of Finance or the Cabinet has first approved.

(*d*) Measures or regulations which might have considerable financial effects may not be undertaken, even if the necessary funds have been included in the budget, unless prior approval is obtained from the Minister of Finance, or if this minister objects, from the Cabinet.

The special position of the Minister of Finance was further formalised in the Accounting Act of 1927, under which he was empowered to prescribe instructions on the manner in which ministers should draw up their estimates. The government budget is presented as one whole to parliament by the Minister of Finance immediately upon the opening of the new parliamentary year; and even after a ministerial budget has obtained parliamentary approval, the Minister of Finance must grant prior authorisation for actual expenditure.[1]

4 *Parliament Has Obtained Increasingly Detailed Documentation of All Aspects of Government Finance*

Since 1906, the traditional budget speech of the Minister of Finance has been replaced by an elaborate written memorandum, the so-called *Miljoenen-nota* which surveys the entire field of government finance. Originally, the estimates were divided along two lines only: the organisational units to which funds were appropriated, and a division of expenditure into 'current expenditure' (which according to older theories of public finance might only be financed from taxes and other sources of direct government income), and 'capital expenditure' (which might be financed from government loans). In the course of time, new classifications were added. A special coding system now allows the regrouping of government expenditure in a number of fields of policy (irrespective of the organisational unit in charge). Newer insights into the relation between budgetary policy and the national economy have led to a differentiation of government income and expenditure into consumption expenditure, income transfers, investment expenditure and capital transfers. On no less than five occasions, parliament receives detailed information on the implementation of its budgetary decisions: on the execution of a budget for the year t, it obtains memoranda (a) in the spring of the year t, (b) in the fall of the year t when the budget is presented for the year $t+1$, (c) in the spring of the year $t+1$, (d) in the fall of the year $t+1$ when the budget is presented for the year $t+2$, and finally in the course of the year $t+2$ when the actual accounts over

---

[1] A new Accounting Bill (passed by the Lower House in 1970, but defeated by the Upper House—below, p. 279) would have legalised the growing practice by which the Minister of Finance instead reserves decisions on actual expenditures from particular appropriations, leaving other ministers free to spend moneys which he did not so indicate.

the year *t* are submitted to parliament for approval. Information is also offered on the overflow of expenditure across fiscal years, and departments are required to spell out future commitments which may be expected to arise from decisions taken in a given year. Since 1970, the budget memorandum also contains three-year forward estimates calculated on the basis of existing policies, while the Central Planning Bureau provides aggregate estimates on the levels of government expenditure expected for a period up to five years ahead. Parliament has become increasingly restless over the divergence between budgetary figures and actual expenditure which necessitates supplementary estimates.[1] All in all, parliamentary concern has therefore led to tighter forms of financial management and reporting by the executive – practices which are a condition for as well as the result of parliamentary control.[2]

5 Political Pressures in Parliament Have Contributed to Further Reforms in the Overall Organisation of Financial Control.

The government established in 1956 what was known as the Simons Committee to enquire into the need for an overhaul of the Accounting Act of 1927. Following the report of this Committee (1960),[3] the government introduced a new Accounting Bill in 1964 which envisaged a number of further reforms.[4] The more important of these are:

(*a*) The introduction of a system of cash budgets, accompanied by estimates of longer-term commitments which the government expects to enter into during the coming budgetary year; this reform

---

[1] Between 1960 and 1970 supplementary estimates amounted to the following percentages of the budgets initially introduced: 1960: 8·9 per cent, 1961: 16·7 per cent, 1962: 6·3 per cent, 1963: 7·7 per cent, 1966: 12·2 per cent, 1965: 15·3 per cent, 1966: 8·8 per cent, 1967: 5·0 per cent, 1968: 8·9 per cent, 1969: 5·4 per cent, 1970: 5·2 per cent. See *Witte Stukken* (*Comptabiliteitswet*), no. 7760, no. 6 (11 September 1968), p. 5 (the term *Witte Stukken* refers to the Dutch equivalent of the British Parliamentary Papers); for later years data provided by the Ministerie van Financien in a letter to the authors dated 5 January 1973.

[2] When it became known in the summer of 1971 that the deficit on the current budget might become much greater than more optimistic forecasts had led politicians to expect at the time of the national elections in the spring of the same year, the Dutch Lower House charged its Committee on National Expenditures to inquire into existing methods of controlling, reporting and forecasting expenditures. See the reports of this Vondeling-Committee in *Witte Stukken*, session 1971–2, nos 11515 and 11862.

[3] See the *Rapport van de Commissie tot Voorbereeiding van een Herziening van de Comptabiliteitswet* (Den Haag, Staatsuitgeverij, 1960).

[4] *Witte Stukken* (*Comptabiliteitswet*), no. 7760.

is to simplify financial management, to expedite the closing of the accounts for each year and to cut the number of supplementary estimates.

(b) A regulation of the degree of freedom which ministers enjoy in transferring surpluses from one estimate to another within their ministerial budget. Ministers did not have this authority except from a special reserve contained in each departmental budget. To increase flexibility, the government had proposed in the new bill to grant ministers the liberty to transfer sums from a large number of estimates to other ones provided such transfers would not exceed 10 per cent of the estimates concerned. When this proposal was debated in parliament, the Lower House successfully insisted on a limitation of such discretionary transfers to 5 per cent of an approved estimate only.

(c) Abolition of the practice by which unspent surpluses from any budgetary year on assigned estimates could be spent freely in the next financial year. Under the new Bill, the minister would still have the power to authorise such transfers. But these were tied to a maximum, and in all cases parliament must be notified as before of the amounts so handled.

(d) Increased control over the government's financial actions under ordinary civil law such as capital loans, the establishment of private companies etc.

(e) An extension of the power of the General Auditing Court; its powers to initiate investigations into the degree of overall efficiency of government operations were increased and the court was given the discretion to suggest any reforms to parliament which it might deem useful.

This new Accounting Bill met with a favourable reaction in the Lower House in 1970. But it was defeated in the Upper House on 11 January 1972 for constitutional reasons. The new Bill contained a clause under which the government would be free to spend up to 50 per cent of any estimate (old or new) as soon as it had obtained approval by the Lower House. This went beyond existing law which allows ministers to spend up to one-third of last year's estimates in case parliament has not passed the budget before the fiscal year begins. The Upper House considered a blanket authorisation to spend moneys on new items which it had not previously debated to be an unacceptable breach of its constitutional right to pass the budget. A new Bill will probably be introduced which will leave out this particular clause, while maintaining most other reforms.

1 *The Presentation of the Estimates*

All budgetary proposals are submitted first to the Lower House. The annual budget is introduced on the same day as the opening of parliament on the third Tuesday of September, and is accompanied by the *Miljoenen-nota*. The budget is divided into eighteen separate chapters: the civil list, the chief organs of State (such as parliament, the Council of State and the Auditing Court, the department of the prime minister), the other departments, Surinam and the Antilles, the national debt and a general reserve. In addition parliament has to approve separate estimates for a number of independent government funds and State enterprises (notably the Civil Service Pension Fund, the Road Fund, the Agricultural Equalisation Fund, the funds for the provinces and the municipalities, the Government Printing Office, the Post Office, the Government Mint, the Fishery Harbours Authority and the Ordnance Factory). Parliament does not vote on most social security funds as these are administered under special arrangements in which interested parties often have direct representation.

A normal budget contains as many as 2,000 separate votes. Funds are appropriated according to the organisational units which have executive authority to spend them.

The budgetary debates are always inaugurated by a general debate on government policy in which the party leaders review the general political situation and the various party financial specialists discuss the general financial outlook in the presence of the full Cabinet. Following this, the departmental budgets and the special funds are debated in the presence of the responsible minister and under-secretaries. Members of the Lower House can spell out their budgetary views in two ways: they can introduce specific amendments, or they can introduce motions. The Lower House has the right to increase and to lower estimates. But when the Lower House increases an estimate by amendment, the minister need not actually spend such appropriations. Similarly, motions may insist on the need for future increases in particular estimates, or demand policy changes. But ministers are not compelled to honour such motions, as long as they retain the general confidence of the House. All budgetary proposals approved by the Lower House are sent to the Upper House which can only pass or reject them.

Within this formal framework two major procedural bottlenecks have occurred: the massive complexity of the budget has forced great changes in the committee structure of the Lower House but even so it has proved difficult to pass the budget through both Houses before the new fiscal year begins on 1 January.

2 The Reforms of the Committee System

Dutch parliamentary traditions were for long opposed to the establishment of special committees. Until 1950 budget Bills (as other Bills) were discussed simultaneously in five sections in which the membership of the chamber was distributed by lot. These sections deliberated in private. Each section appointed a *rapporteur* for a particular Bill. The five *rapporteurs* then met to consolidate all queries and observations in one published report. This was sent to the minister, who would subsequently reply by a public countermemorandum. Only when the sections were satisfied that the debate was sufficiently prepared by such written exchanges would bills be taken up in the plenary session of the Lower House.

This system was rationalised somewhat in 1909. The chamber then decided first to appoint five specialist members for each budget chapter who would prepare the discussions in the sections and act as their *rapporteurs*. But in practice this procedure became an empty shell. More and more, party specialists came to prepare their party's observations in writing and their reports would be included in the final report of the sections without much further discussion. Mounting pressure of business and the desire to bring specialist knowledge to bear more directly on individual departmental estimates finally led in 1950 to the formal abolition of the discussion of the budget by the sections (at least as far as the more important budgetary proposals were concerned).

The sections were replaced by a system of specialised committees for each of the main government departments and for some other budgetary units which present separate estimates to parliament. Parties were (and are) represented in these committees in proportion to their relative strength. They originally met in closed session only to prepare the debates *in pleno* in a manner resembling the earlier system of written exchanges with the responsible ministers.

This system also proved too laborious. After some experiments in the early 1960s it was therefore decided in 1966 to restrict the closed committee sessions to a drawing up of a list of points on which the committee wanted further information or which they wanted to discuss with the minister. The committee then met in public session, with the ministers who could bring their senior official advisers with them. The rights of the House would be safeguarded, as amendments of the estimates (as distinct from the report of the committee itself) could only be decided by the whole House in plenary session. Moreover, members of the House who were not members of the particular committee could attend its sessions and take part in the debates but they could not vote on committee business. It was hoped that the committees would thus be able to define the chief issues sufficiently to enable the House to confine its attention to the main points of controversy.

The new reforms again proved only half successful. Public committee sessions enlivened proceedings and allowed more specific probes, but they did not succeed in focusing debates sufficiently. Instead of shortening the procedures, the new system in fact provided opportunities for debating the same issues twice and with the same participants, first in the public committee sessions and then in the whole House. The time-span of the budgetary debates became longer. Table 15.2 details the number of hours which the Lower House spent on budgetary debates – in public committee sessions and plenary sessions – between 1965 and 1969. Clearly, the experiment did *not* result in a curtailment of the number of hours spent on plenary debates; the *total* number of hours spent on budgetary debates tended to increase rather than decrease.

Table 15.2 *Number of Hours Spent on Budgetary Debates in the Dutch Lower House between 1965 and 1969 (in Committee Sessions and Plenary Sessions)*

Parliamentary session	Number of hours in public committee sessions	Number of hours in plenary session	Total
1965–6	159	115	275[a]
1966–7[b]	—	—	—
1967–8	209	134	343
1968–9	145	189	334

[a] Difference due to rounding of minutes.
[b] Data on 1966–67 session are not included, as the normal budgetary debates were interrupted by a Cabinet crisis and a dissolution of parliament.
Source: Griffie, Twedde Kamer der Staten-Generaal.

A new reform was therefore introduced in 1969. Henceforth the specialised committees were to meet in closed session to draw up a list of contentious issues only. The debates on a particular departmental estimate would then be held directly in plenary session, so that votes could be taken without further delay. The order of the plenary sessions and the committee sessions was in fact reversed: after the passing of the budget the committees would still meet in public sessions with the minister to debate general departmental policy or particular issues. But these debates would no longer delay the despatch of the budget itself. The new system proved technically successful. The number of hours required for debates *in pleno* was 231 hours in the 1969–70 session, and amounted to 226 hours in the 1971–2 session. (No data are given for the 1970–1 session as budgetary debates took place in a pre-election setting.) For the first time in many years, the Lower House succeeded in passing practically the whole of the 1971 and 1972 budgets before Christmas 1970 and Christmas 1971 respectively.

3 *The Disputed Role of the Upper House*

The Upper House may only debate budgetary proposals after they have received the assent of the Lower House. As Figure 15.1 shows, the Upper House was therefore often still debating budgetary proposals in the mid-1960s long after the new fiscal year had began on 1 January. This protracted procedure led to serious criticism. Numerous observers have argued that the need to pass the same budget through two houses causes unnecessary delays, claiming the precious time of ministers and of civil servants for debates which are merely duplications and which are in fact superfluous as the Upper House lacks the right of amendment and inevitably passes the budget unchanged. Many authorities, including two prestigious Committees on Constitutional Reform,[1] have therefore proposed to curtail the budgetary powers of the Upper House – a sentiment which found favour with as many as 55·3 per cent of the members of the Lower House and an even larger percentage (57·1 per cent) of the members of the Upper House themselves in the Leiden University survey of 1968.[2] Various proposals have been made for specific reforms, e.g. the restriction of the budgetary powers of the Upper House to one omnibus debate and vote only, or even the complete abolition of all powers of financial review on the part of the Upper House. The latter implies a change in the Constitution which would require the assent (in a second reading after a dissolution of parliament) of as many as two-thirds of the members of each House separately. As many members of the Upper House regard their constitutional right to review the budget as a guarantee of their right to scrutinise government policy in general, such a

[1] See *Eindrapport van de Staatscommissie tot Herziening der Grondwet* (Van Schaik Committee) (Den Haag, Staatsuitgeverij, 1954), p. 48, and *Eindrapport van de Staatscommissie van Advies inzake de Grondwet en de Keiswet* (Cals-Donner Committee) (Den Haag, Staatsuitgeverij, 1971), pp. 91 ff.

[2] Unpublished data from Leiden University survey among members of parliament (1968).

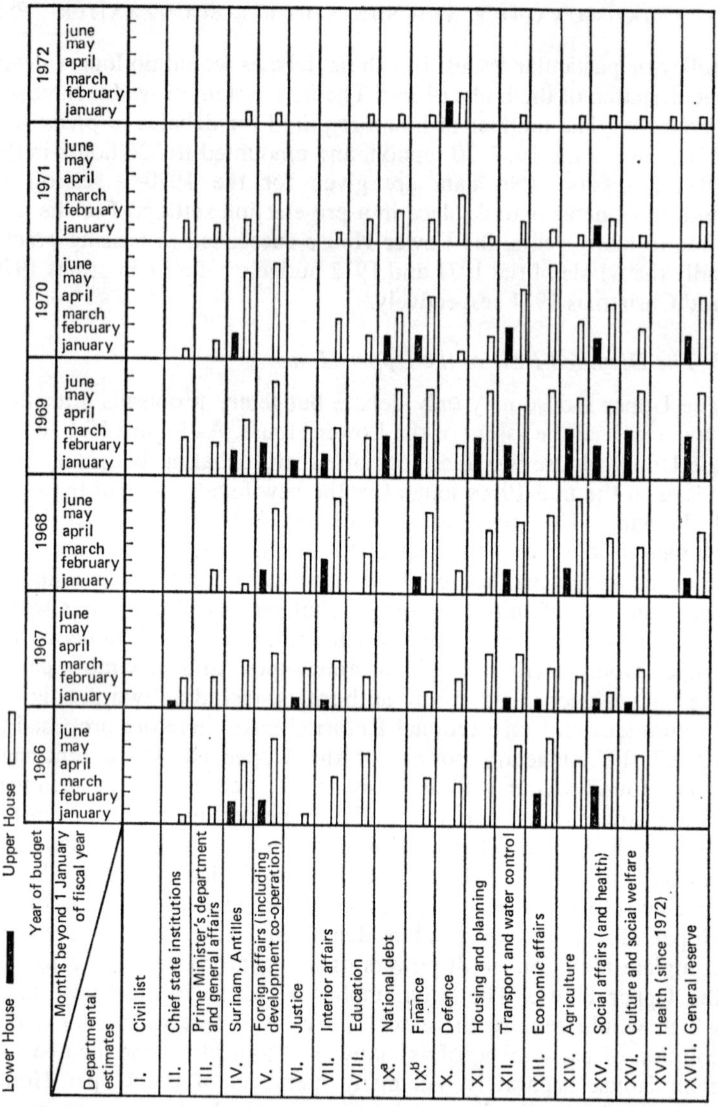

Lower House ▆▆▆ Upper House ▢

Year of budget	1966	1967	1968	1969	1970	1971	1972

Months beyond 1 January of fiscal year: june, may, april, march, february, january

Departmental estimates

I. Civil list
II. Chief state institutions
III. Prime Minister's department and general affairs
IV. Surinam, Antilles
V. Foreign affairs (including development co-operation)
VI. Justice
VII. Interior affairs
VIII. Education
IX.ᵃ National debt
IX.ᵇ Finance
X. Defence
XI. Housing and planning
XII. Transport and water control
XIII. Economic affairs
XIV. Agriculture
XV. Social affairs (and health)
XVI. Culture and social welfare
XVII. Health (since 1972)
XVIII. General reserve

FIGURE 15.1 Continuation of Budget Debates beyond 1 January into Actual Fiscal Year, Dutch Lower House and Upper House, Budgets 1966–72
Note: The departments are presented in this table according to the chapter number which each departmental budget habitually carries in a Dutch budget. For a possible reordering of these departments into certain groups of government activity, see Tables 15.3, 15.4 and 15.5.
Source: Parlement en Kiezer, Den Haag, Nijhoff

formal assent will not be given easily. But insistence on principle has proved not incompatible with measures of voluntary restraint.

In this, the Upper House has tended to follow precedents set by the Lower House. Thus, the Upper House replaced its older sections by specialised committees per department. These committees in time altered the once elaborate written exchanges with the ministers by less time-consuming procedures, notably a drawing up of lists of queries and contentious issues which might guide plenary debates. And in the 1971–2 session it took a drastic step indeed: the leaders of the Upper House parties agreed to pass the budget without debate and formal roll calls, on the condition that ministers would agree to meet with the Upper House in later specialised sessions to debate the policy of their department. As in the Lower House, the Upper House thus authorised expenditures in exchange for a formal guarantee for later policy debates outside the budgetary framework.

4 *Further Measures to Shorten Parliamentary Debates*

In addition to changes in committee procedure and the possible curtailing of Upper House powers, further reforms have been canvassed. Some observers have proposed a return to the system of bi-annual budgets which existed between 1840 and 1848 and which was made constitutionally possible by a revision of the Constitution in 1922. Most participants in the actual process of budget-making have resisted this suggestion, arguing that it would make for unrealistic rigidity at a time when increased flexibility is what is needed. Any gains from having budgetary debates only every second year might be lost by the increased need for supplementary estimates. Others have advocated a system by which the Lower House would rotate different departmental budgets. Though the budget as a whole would still be submitted annually, parliament might decide to investigate only some departmental estimates in detail in any one year, leaving others for closer scrutiny on another occasion. The Lower House carried out some experiments in this direction in the late 1950s and early 1960s. But the shifting tides of political conflict made such neat plans generally ineffective.

5 *The Actual Treatment of a Normal Budget*

This section is concluded with a short review of the manner in which the Dutch parliament treats an actual budget. For this, we have chosen the 1972 budget which was submitted to the Lower House on 21 September 1971. Altogether the Lower House took

Table 15.3 *Time Spent on Different Estimates in Dutch Lower Houses*

	% each estimate forms of total budget (1972)	% of time spent on particular estimates in 1972 budget	% of time spent on particular estimates, average 1968, 1969 and 1970 budgets	% of time spent on particular estimates in 1972 budget by five government parties	% of time spent on particular estimates in 1972 budget by three Opposition parties
	1	2	3	4	5
A. General policy debated	—	9·7	7·4	13·8	13·3
B. General organisation of the government					
Civil list	0·005	—	—	—	—
Chief State institutions	0·1	—	—	—	—
Prime minister's department and general affairs	0·03	1·7	1·8	1·8	1·4
Interior affairs	9·9	} 12·3	12·2	9·7	11·1
Justice	2·7				
Finance	3·1	3·4	5·2	3·7	3·5
	15·8	17·4	19·2	15·2	16·0
C. Foreign affairs, overseas affairs and defence					
Foreign affairs (including development aid)	2·0	11·0	10·9	11·5	9·5
Defence	12·3	7·3	7·3	8·2	8·0
Surinam, Antilles	0·5	2·9	2·2	5·6	3·4
	14·8	21·2	20·4	25·3	20·9
D. Economic affairs					
Economic affairs	2·4	7·2	8·3	6·6	7·0
Agriculture	3·0	3·9	6·9	3·9	5·0

Transport, roads and water control	10·7	7·1	6·7	4·4	6·5
Housing and planning	9·5	5·2	6·2	4·9	5·7
	25·6	23·4	28·1	19·8	24·2
E. *Education, culture and social affairs*					
Education	23·5	9·5	8·5	7·3	7·5
Social affairs (incl. health)	7·6	12·0	9·8	11·3	11·2
Culture and social welfare	5·1	6·9	6·5	6·8	7·2
	37·2	28·4	24·8	25·4	25·9
F. *National debt and general reserve*					
National debt	7·4	—	—	—	—
General reserve	0·1	—	—	—	—
Total	37831 million D. fls.	100·1	99·9	99·8	100·0

thirty-four days to discuss this budget, sending up all chapters to the Upper House before Christmas except for the defence budget which it debated and approved on 1, 2 and 3 February 1972. The Upper House passed the different chapters in three batches on 21 December 1971, on 18 January 1972, and on 29 February 1972. As we saw, that House did so without debates or roll call votes (though some Opposition parties asked to have it recorded that they were against specific estimates).

In conformity with earlier practices, the leaders of the party groups in the Lower House agreed on informal consultation on the order of business for the budget debates, on the number of days allotted to each departmental estimate, and on a fairly strict distribution of speaking time among the fifteen separate party groups in the Lower House. This distribution of time is based on a points system which relates total time allotted to the size of the party group in the Lower House; the maximum time allotted to the two largest parties was some $11\frac{1}{2}$ hours *in toto,* as against a minimum of about 3 hours for the smallest two-man parties. Parties may distribute their total time-ration over different estimates at their own discretion; but tabulation of actual time used suggests that only the very small parties used this right in any very specific manner (thus the Left-Radical PPR used about half its time on foreign affairs, the West Indies and defence matters, while some right-wing splinter parties concentrated almost exclusively on defence and economic affairs). Ministers and under-secretaries (who are responsible to both Houses of parliament, but who are barred by the Constitution from membership of either House as long as they are ministers) are not rationed in their speaking time. Calculations about the amount of time taken up by the government and the party spokesman in the debates on the 1972 budget suggest that the government required only little less time than the members of all parties collectively: 38·5 per cent of all speaking time was taken up by party spokesmen, 32·2 per cent by ministers, 23·1 per cent by government *and* party spokesmen debating matters in the second instance, and 6·6 per cent votes and vote declarations.

Table 15.3 contains more specific information on the amount of time spent on each of the departmental estimates. Column 1 lists the percentage share of each departmental estimate in the 1972 budget, column 2 the percentage of total time which the debate on this estimate demanded, and column 3 the *average* time demanded for each estimate in the debates on the 1968, the 1969 and the 1970 budgets. Comparison between column 2 and column 3 suggests great continuity: parties spent somewhat more time in the 1971–2 sessions on debating the budget for the West Indies, health and culture and social welfare, and marginally less for economic affairs, agriculture, and finance. But the overall pattern proved remarkably stable in the last few years. Column 4 and column 5 show the same percentage distribution of speaking time for the members of the five government parties and the three Opposition parties. Here again there is relatively little difference: Opposition spokesmen spoke slightly more on foreign affairs and the West Indies, spokesmen on the government side somewhat longer on economic affairs, agriculture, and transport and water control. But for the rest, members of the main parties tended to follow the overall distribution of time agreed upon for the debates generally.

To what specific actions did these debates lead the Lower House? Members of different parties (mainly belonging to the Opposition) called for no fewer than 155 amendments, most of these during discussions of the estimates of the Ministries of Culture and Social Welfare, Defence and Education. Of these, only twenty-one (eighteen of them introduced by members on the government side) were accepted. They implied a shift of 12,500,000 guilders within the budget for the Department of Transport, Roads and Water Control, and a little over 1,500,000 guilders within the budget of the Department of Culture and Social Welfare. In addition, the Lower House increased the latter budget by 400,000 guilders. The total immediate changes in the figures as originally presented by the Cabinet referred therefore only to a little over 14,400,000 guilders or only 0·04 per cent of the total.

Table 15.4 contains a breakdown of amendments and Table 15.5 presents the same data on motions, brought to a vote during the debates on the various estimates. Comparable data are presented on amendments and motions for earlier years. These tables make clear that there has been a massive increase in the number of amendments in recent years, and a comparable, if slightly less drastic, increase in the number of motions. But the tabulations also suggest that motions have not been more noticeably successful than amendments. Of seventy-six motions introduced during the debates on the 1972 budget, only seventeen were accepted. Seven of these were introduced by members on the government side, ten by the Opposition. But of the latter, no fewer than nine were in the realm of foreign affairs – a field which until recently tended to be beyond the pale of party politics in the Netherlands. The fate of amendments and motions on matters of domestic policy therefore mainly served to underscore the power of the Cabinet to keep its followers in line, and the ineffectiveness of the attempt by the Opposition parties to introduce an alternative budget of their own (see p. 297).

III PARLIAMENT AND THE POLITICS OF BUDGETING

1 *The Apparent Dominance of the Executive*
The legal powers of parliament to amend the estimates have in the short run proved largely abortive against the realities of executive dominance in the field of budgeting. Once the estimates have been approved by the Cabinet, they are likely to pass through parliament practically unscathed. The influence of parliament (such as it is) is therefore exercised not through a direct use of its formal budgetary powers, but through its indirect impact on longer-term decision-making processes.

How to account for the relatively passive stance parliament has taken towards the executive in direct budgetary legislation? To some extent this attitude is deeply rooted in past political culture which for long tended to insulate the executive from too direct control by parliamentary party politics.[1] Such traditions have been

[1] See Hans Daalder, 'The Netherlands: Opposition in a Segmented Society', in Dahl, *op. cit.*; and Arend Lijphart, *The Politics of Accommodation—Pluralism*

K

Table 15.4 *Amendments, Brought to a Vote during Debates on the Budgets for 1966 to 1972*

N — total brought to a vote
+ — total passed

	1966 N	+	1967 N	+	1968 N	+	1969 N	+	1970 N	+	1971 N	+	1972 N	+	Total N	+
A. *General policy debates*	—	—	—	—	—	—	—	—	—	—	—	—	—	—	—	—
B. *General organisation of the government*																
Civil list	—	—	—	—	—	—	—	—	—	—	—	—	—	—	—	—
Chief State institutions	—	—	—	—	—	—	—	—	—	—	—	—	—	—	—	—
Prime minister's department and general affairs	—	—	—	—	—	—	—	—	—	—	—	—	—	—	—	—
Interior affairs	—	—	—	—	—	—	—	—	—	—	—	—	—	—	—	—
Justice	—	—	—	—	—	—	—	—	—	—	—	—	—	—	—	—
Finance	—	—	—	—	—	—	—	—	—	—	—	—	—	—	—	—
Total	—	—	—	—	—	—	—	—	—	—	—	—	—	—	—	—
C. *Foreign affairs, overseas affairs and defence*																
Foreign affairs (incl. development aid)	—	—	—	—	—	—	—	—	—	—	—	—	12	—	12	—
Defence	—	—	—	—	—	—	2	—	—	—	6	6	31	—	39	6
Surinam, Antilles	—	—	—	—	—	—	—	—	—	—	—	—	—	—	—	—
Total	—	—	—	—	—	—	2	—	—	—	6	6	43	—	51	6

Table 13.4—continued

Departmental estimates	1966		1967		1968		1969		1970		1971		1972		Total	
	N	+	N	+	N	+	N	+	N	+	N	+	N	+	N	+
D. Economic affairs																
Economic affairs	—	—	1	—	1	—	2	—	—	—	10	—	15	—	29	—
Agriculture	—	—	—	—	—	—	—	—	—	—	—	—	—	—	—	—
Transport, road and water control	—	—	—	—	—	—	—	—	—	—	12	—	13	2	25	2
Housing and planning	2	—	1	—	—	—	—	—	1	—	7	—	8	—	19	—
Total	2	—	2	—	1	—	2	—	1	—	29	—	36	2	73	2
E. Education culture and social affairs																
Education	—	—	1	—	7	—	—	—	5	1	16	2	19	—	49	3
Social affairs, (incl. health)	—	—	—	—	—	—	—	—	—	—	—	—	8	—	8	—
Culture and social welfare	—	—	—	—	1	1	1	—	2	1	8	4	55	19	67	25
Total	—	—	1	—	8	1	1	—	7	2	24	6	82	19	124	28
F. National debt and general reserve																
National debt	—	—	—	—	—	—	—	—	—	—	—	—	—	—	—	—
General reserve	—	—	—	—	—	—	—	—	—	—	—	—	—	—	—	—
Total	—	—	—	—	—	—	—	—	—	—	—	—	—	—	—	—
Total	2	—	3	—	9	1	5	—	39	2	155	12	222	21	—	36

Table 15.5 Motions, Brought to a Vote during Debates on the Budgets for 1966 to 1972
N = total brought to a vote
+ = total passed

Departmental estimates	1966 N	1966 +	1967 N	1967 +	1968 N	1968 +	1969 N	1969 +	1970 N	1970 +	1971 N	1971 +	1972 N	1972 +	Total N	Total +
A. General policy debates	2	—	1	1	3	—	5	—	7	—	4	—	9	—	31	1
B. General organisation of the government																
Civil list	—	—	—	—	—	—	—	—	—	—	—	—	—	—	—	—
Chief State institutions	—	—	—	—	—	—	—	—	—	—	—	—	—	—	—	—
Prime minister's department and general affairs	—	—	—	—	1	—	—	—	1	—	1	1	—	—	3	1
Interior affairs	—	—	1	—	7	—	4	—	5	1	5	1	4	—	22	1
Finance	1	—	2	2	1	—	7	—	5	—	—	—	1	—	17	2
Total	1	—	3	2	9	—	11	—	6	—	6	1	5	—	42	3
C. Foreign affairs, overseas affairs and defence																
Foreign affairs (incl. development aid)	1	1	1	—	12	5	5	1	10	4	8	2	14	10	51	23
Defence	—	—	2	—	3	—	2	—	3	1	10	3	8	—	28	4
Surinam, Antilles	—	—	—	—	—	—	1	—	4	—	—	—	1	—	6	—
Total	1	1	3	—	15	5	8	1	17	5	18	5	23	10	85	27

	1	2	3	4	5	6	7	8	9	10	11	12	13	14	15	16
D. *Economic affairs*																
Economic affairs	—	—	2	—	4	1	10	7	6	2	5	3	—	—	27	13
Agriculture	—	—	1	—	—	1	1	—	1	—	1	—	—	—	4	1
Transport, road and water control	—	—	1	—	1	1	3	1	6	1	5	1	—	—	16	3
Housing and planning	2	1	—	—	1	—	4	1	3	—	4	—	—	—	16	2
Total	2	1	1	—	5	—	6	1	18	10	16	2	15	4	63	19
E. *Education, culture and social affairs*																
Education	4	1	1	—	3	—	1	1	12	3	3	—	7	1	31	6
Social affairs (incl. health)	1	—	2	—	4	1	2	—	8	1	9	—	5	—	31	2
Culture and social welfare	2	—	—	1	—	—	2	—	5	2	1	1	10	2	20	6
Total	7	1	3	1	7	1	5	1	25	6	13	1	22	3	82	14
F. *National debt and general reserve*																
National debt	—	—	—	—	—	—	—	—	—	—	—	—	—	—	—	—
General reserve	—	—	—	—	—	—	—	—	—	—	—	—	—	—	—	—
Total	—	—	—	—	—	—	—	—	—	—	—	—	—	—	—	—
Total	13	3	11	4	39	6	37	2	75	21	60	11	76	17	311	63

reinforced by the increased complexity of modern public finance: few members of parliament feel capable of confronting the massive expert resources of a modern executive with rival insights and information: they lack the support of a specialised parliamentary staff, and feel hesitant to set up their personal skills against the much better prepared government.[1] But perhaps the most important factor is the curious nexus which unites a cabinet with the parliamentary majority in a parliamentary system. For in a complex multi-party system,[2] members of governing parties are well aware that they may not only control a cabinet, but that they must also sustain it. This greatly limits their freedom of manoeuvre as they must at all times weigh their own particular desires against the very real danger of a resignation of ministers. Sometimes, members of one or more governing parties may actually desire such a crisis (as in 1958 and again in 1966 when the Catholics terminated a coalition with the socialists on what appeared at first sight relatively minor

and Democracy in the Netherlands (Berkeley, University of California Press, 1968), passim.

[1] Total expenditures for the Dutch Lower House amounted to a little over 20 million D. fls. in 1973: of this 3 million went to personnel expenditures for the clerks and assembly services, and 2 million for staff aid of the parliamentary groups. The number of actual clerks and assistant-clerks was seven in 1972; in addition there was one assistant to the clerks, and one clerk for delegations of both Houses to international parliamentary assemblies. The total staff aid, including secretaries, for the fifteen parliamentary groups consisted of some sixty persons; many of these worked part-time only.

[2] The Dutch party system is indeed highly fragmented: after the November 1972 elections only one party (the Socialist PvdA, with 43 seats) occupies more than a quarter of the 150 seats in the Lower House. In addition to the Socialists there are four more parties on the left: Communists (7 seats), Pacifist–Socialists (2 seats), Radicals (PPR, 7 seats), and Democrats '66 (6 seats)—the latter two parties form a coalition with the Socialists. These five left-oriented parties face six religious parties: Catholics (27 seats), Anti-revolutionaries (14 seats), Christian–Historicals (7 seats), two right-oriented Calvinist splinter parties of 3 and 2 seats respectively, and one Conservative Catholic splinter of 1 seat. The rest of the political spectrum is occupied by the Liberal VVD (22 seats), Democrats–Socialists '70 (6 seats), and a right-oriented *Boerenpartij* (3 seats). For decades Dutch cabinets have been composed of the three larger religious parties with either socialists or liberals as a partner. The strong centre position of the religious parties is rapidly being eroded however: their combined percentage of seats in the Lower House declined from just over 50 per cent in 1963 to 32 per cent in 1972.

For an analysis of the Dutch party system, see in addition to the publications by Daalder and Lijphart mentioned in note 12, P. R. Baehr, 'The Netherlands', in Stanley Henig and John Pinder (eds), *European Political Parties* (London, P.E.P., Allen & Unwin), 1969, pp. 256–81, and Hans Daalder and Jerrold G. Rusk, 'Perceptions of Party in the Dutch Parliament', in Samuel C. Patterson and John C. Wahlke, *Comparative Legislative Behaviour—Frontiers of Research* (New York, Wiley, 1972), pp. 143–98.

issues connected with government finances). At other times, a party may push a particular minister or cabinet to the brink, trusting (with some reason) that a general desire to maintain the cabinet may force the cabinet to bow on a controversial issue. Thus the socialists in 1955, and the anti-revolutionaries in 1960 forced a temporary government crisis as they dissented from a particular government proposal relating to housing; in both cases a new compromise was found which allowed the cabinet to return to office after a temporary resignation.[1] Occasionally, there may be a miscalculation resulting in the unintended fall of a minister or the Cabinet. But generally members of governing parties prefer to play safe: they bark rather than break. In exchange for such loss of immediate independence, members of governing parties receive some compensation by opportunities for informal influence in other places. Thus members of governing parties have a strong voice in the very lengthy and detailed inter-party negotiations which usually precede the formation of a Dutch Cabinet; if they are tied eventually to the results of this bargaining process, so generally are ministers. Once cabinets have been formed, the leading ministers and the leaders of the parliamentary groups may meet to consult on politically sensitive issues. Ministers and members of the same party may maintain special contacts. And specialised members of all parties may use the instrument of specialised parliamentary committees to pressure individual ministers. If parliament therefore seems to agree easily with government proposals, this may also be due partly to the operation of Carl Friedrich's 'rule of anticipated reactions',[2] ministers are aware of specific parliamentary desires and potential veto positions. And they frame their budget to a considerable extent with this awareness in mind.[3] Most budgetary appropriations are the result, moreover, of laws and policies to which parliament itself earlier assented.

2 The Ambiguous Position of the Minister of Finance

In the actual process of budget-making within the executive the

[1] All in all, three out of twelve postwar cabinets fell over interparty disputes on general budgetary policy (1958, 1966, and 1972). A further two faced an intermediate cabinet crisis which was later patched up (1955 and 1960, see above). In addition, some ministers resigned individually over similar issues without provoking the fall of the Cabinet.

[2] Carl J. Friedrich, Man and his Government—An Empirical Theory of Politics (New York, McGraw-Hill, 1963), pp. 199–215.

[3] In addition, ministers may initiate changes in budgets already submitted to the Lower House, possibly to meet parliamentary demands voluntarily. Supplementary bills introduced at the time of the 1972 budget affected as much as 7 per cent of the total budget.

Minister of Finance occupies a key position. It is his special responsibility under the overall authority of the Cabinet to ensure that demands for increased expenditures do not overstep such limits as the overall state of the government finances and of the national economy are thought to require. To fulfil his task, he has (as we saw) extensive powers. Yet for all his instruments, the minister's political position is not as strong as appearances suggest. Individual ministers jealously guard their autonomy in the running of their own departments, and push their special claims hard in bilateral encounters with the Minister of Finance. In the last instance, the Cabinet must decide. But there again the minister is in a difficult position. He is after all only one minister in a coalition Cabinet which consists very much of equals. Other departmental ministers tend to refrain from taking sides in conflicts between one of their colleagues and the Minister of Finance partly because they know too little of the merits of the dispute, partly because they know from introspection that such interference would not be welcome. The particular case of the Minister of Finance is not likely to be a popular one; he must keep ministers from collectively overspending by suggesting cuts in individual expenditures which are bound to be dear to one or other minister. He is therefore somewhat of a lonely fighter in Cabinet. His only hope is for support from the Prime Minister who is himself little more than a *primus inter pares*. The absence of hierarchy in the Dutch Cabinet also does little to foster a sense of solidarity among ministers with the Minister of Finance. Dutch ministers know that they are unlikely to rise to other offices, and consequently they live largely on the assumption that they will be judged solely on their record in their own department.

The special position of the Minister of Finance is reflected in the recruitment pattern of that office. Many prominent economists have been called to the department and have filled the role with distinction.[1] But parties have often hesitated to take the office, judging it a possible political liability. As we shall see in the next paragraph, ministers of finance have sought to capitalise on their role as technical experts. But for the rest, their position has rested chiefly on their own self-confidence, buttressed by the knowledge that their own

[1] Since 1945 three leading economics professors (Professor P. Lieftinck, Professor J. Zijlstra and Professor H. J. Witteveen) have served a total of more than sixteen years in the Ministry of Finance, while another one-time Minister of Finance (H. J. Hofstra) was later appointed Professor of Tax Law at Lidene University. The present minister is a young economics professor of the University of Amsterdam, with no parliamentary experience. Professor P. Lieftinck later become director of the International Monetary Fund, and Professor J. Zijlstra, President of the Bank of The Netherlands in 1967.

continued association with the Cabinet might be as vital to its
further existence as that of any other minister.

The ambiguity of the minister's position is reflected in his relation
with parliament. Although he is likely to be the greatest economiser
in the Cabinet, he may be attacked by the finance specialists of all
parties for yielding too easily to the spending desires of his colleagues. But when a spending minister defends his particular
departmental budget in parliament, an inter-party coalition of
members specialised in that particular field may insist with equal
conviction that the minister has knuckled under too quickly to the
heartless drive of the Minister of Finance for unwarranted economies. Some observers have therefore spoken of the 'financial
schizophrenia' of parliament.[1]

3 *The Abortive Attempt to Establish a General Budget Committee in the Lower House*

Unease about this equivocal stance of parliament, as well as a
desire to underscore its constitutional independence, led the Lower
House to establish in 1966 a new General Budget Committee
(Algemene Begrotings-Commissie, popularly known as the ABC).
This committee was composed of the leaders and financial specialists of all parliamentary parties. It was to meet after all departmental budget committees had met and had debated particular
changes in the government budget. The ABC was then to collate
these individual committee wishes, and to advise the Chamber on
priorities. It was thought that this committee would provide the
Chamber with an opportunity to confront the government with its
own weighting of priorities, and thus to make it less dependent on
Cabinet proposals.

The experiment proved abortive: it was conceived from a mis-
taken reification of the institutions of government and parliament,
and did too little justice to the dominating differences between the
government parties on the one hand and the opposition parties on
the other. In practice, amendments in the specialised parliamentary
budget committees originated mostly with the Opposition parties.
They were already defeated in those committees before they reached
the ABC. The government majority on the latter committee at first

[1] This point has been argued with particular force by the Socialist W. Drees
Sr., when he was Prime Minister between 1948 and 1958 (see his *De Vorming
van het Regeringsbeleid* (Assen, Van Gorcum, 1965), ch. IV), and by his son
W. Drees Jr. For the latter's views see his dissertation *On the Level of Govern-
ment Expenditure in The Netherlands after the War*, op. cit., notably part II,
Budgetary Behaviour, pp. 59 ff.; and below, pp. 307–8.

wanted to discuss only the few committee amendments which had escaped this fate. When the full Chamber insisted that it should nevertheless consider all departmental committee amendments *de novo*, the ABC majority simply proceeded to vote down all Opposition amendments again, thus signalling their feeling that there was little use in duplicating the elaborate setting of priorities by the Cabinet, or in re-examining matters which had received previous attention in the specialised committees. The ABC soon atrophied. Its chief effect may well have been to force members of parliament on the government side to ally themselves more closely with specific government proposals than had been their psychological inclination before.

4 *The Attempt to Strengthen the Instruments of Central Control*

To counteract the upward pressure for increased government expenditures, successive ministers of finance have resorted to a variety of quantitative methods which seek to put conflicts between demands and resources in more concrete terms.

Over the last decades, the Central Planning Bureau has provided increasingly refined methods of forecasting the more important economic indicators, both on a short-term and a longer-term basis. Policy-makers have thus been forced to pay greater attention to the economic implications of specific budgetary policies, and in turn to consider the effect of future economic developments and overall government finances.[1] Various attempts have been made to relate the expected growth of the rise of government expenditures to expected increases in the national income. Thus, in the late 1950s it was argued that government expenditures should rise at no greater (and preferably a lesser) rate than the growth in real national income. This rule of thumb – known popularly as the *Romme-norm* after the intractable leader of the Catholic Party at that time, Professor C. P. M. Romme – was replaced in 1960 by a more refined measure, named after the then Minister of Finance, Professor J. Zijlstra. The *Zijlstra-norm* is based on the following reasoning. Assuming an equilibrium in the economy between the total savings required for government and private investment as well as an acceptable balance of payments, governments can freely dispose of any additional revenue which results from a rising national income. Because of the rate of progression in some of the more important

---

[1] Faint attempts at anti-cyclical budget policies were abandoned as impracticable around 1960: budgetary commitments proved too rigid, as distinct from other instruments (such as monetary policy, short-term tax measures, or specific expenditures in favour of regions with high levels of unemployment),

taxes, a rise in national income will result in a more than proportionate increase in tax revenues by a factor (the so-called progression factor) which was generally put at about $1\frac{1}{4}$ times the percentage growth of the national income.[1] This additional income would be available either for increasing expenditures or for tax remissions. By calculating the sum of total additional income minus the expected increase of expenditures on existing legal, contractional and policy commitments, a measure was provided which clearly indicated at what moment new policies allowed tax remissions or demanded further increases in taxation.

The Ministry of Finance has also attempted to put the need for hard-headed policy decisions in a longer-term perspective. It has calculated, on the one hand, three-year estimates of the prospective financial consequences of *existing* legal, contractional and policy commitments; it has sought (unsuccessfully so far) realistic quantitative estimates of the possible financial costs of *new policy proposals*; and it has calculated *the degree of freedom for forward expenditure* given the expected increase in national and government income according to the *Zijlstra-norm*. It has thus attempted to visualise – to the presumed benefit of ministers and parliament alike – the conflict between existing policies, new policies, and a desire to avoid new tax burdens.

New instruments have also been developed to keep particularly costly government programmes under some measure of control. Thus successive cabinets have fixed ceilings for the forward expenditures of particularly expensive programmes. This was effective in the field of defence, but proved less successful in the field of higher education and various public works programmes. By presenting proposals to parliament for approval in principle, the Cabinet attempted to free certain programmes from the annual bickering over the estimates, while at the same time focusing attention on longer-term implications. Some observers have canvassed the introduction of new forms of alternative budgeting, suggesting that ministers should in future present differing estimates based on differing assumptions of the state of government finances, specifying the consequences of possible cuts, or indicating priorities if future

[1] Calculations about the actual size of the so-called progression factor have forced experts to scale down their initial estimates from some 1·33 in the early 1960s to 1·14 for 1973. The net average effect was proved to have been slightly above 1·20 between 1956 and 1965 and only 1·07 in the period 1965–70. See the report of a special Committee of Experts as presented to parliament by the Minister of Finance on 13 April 1972, *Witte Stukken*, no. 11.780. See also J. J. Vis, 'Somber Begrotingsperspectief', *Nieuwe Rotterdamse Courant-Algemeen Handelsblad*, 25 and 26 April 1972.

revenues should prove unexpectedly generous.[1] In practice, the
state of government finances was so strained as to make only minimum forecasts politically volatile. In an attempt to force further
economies, just to free resources for new policy proposals, an
Opposition proposal recommended the inclusion of a clause in the
new Accounting Bill in 1970 which would force ministers to indicate
which 5 per cent of their estimates they regarded as the least essential; an amendment to this effect was not accepted by the government parties. Finance specialists of all parties, and officials within
the Finance Ministry, have sought solace in proclaiming the need to
introduce new forms of programme budgeting within the government, which presumably would allow a closer evaluation of existing
and desired government programmes.

What effects did such reforms have on the policy process? Para-
doxically the most immediate result may be a tendency to give a
special place to economists – and economic reasoning – in the determination of budgetary policy. Economists play an important role
throughout the government apparatus: in departments, in the
Budget Office, in the Central Planning Bureau, in the key institution
of the Bank of The Netherlands, in important advisory bodies like
the Social-Economic Council, and also in the councils of the more
important interest group organisations such as the employers and
trade union federations. Although their personal and institutional
views make for considerable political argument on technical and
policy questions – and subjective political choice must overshadow
technocratic argument in the last analysis – their presence has
tended to raise the level of discussion on the choice of priorities,
while drawing attention to financial and economic restraints. This in
turn has affected the behaviour of party politicians. Spurred on by
the Central Planning Bureau's quantitative studies of the potential
costs of new policy demands, political parties have become increasingly specific in their election campaigns: they have been forced to
face costs, to be clearer about priorities, and even to spell out the
need for increased taxation to counterbalance their advocacy of new
government expenditures. A similar trend has occurred in parliamentary debates. In 1965 the Liberal Party, then in opposition,
presented for the first time an alternative budgetary plan (the so-
called Joekes-plan) to parliament, in reply to the government budget
introduced by the Cals-Cabinet composed of Socialists, Catholics
and Anti-Revolutionaries. This alternative budget indicated how,
according to the Liberals, the government could cut expenditure by
some 900.000.000 guilders. The proposal was voted down by the

[1] On alternative budgets see W. Drees Jr., op. cit., pp. 86ff.

government parties, but the precedent was followed in later years by the left parties when the Socialists returned to the Opposition benches (as in the counter-budget in the Pescher-plan of 1968, or the alternative Opposition budget prepared by the chief three Opposition parties shortly after the elections of 1971). In addition, parties have tended to become increasingly specific in debates on particular departmental budgets: more and more demands for specific increases are accompanied by indications of compensatory savings elsewhere.

The new trend towards greater specificity has therefore to some extent contributed towards a rationalisation of political discourse. But there are considerable practical limitations to this. It was easy to agree on priorities as long as government income expanded rapidly. But when new resources became scarcer (as economic growth lessened and inflation increasingly strained government finances), attempts to depoliticise issues by means of quasi-objective quantitative formulas began to touch more vital political nerves. The somewhat esoteric nature of the decision-making process which may assist the reaching of consensus at the élite level proves a liability in relations with the population at large, and parliament is to some extent caught in the middle of these cross-pressures. For on the one hand it has to pay due respect to objective limitations. But on the other hand a variety of new developments has made parliament more sensitive to its expressive functions. Direct action tactics have increased, as the pleas and protests of interest groups have been magnified by a barrage of publicity on the part of the mass media. To some extent this has destroyed the equanimity of the political leaders which in turn feeds further pressures on the system. The party system is becoming increasingly fragmented, which feeds inter-party competition and makes the decision-making process less calculable. Some observers have hoped that the entry of an increasing number of economists to the Lower House might help to offset such developments.[1] But their number has been too small, and their disagreements have been too great, to allow them to play a role on the floor of parliament which is at all comparable to that within the executive branch.

5 The Steep Rise in Collective Claims

In the last fifteen years, Dutch cabinets have consisted for 90 per cent of the time of centre-right coalitions, with the Socialists and

[1] The total percentage of economists among the members of the Lower House was 3 per cent in 1945, 6 per cent in 1950, 9 per cent in 1956, 1960 and 1965, 14 per cent in 1968 and 12 per cent in 1971.

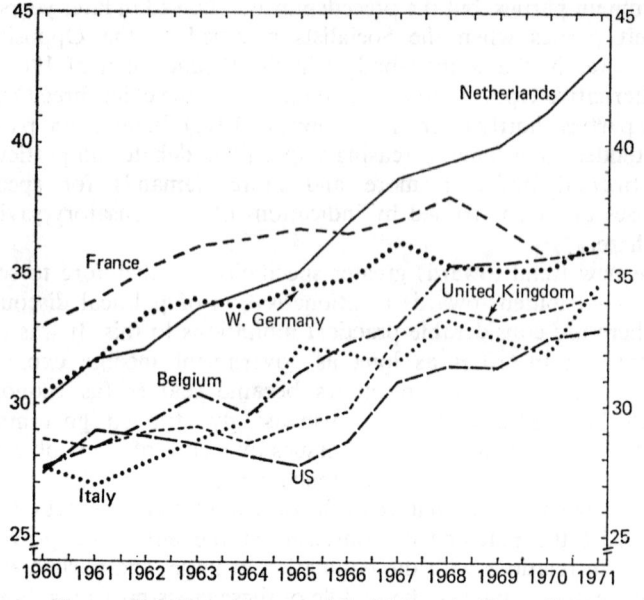

FIGURE 15.2 Government and Social Security Expenditures
(annual figures in per cent of gross national product)
Source: Bank of the Netherlands, annual report for 1971, as quoted in the
Miljoenen-nota 1973, p. 13

other left-oriented parties in opposition for all but sixteen months.
As will be evident from Figure 15.2 however, both government
expenditure and social security expenditure have risen more steeply
in the Netherlands as a percentage of GNP than in many comparable industrial countries. Taxes and social insurance premiums now
demand close to half of the net national income, and further commitments in both sectors are expected to claim the whole or more of
the further growth in resources expected over the next few years,
leaving virtually zero opportunity for an increase of direct incomes
in wages and salaries. As a result major political conflicts are
emerging both on the issue of redistribution of private incomes, and
on priorities on expenditures in the collective sector.

Why this steep rise, which runs counter to the professed goals of
most political spokesmen in the late 1950s and early 1960s?

(*a*) Many increases in expenditure are the automatic results of past
legislative commitments, of exogenous factors like demographic
growth and international undertakings, and of the effects of growing
economic prosperity itself. The active working population in the

Netherlands supports a large number of dependents because of relatively high birth rates, a very low mortality rate, and a very limited participation of women in the production process. Yet the demand for better housing and more education soars. A densely populated country has entered the motor age. Metropolitan cities are becoming virtually unmanageable conglomerates. The need for recreational facilities and social welfare programmes is reaching new dimensions. The protection of the environment demands new policies, and international commitments within NATO, the EEC, and development aid require large expenditures.

(b) Apart from such exogenous factors, the internal rigidity of government finance takes its toll. Budgets tend to be shaped on the basis of last year's figures. Political controversy centres on new programmes rather than on a re-evaluation of existing commitments. Usually, insufficient attention is paid to the expansionary nature of many government programmes, and sometimes such programmes may even have been underbudgeted to secure their initial adoption.

(c) There has been a constant upward pressure on government expenditure from the specialised parliamentary committees. Their constant pleas for new provisions in their particular sector have bolstered the political position of specialised bureaucrats and ministers in the long-term bargaining over new budgetary appropriations.

(d) An even more powerful factor may have been the working of that very powerful advisory agency in the Netherlands, the Social-Economic Council (SER, Sociaal-Economische Raad).[1] This body includes fifteen representatives from employers' federations, fifteen representatives from workers' organisations, and fifteen independent experts, appointed by the government and usually including the Director of the Central Planning Bureau and the President of the Bank of the Netherlands. It regularly advises the government on all matters relating to industrial relations, including incomes policy and social security arrangements. It has tended to develop into a powerful forum in which far-reaching decisions tend to be taken on the distribution of the fruits of a growing national income. Many new social security provisions, and also certain direct allocations in the government budget, find their origin in the SER's prestigious reports. Its net effect has been the establishment of a climate of rising expectations which usually results in ever-growing claims for

[1] On the powerful role of the SER, see the excellent study by John P. Windmuller, *Labor Relations in The Netherlands* (Ithaca, Cornell University Press, 1969), *passim*.

new collective programmes, *in addition to* increased private income demands.

(e) Finally, a peculiarly Dutch factor may explain part of the very rapid increase in the collective sector. In the Netherlands many activities that in other countries are taken care of either by one government agency, or by unsubsidised voluntary societies, are performed by a plurality of subsidised ideological organisations. This phenomenon of pluralist segmentation, 'Verzuiling'[1] originated in the late nineteenth century when Calvinists and Catholics began to press for State aid for parochial schools. This principle was accepted by all parties in 1917, and since then it has been extended to so many other fields that Dutch society may now well be dubbed 'the subsidy State'. Obviously, such a pattern of social organisations need not lead to comparatively higher expenditure, in as far as they may tap private efforts in addition to presenting claims on government resources. But the tight organisational structures may have led to an adumbration of tasks in a variety of social sectors well beyond what might have occurred in their absence. Each of these specialised organisations tends to have special access not only to special bureaucratic agencies, but also through related ideological parties to the centres of power in the Cabinet and in parliament. The government exercises some form of administrative tutelage over the ideological social organisations which it subsidises. But they often present a united front, and *in toto* they represent a massive momentum for the expansion of government expenditure.

6 *The Budgetary Strains of Inflation*

In recent years the rate of inflation has increased, from an average rate of 5·2 per cent between 1963 and 1969 to 7·5 per cent in 1969, 4·3 per cent in 1970, 7·6 per cent in 1971, and 7·8 per cent in 1972. Inflation causes great difficulties in government finances. Expenditure on existing commitments soars because the government's own price index compares unfavourably with that of other sectors of the economy. Salaries represent a large part of the costs of government. The salaries of government employees (and of comparable personnel in State-subsidised institutions) are tied not only to cost of living indices, but also to the average trend in rises of contractual wages in the private enterprises above 10,000 employees. But in contrast to private enterprise, State activities offer little scope for compensatory rise of productivity per employee.

Inflation also causes difficulties on the income side. Although

---

[1] For a trenchant analysis, see Lijphart, op. cit., *passim*.

government revenues rise with inflation, they do not do so at the same rate as expenditure. Some taxes are rigid in the short run, while others increase less than proportionately. Income taxes rise more than proportionately because of the net effect of progressive taxation rates. But under a new Act passed by parliament in 1971 the effect of these progressive rates has been lessened. The government must by law return to the taxpayers at least 80 per cent of the increased revenues which it derives from the mere incidence of progression on rises in income in purely monetary as distinct from real terms. As this concerns increasingly sizable sums of money, this legal stipulation is subject to increasing political controversy.

Difficulties on the revenue and expenditure side caused by inflation are compounded by a decline in the rate of economic growth. New calculations indicate moreover that the favourable effect of economic growth on government revenues, as calculated by the *Zijlstra-norm* (above, p. 298) have been overestimated. Thus rising costs of existing programmes face disappointing results on the income side, while there is simultaneously great political pressure for a further expansion of government tasks. This forces the government to seek a way out in three directions: drastic cuts in existing government activities, increases in taxation, and the raising of charges for services to particular beneficiaries of government services.

These measures lead to acute political conflict. For cuts in specific government expenditures often touch vested interests that past government policies have themselves helped to build up. The raising of payments for particular government services (for instance on such sensitive points as school fees and university tuition) meet with similar negative reactions from groups directly affected. Their protests have often been taken up by individual members of parliament and ministers have sometimes wavered in the face of such actions of protest, thus whetting the appetite of other groups to use similar tactics.

Difficulties are also encountered by the raising of taxes. The increase in direct taxation, indirect taxation, and social security contributions has now reached such a magnitude that in the view of many economists they are in fact being devolved on to the weaker groups of society through inflationary wage demands and rising prices. Nevertheless, the pressure for new government policies and for increased social security provisions goes on unabated. Most forecasts suggest that the total incidence of taxes and social security premiums will rise from 47·7 per cent of net national income in 1973 to well over 50 per cent in 1976.

7 *Government, Parliament, Parties and the Major Interest Groups*

The steep rise in the collective sector, and the quickening of the inflationary spiral, lead to new forms of entanglement between government on the one hand, and the major interest groups (notably employers and workers) on the other. The government has both a direct and an indirect stake in the curbing of inflation. A direct one: for its own expenditures are dependent largely on the level of salaries for government employees if its budgetary figures are to retain reality. And an indirect one: for the government has both a general responsibility for the overall state of the economy, and a particular responsibility for the weaker groups in society which threaten to fall victim to the redistributive effects of rampant inflation. But the instruments of government for a successful incomes policy have become blunted: earlier physical controls over wages have been dismantled and measures of price control have been half-heartedly applied, and fairly ineffective in results. In the prevailing free enterprise climate, unions of workers and other interest groups have become more militant. And within the field of trade union organisations, power seems to be shifting slowly from the once dominant national federations to separate industrial unions. Government policy has therefore vacillated between an attempt to obtain the voluntary co-operation of industrial partners for a policy of restraint, and a grudging recognition of the need to reimpose some controls. Unions on the other hand have equally hesitated between a desire to exploit their market position to the full in favour of immediate wage demands, and an acknowledgement that the situation is fraught with so many long-term economic dangers that some form of co-operation with the government must be sought. In general, unions have chosen the latter course, but they have demanded very specific concessions on the part of the government in exchange for a policy of voluntary restraint. They have demanded, for instance, increased expenditure on the further education of young industrial workers, the abandonment of a proposed increase in the value-added tax on essential goods, etc.

The accumulation of problems generates great strains within the government coalition, and among parties generally. For while workers are united in their demands even though they may belong to different Socialist, Catholic or Calvinist unions, this unity was not found in the political arena until 1973. Since 1966 the Socialists and some other left-orientated parties have been in opposition, while the Catholic party, the two Calvinist parties and the Liberal party have been in government together. The Socialists increasingly sought to polarise politics, declaring that they wanted to replace the traditional system of shifting, low-keyed coalition politics by a new system in which the electorate is given an immediate choice between rival coalitions. This new strategy made life for the religious parties very uncomfortable. For they have large working-class clienteles of their own and had every reason to fear an Opposition which tried to make itself into a strong champion of union demands. A conflict therefore arose between the need for accommodation on the industrial front, and the new polarised politics in parliament.

This complicated situation was made even more difficult when the governing coalition of the Liberals and the three religious parties lost their absolute majority in parliament in the elections of April 1971. Although the left parties made some headway, the chief winners of that election were a new party, Democratic-Socialists '70. This party had originally split off from the Socialist party in protest against its new left tendencies. It was led by W. Drees, the son and namesake of a veteran Socialist Prime Minister who had been identified with careful financial policies in the 1950s. Dress Jr was a former director of the Bureau of the Budget, and an influential part-time Professor of Public Finance. He campaigned on a tough anti-inflation programme, and demanded a massive overhaul of existing government policies. The party won a sufficient number of seats (8 out of 150) to give it a decisive bargaining power. After some arduous negotiations a new five-party cabinet was formed which in addition to the Liberals and the three religious parties included Dress Jr and another DS'70 minister. The new Cabinet proposed massive economies which provoked a barrage of protests from interest groups directly affected.

Within a year two related conflicts caused the break-up of the new coalition. The ministers proved unable to agree on the estimates; and they did not see eye to eye on the way the government should deal with the unions. The DS'70 ministers (harking back to the active interventionist policies of the 1950s) demanded a reestablishment of direct controls over incomes and prices, reasoning that it would not be possible even to draw up a realistic budget until the government had made sure that it would effectively restrain the rate of inflation in the following budgetary year. The ministers of the religious parties, on the other hand, and to a lesser extent the Liberal ministers, wanted instead to negotiate with the representatives of employers and workers for a social contract in which the government and both sides of industry would agree on overall priorities, including if need be specific tax and expenditure policies on the part of the government. The Cabinet fell in July 1972 when the

DS'70 ministers resigned over budgetary conflicts. The rump-Cabinet decided to dissolve parliament with new elections to take place in late November.

These political developments led to very curious scenes in parliament. The outgoing Cabinet presented the 1973 budget in September 1972, knowing that it would be only partly debated before parliament was adjourned. The budget contained a number of proposals which the unions had declared unacceptable, if realistic talks for a social contract were to take place. The Opposition parties took up the main grievances of the unions, and introduced amendments to the estimates which the government had presented to parliament. The Cabinet wished to keep its hands free for the forthcoming negotiations and mobilised its supporters to defeat all Opposition amendments. But in the actual talks with representatives of employers and workers the Cabinet eventually yielded on a number of points which it had refused to consider on the floor of parliament. These events left a bitter taste with many members of parliament. Opposition members complained that their proposals had been voted down in parliament, while they had later been accepted in talks with extra-parliamentary interest groups. Members of governing parties equally felt that they had been told to be steadfast by a Cabinet which itself was later to yield in another place, and all political participants had the uneasy feeling that the political system as a whole had proved insufficiently effective. For its attempt to curb inflation, the Cabinet had had to rely on the voluntary support of outside agents who seemed more powerful than the formal institutions of government, and whose actual restraint fell far short of the figures which the Cabinet itself had stipulated as vital to the national interest when it drew up its budgetary proposals.

The elections of November 1972 further reinforced this climate of defeat: for the religious parties who had formed the traditional centre of Dutch politics for two generations lost heavily, to the advantage of the left parties on the one hand, and the Liberals who carried on a bitter anti-Socialist campaign on the other. A period followed of arduous inter-party negotiations during which time the outgoing Cabinet transacted the remainder of the departmental budgets with the newly elected Lower House. These debates resulted in a few changes, notably in increases in appropriations for the Ministry of Transport and of Culture and Social Work, affecting in all 0·3 per cent of the original budget proposals. The Upper House assented without debate as it had done in the previous year.

Finally, on 11 May 1973, after an unprecedented period of negotiations of 164 days, a new Cabinet entered office. It included ministers of five parties, and rested on the explicit endorsements of the three main left parties and on tacit sufferance from the Catholics and a majority of the Anti-Revolutionary party. The new Cabinet almost immediately sought certain changes in the already-voted 1973 budget in order to give substance to some of its most immediate policy goals. But these short-term measures were rejected by a majority of the Lower House, due to the critical attitude of the Catholic party. This action, undertaken in a climate of highly uncertain inter-party relations, *may* foreshadow a more active use of budgetary weapons by *ad hoc* parliamentary majorities against a Cabinet which is not assured of a formal parliamentary backing. Against such actions, the Cabinet is likely to bring into play arguments derived from the critical state of government finance, as well as the ultimate sanction of dissolution and/or resignation. The latter would oblige a highly divided parliament to find an alternative government to the one formed after the protracted crisis of 1972–3.

8 *Centrifugal and Centripetal Forces in the Budgetary Process – a Summary*

The budgetary process consists essentially in the allocation of scarce resources and unwanted burdens. In this process some forces and institutions pay particular attention to the cause of special interests, while others are charged with fitting such special demands into some form of overall policy. For want of a better term we shall call the first centrifugal and the latter centripetal forces. Using this simple dichotomy as a lead, we may now summarise Dutch experience with the budgetary process as follows.

The chief centrifugal forces consist of demands on behalf of particular interests (which may be wide or narrow in scope, more or less organised, activist themselves or more the object of concern on the part of others). The demands on behalf of such groups reach the political process in different ways. Most contacts are institutionalised by way of an intricate network of advisory councils and subsidy arrangements. But more direct forms of pressure have also been practised and, because of their newness, sometimes with considerable effect. The chief points at which pressures are directed are ministers, specialised members of parliament, particular sections of the government bureaucracy (and as a vehicle to carry messages to these centres of authoritative power, the mass media). Specialised government agencies have been particularly important. The Dutch bureaucracy has traditionally been very loosely structured. Departments enjoy great autonomy, and within departments special divisions also have a fair degree of discretion. The demands of special interests therefore find easy access. They usually filter through bureaucratic channels, reaching a decisive point in the encounter at the official and ministerial level with the Ministry of Finance. At this stage, members of parliament may exercise an important (if indirect) role. Specialist committees of parliament tend to be manned by persons with a strong personal or even organisational interest in increased expenditures in that particular sector. Such committees therefore become centres for political pressures which often parallel the efforts of interest groups outside parliament, and even the professional concerns of particular sections of the bureaucracy. If such pressures are only marginally effective in any one year, they tend to have a larger impact in following years because ministers will confront the Minister of Finance in future years with the argument that they must meet clear parliamentary demands. These demands are even more effective, because they often enjoy inter-party support. In addition, the Opposition as such tends to be a source for upward pressures in expenditures as they may often take up the demands of particular interests without the hindrance of actual government responsibility.

Against these centrifugal forces, the following centripetal factors may be singled out. The key figure is the Minister of Finance, who cannot possibly meet all demands simultaneously. He is assisted in his co-ordinating tasks by his department, most notably by its budget division which incorporates a special corps of Treasury inspectors, and a planning division which draws attention to the longer-term implications of present policies. The minister also finds support from the Bank of the Netherlands which is likely to warn against the dangers of an expansion of government expenditures for the balance of payments and for inflationary tendencies in the economy. The Minister of Finance must appeal to the Cabinet in case of disagreement with other ministers. In the Cabinet he is likely to find most support from the Prime Minister who has no important spending department of his own. For the rest, the Minister of Finance is only as strong as his personal character, his political position in the Cabinet and the urgency of the financial and economic situation dictates. In his effort to withstand pressures for increased expenditures, the minister will draw attention to facts and figures on the one hand, and to earlier policy agreements on the other. Usually, party leaders will have agreed to some extent on priorities in the arduous negotiations which precede the formation of a new Cabinet. The leaders of governing parties in parliament are therefore to a certain degree hostages to Cabinet decisions: as long as they are prepared to sustain a Cabinet, they are likely to be potential allies of the Minister of Finance in resisting the more outrageous demands by members of parliament, even if these are supported by members of their own party. To some extent the meetings of parliamentary parties (and of their leaders on the government side) provide a modicum of co-ordination at the parliamentary level which vaguely reflects the co-ordinating function of the Cabinet at the ministerial level.

But such political processes do not take place *in vacuo*. Political decisions must be accorded legitimacy by the active political strata. To some extent the chief political actors in the government and of the governing parties in parliament can rely on the sense of trust given to any government in power. But against the pressures of special interests, they must also appeal towards centripetal forces in the society at large. Perhaps the most important in this respect have been the large number of central organisations which exist in modern society. In the last forty years, Dutch society has witnessed the growth of a massive organisational network in almost all of its sectors. Such organisations may provide powerful instruments of specialised pressure, but they also provide important forums for consultation and negotiation: for all their pressure on government they also often help to moderate the more extreme demands of some of their own backwoodsmen.

In the pushing and pulling which make up the actual budgetary process, parliament seems to many of its members to be a helpless victim rather than an independent political actor. Members may ventilate wishes and grievances, but are expected to register and legitimise decisions reached in what seems to most of them a process of transcendental magnitude. In the longer run, members of parliament have an important influence on these decisions – perhaps more so than they themselves think. But this does not prevent them from feeling many a short-term frustration.

Authors' Note

We are greatly indebted for a critical reading of an earlier version of this paper to Mr C. H. van Alderwegen, Professor H. J. Hofstra and Professor Th. Koopmans of Leiden University, to Professor C. J. vn Eijk and Professor L. Koopmans of Rotterdam University, to Mr W. Drees Jr, to Mr D. A. P. W. van der Ende and a number of unknown officials in the Dutch Ministry of Finance, and to Professor A. W. Coats of the University of Nottingham. For general analyses on the budgetary process in the Netherlands, see W. Drees Jr, *On the Level of Government Expenditure in The Netherlands after the War* (Leiden, Stenfert Kroese, 1955); W. Drees Jr and F. Th. Gubbi, *Overheidsuitgaven in Theorie en Praktijk* (Groningen, Wolters-Noordhoff, 1968); L. Koopmans, *De Beslissingen over de Rijksbegroting* (Deventer, Kluwer, 1968); L. Koopmans, *Overheidsfinancien* (Haarlem, Bohn, 1971); and C. N. van Wijngaarden and W. F. van der Griend, *De Rijksbegroting – Verleden en Toekomst* (Alphen, Samson, 1971). An important source in English is the annual *The Netherlands Budget Memorandum*, a somewhat abridged translation published since 1952 of the *Miljoenen-nota*, which the Minister of Finance submits to parliament each September.

CHAPTER 16

PARLIAMENTARY CONTROL OVER PUBLIC EXPENDITURE IN SWITZERLAND

Paolo Urio

The problem of parliamentary control has arisen in Switzerland relatively recently. In 1964 considerable over-expenditure in one of the most sensitive arenas of Swiss politics (defence) led parliament to review the means of control at its disposal.[1] In the resulting debate the defenders of the principle of the separation of powers found themselves opposed by the supporters of more effective control and of the supremacy of the Federal Assembly. This latter principle has been well defined by the *commission de gestion* (committee on the administration) of the National Council.[2] Quoting Article 85 of the federal Constitution, the *commission de gestion* observed that the Federal Assembly, which is:

the authority constituted by the representatives of the people and those of the cantons, and which is consequently the supreme organ of the Confederation, must include in its responsibilities the supervision of all the other organs of the Confederation, both the administrative and the judicial, in order to see that they carry out their work according to popular expectations and as the constitution and law have laid down. Their activities must be in accordance with the political objectives of the Confederation. . . . But when the authority with overall responsibility establishes that federal organs are tending to work in an excessively independent

[1] For a brief description of this crisis see Paolo Urio, 'L'Affaire des Mirages', Annuaire Suisse de Science Politique, Lausanne, vol. 8 (1968), pp. 90–100. For a more detailed analysis see Paolo Urio, *Processus de Décision et Contrôle Démocratique en Suisse*, thesis of Geneva University 1970 (March 1972).

[2] The Swiss parliament, the Assemblée Fédérale (the Federal Assembly) consists of two chambers, the Conseil National (National Council), which represents the people, and the Conseil des Etats (Council of States) which represents the cantons making up the federation. The two legislative councils have the same powers, each decision of the Federal Assembly needing to be approved by both chambers. The executive branch of the Swiss Confederation is headed by the Conseil Fédéral (Federal Council).

fashion, and are elevating the principle of the separation of powers to an absolute status which contradicts its political significance, it is then for that authority to remind these organs of the aims of the Confederation, and to make sure that they function once more in the sense decided by the people.

The *commission de gestion* states further that it is not a question of parliament taking over from the government its normal role of supervision of the administration. Parliament's overall supervisory function involves questions which 'pass beyond the framework of supervision which the government exercises over the administration' and which have been summarised by the *commission de gestion* as follows:

As supreme authority parliament must ensure that the administration carries out the laws and decrees voted by the Federal Assembly in the sense that the Assembly has given them, and does not attempt to extract more from them than this. It must ensure that the administration plays the role given it by the Constitution, and does not extend its powers at the expense of parliament, government, the cantons or the electorate. It is also its duty to see whether the administration is making a reasonable use of its powers. ... Another political objective of parliamentary control is to supervise the administration's use of public funds.[1]

The Federal Council has also clearly defined the limits of parliamentary control as it sees them:

According to well-established theory and practice, when control over the administration creates a difference of view between the two authorities, the Federal Assembly has the right to issue 'invitations' or 'recommendations' to the Federal Council to conform to its own opinion. These directions are not binding on the administration. But it is undeniable that the Federal Council should always do its best to take account of the wishes expressed to it by the *commissions de gestion* and the two legislative councils. Nevertheless, the power of control does not permit the Assembly to give categorical instructions to the Federal Council. It does not give it the right to annul or modify a decision taken by the Council, nor to carry out an administrative act within the

---

[1] *Rapport présenté au Conseil National par sa Commission de Gestion au Sujet de l'Extension du Contrôle Parlementaire*, 13 April 1965, Berne, Chancellerie Féderale, pp. 5–7.

province of that authority. The approval or disapproval of measures taken by the Federal Council and, in a general manner, of the administration, has no juridical basis, but constitutes an act of a political nature.[1]

The 1964 crisis revealed certain weaknesses in the federal administration, in particular its difficulty in dealing with especially complex technical, economic or financial problems.[2] It was consequently decided to carry out a major reform of the defence administration (affecting the structure and techniques of decision-making) and at the same time to reinforce parliamentary controls. What have been the consequences of these two reforms for the exercise of parliament's supervisory role? Is the Swiss parliament, representing the people and the cantons, as well equipped today as in the past to control the public expenditure of the Confederation? In order to answer this question the first part of this chapter describes certain aspects of the Swiss parliamentary system which have some influence over the use of parliamentary controls. In the second part the means of parliamentary control are analysed, both as they existed before the Mirages crisis and as they do today. In the third and last part an attempt is made to analyse the consequences for the exercise of parliamentary control of the rationalisation of decision-making.[3]

I THE BACKGROUND TO THE EXERCISE OF PARLIAMENTARY CONTROL

We do not intend here to describe the Swiss political system in its entirety (although in the author's experience it is not widely understood), but simply to underline some of its more characteristic traits where they are relevant to an evaluation of parliamentary control.[4]

The Swiss political system rests upon a society which is divided, not only in the political sense but also linguistically and ethnically

[1] *Rapport du Conseil Fédéral à l'Assemblée Fédérale Concernant le Projet de Loi Relatif à l'Extension du Contrôle Parlementaire, Présenté par la Commission de Gestion du Conseil National*, 27 August 1965, Berne, Chancellerie Fédérale, pp. 6–7.

[2] In this case it was a question of the development and purchase of a high-performance fighter aircraft.

[3] In Switzerland official terminology has not yet found an equivalent to the French 'Rationalisation des Choix Budgétaires' (RCB) or the American 'Planning Programming and Budgeting System' (PPBS). The terms employed are usually *'rationalisation des décisions'*, *'analyse de systèmes'* or PPBS in reference to the American situation.

[4] Among the many treatises on constitutional law, Jean-François Aubert's *Traité de Droit Constitutionnel Suisse* (Paris, Balloz et Neuchâtel, ed. Idées et Calendes, 1967, 2 vols) may be cited.

as well as in culture, economy and religion. The need to preserve the cohesion of this diverse collectivity, so that the central government can keep the peace and achieve economic development at home as well as defend its borders against powerful neighbouring states, has led to the adoption of certain rules (some formally stated, some not) for the political game. The common aim of these rules is the pursuit of equilibrium between the different parts of the system.

In the first place, the federal system allows considerable autonomy to the cantons and the communes, and the former have parliamentary representation through the Council of States. In the second place, the system is neither parliamentary nor presidential. In effect, parliament cannot bring down the government and the government has no powers to dissolve the two chambers. The Federal President, moreover, has no more powers than his six colleagues who make up the government. He has at most the office of representation. These two characteristics of the system illustrate the preoccupation of the Swiss with the need to avoid giving any kind of supremacy to any person or institution, for fear of resulting tension or conflict.

If we now examine the problem of the representation of political interests within the ruling institution (parliament and the federal government), the same preoccupations reappear. Since the introduction of proportional representation in 1919 the different political interests have been guaranteed seats in the National Council in proportion to the number of votes obtained. At present ten parties share the 200 seats in this chamber. The situation is, however, different in the Council of States, where some parties are underrepresented. This is the case of the Socialist party in particular. This party, which represents a good quarter of the electorate, is usually outvoted by the parties of the centre and right wing in the elections to the Council of States (which occur at cantonal level) and can only exceptionally get one of its own members elected. At the last elections in October 1971 only four Socialists were elected out of forty-four, or less than 10 per cent. The reasons for this are partly historical and ideological factors, but the system of majority voting which prevails in several of the cantons for the elections to this chamber also plays a part.

The principle of proportional representation reappears to a considerable extent at government level. Without going back too far in history, it may be noted that since 1944 each main party has always had at least one representative in the Federal Council.[1] Since 1960, two seats have belonged to the Socialists, two to the Radicals, two

[1] There is only one exception: the absence of the Socialists between 1955 and 1959.

to the Christian Democrats and one to the PAB (the party of peasants, artisans and bourgeois). At the last elections the Socialists won 46 seats, the Radicals 49, the Christian Democrats 44 and PAB 21. The government can therefore count on a comfortable majority of 160 seats out of 200, or 80 per cent. In the Council of States the government enjoys a similar situation. This is a considerably larger majority than is necessary for government.

The distribution of seats during the last five parliaments has in fact been such that only two or three parties out of the governing coalition would have been enough to secure a majority. The coalition does not, it is clear, result from arithmetical necessity, but arises from a genuine desire to confide the direction of federal affairs to the representatives of all the principal parties. This situation, exceptional among multi-party systems, has important consequences for the exercise of parliamentary control over public expenditure. The members of parliament whose parties form the governing coalition have little tendency to disapprove of the actions of the Federal Council. Nor should it be forgotten that as a collegiate organ the government is responsible *in corpore* for all its acts. It is consequently very difficult to attribute responsibility to any single federal councillor (who belongs to one of the governing parties) for a decision which he may have made, but which *de jure* emanates from the Federal Council. Moreover, even if all the deputies of one of the coalition parties were to vote against the government, the three others could nevertheless obtain a majority.[1] The Communist party and the Independents (who sometimes take on the role of Opposition) are also both much too small to affect the vote. The government can therefore only lose its majority in exceptional circumstances, that is if opposed by a coalition which is made up of many of its own party members.

The importance attached to the association of all important political groups with the government of the country is also seen in the pressure groups. These must be consulted, according to the federal Constitution, at the preparatory stage of decisions on economic and social matters. This pattern is not of course exclusive to Switzerland, although its status as a constitutional requirement is perhaps exceptional. Nevertheless, the mixing of political and economic affairs is of particular importance in Switzerland as a result of the small size of the country and also of the 'amateur' status of its

[1] This applies only to the National Council. In the Council of States the Christian-Democrats could bring about a negative vote if all the non-government parties were to abstain or vote against the government. But as all decisions have to be approved by both chambers, the original remark holds true.

parliamentary representatives.[1] The first of these factors requires no comment here, but the second should be emphasised. The Swiss member of parliament continues his normal employment, visiting Berne for parliamentary sessions and meetings of the committees to which he belongs. He has no fixed salary, but is paid modest daily expenses.

The latest figures available relating to members of parliament were collected by Jean Meynaud and refer to the situation as it was in 1961–2.[2] Out of the 196 deputies in the National Council, there were 21 state councillors (cantonal executives), 18 members of municipal councils, 9 university or school teachers, 10 other civil servants, 21 lawyers, 15 writers or journalists, 3 doctors or veterinary surgeons, 3 engineers or architects, 36 officials of trade federations or associations, 15 employees in manufacturing and commerce or artisans, 11 directors of industrial enterprises or administrators of co-operatives, 7 workmen, 25 agriculturalists, and 2 others. Out of these 196 deputies, 109 (or 55·6 per cent) were found to be involved or to have been involved in some pressure group activity.[3] In practice, as Meynaud would admit, in view of the fragmentary nature of his data, a much larger number of deputies are so involved. It is clear that the principal sectors of the economy are well represented in parliament.

The fusion of politics and economics which has just been briefly illustrated can be considered both as a consequence and a cause of the desire to allow all national interests to participate in decision-making.[4] In practice this has led to a search for compromise which starts at the administrative stage of decision-making. At this stage the relevant choices are made with the participation of all the principal interested parties so that they can only be revived with great difficulty at the parliamentary stage, where indeed most of the same participants are to be found again. An attempt to extract even a minor modification to a proposal from parliamentary debate leads inevitably to the whole laboriously constructed bill being referred back to the administration, with consequences that can easily be imagined.

[1] There are of course also historical and psychological factors which there is no room to discuss here.

[2] Jean Meynaud, Les organisations professionelles en Suisse (Lausanne, Payot, 1963), pp. 289–90.

[3] A similar though slightly different, situation exists in the Council of States. See Meynaud, op. cit.

[4] There are, of course, other factors (which have not yet been subjected to systematic analysis), for example the unpopularity of professionals of all sorts, and of the ostentatious use of money in politics.

These observations apply in particular to economic and social proposals. In other sectors of State activity (e.g. monetary policy, defence) these tendencies are avoided to some extent. Budgetary proposals, however, are especially affected in this way, and the annual budget, which covers all aspects of national activity, is heavily based on previous compromise; so much so, that not only do the budget and accounts nearly always receive approval from parliament, but expenditures voted by federal decree (and which are subsequently included in the budget) usually also pass without challenge.

There remains the role of the people. In general, the citizens of Switzerland have the power to intervene in decision-making at two points, which is one of the outstanding characteristics of the Swiss political system. The right of 'initiative' confers on the people the power to propose and eventually to take a decision, while the referendum allows the people the last word on any law already voted by parliament. In the realm of public expenditure it is the latter power which is of interest. However, only federal laws or federal decrees of general application are subject to referendum, and as all legislation relating to expenditure takes the form of simple decrees, the budget and all financial decisions by the Confederation are consequently excluded from direct popular control.

In conclusion, the exercise of parliamentary control cannot be dissociated from a number of factors which in turn determine the functioning of the political system. The Swiss political system is usually successful in producing a broad consensus in most governmental activities, and this tends to reduce the importance of parliamentary intervention in budgetary affairs (and not only in these). Thus it may be speculated whether the real control over public expenditure does not take place outside parliament altogether. We cannot be more precise without more systematic research in this field. It remains true however that parliament, the only organ of government which is almost entirely directly elected,[1] must be able to play the part of supreme authority even though a consensus may have been reached before it receives a proposal. Moreover, for various reasons the main pressure groups are not interested in the preparation of all legislation, and for this, parliament's capacity to intervene could assume a fundamental importance. The budget and national accounts can as a result of their global character include decisions falling into either of these classes. It therefore seems essential that parliament should be in a position

[1] In two cantons deputies to the Council of States are not elected by popular suffrage but by the cantonal parliament.

to intervene effectively, and with full knowledge of the facts, in this
essential arena of the political life of the country.

II PARLIAMENTARY CONTROL IN SWITZERLAND

The Situation Prior to the Mirages Affair

Parliamentary control is exercised by means of the election of
federal councillors, *interpellation* (questions to ministers), parliamentary questions, work in committee and the examination of
certain reports (from the *commission de gestion* and other special
committees) or of government proposals (relating to expenditure,
the budget and accounts). As far as the first of these methods is
concerned it is sufficient to note that it is virtually never used;
indeed it may be assumed that a federal councillor stays in office as
long as he wishes.

According to the rules of both chambers, any deputy can request
an explanation from the Federal Council on any federal matter by
using the right of *interpellation*. *Interpellations* must be made by at
least eleven national councillors or four state councillors. They
require the government to reply to the question immediately or in
the very near future. But the Federal Council has the right to
adjourn its reply, and even once this has been given, parliament
makes no decision, the *interpellation's* principal author being
limited to saying whether he is or is not satisfied. Like *interpellations,* questions (also known as *'petites questions'*) ask for explanations from the government, but these require only one signature.
They differ from *interpellations* in that their only outcome is the
Federal Council's reply, which may be oral or written.[1]

The work of the parliamentary committees in Switzerland has
many analogies with that of other European countries. It may however be noted that Swiss committees are set up, in accordance with
the Swiss political system, to give political, regional and linguistic
balance; their sessions are not public, they have only consultative
powers, and they depend to a very large extent on the information
provided to them by the federal administration.

The Federal Assembly also has the power of reviewing the record
of the Federal Council over the past year as a whole at the time of
the debate on the *'rapport de gestion'* (report on the administration)

---

[1] It may be noted that parliament does have two other methods by which it
could in a general sense exercise control, but which technically are the instruments
of parliament's right of initiative. These are *'motions'* and *'postulats'*; the first
oblige the government to table a draft Bill, the second to consider whether a
proposal should be presented to parliament.

which the government presents annually. Parliament has the power to accept or reject this, but in practice it always accepts it. Parliament has in addition the power to request at any time a 'special report' on a specific subject.

It is normal practice that the representatives of the taxpayers should be able to control the expenditure of the Confederation, and especially that the allocation of resources should be a question of political appraisal, based on the way society has ordered its objectives. It is possible to distinguish four types of expenditure: (1) that provided explicitly by the Constitution or laws, (2) that required by the Constitution or laws, but of which the exact amount depends on other circumstances over which the Confederation has no power (for example the subventions made to the cantons in proportion to their own expenditure), (3) expenditure required by the Constitution or law of which the amount is fixed by the federal authorities (for example, subsidies for major roads), and (4) expenditure which arises from certain objectives fixed by the Constitution, but where the latter leaves the relevant authority a choice of means (for example the purchase of defence equipment). Parliament intervenes at different stages, depending on which type of expenditure is concerned. Its approval is required for changes in the constitution or the law, and for decrees (*arrêtés*) which enable public purchasing or public works to be undertaken, and finally for all expenditure provided for a certain period ahead, which is included in the budget. It should be noted that the votes on expenditure and the approval of the budget take the form of simple decrees, which are not subject to referendum.

The budget is drawn up by the different civil service departments and presented to the legislative councils by the Federal Council. Unlike procedure over the *'rapport de gestion'*, parliament is not limited to accepting or refusing the budget as a whole, but has powers of amendment. In practice parliament makes a very moderate use of these powers. The changes proposed usually affect negligible percentages of the total amount. In particular, parliament is not in the habit of making any change at this stage in expenditures which it has previously voted in decrees. The budget debate is not normally the occasion for much argument, especially since certain items of expenditure which could give rise to altercation (like the defence programmes) are discussed on another occasion.

After the necessary expenditure has been authorised by parliament, the government is responsible for its allocation to the items intended. The Assembly has the opportunity of checking on this allocation by the Federal Council and the administration when it

L

examines the national accounts. But this form of financial control is not exclusively parliamentary; the administration itself makes a preliminary check through a division of the Department of Finance and Customs known as the Contrôle des Finances, which collaborates with the financial committees of both councils, and also with a body representing these, the Délégation des Finances. Financial control in Switzerland is consequently an administrative and parliamentary responsibility, but not a matter for the judiciary, as it is for example in France with the Cour des Comptes. The two councils can only accept or reject the national accounts, and to date they have always accepted them. The power of parliament is therefore very limited. However, its checks on the use of funds are not limited to the reception of the national accounts. If the government exhausts the funds allocated under a certain heading it has to go back to parliament to ask for a supplementary credit. Deputies can then ask the Federal Council for the reasons why the original vote was not sufficient, and if the explanations are not thought satisfactory the additional finance can be refused or the original decision altered.

In conclusion it should be noted that, until the Mirages affair, parliament was not able to question federal civil servants without the government's agreement, and there had been no investigations comparable to the hearings of the US parliamentary system. The non-professional character of the Swiss parliament, and its lack of any kind of information-providing service, were making it more and more difficult for the Assembly to deal with any complex problem. Difficulties were already becoming apparent in the 1950s, but it was only at the time of the Mirages affair that the full limitations of parliamentary control became apparent. Parliament then voted some 870 million SF for the purchase of 100 Mirage fighter aircraft. Three years later, as a result of modifications to the aircraft decided by the Defence Department, this was not enough and the government came back to parliament to ask for supplementary funds of over 500 million SF. Parliament, which felt that some deceit had been practised, refused; an investigatory commission was set up and on the basis of its report it was decided to reduce the costs of the operation by buying 57 aircraft instead of 100. Parliament was convinced that the behaviour of the Defence Department had been unscrupulous, but at the same time realised that on its own part efficient control over the administration had been lacking. Consequently, at the same time as requesting the Federal Council to institute a reform of the Defence Department, it decided to set the two *commissions de gestion* the task of preparing new legislation to strengthen parliamentary control.

The Strengthening of Parliamentary Control

In the debate on the strengthening of parliamentary control the following main points were stressed:

1   The establishment of a *'service de documentation'* for parliament.
2   Regularisation of procedure for preparing proposals for submission to parliament.
3   The powers of parliamentary committees and in particular their power to hear evidence from federal civil servants.
4   The powers of the *commissions de gestion* and *commissions des finances* and in particular their power to examine government documents and to obtain further information.
5   The possibility of establishing committees of enquiry.

1   *The creation of a 'service de documentation'.* This first point was the least controversial. The idea of setting up such a service was in fact rapidly approved by all parties and made law in Article 40A[1] of the legislation on relations between the two houses of parliament. A simple federal decree, which came into force on 1 January 1968, lays down the requirements and organisation of the service. The service is at the disposal of the legislative councils, their committees and their members (Article 1). Instructions can be given to it by the presidents of both houses, by parliamentary committees and political groups as well as by individual deputies (Article 3). The service must collect the documentation required,

> draw the attention of the committees and of members to important publications relating to a particular project or to questions of general political interest, or provide them with these publications, keep a record of the subjects discussed by the Councils and their committees and be at the disposal of the committees and of deputies to prepare parliamentary questions and study questions of law. (Article 1).

The *service de documentation* may use the library of parliament and the different libraries and research departments of the federal administration, which is obliged to supply all possible assistance

[1] Federal law on Federal Assembly procedure, 23 March 1962 (state at 31 October 1966), Berne, Chancellerie Fédérale, p. 11.

(Article 5). The *service* can also, if the body or person who requires the information agrees, ask federal departments for

> information on questions relating to technical or legal matters. The departments and divisions are under an obligation to supply such information. The Federal Council can relieve civil servants of their official secrets restrictions, including defence secrets, and authorise them to produce official documents. (Article 6).

It may be noted that this latter provision was not proposed by the Federal Council, but was introduced by the Council of States and approved by the National Council. However in spite of this useful article members of parliament still depend on the goodwill of the administration for the information they require. Article 7 appears to open a loophole in this provision. It provides that 'if the *service de documentation* is not able, even with the assistance of civil service departments and divisions, to provide the information required, it can (as an exception) pass the request on to non-civil service experts.' Apart from the 'exceptional' character of this provision, it will be realised that recourse to outside experts is expensive, and it seems unlikely that the *service*'s budget could cover such costs. Questions on technical problems, which are more likely than legal problems to require the use of outside expertise, have moreover been rare up to date. Having made this observation, we shall now examine the record of the *service* so far.

The director of the *service*, M. Ezio Cattaneo, took up his post on 1 April 1968. He was allocated an assistant for press analysis on 1 May 1968, a scientific assistant to deal with foreign affairs, science, research and historical research on 10 October 1968, a secretary on 1 January 1969, and an assistant qualified to deal with economics on 15 April 1969. In view of this very limited staff, it is understandable that the *service* has concentrated on satisfying requests rather than on the *ex officio* activity suggested in the Federal Council's decree. Deputies have made use of the *service* since its beginning. From 1 April 1968 to 30 September 1969 the members of the two chambers supplied it with 733 requests for information,[1] of which 476 were during sessions and 257 outside session time. The number of requests continues to increase, but this cannot go on indefinitely without an enlargement of the *service*'s staff. The 733 requests were

[1] Secretariat of the Federal Assembly, Service de Documentation. *Données Statistiques sur l'Activité du Service de Documentation de l'Assemblée Fédérale*, Berne 6 October 1969. All figures are drawn from this document, and it may be noted that the work of the secretariat is not included in the number of requests dealt with.

supplied by 157 deputies, of which 131 were national councillors, and 26 state councillors; 42 deputies made one request each, 75 two to five, 22 six to ten and 18 more than ten each. In addition, 15 parliamentary committtes were sent papers.

The contents of these requests have been essentially legalistic. There is no precise explanation for this, but two hypotheses can be put forward. It could be that members of parliament are more likely, in view of their background and experience, to interest them-selves in the legal aspects of different proposals. On the other hand, it would seem that, at present, members who are concerned with the technical aspects of projects can more easily obtain the necessary information via parliamentary committees, from the evidence of civil servants or independent experts. With its present resources, the *service* could not in fact satisfy technical questions above a certain level of complexity. Nevertheless the service proposes to extend its activities to the analysis of scientific journals in order to provide deputies with more specialised information; it hopes to collect and distribute among deputies certain government papers which should be more widely known, and to make a more systematic analysis of press coverage of current problems. Even if, however, the depart-ment does manage by means of increased resources to provide a satisfactory information service extended to the technical as well as legal aspects of the problems studied, the members of parliament would have to find enough time to absorb this information. It is inconceivable that the *service* could be made responsible for draw-ing deductions from the information collected, since this is essen-tially a political task which could only be performed by someone with the same political ideas as the deputy in search of the infor-mation.[1] It must be admitted that members do not have time to consider all proposals in detail, at least in Switzerland.

There are two possible solutions to this to be considered :

(*a*) depending on whether members of parliament remain amateurs or semi-professionals as they are now,
(*b*) or become full-time professional politicians.[2]

In the first case political parties could establish secretariats which would be responsible for permanent liaison with the *service de*

[1] This does not of course exclude recourse to outside experts.
[2] It is true that certain federal deputies are full-time politicians, since they are also members of cantonal executives. But at the federal level professional parliamentarians can be defined as those who occupy themselves with federal politics on a full-time basis.

documentation and for analysing the papers received from it. The objection to this solution is that it would involve too great a central-isation of party affairs at the expense of linguistic and regional diversities.[1] This could be avoided by requiring the secretariats to include employees from the three linguistic regions, at least on a rota. However, the most serious objection to this proposal would appear to be its cost.

Alternatively members of parliament could become full-time pro-fessionals paid by the State and be enabled to employ personal assistants. This is the most expensive solution and the one which is least likely to be adopted. It nevertheless deserves serious exami-nation and should not be rejected simply on the grounds of the unfortunate results obtained in other countries. Everything else being equal (in particular, the integrity of members), this would be the best method of solving the problem of members of parliament's levels of information. It would not only give them more time for their work but also provide them with chosen and reliable assist-ants. The *service de documentation* could continue to function as it does at present[2] and would ensure among other things liaison between deputies and the administration. The political parties' sec-retariats could therefore be much smaller, and fill a mainly co-ordinating rôle while parliament or its committees were sitting.

In conclusion, it seems clear that the effectiveness of the *service de documentation* does not depend only on its organisation and resources, or on the number of requests for information it has to satisfy. It is also necessary for members of parliament to be able to analyse the information provided more effectively than at present.

2 *The regularisation of procedure in preparing proposals for parlia-ment.* Proposals were put forward by both the legislative councils which were designed to require the Federal Council to follow a stricter procedure in pre-parliamentary drafting. The object of this campaign was to give the Federal Council, and especially the Federal Assembly, full liberty to make their own decisions. The deputies considered in fact that the consultation between interested groups in the course of the drawing-up of legislation could lead to

---

[1] See René Helg, 'La Haute Surveillance du Parlement sur le Governement et l'Administration', *Revue de Droit Suisse*, 1966, 11, pp. 85–164. See also Richard Baumlin, 'Die Kontrolle des Parlaments über die Regierung und Verwaltung' *Revue de Droit Suisse*, 1966, 11, pp. 165–319.

[2] With, however, an increase in personnel.

compromise which would bind the executive, and, more seriously, the legislature.[1]

The proposal from the National Council would have given the Federal Council the power to regulate by ordinance the procedure for drawing up projects for legislation. The executive was given the responsibility of laying down general rules to govern expert committees (their convocation, terms of reference, objectives and methods of work) and to regularise the procedure for consulting the cantons and interested organisations. This ordinance would have had to be approved by the Federal Assembly. The Council of States, while in principle adopting the proposal of the other chamber, did not want the general rules described above to be included in the ordinance. However, with the object of 'compelling the authorities to pay more attention to preliminary procedure' it suggested that 'the Federal Council should conduct preliminary procedure itself, and as strictly as possible', and that 'parliamentary committees should have complete access to the working materials used in preliminary procedure'.[2]

The Federal Council, with the support of federal judge Favre, rejected this part of the proposal *en bloc*, and eliminated the relevant articles.[3] The executive's conception of parliamentary procedure was as follows:

What is essential is that good laws should be passed. The Federal Council provides for this in drawing up a preliminary proposal which outlines its own conception of the law. It gathers information and reconciles the different interests in order to guarantee that the law is in accordance with the practical situation it will affect. It is the role of parliament to examine the proposal with especial attention to its legal and political aspects, and to either accept or reject it. It will refuse its consent if it appears that despite the efforts of the government the interest of a group has overruled the interest of the public. Parliament's task in reaching a conclusion will be facilitated by the new arrangements by which parliament can obtain information from experts unconnected with any interested group.[4]

[1] See *Rapport Présenté au Conseil des Etats par sa Commission de Gestion au Sujet de l'Extension du Contrôle Parlementaire*, 12 February 1966, Berne, Chancellerie Fédérale, pp. 7–9.

[2] ibid., p. 16.

[3] Antoine Favre, *Avis Provisoire au Conseil Fédéral sur l'Extension du Contrôle Parlementaire*, Berne, Chancellerie Fédérale, 31 May 1965, pp. 16–19, and *Rapport du Conseil Fédéral* of 27 August 1965, op. cit., pp. 12–15.

[4] ibid., p. 14.

The reasons given by the Federal Council for its opposition to the legislature's proposal can be summarised as follows. First, the preparation of laws and decrees (i.e. preparliamentary procedure) is the responsibility of the Federal Council and not the Federal Assembly.[1] Secondly it is impossible to define the general laws asked for by the legislative councils. Thirdly, the proposal would conflict with the principle of the separation of powers, and fourthly, pre-parliamentary procedure is the exercise of the art of politics, which could not be replaced by a set of regulations. These arguments soon found a majority in the legislative councils, so the articles in question were struck out of the two projects.

It must be admitted that the Federal Council's arguments were well founded, especially in law. On the other hand, there are two observations to be made against them on political grounds.

If it is true that parliament can always refuse to vote for a proposal drawn up by the government, it should be able to do so while being fully aware of the reasons why. In the first place, parliament should become informed on the drafting of a proposal at a very early stage, unless this inconveniences the work of drafting. This would allow parliament to become aware of the background to different proposals and to do its own work more rapidly, because the debate, the vote in the committee stage and a full session could follow each other more quickly. This would undoubtedly be an advantage in urgent decisions (for example in economic or defence legislation). Secondly, parliament should be associated officially with the preparliamentary procedure, even if only as an observer. The claim made by the Federal Council that it had consulted 'experts drawn from among the members of the Federal Assembly' was inadequate. Thirdly, members should be given the resources necessary to enable them to follow preparliamentary procedure effectively.

These observations lead to another problem. Inevitably an increase of responsibilities and hence of the resources needed to

[1] ibid., pp. 13–15, where the Federal Council adopts Favre's opinion (from Favre, op. cit., p. 18): 'The preparation of legislation is the Federal Council's responsibility. In the execution of this function, the Federal Council has a discretionary liberty limited only by the constitutional provisions which reserve the right of the cantons and professional groups to be consulted over some aspects. This constitutional right has been defined in a body of practice which stretches over more than a century. It cannot be restricted by new legislation. Contrary to what is stated in the Report [of the National Council's *commission de gestion*] this is not a procedure which is eroding the constitutional powers of the Federal Assembly, since the latter is free to do as it thinks best with a proposal drawn up by the Federal Council.'

carry them out would lead to considerably more work for deputies. Once again this raises the question of whether Swiss members of parliament do in fact have the time to take up these responsibilities and use the resources concerned.

3 *Increasing the powers of parliamentary committees.* The legislative councils considered this problem under three headings: the powers of all the committees, the powers of certain committees particularly important for parliament's supervisory rule (the *commissions de gestion* and the finance committees), and the powers of parliamentary commissions of enquiry.

(*a*) *The powers of parliamentary committees in general* The National Council's proposal (Article 47a) envisaged the possibility of asking 'advice from experts on subjects' which call for special knowledge' and of summoning 'civil servants and experts from outside the administration in order to question them on particularly difficult details'. It considered that when a civil servant was to be involved the Federal Council should be informed in advance. The executive branch would need to free civil servants from their oaths under the official secrets acts, and in this case 'members of committees, secretaries and minute-takers' would themselves swear official secrecy'. (Article 54, 7e) The Council of States more or less accepted this proposal but went into more detail. The principal difference concerned the conditions under which civil servants could give evidence.

The Federal Council was opposed to the National Council's plan, invoking the separation of powers. It stated that 'the freedom which would consequently be given to committees ... would give them some of the directing and executive powers of the confederation. Administrative civil servants are exclusively under the control of the Federal Council. It is from their superiors alone that they can receive instructions and orders.' Moreover, the executive envisaged that this provision would 'put civil servants in an equivocal relationship with the Federal Council, which would undermine the hierarchical structure of the administration and its day-to-day operation. It would permanently impair the confidence ... between the Federal Council and the administration'.

The Federal Council consequently proposed that evidence from civil servants should be given subject to its own consent. The Council of States, while taking these views into consideration, would not abandon its intention of giving committees the power demanded. The Council of States observed that provisions had already been introduced which would take account of the Federal Council's position; effectively,[1] evidence from civil servants was to be limited to cases where it was necessary to elucidate particularly difficult points, the right to relieve civil servants from official oaths was to be expressly reserved to the Federal Council which had to be informed of the hearing, and the Federal Council had the right to be represented at the hearing and to express an opinion. The Council of States felt that in proposing that the Federal Council should not only be 'informed' but also 'heard', a compromise solution had now been reached. The executive could be reassured as to possible abuse of the situation, while committees would have the means of access to civil servants when they felt this necessary.

This solution, approved by both legislative councils, is very close to the original proposal from the National Council. While reassuring the executive, it does in fact give the committees full right to question civil servants even if the Federal Council disapproves. However, for matters of particular importance, which are covered to a large extent by official secrets or defence secrets provisions, the Federal Council alone can authorise civil servants to provide the information requested.

(b) *The powers of the commissions de gestion and commissions des finances* The National Council's proposal was for the *commissions de gestion* to be empowered 'to maintain supervision at all times over the different parts of the administration ... and to require all federal departments to supply necessary information.' The *commissions* (and parliament) were not however allotted the power to abrogate or modify decrees and decisions made by the Federal Council, the federal departments or their divisions. It was also envisaged that the *commissions* would have a permanent secretariat at their disposal.[2]

The Federal Council was not altogether happy about this proposal, seeing its provisions as too extensive and involving some risk to both public and private interests. It also believed, holding once again to the principle of the separation of powers, that the proposed solutions involved some invasion of confederal affairs. In the face of this opposition, which was shared by certain deputies, the National Council had to give the executive certain guarantees, which were subsequently taken up again by the Council of States. The article thus rewritten was approved by both chambers. The right of

[1] *Rapport du Conseil des Etats*, 12 February 1966, op. cit., pp. 22–3. The report here alludes to the Imboden proposal approved by the National Council in the autumn session of 1965 by 102 votes against 22.

[2] Article 47(4) of the proposal by the National Council.

requiring the administration to produce all official documents was maintained, but made conditional on hearing the Federal Council's opinion. Moreover, when an official secret is involved, or personal interests 'deserving of protection', or when a case is not yet concluded, the Federal Council can present a special report instead of the official documents. Finally, as for other committees, members, secretaries and minute-takers of the *commission de gestion* are all sworn to secrecy as regards the confidential documents which are submitted to them.

The articles relating to the finance committees followed the solutions adopted for the *commissions de gestion*. The finance committees also found themselves endowed with 'the absolute right for information at all times from documents relating to public finance, and to require further details from all departments.'[1] Moreover,

> the Contrôle des Finances, in particular, is required to provide the committee on a regular basis with all the details requested and to this end to put at its disposition all audit reports, evidence taken and correspondence between the Department of Finance, Customs and the other departments, the Federal Chancellery and Federal Courts, as well as all decrees by the Federal Council which affect the supervision of budgetary expenditure and the general financial administration of the Confederation.[2]

Finally, the finance committees were provided with a permanent secretariat.

The solution adopted undoubtedly makes definite progress. The position of the Federal Council was untenable; it is in fact impossible to conceive of an effective supervision over the administration within the narrow limits which the executive attempted to lay down. The *commission de gestion* of the Council of States recognised this and put the point well in its report:

> In principle, the operation and exercise of executive powers cannot be controlled and assessed unless consideration can be given to the way the executive power carries out its function ... It is therefore not possible to draw a clear line between the overall supervision exercised by the Federal Assembly and the supervision exercised by the Federal Council. It must moreover be possible to exercise overall supervision in depth. As a result there is bound to be some overlap. Up till now this factor has been

[1] Federal law of 23 March 1962, op. cit., p. 15, Art. 50(6e).
[2] ibid. (7e).

generally admitted. The activity of the finance committees and of the *délégation des finances* shows very clearly how the supervisory and executive powers are intertwined; some part of the financial control exercised by the parliamentary institutions goes beyond the limits of general supervision of the administration, and must be considered as participation by parliament in the financial management of the State.[1]

The question is whether these new measures are sufficient for their purpose and can be effectively exploited. As Helg has correctly observed: 'to imagine efficient supervision as depending exclusively on the personal action of deputies, is to ignore the complex and constantly evolving nature of the modern State.[2] Here again two solutions seem possible. Either the *commissions de gestion* can be given research services, or members of parliament can become full-time professionals. In the first case an administrative service department, on the lines of the Contrôle des Finances, could be established to assist the *commissions de gestion*. In this case it could be objected that once again members of parliament would be dependent upon the administration for their information. The establishment of a service dependent on the administration would not solve all problems, in particular those relating to the analysis of information and the drawing-up of recommendations. Would deputies feel it right to entrust the collection, classification and analysis of information to such a service? If they did not, would they have the time to carry out the analysis themselves? The growing technicality of problems of government and the volume of activity of modern states, cited earlier as the explanation of the preponderance of the executive branch, and the declining importance of parliament, require a level of attendance and a volume of work from deputies which are hardly compatible with private occupations. The establishment of supplementary services outside the civil service could be a solution, if the object is to preserve a parliament of amateurs at any price. But would members of parliament agree to dispossess themselves still further in favour of a new bureaucracy?

(c) *The possibility of establishing committees of enquiry*
Eleven new articles have been added to the law on relations between the councils to provide the institution of parliamentary committees of enquiry. The Federal Council resigned itself to this innovation in the face of parliament's determination, and was unable to obtain, as

---

[1] *Report of the Council of States*, 12 February 1966, op. cit., pp. 26–7.
[2] Helg, op. cit., p. 112. See also the interesting remarks on pp. 109–11.

we shall see, more than minor amendments to the initial proposal. In his report to the Federal Council, Judge Favre introduces the part dealing with committees of enquiry as follows:

> According to the opinion expressed in a report presented to the Congress of German Lawyers in 1964 and which is accepted in the report [of the *commission de gestion* of the National Council], parliamentary enquiry could in no circumstances be rendered superfluous by executive controls. This opinion does not compel recognition.

And later: 'it is evident that without the Mirages affair it would not have occurred to anyone to settle issues by hypothetical inquiries.'[1] But the Mirages affair did happen, parliament decided that it was necessary to arm itself against future cases of this sort, and the Federal Council had to give an opinion on parliament's proposal.

After concluding that 'such enquiries allow the legislative authority to impinge on the government's powers ... and that such an action is derogatory to the principle of the separation of powers', the executive maintained that 'our constitution includes no provision' which could serve as a legal basis for parliamentary enquiries.[2] It admitted at most that some weight could be put on Article 85 no. 11 of the federal Constitution, which appropriates to the councils the overall supervision of the administration.[3] The Federal Council nevertheless believed that the *délégation des finances*, the existing parliamentary committees and in particular the *commissions de gestion*, 'have at their disposal means which have been enlarged and strengthened for the purpose of exercising their role of overall responsibility',[4] and that this made it unnecessary to establish commissions of enquiry. If the two chambers nevertheless persisted in wishing to set up such institutions, the Federal Council believed that it would be 'legitimate to lay down certain conditions for the initiation and procedure of such an enquiry' in

[1] Favre, op. cit., pp. 14–15. This author also thinks that 'the institution of a parliamentary enquiry procedure, such as is laid down in Art. 54b–f [of the proposal of the National Council] constitutes in all cases an invasion of the authority of the government.' (ibid.)

[2] *Report of the Federal Council*, 27 August 1965, op. cit., p. 21.

[3] On the basis of this concession, the Federal Council affirmed that the function which committees of enquiry would eventually exercise 'is thus a form of the function of overall supervision'. ibid., pp. 21–2. See also below in the discussion of the main proposals relating to commissions of enquiry, approved by parliament. See also *Report of the Council of States*, 12 February 1966, op. cit., p. 45.

[4] *Report of the Federal Council*, 27 August 1965, op. cit., p. 21.

order to 'prevent any unjustifiable invasion of the competence and authority of the government'[1]

According to the new proposals, committees of enquiry could be set up, after the Federal Council had given its opinion 'if factors of considerable importance arising within the federal administration require that the Federal Assembly should clarify the situation' (Article 55, 1 and 2). The committees can ask the Federal Council to provide them with the necessary personnel to carry out an enquiry or engage staff themselves, question persons able to provide information, hear witnesses and enforce the production of documents, call experts and visit sites, obtain 'all the official documents concerning the case from the federal administration' and 'collect written and oral information from authorities and departments, and from members of authorities, civil servants and private individuals.' They can also 'require formal evidence from witnesses' if the other measures do not result in a satisfactory elucidation of the facts.

Evidence from federal civil servants is complicated when they are questioned on subjects covered by official secrets regulations. The Federal Council stated once again on this point that it alone had the power to release civil servants from their official oaths.

After putting forward various suggestions, the two councils finally acceded in part to the wishes of the executive, laying down that 'the opinion of the Federal Council must first be heard. If it insists on secrecy, the commission of enquiry shall decide.' This is probably the most important power attributed to commissions of enquiry. The *commission de gestion* of the Council of States has explained this as follows:

> When the civil servant giving evidence is asked to reveal an official secret, the opinion of the Federal Council must first be sought. It would be wrong to accept straight away that there should be no objection to the communication of official secrets. But the Federal Council should not be able to impose secrecy in all circumstances. If a commission of enquiry, passing over its objections, decides that it must hear the secret information, it must be submitted.[2]

Moreover, it is accepted that as with other committees, the members, secretaries, etc of committees of enquiry should all swear official secrecy.

These proposals give parliament greatly extended powers, while providing the Federal Council with important guarantees. They

[1] ibid.
[2] *Report of the Council of States*, 12 February 1966, op. cit., p. 43.

should enable parliament to deal with the exceptional situations for which they were devised. In the absence of a case in which they have been applied in practice, it is difficult to give an accurate assessment of the effectiveness of the solution adopted. A few comments are all that is possible for the moment.

The opportunity of setting up committees of enquiry was introduced to deal with such cases as elude, for different reasons, normal parliamentary checks. To prevent such cases arising, it is necessary for parliamentary supervision to be exercised more effectively in relation to the work of government and administration. The errors perpetuated at the time of the Mirages affair were not revealed in time not only because of certain deficiencies in the organisation and method of the administration, but also because parliament was not in a position to exercise effective control at all levels of decision procedure (drafting, choice, application). As has already been explained, it is not enough to provide parliament with legal and material resources to assist its exercise of its supervisory function. In addition to this, members of parliament must have the conditions enabling them to make use of these resources. Above all, deputies should be able to analyse the relevant information and draw their own conclusions, with the help of specialists, whether temporary or permanent, and the co-operation of the administration. Up to now the increase in the volume of activity and complexity of the work of government which falls under parliamentary control has not been accompanied by a corresponding increase in information *collected and analysed* by parliament and its committees. On the contrary, indeed, parliament has become increasingly accustomed to work too fast on data collected and sorted by the administration, and on alternative solutions to problems drawn up by it. Clearly, the role of parliament does not consist of reducing the work of the administration, but effective control requires that a project should be followed throughout its development by those who are aware of its implications, its logic and its outcome. This activity requires in the first place technical knowledge (which deputies could possess themselves or derive from trusted assistants), but also and above all adequate time. Will Switzerland ever see professional parliamentarians who can devote all their time to public affairs? In the opinion of the author, sooner or later the evolution of political affairs will make this necessary. Otherwise parliament will transform itself into a sort of political registry, contenting itself with a few grand debates and occasional commotions.

III–THE RATIONALISATION OF DECISIONS AND PARLIAMENTARY CONTROL

Modern decision-making techniques were not introduced into Switzerland until the Defence Department adopted them following the Mirages affair. A sweeping reform of the law of 1914 relating to the organisation of the federal administration is currently being examined, but for the present no substantial modification has been introduced, outside the Defence Department, either to the preparation of the budget and accounts, or to the preparation of individual bills. Since the problems of defence planning and of choice of weapons have financial consequences of great importance, and lend themselves better than others to the application of certain techniques of rational decision-making, it is not without interest to give some consideration to the reforms carried out in this sector.

The reform of the Defence Department[1] started from two basic requirements: on the one hand, to reduce the number of subordinates directly dependent on one official, and, on the other, to give adequate powers to the departments which were to be engaged in the new techniques of decision-making. These two principles led among other things to a decentralisation of direct authority (necessary to relieve departmental heads of burdens which were too numerous and heavy, and to the creation of a directing staff (necessary to ensure better co-ordination and more effective supervision). The new techniques (systems analysis, operational research, cost-efficiency analysis, the PERT method, critical path analysis) have been applied in the choice of a tactical support aircraft.[2] Although the final choice had not been made at the date of writing, this has been the only case of any importance which permits an evaluation of post-Mirages parliamentary control. The conclusions to be drawn from a study of this case are clearly provisional, but are not without interest.

The process of the decision on the new aircraft has shown parliament in a more active role. On the one hand parliament has been better informed about the process of the decision, and on the other hand has itself taken the initiative in deciding to collect supplementary information by organising a grand 'hearing' in September 1969. The members of the two parliamentary defence committees met in joint session and heard representatives of the Swiss aircraft industry, scientific and economic witnesses, represen-

[1] See *Urio, Processus de décision et contrôle democratique en Suisse, op. cit.,* Ch. IV.

[2] For more details see Paolo Urio, 'Rational Decision-Making and National Defence in Switzerland', *Annuaire Suisse de Science Politique, Lausanne,* vol. 11, 1971, pp 25–42.

tatives of the Defence Department, and of the Finance Department and other federal civil servants. Moreover, members of parliament then obliged the government to subject other types of aircraft to a fresh analysis (June 1970). It can be speculated whether this latter initiative will not be prejudicial to national interests in that it will certainly prolong the evaluation phase and consequently delay the delivery of the aircraft finally chosen. It should be noted that the hearing of September 1969 made clear the difficulty experienced by the great majority of deputies in mastering problems relating to so complex a question. Moreover, it is significant that the discussion only covered the problem of construction under licence, easier to grasp than problems of a choice of model. Finally, the differences which arose between the Defence Department and certain deputies on the choice of aircraft were based on facts which it would have been preferable to have elucidated before embarking on an analysis of the different types of aircraft available. Certain fundamental questions were involved, such as the country of origin of the aircraft chosen (the choice of country having possible repercussions for commercial and diplomatic relations) and the planned use for the aircraft (which affected the decision between a supersonic or sub-sonic plane). The choice of this aircraft has consequently revealed on the one hand parliament's inability to deal with technical problems such as cost-efficiency analysis, and, on the other hand, the limits of techniques of decision-making based on a mathematical approach (for example operational research) implying as they do the use of quantifiable variables. Other non-quantifiable elements can influence such a decision, but it is necessary that these should be taken into consideration in good time, since parliament will otherwise believe itself to have been presented with a *fait accompli* and could be led to take initiatives which may not turn out to be particularly happy.

It may be concluded that the need to strengthen parliamentary control has become more urgent since modern decision-making techniques have been adopted by the federal administration. These techniques threaten to increase the gap between civil servants and members of parliament, for they involve specialised knowledge which members do not generally possess. Moreover they tend to diminish still further the importance of parliamentary intervention after the end of the administrative phase, in so far as they substitute the concept of rationality for that of compromise. Since it is already difficult for deputies to put forward a compromise during this phase, it is even more difficult for them to oppose a 'rational solution', which gets itself accepted by definition. This point deserves to be further developed. A decision may be defined as the action of choosing among several alternatives in a situation of incomplete information. The rationalisation of decision consists of reducing and, as far as possible, eliminating uncertainty in collecting together all the necessary information and in setting up one or more methods of processing this information. Once the limit has been reached, the solution is automatic and no decision is possible or necessary. An apparently paradoxical, though perfectly logical conclusion is reached, namely, that a rational decision is not a decision, since it implies no choice. In these circumstances one could more sensibly refer to rational solutions to problems, rather than to 'decisions'.

As the deputies are mainly excluded from the administrative phase which deals with the rational solution of problems, there is a risk that parliament will adopt one of two attitudes: either it will restrict itself to the registration of the solutions prepared by the administration, which implies that it will cease to control anything, or it will refuse to accept the solutions proposed, for reasons irrelevant to the problems in question, which will delay the implementation of the solution and at worst lead to the wrong decisions.

This situation is still far off; situations in which information is complete are still hardly known in political life. Moreover the definition of problems and their solution depend on the recognition of needs as well as on the identification of the objectives which arise from them. It is consequently indispensable that parliament, the representative of the people, should be associated with all stages of the process of decision-making. The measures which would make this association as effective as possible have been listed in the second part of this study. It is enough to recall the most important: the professionalisation of the work of the deputy, the development of parliament's information services, including the possibility of using experts from outside the administration, the association of parliament with the definition of needs and objectives, for example during the administrative stage of the process of decision-making on new proposals. These improvements would allow parliament to make effective use of its legal means of control and to find the necessary time to do this. This in my opinion is the only way to stop the dispossession of parliament which has been so prominent a feature of recent years.

CHAPTER 17

NEW DEVELOPMENTS IN BUDGETARY DECISION-MAKING: A REVIEW

Peter Else

INTRODUCTION

An earlier chapter on the scope and content of government expenditure concluded with a brief discussion of the implications of the expanding role of government expenditure for its control, and it was implied that up to four particular aspects of control could be distinguished, reflecting different needs or requirements.[1] First of all, there is a need for control in the sense of setting limits to the amount and scope of expenditure and enforcing those limits, which, since the emphasis is on legal regularity, gives rise to what can be referred to as the 'legal' aspect of control. Secondly, there is a need to ensure that government departments and agencies carry out their various duties efficiently, which, since internal efficiency is basically a problem of management, suggests a 'managerial' aspect of control. Thirdly, there is a need for the behaviour of government expenditure in the aggregate to be reconciled with the objectives of macroeconomic policy, implying a 'macro-economic' aspect of control, and fourthly there is a need for control over the allocation of expenditure between the various areas of government activity.[2] These various aspects of control are not, of course, unrelated. The legal and macro-economic aspects of control, for example, clearly raise questions of efficiency and have implications for the allocation of expenditure. Nevertheless they may also be competitive in the

---

[1] See Chapter 2, pp. 43–45.

[2] Walkland (Chapter 10, p. 180), following American observers (e.g. A. Schick, 'The Road to P.P.B. The Stages of Budget Reform', *Public Administration Review* (December 1966), pp. 243–58), combines the third and fourth aspects of control under the general heading of strategic planning. In a discussion of European experiences, it is useful to keep them separate as a number of countries have developed procedures which are primarily oriented towards macro-economic objectives.

sense that an emphasis on one aspect of control may lead to the development of budgetary procedures which hinder rather than help the effective exercise of the others, and, by making large claims on the time and energy of those concerned, may also limit the resources that can be devoted to them.

Historically, a common starting point in attempts to establish effective control of government expenditure has been a desire to keep it within reasonable bounds and prevent the misappropriation of funds, in order to limit the tax burdens imposed upon citizens. In other words the initial emphasis was on the legal aspect of control, as defined above, and in some countries budgetary procedures still very much reflect this initial approach. In others, however, as will have become apparent from the preceding chapters, the problems raised by the widening scope and increasing scale of government expenditure have led to the introduction of new budgetary procedures, which take account, explicitly or implicitly, of other aspects of control. The present chapter attempts to consider the budgetary approaches which seem most appropriate to the different aspects of control outlined above, and, drawing on material from the chapters on individual countries and other sources, to compare the extent to which they have been used in the six countries and their influence on parliamentary procedures.

LEGAL ASPECTS OF CONTROL AND TRADITIONAL BUDGETARY SYSTEMS

The early emphasis on the legal aspects of control led typically to the establishment of a budgetary cycle which divides naturally into two parts. In the first, expenditure proposals are drawn up, discussed and eventually sanctioned (in their original or amended form) through some legislative act; the second part is concerned with ensuring that expenditure is as provided for by legislation, usually by means of controls over the disbursement of funds and a post-expenditure audit. The basic elements of this cycle can be found in all the six countries covered in this symposium, although, as might be expected, the details differ. For example, whilst parliaments are always involved in the sanctioning of expenditure plans, the part played by them varies with, at one extreme, the United Kingdom parliament giving more or less automatic approval to the government's proposals,[1] and at the other, countries like the Netherlands, where the problem of getting the budget through parliament in the allotted time seems a perennial one.[2] Again in the

1 See Chapter 10.
2 See Chapter 15, p 281 et seq.

second part of the cycle at one extreme there is France, where checks on the regularity of expenditure are left largely to judicial bodies, presumably on the principle that the enforcement of expenditure laws, like the enforcement of other laws, is basically a judicial function and should therefore be the concern of judicial organs rather than the legislature, and at the other is the United Kingdom, where the underlying principle is that the government through its ministers is accountable to parliament for all its actions, and where checks on the regularity of its expenditure are the responsibility of the Comptroller and Auditor-General who is an official of parliament and who reports to parliament.[1] The other countries appear to fall between these extremes.

The emphasis on the legal aspects of control has tended to lead to the use of a form of accounts in which expenditure is apportioned on an organisational basis and then further analysed in terms of input or items of expense (wages and salaries, equipment, etc).[2] This facilitates checks on regularity since it is clearly easier to check that Department X has spent £y on employing a typist or buying a typewriter than to check that they have been used for some particular purpose of government. Further, as long as the prevailing view was that the proper role of government was limited to providing certain basic services and that any government expenditure above the minimum necessary to provide them simply diverted resources from more productive uses, the information was perfectly adequate for the scrutiny of expenditure proposals since the aim would be simply to ensure that no more resources were used than necessary, and this could be done by looking at the proposed expenditure on individual inputs. However, as governments assumed wider responsibilities and as parliaments became more interested in increasing expenditure than in saving candle-ends, interest in the control of expenditure began to extend beyond its narrow legal aspects and the limitations of the traditional form of accounts became apparent. It could, for example, provide little guide to the efficiency with which a government department was carrying out its duties, since expenditure was not related to function, and it could provide little information about the relationship between the expenditure proposals and a government's general policy objectives, because expenditure was not related to objectives. Further, whilst as far as macro-economic considerations are concerned, it is aggregate

---

[1] See Chapter 9, p. 173.

[2] E.g. see Chapter 10, pp, 181–182, but it should be noted that not all countries have estimates of cash requirements as in Britain. In some the estimates are related to liabilities to be incurred in the relevant period.

expenditure rather than its detailed breakdown which is important, it is helpful to have some breakdown of expenditure by economic category, which again was not provided with this form of accounts. The kind of additional information necessary to overcome these limitations will be indicated in the following sections.

MANAGERIAL CONSIDERATIONS

The exercise of the more legal aspects of control discussed in the previous section can lead to scrutiny before expenditure takes place, when it takes place, and afterwards, but concern with the managerial aspect of control is likely to lead to more emphasis being placed on post-expenditure scrutiny. Bygones may be for ever bygones and past spending cannot normally be unspent, but an organisation is likely to use the resources at its disposal efficiently in the future only if its current practices are sound or if it is aware of its deficiencies and knows how to overcome them. Hence investigations into the efficiency with which government departments and agencies carry out their duties will naturally be concerned with current managerial practices, the results obtained with them in the recent past and the possibilities for improvement in the future. It follows, therefore, that if parliaments are to be interested in the managerial aspect of control, they must have at their disposal some means of carrying out this kind of investigation, but as will have become apparent from preceding chapters, in most of the parliaments studied, financial procedures place more emphasis on pre-expenditure than post-expenditure scrutiny. However, the Mirage crisis in Switzerland has drawn attention to the problem there,[1] and the financial committees of the House of Commons in the United Kingdom have a long tradition of interest in this kind of work. In fact Walkland has described how the Public Accounts Committee (of the House of Commons) began to turn its attention towards managerial problems from about 1900 onwards and how that even the Estimates Committee, which was originally set up to give the estimates the kind of searching scrutiny that was not possible on the floor of the House of Commons, increasingly concerned itself with enquiries into the management of the activities covered by particular blocks of expenditure rather than detailed scrutiny of the estimates themselves.[2] An obvious difficulty faced by both committees, however, was that the basic information on government expenditure on which they had to work, the estimates and accounts, was not in

1 See Chapter 16, p. 322.
2 See Chapter 10, p. 184.

the most appropriate form for the task they had set themselves. Ideally they required details of expenditure relating to function, whereas the estimates and accounts were in the traditional form with expenditure divided up on an organisational basis and further analysed by categories of input.

A parallel concern with the efficiency of government spending in the United States in the 1930s and in the immediate postwar period led to the development of what came to be known as 'performance budgeting'.[1] In a performance budget expenditure is analysed on the basis of functions and the various tasks which are undertaken in carrying out those functions. The aim is then to relate the expenditure to measurements of actual performance, the monitoring of which may give some indication of the efficiency with which a department or agency is carrying out its duties. There do not, however, seem to have been any comparable developments in Europe, and even in the United States the impact of performance budgeting does not seem to have been a lasting one, partly because it eventually became overshadowed by the development of planning, programming, budgeting systems, which are discussed in more detail below, and partly, no doubt, because by its nature it tends to concentrate attention on the minutiae of government activities. However, important though the functions of government may seem, its activities at the level at which performance can be measured tend to be rather mundane. The costs of processing tax returns or issuing passports are hardly likely to be the most burning issues of government finance, and the reported reaction of a New York legislator ('Who the hell cares how much a pound of laundry costs?')[2] would doubtless be echoed by legislators the world over. Indeed it can be argued that such detail is really the concern of the internal management or agency responsible and that external supervisory committees would be more effective if they concentrated their attention on managerial practices and procedures, rather than attempt to get to grips with large amounts of detailed financial information.

This argument receives added force when it is recognised that issues which have caused particular concern in a number of countries in recent years have been connected with the escalating costs of the products of advanced technology where governments are buying from outside contractors and suppliers. The case of the Mirage fighters in Switzerland[3] and the Concorde airliner in the

1 For a recent appraisal of this development, see A. Schick, *Budget Innovation in the United States* (Washington D.C., Brookings Institution, 1971), pp. 44–86.

2 Recorded by Schick, *Budget Innovation in the US*, p. 65.

3 See the contribution by Paolo Urio, Chapter 16 above.

United Kingdom are two particular examples. In such cases it is not internal departmental costs which are of interest, but the initial estimating procedures and subsequent contractual arrangements and whether such apparently unforeseen and uncontrollable increases in costs can be avoided. In the United Kingdom, the Public Accounts Committee has taken a particular interest in problems of this nature; its recent report on the costs of Concorde is merely the latest of a number of critical reports in this area and in fact is the most recent of a number commenting on the Concorde project.[1]

The Estimates Committee in the United Kingdom, however, which has been more concerned with areas of expenditure than with individual items, has on a number of occasions felt that its work has been handicapped because the estimates and accounts have not been in the most helpful form for its purposes, and has argued the case for more functionally based accounts. Whether they would have wanted to go as far as performance budgeting is not clear, but in any case the Treasury always opposed their suggestions on the grounds that the traditional forms were convenient for the purposes of internal administration and Treasury control of the expenditure of other departments.[2] Nevertheless, in recent years financial and administrative procedures within government departments have been subject to reform, and the government is proposing revisions to the form of the estimates (to take effect in 1974) which will give them more of a functional bias.[3] Moreover cost accounting and performance data is being compiled for internal management purposes, and it is possible that some information of this nature might be made available to parliamentary committees in connection with particular enquiries.

MACRO-ECONOMIC CONSIDERATIONS

The early postwar discussion of Keynesian policies emphasised the role of government expenditure and fiscal policy generally in the context of short-run stabilisation policies, but the difficulties encountered in attempts to vary public expenditure counter-cyclically together with the continually rising demand for public

[1] Public Accounts Committee 1972–3, *Sixth Report*, HC 335.

[2] For an account of these exchanges see P. K. Else, *Public Expenditure, Parliament and PPB*, PEP Broadsheet 522 (November 1970), pp. 20–5.

[3] Expenditure Committee 1972–73, *Eighth Report*, Revision of the Form of the Supply Estimates HC 209, Evidence, pp. 1–11 and Appendices. It should perhaps be added that the main purpose of the revision is to facilitate comparison with the annual public expenditure White Paper.

sector services brought to the fore in a number of countries the problem of the longer-term relationship between the growth of public and private expenditure. Too fast a growth of government expenditure can lead to what some people would regard as unacceptable restrictions being placed on private consumption and investment if inflationary pressures induced by excess demand are to be avoided; conversely a slower rate of growth of government expenditure may lead to what may be regarded as inadequate provision of public services. What constitutes an 'unacceptable' restriction on private expenditure or an 'inadequate' provision of basic public services is, of course, a political question, but it is one that ideally needs to be answered in the light of an informed appreciation of the implications of more (or less) government expenditure for the achievement of the other goals of macro-economic policy.

Traditional budgetary practices have not, in general, been designed with the problems of short-term or longer-term macroeconomic policy in mind and have, therefore, been found wanting in a number of respects. First of all they do not, typically, cover the whole of government expenditure. The central government's budget is naturally primarily concerned with its own expenditure, although it does not in all cases cover the whole of that,[1] and it excludes expenditure by non-central governments which may be substantial. Secondly it may exclude expenditure by semi-autonomous bodies such as public enterprises which the government may be able to control. Thus in the United Kingdom, for example, the government controls the investment expenditure of the nationalised industries. In other countries control over the activities of public enterprises is often looser, but in the following discussion the term 'public expenditure' will be used, in line with the conventions used by the British government, to cover this kind of expenditure, where it is within the government's powers to control it directly, in addition to government expenditure as defined in Chapter 2. Thirdly, traditional procedures tend to concentrate attention on expenditure in the year ahead, whereas government expenditure decisions frequently imply longer-term commitments. Fourthly, since budgets are essentially instruments of finance they naturally emphasise financial flows, whereas for macro-economic purposes it is the use and availability of real resources that are most relevant. Measurement problems apart, this last problem can be met without too much difficulty, and it is in fact a common practice for governments to support their

[1] See e.g. Chapter 14, p. 255 for the situation in Italy. The British estimates do not cover interest on the National Debt, loans to local authorities and the nationalised industries, and a number of other items.

budget proposals with background information on the state of their respective economies and an indication of how the budget fits in with their overall economic policy objectives. The others are less easily dealt with and require rather more fundamental changes in budgetary procedures. In particular, what is required is some procedure for examining the implications of present (and planned) policies for the whole of public expenditure over a number of years ahead. These can then be looked at in relation to forecasts of the prospective growth of the economy as a whole, and if as a result it is felt that public expenditure seems likely to be claiming too high or too low a share of the total resources available, the necessary corrective action can be taken in time for it to have an effect.

Of the six countries covered in this study, three, France, the United Kingdom and West Germany, have developed procedures for taking the necessary wider and longer-term view of trends in public expenditure. In the United Kingdom and West Germany particularly the impetus has been a widespread feeling that the growth of public expenditure was becoming excessive in relation to the resources available and that its growth could not be controlled adequately by existing procedures. The same problem has also become apparent in the Netherlands, which, after a period of experimentation, seems set to follow the same path as the United Kingdom and West Germany. In Switzerland, the problems posed by the growth of public expenditure have perhaps not been so acute, since total government expenditure amounts to a much smaller proportion of gross national product than in other countries and the federal government is only responsible for about a third of that.[1] Further, in Italy, whilst the deficiencies of the budget as an instrument of macro-economic policy are widely recognised, in the prevailing political situation reform is rather more difficult.[2] For the rest of this section, therefore, attention will be concentrated on developments in France, the United Kingdom, Germany and the Netherlands.

Of these four countries, France is in a rather special position because of its long-standing commitment to a form of economic planning. Any reasonably comprehensive plan must inevitably take account of public expenditure and therefore automatically provides a means by which the trend in public expenditure for the years covered by the plan can be looked at in its macro-economic context. However, French planning is basically of the indicative type, in which the emphasis is on the identification of feasible targets for

[1] See Table 2.6 in Chapter 2.
[2] See Chapter 14.

particular sectors of the economy rather than on actually making decisions about the allocation of resources. Hence, although the *Commissariat du Plan* has been able to influence the course and direction of public expenditure, the actual decisions have remained the responsibility of individual government departments and the Ministry of Finance which retains overall responsibility for the budget. Indeed it was not until the Fourth Plan that ministers had explicit instructions to prepare their estimates in the light of plan targets.

In the first two plans particularly the emphasis was in any case on expansion and the planners were probably more concerned to ensure that targets were achieved than about the possible dangers from their being exceeded. Towards the end of the period covered by the Second Plan, however, government expenditure on new schools, housing, hospitals and the like considerably exceeded its forecast, and that coupled with an unforeseen increase in defence expenditure arising from the Algerian situation was later diagnosed as a major contributory factor to the rapid rise in prices and worsening balance of payments after 1956. As a result, in subsequent years the enthusiasm of departments to exceed their targets had to be tempered by the government's determination to pursue a less inflationary budgetary policy. Moreover, the increasing sophistication of the forecasting techniques used by the planners produced a greater awareness of the costs of continued expansion of public expenditure in terms of the constraints on private expenditure which it might make necessary. Even so, there were occasions when the short-run situation was felt to require cuts in the planned level of public expenditure, particularly in 1963–4, but with the help of the plan it was possible to make selective cuts minimising the effects on programmes which seemed most important from the point of view of the long-term development of the French economy.[1]

Whilst the problem of planning the growth of public expenditure came naturally under the umbrella of the established planning machinery in France, in the United Kingdom it was necessary to develop new procedures. The growth of public expenditure began to create problems, as in France, in the second half of the 1950s. Before that, a reduction in defence expenditure, following the end of the Korean War, allowed simultaneously for some increases in other public expenditure and reduction in taxes. As the decade progressed, however, expenditure plans drawn up on the assumption of

[1] For a more detailed account of French planning see G. Denton, M. Forsyth and M. Maclennan, *Economic Planning and Policies in Britain, France and Germany* (London, PEP and George Allen & Unwin, 1968) and references cited.

continuing expansion had to be cut back in the interests of controlling inflation and improving the balance of payments. At the time, the Treasury was attempting to keep watch on the trends in public expenditure through its annual estimates review, through its control of new expenditure and with the help of unofficial estimates of departmental requirements for up to two years ahead. The feeling was widespread, however, both within government circles and elsewhere, that these procedures were not adequate and that the apparently indiscriminate chopping and changing of expenditure plans in the interests of short-run economic policy was not conducive to the efficient planning and operation of vital public services. These feelings were voiced most notably by the House of Commons Estimates Committee,[1] and their recommendations led to the setting up of the Plowden Committee to look at the whole problem of the control of public expenditure. The latter's reports[2] laid the foundations for the system now in operation.

The details of the system are described by Walkland[3] and need not be repeated here, but the overall aim is to provide a means by which decisions on future public expenditure are made in the light of projections of continuing existing policies over the whole field of public expenditure, the impact of other possible demands on public expenditure and a medium-term assessment of the prospects for the economy as a whole, giving some indication of the resources likely to be available. In contrast to the French system which plans for a fixed period of time, it is an annual exercise producing a five-year plan of expenditure which is rolled forward every year. The figures for the first two or three years reflect firm decisions, but for later years, depending, of course, on the nature of the expenditure concerned, the figures are sometimes little more than projections. Potentially, therefore, it would appear to be more adaptive to short-term requirements than the French plans, but this has not obviated the need for sudden changes. One continuing source of difficulty has been a tendency to underestimate the future costs of public expenditure programmes; another has been a tendency to overestimate the potential growth of the economy. Ironically the latter proved to be most serious during the period in the mid-sixties when attempts were being made to develop an indicative economic planning system somewhat on the French pattern. A rate of growth of the national

[1] Select Committee on Estimates 1957–8, *Sixth Report*, HC 254.

[2] Its main recommendations were conveyed in a series of confidential reports, but they were later summarised in *The Control of Public Expenditure*, Cmnd. 1432 (HMSO, 1961).

[3] See Chapter 10, p. 186.

product which had originally been regarded as feasible, given favourable conditions, was adopted as a target, and then used as a forecast, even though the necessary favourable conditions did not seem to be materialising, and there was really no solid evidence to indicate that that rate of growth could be achieved.[1] Public expenditure was planned on the assumption that it would be achieved and hence had to be cut back disruptively in 1965 and 1966, when the foreign exchange reserves were under pressure, and again in 1968, following the devaluation of the pound in November 1967. As a result of these experiences, indicative planning fell rather into disfavour and was quietly dropped. The public expenditure survey system, however, has continued using the Treasury's own less publicised macro-economic forecasts and has been further developed. Indeed the government became sufficiently confident of its techniques to give more publicity about the whole exercise and invited the House of Commons to consider how its procedures might be amended to take account of it. Hopefully the lessons of the 1960s will have been learned, but the temptations for politicians in office to take an optimistic view of the costs of their programmes and of the prospects for economic growth is likely to be always present.

Attempts to devise ways of preventing the growth of public expenditure from outstripping the resources available started later in West Germany than in France or the United Kingdom. Throughout the 1950s in Germany, it proved relatively easy to finance public expenditure because of the high rate of economic growth. In fact, budget surpluses accumulated, and these proved to be a useful, if unintentional, factor in containing inflationary forces.[2] In the 1960s, however, the rate of growth of national income and tax revenue began to fall, but at the same time, the rate of growth of government expenditure began to increase.[3] Consequently the budget went into deficit, undermining the efforts of the Bundesbank to counter inflationary tendencies with monetary policy. To meet this situation, a deliberate attempt was made by the federal government in the 1960s to bring budgetary policy more into line with monetary policy, but this was frustrated by its apparent inability to control government spending. Controlling government expenditure is in any case an inherently more difficult task for the German federal government than its British and French counter-

[1] Denton *et al.*, op. cit., p. 221.

[2] ibid., p. 226.

[3] GNP rose by 75 per cent between 1955 and 1960 and 65 per cent between 1960 and 1965, over the same periods federal government expenditure rose by 52 per cent and 72 per cent. *OECD National Accounts of OECD Countries 1953–69*.

parts. Not only is it responsible for a smaller proportion of total government expenditure, but the federal Constitution gives it rather less influence over the behaviour of state and local governments than the British and French central governments have over the lower-tier authorities in their more centralised states.[1] Moreover the nationalised sector of industry is considerably freer of government control and intervention than in Britain. Nevertheless both federal and state finance ministries came to realise that government expenditure and revenue could be brought into a proper relationship only by looking several years ahead, and a start was made by preparing multi-annual budget projections of the resource costs of current programmes. This by itself, of course, did not go far enough, but it was followed in 1967 as a result of a serious financial crisis[2] by legislation which established medium-term financial planning as an integral part of the budgetary process, gave the federal government more power to use fiscal policy for stabilisation purposes, and at the same time established the means for greater co-ordination between federal, state and local governments on both short-term and medium-term aspects of budgetary policy.[3]

Medium-term financial planning in this context means that annual budgets are presented in the framework of a rolling five-year annual plan. Thus the federal government's financial plan sets out the projected development of federal expenditure and revenue over the period and relates them to the overall macro-economic trends. The state governments have similar financial plans covering their activities but there is no joint planning of federal and state pro-grammes. A Financial Planning Council, consisting of the federal and state ministers of finance and representatives of the munici-palities, has been set up to take an overall view, but it can only make recommendations for the co-ordination of the various plans and these have to be unanimous. Consequently, whilst the various reforms provide a means of keeping a watch on the overall trends of public expenditure, it is possible that they will not be sufficient to enable the federal government effectively to impose limits on the growth of public expenditure.[4]

[1] See Chapter 3.
[2] See Chapter 4, p. 75.
[3] See Chapter 4, pp. 75–77.
[4] See Chapter 3, and for a more detailed study see Zunker's *Finanzplanung und Bundeshaushalt* (Alfred Metzuer Verlag, 1972). See also Karl M. Nettage, 'The Problems of Medium-Term Financial Planning', *Public Administration*, vol. 48 (autumn 1970), pp. 263–72.

In the Netherlands, concern with the rate of growth of government expenditure began to be expressed in the late 1950s as in France and the United Kingdom, but the initial attempts to contain it involved the establishment of so-called 'norms' for annual budgetary changes rather than the planning of expenditure over a longer term.[1] The first, the *Romme-norm*, postulated that government expenditure should rise at a rate no greater (and preferably less) than real national income. Presumably that was found rather difficult to maintain, since the tendency for government expenditure to rise relatively to national income seems to have been more marked in the Netherlands than elsewhere,[2] and in 1960 it was replaced by the more sophisticated and less restrictive *Zijlstra-norm*. This implied, in effect, that normally the planned increase in government expenditure in any year should not be greater than the prospective increase in revenue from taxes and other sources. The latter would be greater than the increase in the national income because of the progression of the tax system, but the idea was that an explicit decision should be made each year as to how the expected increase in revenue, the budget-margin, should be divided between new expenditure and tax reductions. Inflation, the rate of which has increased in recent years, rather spoils the apparent simplicity of this norm, and whilst attempts are made to counter it by making the calculations in real terms, it is possible that the implications of inflation for the operation of the norm have not been fully understood.[3] Certainly, the tendency for actual government expenditure to exceed budgeted expenditure has been a continuing source of concern.[4] Moreover when the demographic effects on the costs of past commitments, and the various social and political pressures for increased expenditure, described in detail by Daalder

[1] See Chapter 15, p. 298.

[2] See Chapter 2, Table 2.1.

[3] For example, an assumption that the real rate of growth of national income will be around 4·8 per cent per annum coupled with a regression factor of about 1¼ per cent seems to imply that government expenditure can increase by just over 6 per cent in real terms. But this is true only if costs in government services are rising at the same rate as costs in other sectors. Allowing for the fact that the opportunities for increased productivity tend to be less in government services than in other sectors (particularly manufacturing), costs in government services may be expected to rise more steeply. The real increase in government expenditure must therefore be less than 6 per cent to keep within the budget margin. In Britain, the government attempts to allow for this factor by adding a 'price effect' to its estimates of future government expenditure in real terms. See *Public Expenditure: A New Presentation*, Cmnd 4017 (HMSO, 1969), Appendix II, paras. 9–16.

[4] See, for example, *The Netherlands Budget Memorandum 1968* (abridged English version), pp. 14–17.

and Hubée,[1] are added to the problems arising from inflation, it is not entirely surprising that successive Dutch governments have found it increasingly difficult to keep expenditure within the confines of the norm.

The emphasis in these norms on the annual budgetary process may partly reflect the short life-expectancy of Dutch governments, but at the same time there has been increasing interest in longer-term aspects. In 1963, the Central Planning Bureau (which in fact is more concerned with forecasting and the consideration of the implications of alternative strategies than actual planning, and which hitherto had been mainly preoccupied with short-term problems) was asked to look more systematically at the medium-term prospects for the development of the economy. Against this background, budget memoranda began to include some discussion of long-term strategy, and eventually gave some estimates of expenditure on certain selected items up to two years ahead.[1] Meanwhile behind the scenes the Ministry of Finance has been working with other government departments on estimates of the financial consequences over a five-year period of existing legal and policy commitments and new policy proposals. Its techniques are still in the process of development, but it seems likely that in future Dutch ministers will increasingly be able to draw up their expenditure plans in the light of their longer-term implications. Whether they will then find it easier to contain the growth of government expenditure depends, of course, on a number of other factors as well.

So far, in this section, the emphasis has been on the more technical developments in the area of macro-economic control and their use by governments. It remains therefore to consider the role of parliaments and particularly the extent to which parliamentary practices have been modified to take account of the longer-term perspectives of budgeting.

From a purely formal point of view, it might appear that parliaments are not likely to be at their most effective in dealing with medium- to long-term plans. Their formal powers are derived to a considerable extent from their role as legislative bodies, since if their views on legislative proposals are not sufficiently heeded they have the power to reject them. This sanction can be applied to annual budgets where spending requires legislative authorisation, but not normally to longer-run expenditure plans because no special powers are required at that stage. Moreover, it can be argued that longer-term expenditure plans are not, in practice, sufficiently final

[1] In Chapter 15.
[2] *The Netherlands Budget Memorandum 1969.*

to be enshrined in legislation.[1] Whilst some of the figures may reflect firm commitments already entered into, considerable flexibility may be attached to others. In any case, the figures tend to be rather hypothetical, showing, for example, what expenditure might be if prices were to remain unchanged. With no legislative act to be carried out, however, parliamentary examination of the details is likely to be less thorough and the whole discussion may lose some of its bite. A vote against the whole plan would, of course, raise questions of confidence in its sponsors, but where proposals are made to amend details, a government can simply parry them with a promise to reconsider the matter without making any definite commitment one way or the other. On the other hand, if parliaments are to be able to influence the pattern of future public spending they need an opportunity to discuss expenditure plans whilst options remain open, and they need to be able to express a reasonably coherent view.

In fact, the opportunities presented to parliaments to discuss their longer-term expenditure plans differ. In the Netherlands, the details of the longer-term plans that are published are in the annual budget memorandum, the main concern of which is the explanation of the budget proposals for the year ahead. In West Germany, the federal government's medium-term financial plan is published in considerably more detail[2] and has the status of a particularly important policy statement, but it is again tied up with the annual budgetary procedures. Indeed, the annual budget has to be presented within the framework of the financial plan. From one point of view these arrangements make sense, but there is a danger that the discussion of the longer-term plans may be overshadowed by the arguments over the more immediate budget. In France, however, there have been fewer opportunities to discuss longer-term public expenditure strategies, because economic plans are drawn up only every five years. Moreover, the early plans were not laid before parliament until they were in such final form that amendment would have raised considerable difficulties. With more recent plans, parliament has had an opportunity to discuss them at an earlier stage, but of course, public expenditure is only one aspect of the whole plan to consider. By contrast, as a result of recent changes in financial procedures the United Kingdom has an annual debate in which its attention is directed solely to the government's plans for public

[1] In fact, even annual budgetary provisions frequently need supplementation before the end of the budgetary year.
[2] But some shortcomings in the information provided are pointed out by Schmidt in Chapter 5, p. 97.

M

expenditure over the next five years as set out in its White Paper.[1]

Nevertheless, it is one thing for parliaments to have the opportunity to discuss longer-term expenditure plans, and another for them to use those opportunities effectively, and here the nature of the plans is an obvious source of difficulty since they raise so many issues, some of which are purely technical and some of which are highly political. For example, there are the broad macro-economic problems of the planned size of public expenditure and its implications for taxation and other aggregates such as private consumption and investment; there are the technical problems related to the forecasting of future economic growth; there is also the planned allocation of expenditure between broad sectors such as defence or social services, and the allocation of expenditure within sectors. Consequently it is easy for the debate to be a rather rambling affair, hopping from one thing to another without focusing effectively on any one issue. This certainly has been the case in the House of Commons debates so far, and whilst individual members have made pertinent contributions the debates as a whole have not yet fulfilled the hopes of the Select Committee on Procedure that they 'should come to occupy as important a place in parliamentary and public discussion of economic affairs as that now occupied by the annual budget debate.'[2] The debates would perhaps have had more focus if the opposition had taken a specific line on the government's proposals, concentrating on a small number of specific issues, but so far, neither major party when in opposition has chosen to do this.

However, from the point of view of the detailed examination of the British government's expenditure plans, a more important innovation was undoubtedly the setting up in 1971 of an Expenditure Committee to supersede the old Estimates Committee to examine matters relating to public expenditure as a whole. One of its subcommittees is charged with the job of considering the form and content of the papers on public expenditure presented to parliament and the broad macro-economic issues raised by the expenditure plans set out in the government's annual White Paper, and it is this sub-committee which has so far made its presence most obvious, if only for the number of reports it has made. Initially it concentrated largely on the information contained in the White Paper and made a number of suggestions for improvement. A number of these have been incorporated in the more recent White Papers and the sub-committee has now turned its attention more to the actual proposals

[1] See Chapter 10, pp. 186.
[2] Select Committee on Procedure, 1968–69, *First Report*, HC 140, para. 13.

and the assumptions underlying them.[1] In this work, which touches on some of the more technical problems of economic forecasting, the sub-committee has undoubtedly been helped by having an ex-Treasury official as specialist adviser, but if, as suggested above, governments might be tempted to over-optimism in these matters, then it is surely important for parliament to have some capacity for discovering the extent to which a government's plans are based on wishful thinking.

The financial committees in the other parliaments seem to be more preoccupied with the annual budgetary process. But clearly, as government's expenditure decisions are increasingly made some years in advance of the actual expenditure, if parliaments are to have any influence on the course and direction of public expenditure, their financial procedures need to be less closely tied to the annual budgetary cycle and more to the actual time-scale of decision-making within the government.

ALLOCATION ASPECTS OF CONTROL

Many of the goods and services supplied through the public sector are, as implied in Chapter 2, provided publicly because they are goods and services for which the market system would not work, or would at best work imperfectly, or where it is felt that the consequences of the working of market forces would not be satisfactory for one reason or another. However, one of the features of a properly functioning market system is that its operations automatically yield the kind of information which is necessary for an efficient allocation of resources. Once goods and services are taken out of the market sector this kind of information is no longer so readily available, but it is still relevant. This section will therefore approach the problem of allocation in the public sector by considering briefly with reference to the operation of a market system the kind of information that is relevant to allocative decisions and the kind of budgetary approach necessary to provide it, and it will then go on to consider the extent to which the six countries in the present study have adopted that kind of approach.

In a market system, to take a somewhat simplified view, there are on one side buyers who have certain wants which can be satisfied to a greater or lesser extent by the goods and services which the sellers are willing to provide. The prices asked for the various goods and services on offer then provide a basis from which each buyer can work out the best way of satisfying his various wants, estimate what

[1] See, for example, Expenditure Committee 1972–3, *Fifth Report*, HC 149.

it costs, and decide how he should spend the limited resources at his disposal. The amount he buys of any one good will then reflect the priorities which he attaches to his various wants, the total amount he can spend, the price he has to pay for the good in question and the prices of other goods and services which provide alternative ways of satisfying the same wants, or may satisfy different wants. On the other side of the market, sellers are willing to sell goods and services, provided that the prices they can sell them for are high enough to make it worthwhile. Whether a particular price is high enough depends on the costs of the resources which have to be employed to produce the good or service in question and bring it to the point of sale, and what could be obtained if the resources were put to some alternative use. Hence whether a seller is willing to supply a particular commodity and the amount he is willing to supply will depend upon the price he can expect for it and the price he could expect by using the resources at his disposal to produce other things. In the 'market' itself, if it is functioning properly, prices adjust to bring the amounts purchasers want to buy into line with the quantities producers are willing to sell. It thus provides a means by which resources are allocated in a way which takes account of buyers' wants, the priorities they attach to them and the costs of providing for them. Moreover, in all this, prices have an important part to play, since they pass information to buyers about the costs of providing particular goods and services, and they also pass information to sellers about consumers' wants and preferences.

All this is perfectly straightforward, but the point is, that once responsibility for the provision of particular goods and services is taken away from the market, prices are no longer available to transmit information about wants, preferences and costs to those whose decisions determine the allocation of resources. Yet such information is clearly still relevant, and if it is to be used has to be provided internally. Traditional budgetary methods in the public sector with their emphasis on the expenditure of organisations and the inputs used by them clearly do not provide this kind of information, but the kind of approach involved in what is referred to as 'planning, programming, budgeting' (PPB) could, potentially at least, help to meet this deficiency.

In outline, planning, programming, budgeting systems[1] involve, first, the identification of the objectives of particular areas of

1 PPB was developed in the USA in the 1950s and adopted first in the Department of Defence and then in other departments in the 1960s. The literature on it is now voluminous, but for a recent assessment see Schick, *Budget Innovation in the United States*, op. cit.

activity; secondly the identification of the activities which contribute towards those objectives; thirdly, the measurement of the costs of the resources devoted to those activities; and fourthly some analysis of the relationship between expenditure and what is being obtained for it. The identification of objectives requires some articulation of the 'wants' the expenditure is meant to satisfy; the identification of the activities which contribute to a particular objective (which together constitute a 'programme') implies consideration of the different ways of satisfying particular wants, and the subsequent analysis of costs and what is being obtained should give an indication of the costs of doing things in different ways. Moreover the analysis of costs would, where appropriate, take into account the costs incurred over a number of years rather than those in a single year. The aim is thus to allow expenditure plans to be drawn up, as they might be under a market system, in the light of the various wants the expenditure can meet, the alternative ways of meeting them, the full costs involved, and the priorities which are attached to the various wants.

When set out in this form, PPB seems an obvious requirement of a rational budgetary process, but in practice, putting it into operation is no simple matter, as the Americans have found, and indeed some critics have raised serious doubts as to whether PPB systems can work in a political context. In a market system, priorities are determined by the preferences of the individual consumer or household. With public expenditure the situation is more complicated because of the division of responsibility between the various levels of government, and, perhaps more importantly, because it necessarily involves some people making decisions which take account, to a greater or lesser extent, of the preferences of others. Hence, although a budget may typically be drawn up and settled in all but a few details by government ministers and their officials, they have to take account of what parliament and the country at large will accept or can be persuaded to accept. Furthermore, the extent to which they take account of others' preferences may be very much influenced by relatively short-run political factors such as the morale of the government's parliamentary supporters, the proximity of elections, and the like.[1] This does not of itself detract from the potential

---

[1] Cost-benefit analysis, which is often seen to have an important role to play in PPB systems, is concerned with measuring the value to the community as a whole of the benefits and costs of particular projects, and would thus appear to be a means of avoiding the influence of political factors. However, in the absence of market information, the analysis frequently involves the use of arbitrary assumptions based on political judgements, even if they are not explicitly recognised as such. See also below, p. 360.

usefulness of PPB systems provided that objectives can be defined and appropriate programme structures developed, but it has been argued that the spelling out of objectives in more than vague terms is not really to be expected. Political action primarily involves getting support for particular courses of action and such support may be obtained from groups whose objectives are divergent or even conflicting. Hence it is argued that focusing attention on objectives will emphasise the differences between potential allies rather than their common interests, and so hinder effective political action.[1] This view perhaps underestimates the awareness of politicians about the realities of the situation in which they operate, but in any case budgetary decisions predominantly relate to on-going, well established programmes for which it is not so much objectives that are likely to be in contention as the priorities attached to those objectives.

A more substantial objection to the use of PPB is that expressed by Wildavsky[2] who agrees that it is important to analyse the objectives of particular programmes, the alternative ways of attaining them and the costs and benefits involved, but argues that it is undesirable to tie this essential policy analysis to formal budgetary procedures. Indeed he suggests that the establishment of PPB systems is detrimental to good policy analysis, because it diverts scarce analytical resources to the more mundane tasks of working out programme structures, rearranging data and compiling routine budget documents, and subjects it to the artificial constraints of the annual budgetary timetable. Against this, Schultze has argued that one of the objects of a PPB approach is to create a system in which policy analysis is brought to bear as a matter of routine on budgetary decisions, and is stimulated by questions raised in the course of budgetary decision-making.[3] Whilst Schultze has a point, it nevertheless has to be recognised that a considerable volume of analytical spade-work needs to be done before policy analysis can be brought to bear 'as a matter of routine' on budgetary decisions, so the benefits of a premature introduction of PPB may be small.

Whether it is for this kind of reason, the mixed fortunes of PPB in

[1] One of the leading advocates of this kind of view, C. E. Lindblom, has written a number of books and articles on this and related topics. See, for example, David Braybook and Charles Lindblom, *A Strategy of Decision* (Macmillan, 1963).

[2] A. Wildavsky, 'Rescuing Policy Analysis from PPBS' in R. H. Haveman and J. Margolis (eds), *Public Expenditure and Policy Analysis* (Chicago, Markham, 1971), ch. 19.

[3] C. L. Schultze, *The Politics and Economics of Public Spending* (The Brookings Institute), p. 77.

the United States, or innate conservatism, is not entirely clear, but on the whole European countries have tended to be rather cautious in their attitudes towards PPB. In a number of them there has been some interest in various aspects of policy analysis, making use of systems analysis, cost-benefit analysis and related techniques,[1] but of the six countries studied in this volume, only the United Kingdom and France appear to have gone very much further and their experience of PPB is still fairly restricted.[2]

In fact, in the United Kingdom the Conservative Government 1970–4 showed more interest in policy analysis, under the title Programme Analysis and Review (PAR), than in PPB.[3] Moreover, the PPB systems which have been developed in the central government, particularly those for defence and police services,[4] might not be recognised as such by the purist. Indeed the term 'output budgeting' tends to be used rather than PPB, and the emphasis would appear to be on long-run projections of the costs of existing operations to help in the planning of future developments. As a result, expenditure tends to be analysed in terms of existing functions rather than objectives. The distinction between functions and objectives, or means and ends, can never, of course, be a clear one. For example, whilst hospitals are a means of providing medical care, the provision of medical care is a means of mitigating the effects of particular diseases in the community which in turn might be regarded as a means of increasing the general welfare of the community, or perhaps more narrowly of reducing the labour-time lost for medical reasons. However, the more ultimate the objective, the less easy it is to assess the extent to which that objective is being achieved and to relate expenditure to it. On the other hand, the more closely the analysis of expenditure is related to existing functions, the easier it is to avoid one of the more fundamental aims of PPB, which is to direct attention to the reasons why particular tasks are being performed and to the alternative ways of achieving particular objectives.

In France, the efforts to introduce a more objective-oriented approach to budgetary decisions have come under the general heading of Rationalisation des Choix Budgetaires (RCB).[5] In a sense, of

[1] See for example Chapters 15 and 16, pp. 300 and 336.
[2] Belgium and Sweden have also developed PPB systems.
[3] See Chapter 10, p. 188.
[4] Select Committee on Procedure, 1968–9 *First Report*, HC 410, Evidence pp 58–63, and G. J. Wasserman, 'Planning Programming Budgeting in the Police Service in England and Wales', *O. and M. Bulletin*, vol. 25, no. 4 (November 1970), pp. 197–207.
[5] For a more detailed account see Ducros in Chapter 8 and also P. Huet, 'The

course, the long-established planning procedures can be interpreted as an attempt to rationalise strategic decision-making as far as the general direction of the French economy is concerned, but inevitably the emphasis tends to be on broad aggregates. Further the annual budget came increasingly to be seen, in the 1960s, as a means of ensuring the almost unquestioned continuation of established activities, which given a continuing need for budgetary restraint tended to leave little room for new initiatives.[1] Hence in some areas of expenditure RCB has been used mainly for the assessment of new policies, but it now covers analytical studies of specific major problems, making use of systems analysis techniques, cost-benefit and analysis and the like, together with more general developments along the lines of PPB. The latter has been used particularly in the Ministry of Defence (under the title of Planification, Programmation et Préparation du Budget or 3PB) and the Ministry of Equipment and Housing, but it is also being applied to other departments.

In both Britain and France, the initiative for the development of PPB and other analytical techniques has, as might be expected, come from within the governments concerned and the techniques have been adopted principally to aid these governments' own decision-making. Their use in that context can do little by itself to reduce or increase the influence of parliament on the allocation of expenditure. To the writer of the present chapter, the suggestion of Ducros[2] that the use of RCB will enhance the role of parliament in the choice of ends but reduce it in the choice of means, apart from assuming that a meaningful distinction can be made between ends and means, seems to rest on an exaggeration of the extent to which the choice of means can be reduced to a purely technical matter. Even the most sophisticated cost-benefit analysis involves value judgements about distributional implications and the account which should be taken of particular kinds of costs and benefits, giving plenty of scope for political debate.[3] Nevertheless such techniques can potentially help parliaments to have more informed debates in the same way that they can help governments to make more informed decisions, provided they have access to the relevant information and have the opportunity to make use of it.

In France, the use of PPB has not so far led to changes in basic

Rationalization of Budget Choices in France', *Public Administration* (autumn 1970), pp. 273–87.

[1] Huet, op. cit., p. 279.

[2] See Chapter 8, pp. 152 et seq.

[3] The debate on the Roskill Commissions Report on the site of the third airport is an obvious example.

budgetary procedure, but it has led to some changes in the nature of some of the financial information given to parliament and further developments are expected.[1] In addition an undertaking has been given that the Commission des Finances will be kept informed on matters relating to the use of RCB.[2] Similarly, in the United Kingdom, the defence budget is now published in programme form (alongside the more traditional form), and the annual public expenditure White Paper give some details of broad programmes of expenditure. Ideally what is required, however, is not just expenditure figures set out in programme form but some indication of what these figures imply in quantitative terms and the costs of alternative policies. Various Treasury memoranda have hinted that as a result of the efforts being devoted to programme review more information might eventually be made available to parliament,[3] but for the moment that remains pie in the sky. Despite the considerable improvement in the financial information available to parliament over the past decade, in both quantitative and qualitative terms, the information available relating to the allocation of resources is still somewhat deficient. Indeed generally it seems true to say that whilst governments are experimenting with and in some cases using new techniques to help their decision-making, the developments have not really gone far enough to affect to any great extent the nature of the information available to parliaments on matters related to the allocation of government expenditure.

It is not sufficient for parliaments to receive information, however, they also need to be able to make some use of it. In fact, as the earlier chapters on individual countries have shown, parliamentary influence on the allocation of resources appears slight in the formal sense, since in most countries the government's expenditure proposals are eventually passed with little or no amendment. But there are also more indirect methods and the allocation of expenditure may be influenced in some degree before it reaches the final form of a budget proposal, by views expressed in debates, in committee reports and by other means. The opportunities for this kind of influence are increased where governments publish their longer-term plans for the allocation of expenditure and submit them for parliamentary scrutiny. Thus in the United Kingdom, parliament does have the opportunity to comment on the government's expenditure plans through an annual debate and through its Expenditure Com-

---

[1] See Chapter 8, p. 151.

[2] Chapter 8, p. 158.

[3] For example, see Expenditure Committee 1970-1, *Third Report* Evidence p. 21.

mittee, though whether these opportunities are entirely adequate is doubtful. A single two-day debate and the work of a handful of investigating sub-committees can barely scratch the surface of what is really one of the most important tasks of governments in modern states. Nevertheless, the United Kingdom parliament might be able to make more use of these limited opportunities if it had at its disposal more of the kind of information which this section has suggested would be relevant.

CONCLUSIONS

From the above discussion it is evident that there is a considerable degree of variation in the way the six countries covered in this symposium have responded to the need to consider the particular aspects of the control of government expenditure identified at the beginning of this chapter. The fact that some countries have experimented more than others with new budgetary techniques may reflect a number of factors, such as the political pressure for increased government services, the constraints imposed by the economic situation, and the receptiveness of government departments, particularly those most concerned with finance, to new ideas. The first two factors have clearly been of importance in the attempts of such countries as the United Kingdom, Germany and the Netherlands to devise more effective ways of keeping the growth of government expenditure within the limits of the resources available. By contrast it would appear that the devotion of Italian civil servants to long-established formal procedures may well have been an important factor inhibiting innovation there.

In several countries, the introduction of new approaches has explicitly altered the time scale of budgetary decision-making, in the sense that governments are taking more account of the implications of current decisions for expenditure several years ahead. To keep abreast of these changes, parliaments need to adapt their procedures in a similar way, and perhaps be prepared to spend less time on procedures related to the annual budgetary cycle, so that more attention can be paid to the longer-term expenditure plans of their governments. However, most of the budgetary innovation discussed in this chapter has taken place within the last ten or so years, and within most governments there is still considerable scope for further developments. It is thus early to judge their effects on governments' management of their own activities, and since there is usually some time-lag before the new approaches are considered sufficiently developed to bring to parliament's attention, it follows that it must be even more premature to assess the effects of such innovation on parliamentary participation in the control of government expenditure. It can, of course, be said that potentially parliaments can benefit from the use of the kind of budgetary technique outlined above simply by having more relevant information available. Whether parliaments will in practice be able to take advantage of it will become apparent only during the course of the next ten or so years.

CHAPTER 18

THE ROLE OF PARLIAMENT IN BUDGETARY DECISIONS: SOME GENERAL CONCLUSIONS

David Coombes

The general object of the symposium was to see how far and in what particular ways changes in the purposes and techniques of budgetary decision-making in central government had affected the role of European parliaments. That there were important changes in this aspect of government was taken for granted. What the contributors were asked to consider especially were the ways in which parliaments had sought to cope with them, in view of the traditional importance attached in liberal democracies to parliamentary control of the budget, and in view of the popular impression of a decline in the value and effectiveness of parliaments. As was explained in the introductory chapter, uppermost in the minds of those who initiated the project was the debate, which has continued to hold the centre of institutional discussions in the European Communities, about the budgetary powers of the European Parliament. In this debate there has been a widespread (but by no means universal) assumption that budgetary powers no longer have great significance as an arm of representative institutions, and that classical arguments about the primacy of such concepts as 'no taxation without representation' serve to confuse rather than clarify. We thought that this debate was important beyond the special (though crucial) issue of the institutions of the European Community. Therefore we asked a group of specialists from different European States whether parliament's budgetary powers were still important (including for good measure a state outside the enlarged European Community), and if so, in what ways.

The resulting contributions show that the role of parliament in budgetary procedure certainly is important, not only in the adjustment of parliamentary procedures and practices, but also in the attempt of representative government as a whole to meet changing demands and technology. What is most striking, however, is that no simple or general explanation has emerged, and that the very understanding of our questions has varied from country to country.

As has been explained, this began deliberately as an open-ended symposium in which the authors themselves determined for each country which were the important issues.[1] The style and content were established gradually at a series of meetings and after considerable exchange of draft papers. In view of the collective nature of the project, therefore, the failure to agree either on a general measure or comparison of the budgetary powers of different parliaments, or on a bald assumption that parliament's budgetary powers have declined compared with some earlier period, is most significant.

Nevertheless the authors have taken the apparently simple notion of parliament's 'power of the purse' and have tried to compare it with a highly complex and confusing reality. The one firm conclusion which can be derived from their efforts is that in none of these countries can traditional ideas about 'the power of the purse' be applied in the modern State without major adjustments.

The problem, however, and again this seems to be general, is that the task of adjustment is not simply one of recognising changes in government and seeking to accommodate them. (Indeed in at least one country it is denied that significant changes have taken place in the way budgetary decisions are made.) The survival of traditional notions of parliamentary control seems to have about it a mysterious air of the inevitable, as if some more intractable problem than the efficiency of government were at stake. Two particular aspects of this stand out from most of the contributions and will be considered later in this chapter.

First there is the dislocation between political, economic and constitutional reality, on the one hand, and prevailing attitudes and objectives, on the other. Then there is the point, sustained by most authors here, that parliament's powers should not be judged in their own right, but as part of the wider process of government: for example the very issue of parliament's power of the purse is sometimes seen as important only because it reflects more pressing problems in the public administration itself.

Treatment of these two themes will lead me to offer some personal reflections about their consequences for parliamentary institutions and to try to offer some manner of reply to the debate. Before that, since one of the main achievements of the exercise has been to indicate just how many different influences need to be traced in order to measure changes in the role of parliament, either across

1 See p. 18 above.

different countries, or over periods of time, I shall pick out what seem to have been the main factors causing differences of approach among the contributors.

THE SIGNIFICANCE OF THE BUDGET

Many contributors develop the theme that to focus on the annual budget is to mistake a token for the reality of power. Some go so far as to regard the budget as 'a meaningless document' and parliamentary procedure in relation to it as 'a pointless ritual'. In any event the concept has no simple meaning. This is not only because the document itself or the procedure associated with it differ from country to country; it is simply not possible to break the process of expenditure down into watertight phases or compartments. Moreover, as Peter Else has discussed in the previous chapter, the receipts and expenditure can be financed in a variety of ways, not all of them proving susceptible to approval in an annual statement before parliament.

I shall turn to the consequences of procedural differences later, although I have already explained that the word 'budget' evades consistent definition even in formal terms.[1] We still contrive to mean by 'budget' the formal statement (or statements) of proposed income and expenditure which governments put to parliaments for approval on an annual basis (and we shall continue to leave aside the problems arising from the different ways in which that statement can be finally presented and treated). The preceding contributions show how limited is the significance of budgetary procedure in that sense. Many contributors say that ordinary legislation involving the spending of money is more important than the budget itself. In Italy, for example, it is forbidden by the Constitution to include new expenditure in the budget, and Mortara estimates that 88 per cent of the sums passed in the budget normally arise from previous money laws.[2] Schmidt's article shows how important financial legislation can be in committing expenditure, and in placing constraints on the government's ability to manage its financial activities in relation to conjunctural policy.[3] One of the French contributors says that the bulk of the budget proper is more or less fixed expenditure based on continuing needs previously established.[4]

[1] See Chapter 1.
[2] See Chapter 13.
[3] See Chapter 5.
[4] See Lalumière, Chapter 7. The author presumably refers to the practice of

The budget can also become a mere expression of commitments already made as a consequence of the mechanisms developed by governments for economic planning, whether these go as far as the French plan, or take the more limited form of German financial planning or British public expenditure surveys. There are at least two fundamental reasons why the annual budget is likely to be superseded in this way: first, because governments' financial activity has wide social and economic implications which modern governments need to manage in a broader perspective than that of public administration; and, secondly, because the time covered by the annual budget is too short to be effective as a control of most important government expenditure. Financial and economic planning tend in practice to determine most expenditure formally authorised in the budget, although they do not of course take away the formal right of parliaments in budgetary procedure.[1]

The significance of the budget is also reduced by the form in which it traditionally presents information. The main contemporary criticism, with which a number of our contributors deal and which Peter Else considers at some length,[2] is that parliamentary consideration of the budget is invariably concerned with inputs of resources used in administration, rather than with the objectives or outputs of expenditure. In fact all the countries treated here have had some debate about altering the presentation of the budget to take account of this criticism, but none seems to have gone so far as Great Britain or France in changing the form of its expenditure proposals to make possible better comparisons between types of expenditure and to make more explicit the choices of policy expressed in cash flows. However other countries have adopted the practice of appending extra information to the conventional budget document in the hope of making some improvement.

Some exponents of 'output budgeting' would go much further and attempt to subordinate as much as possible of budgetary decision-making and presentation to a broader process of rationalising decisions about the allocation of resources. The lengths to which this process could go are discussed in Ducro's article.[3] As Peter Else sums it up, nothing so elaborate has been tried in our countries as was introduced in the USA under the title of 'Planning-

debating only *mesures nouvelles* and also to the use of the procedural device known as *vote bloqué*. But see Dupas, pp. 115–116, for a different view.

1 See Lalumière, p. 136; Friauf, p. 74; Onida, p. 235; Else, p. 346. See also Daalder and Hubée, p. 298, on the attempts of Dutch governments to control public expenditure by the use of norms.

2 See Chapter 17.

3 See Chapter 8.

Programming-Budgeting Systems'. Nevertheless policy analysis, the use of special techniques like cost-benefit analysis, and organisational changes like the introduction of 'management-by-objectives' have made a great deal of difference, especially in Britain and France, to the way in which many decisions about expenditure are made.[1] In Britain a majority of MPs, ministers and civil servants probably now believe that the government's annual statement about future projections for public expenditure, expressed largely in 'output' terms, is more important for parliament than the budget itself (whether understood as the Chancellor's statement on 'budget day' or as the estimates themselves).

A word of warning must be given to those who would seek too enthusiastically to elevate the budget into an expression mainly of the fundamental planning and policy-making exercises of the executive. The discussion included in this book of budgeting in Italy should be enough to remind us of the vital administrative significance of the budget for control of expenditure. Whatever one may feel about the need to qualify the annual basis of parliamentary consideration of expenditure or about the limitations of a 'resource budget', the helplessness of the Italian parliament in the face of the failure of administrators to carry out authorised expenditure shows up the dangers of accepting authorisations in principle rather than specific commitments to spend. Some Italian experts have recommended introducing a 'cash budget' in an attempt to solve what seems to be a genuine crisis of administrative inertia.[2] Perhaps one is reminded most at this point of Walkland's statement that what has supported the traditional forms of accounting most of all in British experience has been the desire to maintain a trusted system of *a posteriori* control of expenditure.[3]

We seem to have dwelt on the question of expenditure, but from the point of view of revenue, too, budgets are seen as an inadequate instrument for parliament. All ministers of finance seem to have extra-budgetary means of raising revenue or of otherwise financing expenditure. This is closely related to the macro-economic significance of public finance, and the parliaments we have been studying cannot be satisfied, in view of that significance, with examining taxation only in terms of its relationship with government spending. Some observers in Britain have argued that the House of Commons must look at taxation through a select committee on economic

[1] See Chapter 17.
[2] See Chapter 12.
[3] See Chapter 10.

affairs.[1] Millar argues forcibly that the macro-economic aspect, added to the continuing need to consider both the administration of the tax system, and the choice of methods and sources of government income, call at least for a select committee on taxation.[2] He feels that the traditional British procedures based on the Finance Bill are inadequate from all these points of view, and clearly thinks that Britain lags behind other European countries in this area. Reading the contributions from other countries, however, one is led to doubt whether things are that much worse in Britain, and to think that the arguments upon which his case rests (although perhaps not the specific proposal he makes) could well be taken to heart even in countries with a more elaborate committee system than the British parliament's.

Dissatisfaction with the budget also arises because potentially important categories of public expenditure can be excluded from it. This happens deliberately and in accordance with parliament's own wishes, when semi-autonomous public agencies and corporations are set up and are required to publish their own accounts separately from those of the government. Various forms of State enterprise, including both public utilities and miscellaneous industrial and trading activities, account for a substantial proportion both of public investment and of the gross national product. The type of organisation can vary from one in which all the assets of a particular undertaking are owned by the State to one in which the State is simply a partial shareholder. In either case subsidies and other payments to the undertakings concerned are shown in the budget, as are loans, and in France and Britain figures describing the investment of most public enterprises are published with the budget. However, the normal way for these organisations to obtain their revenue is by selling goods or services in the market, so that the exclusion of their ordinary receipts and expenditures from the State budget is a natural consequence of that type of organisation. Of greater importance for the significance of the budget is when governments use extra-budgetary agencies to carry out activities which are traditionally entrusted to the ordinary public administration (as seems to be happening especially in Italy) or when they set up special financial organisations empowered to make loans or subsidies from public funds in pursuit of regional and social policies (also in Italy and in France).[3] One contribution here gives an interesting example from West Germany of a 'para-fiscal' institution

[1] See Chapter 11.
[2] See Chapter 11.
[3] See Chapters 14 and 7.

N

in the field of social insurance; here the basic principle of organisation seems to be an element of 'self-government' by representatives of socio-economic interests (similar organisations seem to have been important in the Netherlands).[2]

These are the principal reasons why, running through the contributions from every country, is the theme that the traditional budget is no longer the right focus (at least, on its own) for those who would champion parliament's right to control expenditure. Starting from the notion of parliamentary control of the budget, all the writers have wanted to stress other aspects of parliament's role in relation to public expenditure, whatever aspect of public expenditure has been their particular concern.[2] From the legal aspect, much financial activity would seem to escape the limits set by the formal budget. For enforcing what limits can apply, *a posteriori* control through some form of audit seems to be far more useful than an attempt at restrictions in advance. Indeed in all the countries treated here, control of the legality of expenditure seems to have become primarily an executive or judicial function (although in two of them the way this function is performed seems to have been highly controversial in recent years: in Italy, because of 'under-spending', and in Switzerland, because of 'over-spending'). In those States where parliament has a role to play in reinforcing limits to expenditure, its interest seems to be mainly in the 'managerial' aspect. From this aspect, too, however, it seems that parliament cannot confine itself to the formal statement of income and expenditure contained in the budget or to the annual time-scale of normal budgetary procedure. The macro-economic aspect also seems to require a different sort of information and time-scale as does the allocation of expenditure among different activities. There would seem to be a trend to play down the significance of the budget as a legal instrument altogether and to see the financial activities of government flexibly in relation to the policies and the administrative functions which they support. This is certainly not true of all the countries considered here, and it may not be a trend welcomed by all members of parliament or students of it. Even if we were to accept that the budget has never been more than an administrative instrument, an expression in figures of decisions already taken and approved elsewhere, the question remains whether, and if so, why, it is being drained of the political significance attached to it. This brings us to the wider issue of parliament's role in relation to budgetary decisions.

1 See Chapters 5 and 15.
2 We rely here on Else's analysis of the aspects of public expenditure in Chapter 17.

THE SIGNIFICANCE OF PARLIAMENTARY CONTROL

The countries treated in this book all have what would be called parliamentary systems of government, but the diversity of the contributions here are some evidence of the complexity which that phrase conceals. Indeed the symposium's problems of communication arose not just over linguistic differences (some of which regarding the word 'control' itself are considered in the introductory chapter),[1] but also over differences in the use of concepts, and from ignorance about the practices of neighbouring European political systems. In view of the specialised subject of the symposium we have not gone as far as we were tempted into discussion of fundamental differences between one system and another, or into general aspects of constitutional parliamentary arrangements or procedure. The need for greater international confrontation on such themes has been highlighted by our own difficulties. However it is, of course, within and not only between countries that differences of understanding about concepts such as parliamentary control arise. In discussing our particular aspect of that control, two sets of conceptual problems have been especially important: one to do mainly with the notion of control; and the other with ideas about the role of parliament.

It is arguable that the notion of control should not be applied to parliament's function in all aspects of the process of expenditure. This relates partly to the linguistic problem already mentioned, in that in some European languages 'control' strictly means only the activity of checking something's conformity with a given set of standards, while in English (and now in most common European usage) it has the much vaguer meaning including 'restraint' and even 'guidance'. Thus, used in its narrower sense, 'control' applied to the process of expenditure would seem to belong properly only to the aspect of regularity, that is, the various exercises of audit and accountability which are designed to check that expenditure conforms to budgetary (or other) provisions.

The issue is less pedantic than this, however, since it seems that even in this narrow sense none of the parliaments considered here devotes much time to control of regularity or expects to be able to achieve it acting alone. Indeed in most of these countries it does seem as if control of regularity is really a task entrusted to some organ of the executive, like the Treasury in Britain, or the Ragioneria Generale in Italy.

Indeed for the most part we have tried to give in this symposium

1 See Chapter 1, p. 15.

the wider and looser meaning to 'control'. All the same in none of the countries considered here does parliament seem to have much confidence about its influence over the executive's decisions about public expenditure. The formulation of the budget and its presentation to parliament are generally regarded as a task for the executive.[1] Moreover, although all the governments covered by this symposium have to obtain parliamentary approval both for expenditure as a whole and for the allocation of expenditure to different departments or purposes, the significance of this varies in practice.

A distinction can be made here between Britain, where it almost seems to be a constitutional convention that parliament's approval of the estimates is a pure formality, and where the estimates themselves are not even subjected to debate at the time of approval, and other countries where the executives' proposals for expenditure are regularly debated and where it is certainly not unknown for the executive to suffer defeats in parliament on certain proposals, so that they have to be withdrawn or amended. In the Netherlands, and even now in France, voting on proposals for expenditure contained in the budget is an important opportunity to hold a political debate on the performance and policies of different sectors of government.[2] In Britain the procedure has now been rationalised so that the debate formerly held in Committee of Supply has become simply an opportunity for the Opposition to choose any subject for debate; the 'budget debate' so called is an opportunity to debate the government's economic policy as a whole. (On the other hand British governments sometimes have difficulty in getting through their proposals for taxation in the Finance Bill.)[3]

However none of our contributors regards the net effects of parliament's intervention at this stage as significant. In the first place, although it is still possible in some of the countries for a government to be brought down by a vote on the budget, this is considered abnormal; indeed budgetary votes are not usually seen as having much political importance (although the *debates* are so considered). Even where members of parliament do normally succeed in getting amendments carried, these nowhere amount in practice to more than a minute proportion of the total expenditure proposed by the executive. Moreover in most of these countries there is some limi-

[1] However, in the French Third and Fourth Republics the National Assembly did intervene significantly during this phase, since it was the finance committee's draft rather than the government's which was debated in the Assembly. See also Daalder and Hubée's reference to the attempts of the Opposition in the Dutch parliament to produce 'alternative budgets'.

[2] See Chapters 15 and 6.

[3] See Chapters 10 and 11.

tation on the sort of amendments members may put down, or on the obligation for the executive to accept them. Even in the Netherlands where members may move increases in expenditure, ministers are not legally obliged to carry these proposals out.[1] Elsewhere members are either prohibited from proposing increases in expenditure or are required when doing so to provide for compensatory reductions in other parts of the budget or to show otherwise how the extra outlay is to be provided for.[2] (Italy seems to be some exception in practice, since the government often has to accept new expenditure for which no specific provision has been made, if only as a result of money laws.)[3] Most of the executives covered by this symposium seem to be only slightly constrained, if at all, by the limits to revenue and expenditure set by parliamentary approval of the annual budget. The power of the French government to undertake supplementary expenditure by decree, and the ability of the Italian government to make use of *fondi globali* for unspecified purposes and in any year (or rather not to use them), are probably exceptional.[4] Nevertheless the view of one French contributor, that parliament's actual role in approving the budget and the allocations it contains is essentially nothing more than that of a *'chambre d'enregistrement'*, could with only slight qualification be applied to all the parliaments studied here.[5]

In fact the important effect of parliament's intervention in this phase of the expenditure process is best summed up by Friedrich's idea (quoted effectively by Daalder and Hubée above) of the 'rule of anticipated reactions'.[6] In other words, the importance of parliamentary 'control' lies in its consequences for the conventions and procedures adopted by the executive in recognition of parliament's formal powers.

However, once we have focused on the idea that parliamentary control is not an attempt to take the executive's place in making budgetary decisions, nor a source of obstruction to government except in extreme circumstances, then it is possible to have an even broader meaning of control. For there is an implication in some contributions that parliament's best interests are not in the formal or legal aspects of prior approval, but in its means of influencing the way the executive carries out the financial proposals authorised by the budget, which is intimately related to the way those proposals

---

[1] See Chapter 15.
[2] See Chapters 4, 6 and 12.
[3] See Chapters 13.
[4] See Chapters 12 and 7.
[5] See Chapter 7.
[6] See Chapter 15.

are made in the first place. In other words parliament could be seen as having better opportunities to influence budgetary decision-making, in a manner in which it would have something worthwhile to contribute, by taking an interest in the way in which decisions are made and carried out rather than by seeking each year to determine the specific allocations of a particular budgetary exercise in advance. One condition would be that parliament was able to go beyond a narrow interest in regularity and to concern itself generally with the effectiveness with which government policy was being achieved. In one sense parliament's interest would then be in the managerial aspects of expenditure, for the purpose of control would primarily be to influence the management of government departments and agencies. In Britain that has seemed to be the bias of parliament's attempts to control expenditure throughout this century, and the method employed has been mainly that of the parliamentary select committee. Walkland's description of recent reforms, including the development of the Estimates Committee into a Select Committee on Expenditure, gives some indication of what opportunities lie in this direction, especially when the committee concerned can deal with the reasoning and assumptions upon which government policy for expenditure rests. To be influential, control of this kind probably does not normally need to be backed up by formal votes in plenary session or to take the form of a prior authorisation of expenditure (indeed it probably could not take that form).[1]

Carried to its logical conclusion, however, that view implies a role for parliament which would not be acceptable to other contributors. The sharpest difference is between traditionally British and traditionally French attitudes to parliament. Whatever may have happened to parliament's powers under the Fifth Republic, Lalumière's contribution gives us an insight into the French parliament's traditional view of its role, which could perhaps be summed up in the phrase *'résistance au pouvoir'*. Thus deputies and senators seem to have regarded mistrust of the executive almost as a duty and, if under the present régime expressions of this mistrust seem to be less effective, that is more to do with the executive's relative constitutional independence and its influence over the parliamentary majority, than with any fundamental change in parliament's own sense of duty.[2] It seems as if a distinction could be made here between parliament seen as an 'institution of opposition' and the more typically British view of parliament as an 'institution of

[1] See Chapters 9, 10 and 11.
[2] See Chapter 7.

government'. In the first of these conceptions the exercise of government seems to be regarded as conditional upon the active support of
parliament as a whole, while in the second the role of opposition
and the rights of the minority tend to be formalised into the recognised functions of an official alternative government or 'opposition'.
Of course neither of these conceptions is more than an 'ideal type'.
Indeed Dupas expresses a rather different view of the modern role
of parliament in France, which comes much closer to the British
'ideal type'.[1] He and Lalumière seem to disagree in interpreting the
rights of the parliamentary minority, in that Dupas would see the
new intimacy between executive and majority party as, broadly
speaking, favourable for parliamentary influence, while Lalumière
would see it rather as slavish loyalty, if not a conspiracy to deprive
the minority of its rights.

The distinction can be important in procedural terms as differences in the role of parliamentary committees show. Thus the type
of committee seen by Walkland and Millar as playing an important
role in parliamentary control of expenditure in Britain (a type
which seems to be acquiring even more importance there) is a
different sort of institution from that which has played so central a
part in parliamentary consideration of the budget in France, Italy
and the Federal Republic of Germany. The difference is probably
best summed up by describing the former as 'investigatory' committees, and the latter as 'legislative' committees. The British
financial select committees, including now the Select Committee on
Expenditure, are not so much investigatory in an inquisitorial or
judicial sense, as in their essential purposes of inquiring into the
ideas and practices of the administration, reporting to the House of
Commons on the consequences of existing policies and procedures,
and giving their own recommendations. They do not normally divide
on party lines, nor do they normally seek to settle issues which
divide government from Opposition in critical ways. They are concerned rather with the continuing conduct of policy-making and
administration by the executive, than with a particular budgetary
exercise. The continental committees play an essential part in the
process of approving the budget itself and in the three countries
mentioned may well be more important in this respect than the
plenary session itself. (In Italy specialist legislative committees
often decide the fate of money Bills, on which the nature of the
budget itself invariably depends, without reference to the Chamber
as a whole.)[2] Their basic function is clearly to enhance and facili-

[1] See Chapter 6.
[2] See Chapter 13.

tate the exercise by parliament of its political influence over the budgetary provisions for a particular year. The way in which they seek to do this is most important. It is normally by bestowing special privileges and opportunities on particular members (the *rapporteurs* of the committees) who are sometimes expected to act as representatives of the chamber as a whole in relations with ministers and officials. This system may not always have the effect of asserting the rights of individual members or minorities, since the *rapporteurs* may form along with the chairmen of committees and ministers themselves an élite with privileged access to the decision-making process.[1]

Although the practice of parliamentary control does not seem in any of our countries to present a major challenge to the power of the executive to formulate, decide and execute the budget, or in other words to make its own decisions about revenue and expenditure, nevertheless my brief analysis has shown up some interesting nuances in the concept of parliamentary control. To the simple notion of control as assuring regularity, must be added control as obstruction, and then also the idea that parliament should actually influence decisions about revenue and expenditure, and even concern itself more broadly with the effectiveness with which policy is made and administered. In none of these respects do the parliaments with which we have been concerned seem to exercise much power. On the other hand, we have also tried to isolate an even vaguer notion of control in which parliament's influence would depend more on gaining a better understanding of the objectives and the results of budgetary decisions, as well as of possible alternative decisions, than on enforcing legal restraints or commitments on the executive. There seems to be a distinction here between an approach to parliamentary control of the budget which is essentially 'legislative' in purpose and method, and one which is essentially 'managerial'. However, at this point we raise much broader questions about the role of parliament and, in particular, about the relationship between parliament and the executive. Before developing that theme, we need to take into account other factors which make it difficult to rely on meaningful comparisons over space or time.

CONSTITUTIONAL RESTRAINTS ON PARLIAMENTARY CONTROL

We were aware of course that there were important differences in the basic structural and constitutional features of government in the

1 See Chapters 7, 6, 5 and 4.

countries included in the symposium. The contributors were asked to take this factor into account in deciding which aspects should be covered for each country.

Perhaps the most striking exception, and the one with most consequences for parliamentary control of budgets, is the federal system of West Germany. We decided that it was necessary to include one contribution entirely devoted to the consequences of this special constitutional feature. That contribution suggests that it is crucial to understand the federal nature of the West German Constitution before the role of the federal parliament in budgetary affairs can be understood. This is not so much because much public expenditure, which would in other states be made by the central government, is made in West Germany by the *Land* governments, but because it is so difficult in many respects to separate the financial activity of the states from that of the federal government. As Zunker explains, the situation is complicated by the facts that to a large extent federal policy is actually administered by the state governments, and that the federal government tends to participate more and more in decisions about expenditure and revenue taken by the states. However, the more the state and federal governments co-operate in making decisions in joint committees and joint under-takings, the more difficult it becomes for parliaments at both levels to exercise control. Zunker's account makes an indirect but vital contribution to debate about the institutions of the European Community, in the expectation of a growing interdependence between budgetary policies in steps towards an economic and monetary union.[1]

Federalism is also a factor limiting the influence of the national parliament in Switzerland, but Urio's contribution suggests that a more important restraint on parliamentary control of the budget has been the persistence of a notion of the separation of powers, by means of which the federal executive has sought to claim independence of parliament, at least in budgetary and administrative affairs.[2] Similar elements of 'dualism', expressing themselves in a sense of institutional conflict between parliament and the executive, can be traced in the German contributions.[3]

However, the French Fifth Republic probably offers the most striking example of the effects of constitutional separation between parliamentary and executive authority, especially since 1962 when the direct, popular election of the President of the Republic was

[1] See Chapter 3.
[2] See Chapter 16.
[3] See Chapters 4 and 5.

introduced. The various constitutional restraints placed on the French parliament's powers make it in this sense undoubtedly the least privileged of those considered here.[1]

This does not mean that Britain, Italy and the Netherlands can be grouped together as 'normal' in constitutional terms. Although government and parliament seem to be more closely tied in those countries than in the other three, there are very important variations. These are probably most significant, however, when seen in terms of other factors. Indeed, once basic constitutional variations are taken into account, it is often difficult to separate them from other influences, which may alter the interpretation, or at least the weight, of constitutional factors at any one time. For example, the changes in *Bund-Land* relations in the Federal Republic seem to arise from problems in making social and macro-economic policy, posed by the diffusion of the power to spend. Again, the role of parliament in the Fifth Republic might well be different under other political circumstances, for example, if the President faced a hostile majority in the National Assembly.

POLITICAL RESTRAINTS ON PARLIAMENTARY CONTROL

In the symposium two aspects of the political systems considered seem to have been of outstanding importance in influencing the exercise of parliamentary control in practice: the nature of the party system and the influence of interest groups.

In all our countries the relationship between the government and the political parties in parliament influences the way in which parliament exercises its budgetary powers. In Britain, France and West Germany the emphasis is on relations between the executive and members of the majority party in parliament, although in the last two of these countries the relationship has been complicated: in France because the 'majority' technically consists of more than one party grouping, and in the Federal Republic because the majority usually shares office with a minor coalition partner. In all these countries, however, the executive can normally manage if necessary to use the support of the majority to get its budgetary measures (and financial legislation in general) accepted, and hostile amendments reversed. Nowhere is this so much the normal practice as in Britain, for in France it seems that important concessions do sometimes have to be made in order to win the support of dissident groups within the majority (the bargaining over which takes place outside formal parliamentary procedure),[2] and in Germany the executive

1 See Chapter 7.
2 See Chapters 6 and 7.

often has to accept minor amendments to keep its parliamentary supporters happy (while the important illustrations of bi-partisanship in social policy given by Schmidt should not be overlooked).[1] Moreover, neither France nor Germany have such a long experience as Britain of stable majorities in parliament (or of executive dominance in the field of budgetary decisions); and in this respect Germany has been less stable than France under the Fifth Republic.

In both the Netherlands and Switzerland, the pressures for conformity to the executive's intentions are not much different, although the relationship between executive and parliamentary parties is by no means the same. In these countries, just as more parties are usually included in the formation of a government, so the consensus necessary to sustain a government seems to commit a larger proportion of the political tendencies represented in parliament. Here it is not just the numerical majority which matters, but also the emphasis on accommodation and compromise in the political culture in general, and in the formation of governments in particular. The effect often is, however, to present members of parliament with the alternative of accepting unfavourable measures or taking responsibility for bringing down the government. The crucial bargaining in this type of system tends to take place while a government is being formed, and between its constituent party groups, rather than between executive and majority party.[2] However, Daalder and Hubée find an increasing polarisation of political parties in the Netherlands, and attempts to develop an 'alternative government' among opposition parties. It could be that so far this has made it more difficult to form stable governments, and it is particularly interesting for us that in recent years budgetary affairs seem to have played an important part in this conflict.[3]

Italy has something in common with the last two countries, but there are features which set it apart. Above all there is the special role of the Christian Democratic party whose support is essential for forming effective coalitions in government. While the discipline of that party can be assured, then the crucial decisions about expenditure can be settled by a process of bargaining among the parties forming the coalition, a process in which the party secretariats play a dominant part. However, there are not the same pressures towards consensus as in the Netherlands and Switzerland, not even within the Christian Democratic party itself. Much

---

[1] See Chapters 4 and 5.
[2] See Chapters 15 and 16.
[3] See Chapter 15.

depends, therefore, on the extent of dissidence and indiscipline among the disparate groups forming that party. As a result governments seem to have had a lot of difficulty in recent years in getting their proposals for expenditure (expressed in money laws) approved unamended or without great delays, while on the other hand money laws originating in parliament sometimes have to be accepted.[1]

The influence of interest groups can be distinguished according to countries in a fairly similar way. Thus in the Netherlands and Switzerland both the political culture and the working of the system of government seem to give interest groups a specially privileged position independent of the power of parliament. (In Switzerland their right to be consulted is even protected in the Constitution.)[2] However, the Netherlands also shares with Britain, France and the Federal Republic a type of government in which representatives of interest groups have come to play an integral part in the making of the social and economic decisions on which so much financial activity of the executive now depends. One problem is the extent to which the executive relies on the support of major socio-economic interests for the success of its economic policies, so that the demands of parliament seem bound to be less important. However, in Italy interest groups, like the trade unions, also use parliament as a channel for pressing their demands.[3] The 'dualism' of the German parliamentary system also seems to have encouraged interest groups to use parliament as a channel, at least in the case studied by Schmidt.[4] Some groups however are satisfied with direct access to the executive. Lalumière describes the privileged role of interest groups in the machinery of concertation in French economic planning, and the Italian authors feel that large industrial corporations, including the great State enterprises, have privileged access to government.[5]

In a special sense the public administration itself could be regarded as a kind of interest group in Italy, exercising a special kind of power and weakening the relative influence of parliament. It is evident from the symposium that, in terms of the influence of the political system on parliamentary control of the budget, Italy presents unique problems among the countries we have included. Whatever the influences of political parties and interest groups, through parliament or outside it, the crucial factor in determining

[1] See Chapter 13.
[2] See Chapters 15 and 16.
[3] See Chapter 13.
[4] See Chapter 5.
[5] See Chapters 7, 14 and 13.

expenditure in Italy seems to be the role of the public administration, which enjoys considerable independence from both parliament and ministers. The main cause of this seems to be the survival
of highly specialised and complicated procedures for making
expenditure, together with the dominance within the administration
of those who tend to emphasise regularity and economy. The result
is that officials in key parts of the Italian administration are able to
decide not only the timing of expenditure already authorised by
parliament, but also other vital aspects of the way in which budgetary provisions are put into practice.[1]

ECONOMIC RESTRAINTS ON PARLIAMENTARY CONTROL

As Else has already shown, budgetary decision-making is closely
related to economic policy. An important limitation on budgetary
decisions is the incompatibility of a certain amount of public and
private consumption with goals like full employment or stable
prices. Most industrialised Western countries are confronted with
this issue at the present time. In most of the countries under consideration here (the possible exception being Switzerland), the
growth of public expenditure as a proportion of gross national product has been seen as a threat to management of the economy.

This is not only likely to make governments more reluctant to
accept proposals for new expenditure, but might also be thought to
induce both government and parliament to look more rigorously for
ways of justifying continuing, as well as new, public expenditure,
and to pay more attention to the efficiency with which government
carries out its policies.[2] This trend could enhance the 'managerial'
kind of parliamentary control, while it certainly reduces the weight
attached to parliament's role in voting budgetary allocations.

On the other hand anxiety about the relationship of public
expenditure to GNP might not be shared by all forces in parliament,
and might not override other interests which parliamentarians feel
obliged to promote or defend. So it might not of its own accord give
the government an easier time with parliament. At the same time
economic restraints encourage the executive to reform its own procedures for making financial decisions, for example, to adopt long-
term planning of public expenditure or to take discretionary power
to raise or lower certain forms of taxation in response to contin-
gencies. These changes might force a self-denying ordinance on
parliament, in the interests of economic stability.

1 See Chapters 12, 13 and 14.
2 See Chapter 17.

Having given a long analysis in an attempt to simplify the complexity of the results of the symposium, I shall now turn to what seem to me to be the two most striking common themes running through the contributions.

First most of the authors seem to see some conflict between, on the one hand, parliament's purposes and characteristics and, on the other, the needs of financial administration in government.

Most of these parliaments' procedures for dealing with budgetary decisions were designed when parliament and government shared an overriding concern for regularity and economy in public finance. In most countries treated here the right to approve proposals for expenditure and revenue seems to have been grafted on to earlier arrangements, established usually in the mid-nineteenth century, for providing *a posteriori* control of expenditure.[1] This process did not go as far in some countries as in others, and it does not seem as if it was ever particularly effective. Certainly in most of this century, but even during some of the last, members of parliament, where they had power to influence budgetary decisions, saw it primarily as an opportunity to increase expenditure. Thus parliament's own role in budgetary procedure did not itself go far to provide unity, coherence and order in public finances, and did not acquire a good reputation. The essential contribution of parliamentary control was to provide the grounds for reforms in financial administration carried out by executive departments and agencies themselves.

However, as the role of public finance has altered and become more complex, involving as it does now the implementation of social and economic policies upon which the welfare of the whole nation depends, the emphasis of both parliament and government has changed. The main concern now is with the efficiency of government revenue and expenditure in fulfilling social and economic policies, and on the allocation of the costs and benefits arising from the State's financial activity.[2]

This trend seems to have had two important consequences for parliamentary control of the budget. First, the traditional procedures designed mainly for regularity and economy seem more than ever anachronistic and anomalous, while, for the various political and economic reasons already discussed here, governments feel obliged increasingly to by-pass them or to lessen their obstructive influence. (Where they have failed to do so, as in Italy,

[1] See especially Chapters 4, 10, 12 and 15.
[2] See Chapter 17.

the consequence has been ineffective administration.) Secondly, members of parliament themselves become more frustrated by their inability, in spite of their apparently extensive formal powers, to exercise any real influence on the major financial decisions.

At the same time, the emphasis on efficiency in modern public expenditure, and the economic factors discussed previously in this chapter (both treated more fully by Else earlier in the book), keep the need for co-ordination and control of expenditure very much alive. Thus the traditional principles of parliamentary control of the budget certainly have not become irrelevant; it is rather that they need to be applied with some qualification, and need to be seen as a discipline, not only for the executive, but also for parliament itself. It is still important to judge public expenditure in terms of its effects on other components of the gross national product, as well as to relate individual commitments of public expenditure to general objectives of government policy. The right to approve the allocation of expenditure is still relevant as a means of forcing governments to justify the political choices involved and to consider the costs and benefits of different methods of attaining the same objective. Finally, there must be some obligation to review the results of past decisions, although in modern circumstances this should go beyond concern with regularity and take in much broader questions of efficiency.

Some of the writers here seem extremely pessimistic about the ability of parliament to adapt its procedures and practices to these modern needs. The worst problems seem to arise in Italy and are so extreme that they probably form an exception. The feeling of the Italian contributors seems to be that the main effect of parliament's attempts to control the budget has been to hamper government with a tangle of bureaucratic devices, over which parliament has now actually lost control, and which in reality prevent the effective performance of social and economic policy. Although Italian members of parliament seem to be more or less favourable towards positive action by the State and to support public expenditure, the system of control which they themselves still defend frustrates their own interests and objectives. The activity of parliament in influencing the amount and nature of expenditure authorised is shown to be irrelevant in effect, since the machinery does not exist to carry out parliament's wishes, and it might even be harmful (although here the Italian authors seem to disagree) by making it impossible to plan expenditure.[1]

[1] See Chapters 12, 13 and 14.

However, contributions from other countries contain similarly sceptical judgements about the capacity or willingness of parliament to make use of the budgetary system for modern needs. Daalder and Hubée sum the situation up rather well by referring to parliament's 'schizophrenia'.[1]

If one could hazard a generalisation on this important theme, it seems that, although there are enormous political and economic pressures for continuing to regard parliamentary control of the financial activity of governments as having a contribution to make to effective administration, yet there is widespread doubt that parliaments can face up to the demand in its modern form. Explanations and possible solutions vary, according to the complexity of the factors influencing the role of parliament and the nature of budgetary procedure in the countries we have studied. Most reactions, however, lead to another, related common theme.

THE NEED FOR EFFECTIVE GOVERNMENT

Looking back on the symposium as a whole, one can detect a frustration with the very focus of our subject. There is a tendency to feel that the notion of budgetary procedure as it has been developed by parliaments has lost, even if it ever had, significance as an expression of the important decisions of government. If parliaments wish to keep in touch with political and economic reality, then they must recognise the complexity of the factors which determine decisions about revenue and expenditure, and so accept limitations on their own ability to participate in these decisions or at least to make fundamental changes in their own attitudes and objectives.

The main impact of the changing scope and content of public expenditure in institutional terms has been on the executive. Managing the macro-economic consequences of the budget is understandably enough an executive function where discretionary powers are essential. Where executives have sought greater flexibility in budgetary procedure, and greater independence from parliamentary control, these have normally been granted. The need and the ability to take budgetary decisions in the context of medium- or long-term programmes and projections has again strengthened the executive, if only because legislative commitments in public expenditure are more difficult to make, and are less meaningful, over a number of years (for example, because governments change). The search for greater efficiency in government has increasingly been seen as a

[1] See Chapter 15, especially its discussion of the failures to establish a general budget committee in the Dutch parliament; see also Chapters 4, 5, 6 and 8.

problem of finding the right methods and structures of organisation. Accountability to parliament is not always the best means of getting the best performance out of some public undertakings, so that a measure of autonomy will be granted; traditional forms of financial accountability within government departments themselves give way to arrangements such as accountable management. The application of new decision-making techniques calls for specialised skills which are more likely to be found in the public administration than in parliament. The influence of interest groups is one aspect of the way in which governments find it easier to deal with both economic management as a whole, and sectoral policy, in extra-parliamentary consultative bodies, by negotiating with those directly affected and directly informed.

It is tempting to see these trends as supporting what we called before the 'managerial' approach to parliamentary control of the budget. This approach is probably best illustrated in recent British experience, where reforms of parliamentary procedure have tended to rationalise the traditional, legislative aspects of approval of the budget, while making improvements in the supply of relevant information to MPs, developing the committee system to enable MPs to scrutinise more effectively the assumptions upon which decisions are based, and giving the House of Commons as a whole the opportunity to debate at a fairly early stage the government's medium-term projections of public expenditure. We suspect that in France and Germany a similar tendency may be seen, although in both those countries traditional parliamentary attitudes prove more difficult to dislodge (and are very different from those in the British parliament). In many contributions from various countries something of this 'managerial' view is implied by the emphasis on information as a source of parliament's power. If the more sophisticated forms of data and of argument which governments now use could be more readily available to parliament, and if members of parliament were better equipped to interpret it, then, it is felt, a more useful dialogue could take place.[1] Even in Italy, where the problems seem to be so much more intractable, our contributors are concerned primarily with the priority of effective formulation and execution of financial decisions, and look to improved techniques of planning and control within government.[2]

In general the notion of parliament as an 'institution of opposition' does not seem to have come out of this symposium very well. The countries which seem to have been able to cope best with the

[1] See Chapters 16, 6, 8 and 3.
[2] See Chapters 13 and 14.

changing circumstances of modern budgeting are those where the main options of social and economic policy can be settled outside the ordinary proceedings of parliament. This may be because the electorate is seen as having the decisive choice, or because there exists a certain constitutional 'dualism' between parliament and government, or again because there exists an effective and comprehensive means of governing by 'accommodating' most or all parties and groups. In any event, such an arrangement seems in many ways to be better suited to the complexities of modern social and economic policy-making, although it might make redundant procedures traditionally associated with the power of parliaments. Parliaments themselves seem on this theory to be launched into what many would regard for them strange territory. I shall conclude with some thoughts about how they could and should continue to play a role.

DOES PARLIAMENTARY CONTROL OF THE BUDGET REALLY MATTER?

If they took account of the results of this symposium, the founders of a new parliamentary system in Western Europe (such as those concerned with the budgetary powers of the European Parliament) would not take the traditional rules of parliamentary control of the budget at their face value and, paying attention to a number of changes since those principles were enunciated, would make various qualifications. (Whether policy-makers in the European Community seem to be making the right qualifications is another matter.)[1]

The traditional rules were defined earlier as the right to give prior approval to the budget, the right to approve allocations of expenditure, and the right to control the execution of the budget.[2] These are clearly not enough on their own to give parliament effective or meaningful influence over the scope, content and administration of modern public finance.

However, the symposium has shown some ways in which parliaments can extend and adapt their traditional rights to meet modern circumstances. In some countries ways have already been developed for giving parliament better access to information about the assumptions on which budgetary decisions are based.[3] There are a number of suggestions in this book for improving that access, for example, by making the executive's own services for providing background information available directly to parliament.[4] An

---

1 See above, p. 21.
2 See above.
3 See Chapters 10 and 16.
4 See Chapters 6, 8 and 16.

important distinction has emerged however between members of parliament obtaining access to useful information and then actually obtaining and making use of the information itself.[1] The contribution on Switzerland describes how, to help members in the second of these respects, parliament has been given its own *service de documentation* which includes in its functions research and investigation on behalf of parliament.[2] Some contributors see the real need as to alter the qualifications of members of parliament themselves and their own conditions of work.[3] (I might also insert the idea that bodies responsible primarily for auditing public expenditure can be given a much wider role in assisting parliament even before expenditure is approved.)[4] Parliament can even develop means of keeping in touch with the activity of autonomous public enterprises and other agencies (as the experience of the British select committee on nationalised industries suggests), with the government's conduct of macro-economic policy (again by judicious use of the British-type of select committee) and with the longer-term projections of expenditure made by governments.[5]

I shall not attempt to evaluate these various suggestions here. Indeed their applicability to different parliamentary systems must depend on a variety of conditions, the complexity of which has been described in this chapter. There is in practice great variety in the extent to which parliaments have adapted to changing circumstances. This brief survey gives an idea of ways in which they could adapt.

The constructive ideas which have emerged suggest that for one thing we should not think of the budgetary process only as separate phases each marked by some legal act of approval. Thus, if conducted in the right way, a study of continuing administration could help parliament to influence the intentions and assumptions of the executive even before the stage at which it normally plays a part in budgetary decisions. At the same time, as we have already remarked, the legislative element of control needs to be supplemented with means of obtaining adequate information, and parliament needs to be concerned with the procedures and structures employed by the administration in carrying out authorisations.

[1] See Chapters 16 and 6.
[2] See Chapter 16.
[3] See Chapters 8, 16 and 17.
[4] See E. L. Normanton, *The Accountability and Audit of Governments* (Manchester and New York, 1966); and 'Public Accountability and Audit: a Reconnaissance', in B. L. R. Smith and D. C. Hague, *The Dilemma of Accountability in Modern Government* (London, 1971), pp. 311–46.
[5] See Chapters 10 and 11.

Many would see in this process of adaptation a trend towards what we called earlier an 'ideal type' of parliament as an 'institution of government' rather than as an 'institution of opposition', and towards a 'managerial' rather than a 'legislative' approach to parliament's functions. Not all the ideas quoted here or elsewhere in the book fit this pattern. Indeed it is clear from some contributions that such a view of parliament would be simply unrealistic in some of the countries studied here (and in any of them under certain political circumstances). However inconvenient it may seem, parliaments often are the arenas where the resolution of vital social and political conflicts must take place, so that governments may be obliged to accept measures which they regard as 'irrational' or 'extravagant'. Even where constitutional, political and economic factors may have reduced parliament's role in practice to that of ratifying decisions already settled elsewhere by representatives of political parties or interest groups, it should still be asked whether a more active role for parliament is needed.[1]

There is evidence for example that the rise of public expenditure in relation to GNP is not a function of party-political differences. On the contrary most parties seem to have favoured increased public expenditure. The 'rising expectations' sometimes engendered by the privileges accorded to interest groups in the decision-making process also suggest that the 'irresponsibility' of parliamentarians is hardly the main cause of governments' difficulties with economic management.[2] Parliament's function as a 'forum of the nation', where an attempt is made to crystallise competing political demands and interests into support, is in this sense far from redundant.

There are other contributions made by parliament which administrative rationality and convenience might lead us to overlook. As we know it, politics cannot live without an element of spontaneity, both in the sense of freedom to change one's mind and in that of toleration of diversity. Spontaneity cannot of course be limitless and some parliaments have a dismal record in that respect. However, administrations in our sort of political systems cannot always reconcile their own ideas about what is the right time-span for a project or decision with shifts in what people are prepared to accept. Moreover, it is far more difficult than some experts think to reach stable and rational settlements of political differences (and there is

[1] Daalder and Hubée, for example, report a recent survey undertaken by Leiden University showing that a far higher proportion of Dutch members of parliament were dissatisfied with their powers over government expenditure, than were dissatisfied with their powers over legislation or administration. See p. 268 above.
[2] See Chapters 5 and 15.

plenty of evidence in the pages of this book that expert advisers on financial policy invariably get caught up in political arguments among themselves).[1]

Politics also relies on openness and communication, and again parliaments can be vital (although not exclusive) instruments in this respect. The main warning here is that the need for communication with those who do not understand, or who are too obstinate to try to understand, may not always be apparent to those who have been clever enough to find some technical solution to a difficult problem. Also potential critics and opponents might be much more reasonable if they are let in sufficiently on one's preliminary thinking; if, when the problems are genuinely common problems, they are even given a share in helping to solve them.

Finally, there is the point that formal powers do not have to be used to be effective, which brings us back to a comment made earlier about 'anticipated reactions'.[2] Thus parliament's questioning, whether or not it leads to sanction, could be a source of stimulation to the executive, especially when there are internal divisions within the administration itself. Moreover, the recent developments in Switzerland which are described in this book provide a very striking example of how a parliament can assert itself when it feels that the administration has blundered.

These are warnings to those who might undervalue the basic principles of parliamentary control of the budget. Parliaments too, however, as we have already argued, have to accept some discipline and certain restrictions in the way they use their powers. For example, while preserving the right of spontaneous control, parliaments will only defeat their own objects if they fail to realise the meaninglessness of annuality for so many types of public expenditure. Parliaments sometimes also have much to learn where openness is concerned. Parliamentary financial procedure is often itself uncommunicable 'mumbo-jumbo', and in some parliaments, as we have seen, traditional budgetary procedure tends to take place behind closed doors. Parliaments need above all to use their formal powers judiciously and that might also mean sparingly; in dealing with the budget itself it seems in most countries to mean being more selective in the subjects chosen for debate.

In a task such as giving budgetary powers to the European Parliament, the qualifications and exceptions to parliament's rights in European states should not drive out the fundamentals. Above all it should not be forgotten that the actual powers exercised by

1 See Chapters 5, 15 and 14.
2 See p. 373 above.

national parliaments now are partly a consequence of the granting of certain rights which may or may not be invoked as sanctions in practice. We do not know how different the situation would be now, if those rights had not been granted at all. The symposium offers constitution-makers in the Community confirmation that budgetary powers should be exercised in relation to parliament's other powers; and secondly, that the capacities, attitudes and objectives of parliamentarians themselves can be vital in deciding whether such powers are effective (a factor which relates to the role which parliament plays in the political system as a whole). Thirdly, however, what could be most important as a precedent is the way parliamentary financial powers rest mainly on their effect on the role of the executive. Indeed in many of the countries considered here the development of effective budgetary co-ordination and control within government followed parliament's own initiative for reform and parliament's own original demands for public accountability. In this respect, the 'power of the purse' is at least as important as other powers of parliament (like that to approve ordinary legislation), and is certainly indispensable to effective government in open, pluralist societies. Thus we have tried to emphasise in this concluding chapter that the disciplines which parliament's traditional budgetary powers imply are still necessary in modern circumstances, however much they need adjustment. Although parliaments approach the problem in different ways and although some parliaments seem to have adjusted better than others, we should not overlook that basic fact.

INDEX